new

When
Hell
Froze
Over

When Hell Froze Over

*The Untold Story
of Doug Wilder:
A Black Politician's
Rise to Power
in the South*

Dwayne Yancey

Taylor Publishing Company
in association with the Roanoke Times & World-News

Published by Taylor Publishing Company
No part of this publication may be reproduced in any form without
written permission from the publisher.

Library of Congress Cataloging-in-Publication Data

Yancey, Dwayne.
  When hell froze over.

  1. Wilder, Doug. 2. Virginia   Lieutenant-governors
  Biography. 3. Virginia   Politics and government
  1951- . 4. Afro-American politicians   Virginia
Biography. I. Title.
F231.W55Y36 1988   975.5′043′0924 [B]   88-38015
ISBN 0-87833-670-2

Printed in the United States of America
10 9 8 7 6 5 4 3 2

Contents

Preface

The idea for this book came one September evening in 1985 at a roadside diner in Augusta County called the Meadow Muffin. Tim Orwig, then a fellow reporter at the *Roanoke Times & World-News,* and I were on our way back home from Richmond and a day of covering the statewide campaign then in progress. Tim, a proud Texan, lamented the lack of good regional histories and listed many subjects back in the Lone Star state which he felt deserved to be commited to posterity while memories were still fresh. He also pointed out that here in Virginia, the campaign I was covering — Doug Wilder's historic bid to become the first black to win a statewide election in Virginia — ought to be documented for future generations, especially if Wilder could pull off an upset. He did, and this book tells the story of how he did it.

A note about its scope: This book is neither a Wilder biography nor an examination of his term in office. Instead, it is limited to the story of his remarkable campaign for lieutenant governor. Within those limits, it is the intent of this book to tell not only the public, on-the-record story of that campaign, but, as much as possible, to reveal what was actually going on behind the scenes. Toward that end, I have interviewed almost 200 people involved in some facet of the campaign, from the candidates themselves, their campaign managers and assorted campaign workers, to ordinary voters they met along the way.

But humans are imperfect witnesses. They see things differently, they exaggerate, they forget, they conveniently omit, they sometimes even lie, especially when politics is involved and even more especially when the politicians in question are still in office. For that reason, I have made liberal use of direct quotations, so readers can judge for themselves who to believe. In some cases, I have not attempted to resolve conflicting accounts, but instead have set out both sides in their own words. In the case of the conflicts between Wilder and then-Gov. Charles Robb, in particular, readers may find it hard to believe that the two sides are talking about the same thing.

Preface

Although my name alone appears on the cover, there are many others who helped to make this book a reality — especially at the *Roanoke Times & World-News*. Firstly, this book would have been impossible without the support of publisher of Walter Rugaber, executive editor Frosty Landon and managing editor Bill Warren. I am doubly indebted to Bill, who made it possible for me to take a leave of absence to work on the book and who, along with copy editor Pete Mathews, had the herculean job of editing the manuscript. Their skillful touch greatly improved the text.

I also am grateful to Roger Holtman for designing the typography; to Gary Craddock and Bob Adams for shepherding the text from the computer screen to the printed page; to Steve Stinson and John Earle for the cover design; to Don Petersen for the author's photo; to Roland Kidwell, Rich Martin, Wendy Zomparelli and Jane White for their support; and to Melissa Amos, Jenna Conner, Nancy Skinner and Tyrone Smith for their technical assistance.

Outside the newspaper family, I am grateful to Tim Orwig for suggesting that I write this book; to Roland Lazenby and Louis Rubin for their advice in finding a publisher; to Nancy Cook for the cover photo; and to a host of others who assisted along the way: Debbie Armstrong, Jean Cash, Lawrence Emerson, Ellen Fox, John T and Margaret Funkhouser, Calvin and Ruth Koon, Alan Neckowitz, Lee Rose, David Wendelken, Katerina Yancey, and Tyre and Jane Yancey.

1

Richmond Hotels

"Virginia makes the powerful impression of a country living under a spell, in which time has stood still."
— *Arnold Toynbee, British historian, 1947*

Jan. 15, 1952

A heat wave from the Gulf had settled on Richmond, driving afternoon temperatures to a sweltering 75 degrees, but what the city really felt was the hot breath of hope and dread.

For nearly a century, the heavy hush of history had hung over the capital of the defeated Confederacy, a proper city of garden clubs, debutante balls, wrought iron fences and the statues of our late heroes on parade down Monument Avenue.

But now one had only to pick up the newspaper to find unmistakable signs that the South was beginning to stir — and a state comforted by the past was about to be hurried into a future it could scarcely have imagined a decade ago. Or even now.

"Hall Becomes First of His Race on Planning Unit," headlined the afternoon *Richmond News Leader* on a story about the appointment of Wiley Hall to the city planning commission.

But more worrisome news came from the state Capitol, where the General Assembly was in session. Like a Southern Cato inveighing against the growing threat from Carthage, state Sen. Charles T. Moses of Appomattox had declared in public what should have been whispered only in private — the fear that the meddlesome Supreme Court might someday rule Virginia's hallowed system of segregated schools unconstitutional. But Moses — "Uncle Charley," he was called — had a plan to get around whatever the Supreme Court might do. He introduced a bill that would allow local school boards to contract the operation of public schools to private, non-profit corporations that would, he believed, be beyond the court's reach.

Gov. John S. Battle, a Southern man through and through but one with the dignified air of a Virginia gentleman, was unimpressed by such blatant legal chicanery. He called the Moses bill unworkable and said the court would likely regard it as "a deliberate attempt to circumvent the law."

The outcry against the governor's comments was loud and immediate. By morning, Battle would be forced to issue a clarification, insisting he had criticized Moses' bill on technical grounds, not philosophical ones: "My position on maintaining segregated free schools in accordance with the requirements of our constitution is unchangeable. I am unalterably opposed to mixing the races in public schools." And finally: "I sincerely hope the assumption on which his proposal is based, namely the abolition of segregation by court decree, will not materialize."

But the mere fact that the governor was forced to reaffirm one of the basic tenets of Southern political life was a sign of how much the old assumptions were starting to give way. The low rumble of the social and political landscape beginning to shift beneath Southerners' feet could be heard in other ways on that unseasonably warm January day in 1952.

Sen. Robert Taft, the Ohio Republican who was seeking his party's presidential nomination that election year, was in Richmond to make five speeches in a single day. The presence of "Mr. Republican" on the floor of the Virginia General Assembly was a dramatic appeal to Southern Democrats disenchanted with the liberal drift of their national party, and Taft played it for all it was worth.

"Southern thinking's all right if the voting's all right," Taft told the legislators, and the politics of Southern Democrats and the national Republican Party had become "difficult to distinguish." He praised U.S. Sen. Harry F. Byrd Sr., the plantation master of the ruling Byrd Machine, and his colleague, Sen. Willis Robertson. "They are Democrats but I find myself in agreement with them about nine-tenths of the time," Taft said. "I admire their principles."

In case anyone missed his point, Taft railed about federal interference in what rightly should be purely local affairs. "The principle of states' rights protects not only the independence of the state, but of cities, counties and school districts all over the country," Taft declared. "State legislatures must preserve the freedom of the people to maintain their roads, schools and other activities as befits the genius of that particular community."

Virginia legislators roared their approval. The *Richmond Times-Dispatch* described Taft's address as "what twenty years ago would have been regarded as a well-nigh perfect Democratic speech . . . For an overwhelmingly Democratic legislature to invite a leading Republican to address it is evidence that one-party government in the South is breaking down."

Then it was on to the William Byrd Hotel for a luncheon where, with the same wink and nudge, Taft again told his white Southern listeners that it was the Republican Party that could best preserve the local customs they held dear.

In the back of the banquet room that day was a young black man of twenty-one. He had grown up on Church Hill, on the other side of the C&O Railway tracks in east Richmond. Patrick Henry had once declared "give me liberty or give me death" in St. John's Church there, but that was almost two hundred years before. Now Church Hill was Richmond's largest black slum, a place of poverty and despair, a place separate and unequal from the gleaming white Richmond across Shockoe Bottom.

This young black man had grown up playing on Church Hill's unpaved streets, had shined shoes in its barbershops, had washed the windows of its stores, had painted its houses. Nowadays he rode the back of the bus downtown to Richmond's grand old hotels and country clubs. He began by pouring endless cups of coffee for $1 a day at the Hotel John Marshall, just another uniformed black serving boy moving silently through a wealthy white man's world. Now he had clearly moved up — he was waiting tables on the banquet circuit. He studied the trade under the older black men who had spent all their lives working in these hotels, learning when to whisk away an empty plate, when to arrive with more coffee, how to be gracious and polite, all useful skills for a black man in the South in 1952.

It was nearly 3 p.m. by the time he had finished cleaning off the tables and setting up the banquet room for the evening. He and two other waiters — themselves working their way through college — hurried to the bus stop in front of the William Byrd and hoped they still had time.

A small, rumpled white man in a coat and tie came out of the hotel, too. The waiters had seen him at lunch taking notes. He was Guy Friddell, one of the top reporters for the *Richmond News Leader*. While the waiters had been cleaning up after lunch, Friddell had been on the phone in the lobby, dictating his story for the afternoon editions. Now he, too, was checking his watch, in a hurry to get to where he was going. The three young black men at the bus stop caught his eye. They seemed anxious, vainly looking up Broad Street for a bus that was nowhere in sight.

Friddell asked if they needed a ride downtown.

Sort of, they said. They were going to Virginia Union University, the local black college.

No problem, Friddell said. He was going there, too. Taft was scheduled to speak to students in the chapel auditorium at 3 p.m.

That's why they were going, too, the waiters said, and eagerly piled into Friddell's car.

Two of the young men sat quietly, looking out the windows as Friddell drove down Broad and up Lombardy. They were just happy to be saving the bus fare. But the one waiter pestered the reporter with question after question. What did you think of Taft's speech? What was Taft saying back there? Was he saying the Republican Party supports segregation? Are Southern Democrats likely to go along with what Taft says?

Friddell tried to answer the questions as best he could, but finally gave up in exasperation. "Did you listen to Taft's speech?" he asked.

His young interrogator shot back: "I always listen."

The waiter was keyed up for Taft's appearance at Virginia Union. He had heard Taft was going to take questions from the students — and, after listening to Taft at the William Byrd, he was ready with some questions that would be sure to make the senator squirm.

He was in for a keen disappointment. When the students got to the college he found the question-and-answer forum was a set-up. Taft would only take written questions that had been screened by the moderator. This waiter, who had graduated the previous year, protested the arrangement, but to no avail. The format was set — and his pointed questions were hardly likely to be deemed suitable for the polite, deferential session the organizers had planned.

The young man was furious — at Taft, at the moderator, at the political system in general. He sat there seething while Taft gave the black students a soothing, upbeat speech about how he, too, opposed segregation. "The federal government should take an increased part in the steady improvement of the lot of the colored people," Taft assured the students, and listed all the bills he had supported that would help them.

The student couldn't believe what he was witnessing. How could Taft, a United States senator — a candidate for president, no less — be allowed to get away with such double talk? How could he say one thing to the whites at the William Byrd and another to the blacks at Virginia Union?

The crowd was filing out of the auditorium after Taft's speech when the student ran into the reporter who had given him the ride.

Friddell asked what he thought. But if Friddell expected the student to rage against the senator, he was in for a surprise. The young man was still angry, all right, but he was also calm and analytical. He hadn't just listened to Taft, he had studied him. The student went over Taft's two speeches, pointed out all the inconsistencies and poked one hole after another in the senator's sweet-sounding arguments. How could Taft say he opposes segregation when he admits he wouldn't force the states to abolish it? Taft said he supports a Fair Employment Practices Commission, but he would not give it the power to require companies to hire more blacks. Instead, he would ask for "voluntary" cooperation. Now what good would that do? Taft is talking about things, but he wouldn't do anything about them.

Friddell nodded, impressed by the waiter's attention to detail. He suggested that if the young man was upset, one way to help change society was to get involved in politics himself.

Oh no, the waiter said. He wasn't about to get mixed up in anything so crooked and confusing and deceitful as politics, no sir. He had been a chemistry major, he said. The sciences — impartial, empirical — were the way for blacks to get ahead. Besides, he said, he didn't know what the future would hold anyway. His draft number was up and he expected to be sent to Korea, maybe even the front lines. Who knew what would happen to him there?

Friddell listened to his protests and wished him luck. And, as the young black man turned to leave, the reporter asked what his name was.

"Doug Wilder," he said.

Nov. 6, 1985

Doug Wilder's hair was gray now, his anger subsided. He had lived through the Korean hell and come home a hero, only to find he still had to ride the back of the bus downtown from Church Hill. He had graduated from college, only to find that a degree in chemistry would qualify him only to be a cook at a juvenile detention center. He had lived through enough to justify a young black man's anger — or turn it into an older black man's determination to succeed.

Now it was thirty-three years later and he was at another Richmond hotel. The November night was cold and quiet and seemed to go on forever, stuck between the dying of one day and the dawn of another, as if time itself had paused long enough to reflect on this moment before the morning washed out its mystery.

Wilder's voice was almost gone, so he spoke softly, in a low raspy whisper. He had sweated so much under the glare of the TV lights, he had shaken so many hands, that he felt like a wrung-out dishrag.

He tried to sit and relax, but there was still so much nervous energy bundled up inside him that every few minutes he'd get up to pace back and forth behind the chair. He had taken off his shoes; the plush carpet squished beneath his stocking feet.

This time it was Guy Friddell, himself grayer with the passage of three decades, who was asking the questions, probing Wilder's mind to learn what it all meant.

It was 2:30 in the morning, a Wednesday. The polls had been closed for hours, the votes counted, the results broadcast. At the John Marshall, across the interstate out in Northside at the Flamingo Lounge, the victory parties were still going strong — people cheering, people drinking, people dancing, people hugging one another. But in a hushed hotel room overlooking Capitol Square, a subdued Wilder sat in the shadows and wondered himself what it all meant.

His college-age daughter was there. So was his nephew. They said nothing. The three reporters admitted to this private moment spoke in reverential tones. Only one weak lamp was turned on, almost as if no one dared disturb the night, lest it change its mind.

Out there, history had been made. The morning paper already was rolling off the presses to confirm it.

So this is what it's like. The making of history — accompanied not by drumbeats and thunder, but by whispers in the night. In the silence of the Commonwealth Park Hotel, Room 303, if you listened closely enough, you could hear the pages of history turning over.

It was there in the questions the reporters asked and the answers Wilder gave. Only a few hours ago, they were phrased conditionally — what if? how will? Now they slipped into the past tense — how did? how were? — as if discussing something that had happened years ago, as if discussing, well, history.

Only a few hours earlier, Wilder had won his place in that history. And there had been plenty of cheering then.

At the Hotel John Marshall, where Wilder once poured coffee, an expectant crowd had started arriving early, even before the polls had closed. Soon it was far bigger than the crowd that had converged on the

John Marshall four years before, when the Democrats swept back into the Governor's Mansion for the first time in twelve years. They pressed against the ballroom stage all evening, screaming themselves hoarse. Hours went by with no official word. The crowd was too loud to hear what was happening on the big TV monitors. But everyone knew.

Jerry Baliles had won the governorship early; Mary Sue Terry had won her attorney general's race earlier still. But they waited until Wilder's margin for lieutenant governor was assured so they could go down and claim victory together. The exit polls predicted it; the early returns confirmed it. Still, Wilder hesitated, wanting to make sure it was really true, it was so hard to believe.

Just a few minutes before the 11 o'clock news went on, the doors at the side of the stage were flung open and everyone jostled for position to see who was coming out. Yes, there's Baliles, and yes, Terry — and yes, Wilder, too, smiling, waving, flashing a V-for-Victory. Even though they had stood there all night waiting for that moment, the Democrats in that room could scarcely believe what they were seeing.

The next governor seemed almost forgotten in the midst of all the shouting. Everyone knew Baliles and Terry would win. It was Wilder the people wanted to see, to hear, to touch.

Baliles and Terry gave their victory statements and worked the receiving line, then retired to private parties upstairs. But Wilder lingered, as hundreds more pushed up to the stage just to be able to shake his hand, to be able to get close to this man who had made history. There were so many people they nearly pulled Wilder off the edge of the stage. TV lights blinded him. He dabbed his face with a handkerchief, but sweat still dripped off his nose.

An elderly white man seized Wilder's hand and pumped it vigorously. "It's a great day for Virginia," he said, beaming.

A fresh-faced college student followed. "I'm with the Young Democrats," he said, "and I want to thank you for letting me help you make history."

Not until an hour after victory was declared did Wilder get upstairs to the party with his own supporters. The crowd burst into "For He's a Jolly Good Fellow" and mobbed Wilder again, waving scraps of paper, napkins, anything, for him to autograph. Nephew Mike Brown had to pull Wilder out of the crush so he could go to the Flamingo Lounge for the traditional party with the black Crusade for Voters.

The Flamingo crowd squealed as Wilder came through the door. Dignitaries rushed to get on the podium beside him. Wilder reminded them of another night he had been to a victory party at the Flamingo, the night he first won election to the Virginia State Senate. "It was Dec. 2, 1969," Wilder reminded them. "The weather was bad and cold then, too. People said it couldn't be done but we did it."

The Senate had seemed such a big step then. Now Wilder had earned himself a place in history that could never have been imagined by the young waiter listening to speeches in the back of the banquet room that day in 1952.

He was now the first black to win a statewide election in Virginia, the first black to win a statewide executive office in the South since Reconstruction. For the next few years at least, as lieutenant governor of Virginia, he would be the highest-ranking black elected official anywhere in the country. Maybe someday he would become the first black elected governor anywhere in the U.S.

But that was for later. Now it was early morning and Wilder still knew nothing about the nature of his victory except what he had heard on television — he had been so busy being pulled from one frenzied victory party to the next.

Exhausted, he retreated to the Commonwealth Park to savor his victory in private. The room was so quiet it was almost unreal, as if the excitement only hours ago had all been a dream. Only the sound of Paul Goldman mumbling into the phone was proof that it had really happened.

The scraggly-haired New York lawyer who had engineered the victory was scrunched down on the sofa, phone pressed to his ear, calling party workers around the state — "Joe? Paul here. How'd we do out your way?" — and scribbling down the returns on the back of an envelope.

Wilder had always clung to a stubborn, perhaps naive, across-the-board faith that white Virginians would ignore his skin and focus on his Senate record. But when the totals were broken down into the judgments of individual communities, even Wilder found them impossible to understand.

"The areas we carried, you just wouldn't believe," he said softly. "We carried the Sixth [Congressional District]. I just can't believe that." The mountains and valleys of Western Virginia were almost exclusively white and had been Republican territory since the Civil War.

"We carried the Ninth by more votes than [Rep.] Rick Boucher did in 1984. That's what they told me." Wilder had once been advised not to even go into the Appalachian coalfields, that it might not be safe for a black man there.

"We lost the Third [Wilder's home district] by only ten thousand votes. That wasn't supposed to happen." The sprawling suburbs of Henrico and Chesterfield counties were mostly scrub until Richmond's schools were integrated and the white flight began.

Wilder shook his head. "It's amazing. Did we win the Second?"

Goldman nodded and kept scribbling.

Wilder had been considered so easy a target in this seaside suburbia that the Republican candidate for attorney general — a Virginia Beach hometown boy — had ignored his own opponent and made a point of attacking Wilder in TV commercials there.

"What about the First?"

Goldman nodded again.

Eastern Virginia was the old colonial heartland, where magnificent white-columned plantation houses look down on sluggish rivers. Its congressman, a former lieutenant in the Byrd Machine who had led other conservative Democrats in joining the Republican Party, had been a campaign co-chairman for Wilder's opponent.

This time Wilder simply shook his head, unable to find the words, unable to even voice the question. There was no point asking where he won, because he had won so many places. If Wilder had been able to shake another 1,800 hands in the rural Fifth he might have carried the tobacco country of Southside, once the last redoubt of segregation.

Virginia had changed. The South had changed. But no one knew how much until tonight — until Doug Wilder, the former busboy from Church Hill, had given it a chance to prove itself. Now Wilder was a prophet and the reporters strained to capture every word. "How?" they asked. "Why?" Suddenly, all the old assumptions were gone, dramatically cast aside.

Wilder gestured toward the darkness outside. "There wasn't ever that monster that people think is out there," he said, "that monster" being the racism he was repeatedly told lurked somewhere waiting to get him, if not in public, then at least in the privacy of the voting booth. So where was it tonight? Even he seemed to be groping for new landmarks.

Friddell reminded Wilder of the first time they met, when he gave him a lift at the William Byrd. Wilder smiled. Yes, he remembered that. Wilder also remembered another speech he had heard years ago. Once in the mid-1950s, while he was a law student in Washington, he went to hear former Secretary of State Dean Acheson speak to the students. Acheson also had crafted his answers to suit the audience at hand. "I said, 'That's it, no way I'm going to get mixed up in politics now,' " Wilder said, laughing softly.

One floor down in another suite, Wilder's twenty-three-year-old son was pouring the champagne for relatives. When they finally went home, the first pale light of a new day was streaking the sky over Church Hill.

When Hell Froze Over

"If Chichester's alive on Election Day, he's in."
— prominent Republican soon after John Chichester was nominated as Wilder's opponent.

Doug Wilder's story is one even Hollywood would be hard-pressed to imagine: A black candidate, given up for dead by many in his own party, wins election in the South, partly on the strength of votes from Appalachian mountaineers and low-country rednecks.

But it happened.

And it happened in Virginia, a state with a long and ugly history of racial prejudice. Yet Wilder won an impossible-to-believe share of the white vote: 44 percent, only two percentage points less than moderate-conservative Democrat Charles Robb received when he was elected governor in 1981.

At first glance, Virginia — the conservative, hidebound Old Dominion — is one of the last states in the country where a black should have won statewide office.

To begin with, Virginia has one of the smallest black populations of any Southern state — 19 percent, compared with 35 percent in Mississippi and 30 percent in South Carolina.

Beyond that, Virginia is also an unusually conservative state, even by Southern standards. Until the 1980s, Virginia had been one of the most Republican states in the nation. Between 1948 and 1984, Lyndon Johnson was the only Democrat to carry the state. Virginia was the only Southern state not to go with Jimmy Carter in 1976 and was damn proud of it, too. By 1980, the state's congressional delegation consisted of nine Republicans and one old-line Southern Democrat. Only in local offices and the General Assembly did Democrats retain their old majority.

No, Virginia was most assuredly the last place where a black Democrat could win a statewide election. A black who could get the Democratic nomination and command at least some degree of party loyalty might be able to win in some other Southern state — maybe. After all, a black had won the Democratic nomination for Congress in Mississippi in 1982 — but he failed to win even in a district that was 53 percent black.

So why did anyone think that a black could win in Virginia, a state that had none of the prerequisites of black voting strength and Democratic heritage?

And there was yet another coldly practical consideration standing in the way of a black candidacy. Where was this black candidate supposed to come from?

Virginia's political system forecloses the most obvious route to power that black politicians in other states have taken. Virginia's system of local government does not vest much power in mayors — so the mayor of a big Virginia city, whether black or white, has little chance to exert statewide influence and demonstrate executive leadership the way Andrew Young has done in Atlanta or Tom Bradley has done in Los Angeles.

The traditional route to statewide politics in Virginia is through the General Assembly. The House of Delegates, with one hundred seats, has a half-dozen black legislators, but most are junior members that go unrecognized outside their home districts. Thus it happened that Doug Wilder, for thirteen years the only black in the forty-member state Senate, was the only black of any statewide stature — but he was a highly controversial figure, hardly suited for running a statewide race.

Or so it was thought.

Was Wilder's election a fluke? "Maybe it's campaign astrology," says Darrel Martin, who managed Baliles' campaign for governor. "We had a convergence of the planets. Maybe it only occurs once a century, but it occurred in Virginia in 1985."

Certainly everything happened that Wilder needed to happen — a picture-perfect campaign and a bumbling opponent. The presence of the fantastically popular Charles Robb in the Governor's Mansion (and in Wilder's TV spots) cannot be underestimated, either.

Wilder's victory was no mistake, though. He may have been pulled over the 50 percent mark by the tug of the Democratic sweep, but no Democratic trend would have been strong enough to help Wilder if he hadn't already put himself within striking distance. A change of about 2 percent would have meant defeat but it wouldn't have changed the fact that, for a black candidate in the South (or anywhere else, for that matter), Wilder did very, very well indeed.

Wilder's winning 52-48 percent margin was slim but not microscopic. It was bigger than Republican John Warner's margin in the 1978 U.S. Senate race and Republican Paul Trible's margin in the 1982 Senate race — and Baliles' margin in the 1981 attorney general's race, for that matter.

Wilder's victory was geographically and demographically broad. He carried seven of ten congressional districts. His biggest margins came in the two whitest areas of the state: the Washington suburbs in Northern Virginia and the Appalachians of Southwest Virginia. He came within 3,500 votes of carrying rural Southside's Fifth Congressional District, which comes closer than any other Virginia region to resembling a red-clay district of the Deep South.

Most amazingly, Wilder won without a large black turnout. In the 1981 governor's race, 15 percent of the voters were black; in 1985, with a black on the ticket, only 14 percent of those who cast ballots were black. For a variety of reasons, Virginians were apathetic about the 1985 election and even the historic candidacies of Wilder and Terry — the first black and first woman to win statewide election — failed to stir them. White turnout was down dramatically from 1981, but so was black turnout. In 1981, 68 percent of blacks who were registered to vote went to the polls. In 1985, Doug Wilder notwithstanding, barely 54 percent did. Furthermore, there was no concerted voter registration drive among blacks to help Wilder's campaign.

The significance of Doug Wilder's election as lieutenant governor of Virginia in 1985 extends well beyond the state line:

It offers irrefutable evidence of changing racial attitudes in the South.

Wilder's 44 percent of the white vote was about standard for a Virginia Democrat in a statewide race. (Not since 1965 has a Democratic candidate for governor, U.S. senator or president received a majority of the white vote.) And three out of every four votes Wilder received were cast by whites.

Black judges have been elected statewide on long ballots in some Southern states — in Florida in 1972, in Alabama in 1982 and in Georgia in 1984. But not since Reconstruction had a Southern state elected a black to a non-judicial statewide office. Wilder's victory as lieutenant governor was the breakthrough. With it, he automatically became a logical and frequently mentioned candidate for governor in 1989. But winning the governorship after four years of high-profile apprenticeship would not be nearly so surprising as the fact that he won the first time, on the blind faith of white voters.

Wilder's election demonstrates the potential political clout of the emerging black middle class. Doug Wilder represents a new type of black leader — a professional, not a preacher, a career politician with close ties to the white power structure, not a civil rights leader who marched in the streets.

The black ministers who led the civil rights movement spoke for a black community with a common concern: dismantling segregation. But in the three decades since the *Brown* decision, and the two decades since the Civil Rights Act, the black community has become divided — into those who have been able to translate legal protections and educational opportunities into economic success and those who haven't. Jesse Jackson represents the latter. He speaks for the poor and downtrodden and emphasizes race by talk of building a "rainbow coalition." Wilder, though, won election in a conservative Southern state because he espoused solid middle-class values that were neither black nor white. "Doug Wilder worked his way to the top," was the slogan of one of his TV commercials. His is a success story. Voters like a Horatio Alger and Wilder gave them just that, without the threatening overtones of "it's our turn."

Surprisingly, Wilder was no newcomer to the Virginia political scene, a black with no racial political baggage who could make his first impression on voters in an upbeat TV spot. For better or worse, many voters knew who Doug Wilder was long before he ran for lieutenant governor. For sixteen years, he had been the leading spokesman for blacks in Virginia, a position that often had him embroiled in controversy and earned him a well-deserved reputation as a firebrand. His evolution from the loud, militant Doug Wilder with the Afro into the low-key, mainstream Doug Wilder in the banker's gray suit is all part of a larger evolution of black leadership in America. In the end, Wilder won because he struck middle-class white voters as being not much different from themselves. Even what would have been a scandal for a white candidate — charges of being a slumlord — may have indirectly helped Wilder because it reinforced the fact that he is a property owner, a developer, a speculator in the American Dream.

Wilder's victory demonstrates the economic clout of that same emerging black middle class. One rap against black candidates has always been that they can't raise money from "traditional" sources. Wilder's campaign showed that those traditional sources may not be nearly as important as they once were.

Wilder raised more than $700,000, far beyond even his own expectations. More than half of that money, according to Wilder's chief fund-raiser Jackie Epps, came from black contributors, virtually all of them in-state. Wilder's fund-raisers targeted young black professionals, who kept the campaign afloat in its early days. Not until the final months of the campaign, when it became clear Wilder could win, did sizable amounts of "white" money start coming in. Wilder's original budget called for raising $500,000. He came close to that from black contributors alone.

One major lesson of Wilder's campaign, campaign consultant Paul Goldman says, "is that you can raise $300,000-$400,000 indigenously from blacks in a state like Virginia. It's probably not enough, but it's enough to run a credible campaign. It demonstrates to Democrats a source of money to be tapped in future campaigns." And economic power, of course, makes the goal of attaining political power much more realistic. Wilder's fund-raising experience in Virginia suggests that similar black candidates could bankroll serious campaigns for lower-ballot offices in other states without undue reliance on white contributors.

Wilder's election signaled the possible opening of a new era, as black politicians break out of black-majority districts and venture into the virtually unexplored territory of statewide politics.

When Wilder ran in 1985, only three other blacks held statewide elected office, all in lower-ballot positions — Roland Burris, the comptroller of Illinois; Henry Parker, the treasurer of Connecticut; and Richard Austin, Michigan's secretary of state, all of them holdovers from a short-lived heyday of black statewide victories in the 1970s. In 1978, in fact, there had been six blacks holding statewide office, including U.S. Sen. Edward Brooke of Massachusetts and the first two black lieutenant governors in this century, Mervyn Dymally and George Brown (both elected in 1974, in trendy California and Colorado). But by the end of the decade, most of them were out of office.

"For a while there in the 1970s, it was fashionable to vote for black candidates," says Benjamin Hooks, the NAACP's national executive director, "but then that trend cut against us and cut against us rather meanly." Perhaps Wilder's election marks a renaissance of blacks seeking statewide office.

Significantly, those blacks who do win statewide elections — or even local elections in white-majority districts — are likely to be moderates in the Wilder mold, candidates who de-emphasize race and thereby appeal to the white middle-class swing voter. And, again, those successful candidates are likely to be members of the new black middle class — people such as Bobby Scott of Newport News, the Harvard-educated lawyer who in 1982 won in a district that was 68 percent white to become Virginia's second black state senator; and Alan Wheat of Kansas City, Mo., the Grinnell-educated economist who represents a congressional district that is 77 percent white.

In many black communities, there is a generational and demographic fault line forming between the old guard and the new middle class. It was seen in the 1986 Democratic primary for the Atlanta-area House seat between John Lewis and Julian Bond, in which Lewis' old warriors of the sixties were pitted against Bond's "buppies" of the eighties. Thus, Wilder — who grew up in the segregated society of the pre-*Brown* South but was able to present himself as a spokesman of the new middle class — is an important transitional figure for both blacks and whites.

Wilder's candidacy raises the tantalizing question of whether Southern blacks might not want to quit their efforts to eliminate runoff primaries and, in multi-office elections, push for conventions instead. Wilder's campaign in 1985 suggests that blacks might hold more real bargaining power in a convention, even (perhaps especially) a Southern one set to nominate a moderate-conservative candidate for governor. "That flies in the face of a whole lot of conventional wisdom and legal arguments," says Goldman, "but our experience suggests it's true."

In a primary there's no way to make deals to deliver individual voters. In a caucus system, with Wilder seeking the lieutenant governorship, the two candidates for governor always faced the threat of blacks flooding mass meetings to file as Wilder delegates, but either uncommitted on the governor's race or committed to the other candidate.

Wilder's victory suggests the outline of a possible new coalition — an alliance of blacks with white moderates, an alliance that has the potential to redefine the Democratic Party. That runs counter to the Jesse Jackson model — blacks allied themselves with the Democratic left in 1988 — but once again, Wilder's style of black politics represents an alternative to Jackson's.

Wilder's alliance with the political center came when Democrats chose a candidate for governor. Politically, he had more in common with Dick Davis — but Davis had the fatal flaw of being perceived as a liberal in a steadfastly conservative state. Wilder realized that, too, and maneuvered behind-the-scenes to see that the moderate-conservative Jerry Baliles was nominated instead. Baliles at the head of the ticket gave Wilder access to moderate voters he might not have been able to reach with Davis.

But 1985 was not the first time in Virginia that blacks have allied themselves with a moderate-conservative and emerged victorious with far more than they ever expected. The Baliles-Wilder coalition was essentially the same as the Robb coalition of 1981. In 1981, blacks were initially skeptical of Democratic gubernatorial candidate Charles Robb and his claims to be a fiscal conservative yet a social progressive. However, blacks turned out to vote for Robb in record numbers and Robb proved himself to indeed be the new breed of Southern Democrat that he claimed to be — he pleased his conservative supporters by turning in a record budget surplus without a tax increase, but he also appointed the first black to the state Supreme Court and named blacks to scores of other key positions. Robb's centrist politics enabled blacks to make unprecedented gains in Virginia. Is that something which could be duplicated on the national scene?

On a purely Virginia level, Wilder's election serves as the ultimate repudiation of the Byrd machine, once one of the South's most powerful and enduring political organizations. But some important observations on the status of racial prejudice in the South can be found in the machine's last hurrah.

In 1981, GOP gubernatorial candidate Marshall Coleman had been wounded by even his lukewarm association with the Old Guard of the Byrd crowd. Its effect then was limited mostly to blacks, who came out en masse to vote for Charles Robb after former Gov. Mills Godwin had made a thinly veiled racial appeal on Coleman's behalf. But in 1985, for the first time among white voters, a Republican candidate was hurt more than he was helped by his close association with the remnants of the Byrd organization. John Chichester, Wilder's opponent, was on the defensive for his ties to Godwin even among white voters. Upscale, white professionals may have agreed with Godwin's fiscal conservatism but they simply found it embarrassing to be associated with a leader of Virginia's Massive Resistance to integration. And not only did they find it repugnant in public, they apparently found it that way in private, too — Wilder ran surprisingly strong in the white suburbs. If Republicans learned anything from the 1985 election, they are likely to go out of their way to avoid nominating a candidate linked to the conservative Democrats who switched parties in the seventies.

And if nothing else, Wilder's election is the dramatic personal story of how a black busboy in the all-white country clubs of Richmond rose to preside over what is reverently called "the most exclusive club in Virginia" — the state Senate.

The state's premier political analyst, Larry Sabato of the University of Virginia, called Wilder's defeat "the surest thing in Virginia politics." This was, after all, Virginia and Wilder was, after all, black.

Paul Goldman concedes that Wilder should not have won in 1985. "Doug should have gotten 45 percent of the vote and people afterward would have been saying, "Someday it could be possible.' If the Republicans had nominated Marshall Coleman or a smarter candidate [than John Chichester] they might have beaten us, but they gave us an opportunity to get in and move up a generation early." And that brings us back to Wilder as a symbol of the emerging black middle class.

At age fifty-four in 1985, Wilder was a generation ahead of the politicians who would be expected to lead the new black middle class. Wilder felt the full sting of Southern racism growing up in the forties and fifties. He went to dilapidated, segregated schools, was denied admission to Virginia law schools, and had no chance of joining a prestigious law firm. He had none of the advantages blacks growing up in the sixties and seventies started to have. Logically, the first black to have enough connections within the white establishment to win a statewide election in Virginia should have been a member of that generation. "Doug is maybe twenty years ahead of his time," Goldman says. "It should have taken another generation for that to happen."

By forcing himself on a skittish Democratic Party in 1985, Wilder caught the public at a time when racial prejudice, even in the South, had moderated enough to accept a black candidate. Goldman credits television for accelerating that change. "Doug came along when people are seeing more upscale black images," he says. The Huxtables of "The Cosby Show" are the best examples of that. With Wilder projecting those same middle-class values, Goldman argues, he presented white voters with a model they could recognize and even identify with.

In that sense, Wilder's campaign is a blueprint for other black candidates seeking white votes.

Wilder never mentioned race. He hammered away at why he was more qualified until the media and white voters finally had to pay attention. But his campaign never took on the aura of a black crusade. The inherent risk in such a strategy is that blacks won't feel motivated to vote and, indeed, Wilder almost lost the election because black turnout was far lower than expected. But Wilder knew he had to have the redneck and suburban vote to win and he went after it. Wilder ran one of the most traditional, almost chauvinistic, campaigns Virginia has ever seen and Virginians loved it.

Wilder turned racial imagery on its head. His most memorable TV commercial featured a beefy white Southern lawman standing beside his cruiser and testifying in a drawl why he was voting for Doug Wilder. "That commercial won the election for me," Wilder says.

Wilder was a master at using the media to his advantage. His station-wagon tour of the state, a two-month odyssey of barnstorming rural communities to shake hands in country stores, was political theater and "drama works to a candidate's benefit," says Baliles campaign manager Martin. All Virginia was holding its breath for a racial incident that never happened. Instead, Wilder received one enthusiastic reception after another. "His campaign journey became a metaphor," Martin says. "It was not just a campaign schedule. It was symbolic." In the end, Wilder's journey took him back to where he started — in Richmond hotels, listening to political speeches. And that might just be the most telling symbolism of all.

2

Little Douglas

More than one Virginia Democrat has offered this unusual description of the state's most prominent black politician: "He's a Virginia gentleman. He talks like a Southern gentleman. He dresses like a Southern gentleman. He acts like a Southern gentleman."

It's just that his skin is darker than most.

It is a description as accurate as it is misleading, but one that goes a long way toward explaining how Lawrence Douglas Wilder forced his way into the state's history books in 1985.

Doug Wilder is a black politician, make no mistake — he has played the racial card too often for that — but he is no ordinary black politician.

"Much in the story of Doug Wilder is familiar as the legendary dream — the young black, rebuked and embittered by segregation, who comes of age and awareness in war and goes on to succeed through talent, hard work and patience," the *Washington Post* once wrote. "But much is fundamentally different from the accepted truth of contemporary black politics. He has risen to power less through a messianic unifying appeal to blacks than through his ability to understand and work with whites. The key to his success, in fact, is his ability to be totally at ease with whites but not in the least obsequious."

And no one has ever accused Doug Wilder of being obsequious.

Wilder's is a Horatio Alger story, certainly. "When he started practicing law, he couldn't even sit at the same bench or drink from the same water fountain as other lawyers," Del. Chip Woodrum, D-Roanoke, once said. "Nothing's been given to Doug. He's managed it on his own."

And he's managed quite well, thank you. Wilder was the first member of his family to buy a car. Now he drives a Mercedes. His grandparents were slaves. Now he owns $1 million worth of property. He belongs to a country club. He subscribes to *Signature,* "the magazine of preferred living." His law office may still be on Church Hill, the black neighborhood where he grew up, but now Wilder lives in upper-middle-class Ginter Park, in a fifteen-room Georgian house decorated with art and antiques from all over the world. He employs a housekeeper.

"He lives the good life," says Virginia Senate clerk and Wilder confidante Jay Shropshire, "but on the other hand, he's worked hard to live it."

Don't get the impression, though, that Wilder is all show without substance. "I've seen him long enough to know he's animated by some pretty deep passions," says former GOP legislator Ray Garland of Roanoke.

Still, Wilder's aristocratic tastes may be reassuring to some conservative Virginians taken by the superficial gloss. This is no primitive backwoods preacher out leading marches and whipping up the congregations. Here is a professional man of letters, a member of the propertied class, if you will. Wilder's resume and lifestyle signal to the political bosses and captains of industry that he is, in many ways, one of them. This is no black power radical; this is someone they can do business with.

Yet this genteel insider could never be mistaken for an Uncle Tom. For nearly two decades, he has been the most visible spokesman for black Virginians. "Every governor of Virginia has had to go through Doug Wilder," Shropshire says.

And if Doug Wilder has been someone that the conservative establishment can do business with, he also has sometimes been one to drive an especially hard bargain. But other times, when deep passions have bubbled up, Wilder has seemed intent on disregarding common sense and provoking controversy.

Until his 1985 campaign for lieutenant governor, whenever Doug Wilder got his name in the paper, it was usually as a whine, a scold, taking on the state's conservative establishment: attacking a state song he considered racist, sinking a Democratic candidate for the U.S. Senate he objected to, insisting a white colleague take him to the all-white Commonwealth Club, lambasting the House speaker for his "magnolia mentality."

"He's often said someday his children will call him to task: What did you do in the war, Daddy?" says Sandy Bowen, who became secretary of the commonwealth under Baliles. "So he's gone out and been bellicose and shaken the trees and taken pot shots at sacred cows."

Yet the same Wilder who has been quick to shout racism at some perceived slight has also been quick to put white colleagues at ease with racial humor. Once when state Sen. Bill Parker, D-Chesapeake, was just back from his beach house with a dark tan, Wilder put his arm up against the senator's and exclaimed in mock horror, "Damn, Parker! You're darker than I am!" Another time, at a political dinner in Williamsburg, a white legislator asked Wilder who someone across the room was. Wilder shook his head. "I don't know," he said. "All those white people look alike to me."

To conservative opponents, his very name — Wilder — symbolizes how they see him, someone who any minute now might call for razing the Confederate statues on Richmond's Monument Avenue. But while other politicians might have been diminished or even destroyed from such seemingly reckless showdowns, Wilder emerged from each confrontation stronger than before. Some have argued that his race gave him a protective cloak. Perhaps, or it may have been just extraordinary good luck. "Doug Wilder's like a cat," Shropshire says. "No matter how you drop him, he always lands on his feet."

And here he was in 1985, ranked by a Norfolk *Virginian-Pilot* newspaper poll as the fifth-most-powerful member in the Virginia Senate, the state's bastion of conservatism. And here was that most conservative of senators, Finance Committee Chairman Ed Willey, who counted Wilder as both a friend and important ally. "The people who say he's a wild-eyed liberal just don't know his record," Willey said during the campaign. "On the big votes, he's on the right side. He sticks with me on the budget."

So just who is this Doug Wilder?

The *Washington Post* once offered this thumbnail sketch: "Wilder is only 5 feet 9, but he is always noticed. Dapper and high-school trim at fifty-five, he struts any room like a stage, his Richard Pryor mimicry accenting his anecdotes, his grin easy as his handshake, his laugh bursting forth constantly — to show delight or derision. Clothes highlight the act, from the tan silk Countess Mara tie to the beige sport coat to the burnished wing tips and lapis pinkie ring. He does not suffer slights that were the norm in segregated days. Once an elevator operator in the Capitol carrying

Wilder up reversed the elevator when whites got on and took them down first. "You do what you have to do," says Wilder. "I had him *removed!*"

Another time, when state Sen. William Fears, D-Accomack, mentioned that he was going to South America after the session, Wilder said he'd like to go along. "I said 'Well, come on, let's go,'" Fears recalls, and this political odd couple — Wilder, the smooth, urbane, big-city lawyer, and Fears, a drawling, cigar-chewing, motorcycle-riding country lawyer — spent a week sightseeing in Caracas, Venezuela, and Bogota, Colombia. Fears remembers they stopped in a jewelry store and bought some emeralds wholesale as a combination souvenir-investment. "I think Doug's got a lot of personality," Fears says.

Wilder is a charmer, all right. "Some call it charisma," says Ben Dendy, an aide to both Robb and Baliles. Wilder's vivaciousness carries over to almost every aspect of both his political and personal life. He is a flashy dresser. "I could safely say he's a bit of a dandy," says state Sen. Buzz Emick, D-Botetourt County. Wilder's shirts are monogrammed. He sports cuff links bearing the seal of Virginia. In earlier times, he sported an Afro and once wore a leather jacket onto the Senate floor.

Wilder likes to show off in other ways, too.

He learned to shoot pool in the smoky billiard halls on Church Hill and became a master, a talent he demonstrated to the amazement of the good ole boys in Edgar Bacon's basement in the mountains of Southwest Virginia early in the campaign. One image that sticks in son Larry Wilder's mind is going to Richmond's Club 533 some years ago. Like Babe Ruth at the plate, Doug Wilder called his shot and tapped the cue ball. "It curved around the one in front of it and hit another ball," Larry recalls, just as Wilder had said it would.

Tennis and golf are also hobbies, but bridge remains his favorite. Wilder is an amateur artist, occasionally dabbling in oils. Wild animals are his favorite subject. He's also a gourmet cook. "He has all the right pots and pans and sauces and spices," says former State Corporation Commissioner Junie Bradshaw. Once Ed Willey brought back a goose from a hunting trip and offered it to Wilder. Not long afterward, the Willeys were invited to Wilder's home for dinner — and there was the goose, carefully prepared, as the main course.

One gets the feeling Wilder would excel at just about anything he applied himself to. The phrase "Renaissance man" is tough to resist.

In some ways, Wilder is a throwback to a nineteenth-century politician — a spellbinding orator who says his favorite pastime is simply good conversation.

Extraordinarily well-read, Wilder "quotes classical literature at the drop of a hat," says state Sen. Granger Macfarlane, D-Roanoke. Jim Morris, a Richmond lawyer, likes to trick friends by reciting the line "take the cash and let the credit go" to see if they know it's by Omar Khayyam, a twelfth-century Persian poet. Morris tried that on Wilder one day. Wilder quoted him the next four lines.

During the 1985 campaign, Bradshaw invited Wilder to his weekly Wednesday morning prayer breakfast. "He joined right in and contributed in a very scholarly way," quoting Scripture from memory, Bradshaw recalls. "He's a scholar of Scripture." And Bradshaw notes that on election night, Wilder was the only candidate to thank the Lord.

The man's gift for oratory — putting those rare quotations to work — is just as legendary. "Wilder is a cross between a Southern stem-winder and a Baptist preacher on the stump," says Alan Albert, an adviser to Baliles. With a text, Wilder's speeches sometimes come across wooden and laborious. But liberated from the written word, Wilder is a master. Karl Bren, who worked in the Baliles campaign, remembers a eulogy he once heard Wilder give. "It was one of the most powerful things I've ever seen, how Wilder moved that group. He was compassionate, universal in theme. He addressed the family, he addressed those of us there — all without a single note. He didn't go on. It was well-rounded and it just came to me, Doug Wilder's got it. He's got that quality. This man had a depth he could go to I've rarely seen in a speaker and I knew the man had some greatness about him."

Macfarlane lauds Wilder as a man of ambition. "Doug Wilder is not only a man of destiny but it's even deeper than that. Deep down in the very bottom of his heart, his soul, Doug Wilder believes he is a man of destiny. He believes he is slated to do something great."

But where some see ambition, others may see only excessive ego.

So, too, do other attributes sometimes mask a darker side.

Michael Brown, the Wilder nephew who worked in the 1985 campaign, praises Wilder's incredible memory. "Wilder is an encyclopedia," Brown says. "On Chuck Robb, he can tell you from his first political mistake to his first political victory — and the same for all the members of the House and Senate. He could tell you why someone has fallen in disfavor. It may be an incident that might go back to 1960 but he can cite chapter and verse."

A former aide to two Republican governors, Bruce Miller, remembers once being at a Chamber of Commerce dinner in Richmond when he felt a hand on his shoulder. He looked up and saw Doug Wilder smiling at him. "He thanked me for some nicety I had done him years ago," Miller says. Miller had forgotten but Wilder had not.

But that same trap-like memory that serves Wilder so well also is said to remember every slight — real or perceived — and nurse it for years with a vindictive pettiness.

Richmond lawyer and long-time Wilder critic Sa'ad El-Amin once called him "vain, power-hungry and self-centered." One unidentified Democrat once described Wilder as "a showhorse rather than a workhorse." Emick has faulted Wilder for sloughing off issues he's not interested in. But Emick also says Wilder is the only senator he's known who has taken the time to memorize the Senate rules, giving him an edge in parliamentary combat and emphasizing a competitive trait that can manifest itself in both attractive and not-so-attractive ways.

Another senator once said of Wilder: "He wants to be the top black, wants no rivals around." But others have also said: "Had he been white, he would have been governor long ago."

Virginia politicians often recite their genealogy, as if invoking the names of distinguished forebears somehow confers legitimacy and perhaps even honor on their own ambitions. Doug Wilder, too, can trace his lineage back to the plantation. Except the Wilders were part of the estate's inventory, not its first families.

Doug Wilder's grandparents were slaves. He never knew them, but he heard the vivid stories from his father on the rare occasions when that taciturn man would discuss the subject.

"My grandfather and grandmother were married in slavery," Wilder once told the *Washington Times*. "She was sold to a place outside of Ashland [about 18 miles north of Richmond] and they had three children at the time. My grandfather would walk the distance on the weekend to see them. Quite often, he would be late or unaccounted for — I guess you would call it AWOL — and he had to be punished." His overseer, though, was sympathetic to his circumstances. "They concocted a scheme on some occasions, rather than to actually punish him they would whip a saddle and he would act as if he were being punished." As long as the slave's wailing could be heard, the plantation master would be satisfied.

When the Union army took Richmond at the end of the Civil War, James Wilder hid in a silo "scared to death. The owners had threatened him with all the things the Yankees would do if they caught him. He almost suffocated in the silo." Instead, he emerged to find the tales of Yankee atrocities untrue and himself suddenly a free man. James Wilder became a teamster and sold meal. He built a house on Richmond's Church Hill. "My grandfather, a pillar of the church, believed in pride of ownership and hard work," Doug Wilder once told the *Virginian-Pilot* in Norfolk. "And the feeling was that I and those like me would be doing a disservice to the heritage if we didn't continue it."

James and Agnes Wilder's family eventually grew to fourteen children. Despite the laws against teaching slaves to read, Agnes Wilder could — and she impressed her children with the need for an education. One of the boys, Charles, set off to be a doctor. "To be a doctor in those days, what he had to do," marvels Doug Wilder. An older brother, Robert, sacrificed so his sibling could go to medical school. Charles was the family's inspiration. But then the young doctor, only about thirty years old, died. Robert was crushed. "Father just gave up," Doug Wilder once said. "That dashed all his hopes."

Still, Robert Wilder did well for himself. He was an insurance salesman who eventually rose to become a supervisor of agents for a black-owned insurance company, Southern Aid Insurance Co., and built a house of his own across from James Wilder's. The Wilders were middle-class blacks for their day, but their middle-class status was relative. "He never made more than $50 a week," Doug Wilder says of his father, and the family's street was unpaved. Church Hill wasn't that far removed from the backwoods of the Deep South.

"We were poor, but we had a gentle poverty," Wilder once told the *Washington Times*. "We had a large stable affixed to our yard, and it had the darnedest atmosphere. You would think that you lived on a farm because all kinds of animals were in that stable: homing pigeons, ducks, geese, turkeys, gander, guinea and always fresh eggs because we kept chickens. So we never went without food."

Robert and Beulah Wilder had ten children; Lawrence Douglas, born in 1931, was the youngest of the eight who survived. He grew up in a Depression-era, Jim Crow-era household dominated by his mother, an expressive, strong-willed woman. She was the perfect counterpoint to his stern and silent father, who would clamp his pipe between his teeth whenever a subject he didn't want to talk about came up. "I was the only boy in the whole [high] school that freshman year who wore knickers," Wilder told the *Washington Times*. "It used to make me so mad [that] I used to see little children with long pants but I had to wear knickers because my father said I had to wear them. The girls would laugh at me and no one wanted to have anything to do with someone wearing knickers." Not until Wilder was fourteen would his father allow the long pants. "My father used to say, 'Whatever you have, you're better off than I was when I was born. I don't want to hear you complain,' " Wilder once said.

Wilder's mother, the forceful lady that she was, doted on the baby of the family. But rather than smother her young son's identity, Beulah

Wilder instead nurtured his self-confidence.

"She used to tell me, you can do it all," Wilder told the *Washington Post.* "She would tell a story about a 'great little boy.' I would say 'am I that great little boy?' 'Oh yes.' 'Do you know any other great little boy?' 'Ohhh no!' "

His father believed "there was no place in any decision-making for women's talk and children likewise," Wilder said. "My mother loved to talk and had no audience. And I had no audience. So we would just entertain ourselves. She did crosswords. There were very few words you could spring on her."

His mother's daily crossword puzzles played a big part in childhood routine. "One reason he has the vocabulary he has," Shropshire says, "is his mother used to work the crossword puzzle all the time. Back then blacks couldn't go to the movies so they stayed home. She called him 'Little Douglas' and she made him learn a new word every day from the crossword puzzle. At the end of the week she'd give him a test and he had to give her the definition."

Wilder also was learning how to use all these fancy words. His Aunt Kate held grand formal teas at which all the children were expected to perform — either by singing, playing an instrument or reciting poetry. Wilder always chose the poetry, honing the dramatic skills that would later make him such a gifted orator and debater. Thanks to Aunt Kate's teas, Little Douglas would never be one to be embarrassed at speaking before a crowd and, thanks to his mother's crossword puzzles, his choice of words was always impressive.

The elaborate informal education Doug Wilder got at home was a striking contrast to the spartan conditions the state provided for black students, though. Wilder went to the rundown segregated schools of the 1940s. His elementary school had no indoor toilets, no cafeteria, no auditorium and no library. In those sorry conditions, the young Wilder stood out as a star pupil. His native intellect helped, but so did his family's devotion to education. "My parents didn't accept just passing," he once told the *Richmond Times-Dispatch.* "You were expected to excel."

And excel Wilder did. At home, he became a "self-styled philosopher" who wrote his own essays and read Aristotle and Emerson. "I got sidetracked temporarily by Nietzsche," he says. Wilder told the *Post:* "I used to go around the house reciting it and my mother would say, 'Can't you find something else to read? That man's crazy.' "

Doug Wilder was a very rare and very fortunate young man. Strengthened by a family that encouraged education and enterprise, he was able to withstand the poverty and despair of segregation that ground down many of his friends. "I knew any number of classmates who, if they had had the slightest opportunity, could have gone on," Wilder sadly told the *Post.*

While he was learning to recite poetry and quote philosophers at home, Wilder also got a valuable education on the streets of Church Hill. From age thirteen on, he worked a succession of jobs — shoeshine boy, elevator operator, whatever was available for a black youth in those days.

"I learned everything out there as a bootblack," Wilder told the *Times-Dispatch.* "There was everything out there. That's where people gathered and enjoyed themselves. There was a barbershop and a fish market and a place for numbers; I loved it all and I learned a lot about people."

"I used to have a little window-washing business in the neighborhood," he says, "but the ammonia I would use in the water was so strong, the letters on the businesses would come off, not intentionally, so I'd get the job of painting it back on. We hauled the stuff around in a taxicab. The driver used to hate to see us coming with our ladders and paint cans. Eventually he told us we couldn't haul it anymore."

One summer when he was in high school, Wilder got his first job downtown in white Richmond, running an elevator on Main Street, the city's financial district. It was his first real encounter with whites. "I met a couple of very good guys," Wilder told the *Post.* "They went to a different school, of course. But our thoughts were so much the same on so many subjects. And I knew then that if people had a chance to talk and meet there was hope." Still, Wilder knew his opportunities were sharply limited by the complexion of his skin, no matter how much poetry and philosophy he could recite. "I was a constantly boiling cauldron," he told the *Post.* "I was fortunate to have had some degree of discipline." Otherwise, "I don't know what would have happened."

Wilder's mother wanted her son to be a minister or mortician, two respected professions to which a young black man of that era could reasonably aspire. Wilder, though, had other ideas. He thought about being a policeman or a firefighter. He liked to draw and for a while wanted to go to art school, although that was out of the question in those days. When he finished high school at age sixteen, Wilder wanted to join the Navy, but because he was underage, his parents had to sign for him. His mother refused, so he went to college instead — Virginia Union University, a private black college in Richmond, where he majored in chemistry. The sciences were then considered the best way for blacks to get ahead.

Somehow Wilder's mother eked out the first $25 of the $100 tuition and he was responsible for raising the rest. His career waiting tables began, at sixteen. "I got $1 a day for pouring coffee at the John Marshall. They'd have seven hundred, eight hundred, one thousand people there and you just poured coffee. I said I wanted to make more money so I got on as a busboy so I could watch the older waiters and learn the trade, so I learned to wait tables."

For years, he worked the banquet circuit in Richmond, at all the big hotels and country clubs. It, too, was an education, to be a black servant in the classy retreats of the state's white establishment. "Racial jokes were told in your presence; it was like you were an invisible man," he told the *Times-Dispatch.*

Wilder soon learned to like the political functions he worked. Unlike the older waiters, "I would always stay up and listen to the speeches," he says. Many a night he slipped into the shadows of the balcony of the John Marshall to listen to the politics below, not imagining some thirty years later he would be down there on that same stage, making a victory speech of his own.

He especially remembers the time Robert Taft came to Richmond and he got to hear his private pitch to whites at the William Byrd and then his public speech — "entirely different" — later that afternoon at Virginia Union. "I was incensed. That was just too much for me."

By the time Wilder was nearing graduation at Virginia Union, he was becoming an impatient — and often angry — young man. "I realized I wanted to be a lawyer in my junior year of college — not just because the chemistry was so hard. I was encouraged by reading about the likes of an Oliver Hill, a noted civil rights lawyer here; Spottswood Robinson, a federal circuit judge in Washington but a Richmonder," he told the *Washington Times.* "There were so many people [who] said, 'It will never happen; it's a fact of life. It's ordained by God; segregation is meant to be. If God had meant people to be equal, he would have made them so.' All that foolishness, that more emboldened me to do it."

As a college senior, Wilder came to trust less in the legal appeals of the Hills and Robinsons and instead believe that segregation would only fall through armed revolution. "It was the Mau Mau uprising in Kenya. Blacks had been so mistreated, and Kenyatta embarked on this theory of doing away with the oppressors. It fascinated me. In the Army I found some who felt the same way. We would write letters back and forth and sign them 'the Burning Spear.' " Today, Wilder dismisses his revolutionary leanings as "just romantic rhetoric. I had not seen the breakthroughs."

But the family discipline kept the budding militant in line. And there were other pursuits besides politics. Unable at 5-feet-9 and 135 pounds to make the college football team, Wilder was quarterback of a semi-pro team, the Oakwood Steamrollers, that played a crude brand of ball in a neighborhood park. "They almost ran me out of the park," Wilder once said. "Those beefy lineman loved going after me."

Soon Wilder had more deadly concerns than defensive linemen. He was graduated from Virginia Union in 1951 and by 1952 found himself drafted into the U.S. Army and sent to Korea. He could have contented himself with a rear-line assignment. Instead, he volunteered for combat duty so he could cut his Army hitch in half. Ten of his thirteen months in the Army were spent on the front lines with the 7th Infantry Division.

The *Times-Dispatch* once wrote: "Fellow Army enlistees remember him as bookish but a natural leader. Frank Thomas of Richmond, who spent twenty-one years in the Army and served with Wilder, recalls how Wilder used to write and read letters for illiterate servicemen. Despite the integration of the services a few years earlier, blacks didn't have equal opportunities, except in combat.

"Wilder, a platoon leader, and a black sergeant were chosen by colleagues to complain to the company commander about the lack of promotions for blacks. Doug was always a good speaker and so the two of them went to the commander. A few days later, there were promotions for other blacks in the unit," Thomas said.

On April 18, 1953, Wilder's unit was moving up to relieve front-line troops near Pork Chop Hill. The terse, utilitarian prose of the U.S. Army records tells the story:

"Corporal Wilder continually exposed himself to deadly enemy artillery and mortar fire while he aided the wounded from the other units. During the course of the ensuing action, Corporal Wilder moved about the area placing fighting men in fighting positions and assisted in capturing, searching and guarding prisoners."

Later in the day, Wilder's party was cut off, though they didn't know it. Wilder has told the *Post:*

"I had no idea the Chinese had half the hill. I thought we had it all. Next thing I knew," he says, making the quick motion and *brrrp* of an automatic rifle, "the guy next to me was gone. The three of us left fell to the ground, thinking there were only two or three of them. We made them believe there was more, running in different directions and hollering. I threw a grenade and fired a volley but we still didn't know there were nineteen of them. When they started coming out of the hootch, good God, it looked like they never stopped coming. If they had known there were only three of us, I guarantee I wouldn't be here talking."

Instead, Wilder and his two buddies had captured nineteen prisoners.

"Quite frankly, he [one of his fellow soldiers] was instrumental in getting them to surrender," Wilder said in another interview. "He went behind the bunker, pried a hole in the sandbags, and put a thermite grenade in it, and I was covering the front aperture. We thought there were no more than three or four in there. I guess they thought we were a full platoon until they came out."

For this and his bravery earlier in the day, Wilder was awarded the Bronze Star. Later he was promoted to sergeant first class.

Wilder says little about his combat experience. "I don't take any credit for it; a man who was killed deserved it," he told the *Times-Dispatch.* "Whether you lived or died was a matter of luck."

And Wilder was one of the lucky ones. His hitch up, he returned to Richmond, though he never told anyone, not even his family, about his Bronze Star until many years later.

With his college degree in hand and the war behind him, Wilder set off to find a job. His experience in Korea made him believe segregation could be overcome. When he had led his group to the colonel to complain about lack of promotions for blacks, the colonel acted promptly to remedy the situation. And on Pork Chop Hill, he discovered "how easily the reason for prejudice disappears when you have to depend on each other to live." So Wilder optimistically went down to Capitol Square in Richmond one day and applied for a job with the state, citing his degree in chemistry. He was told there were no openings. When he persisted, he was indeed offered a job — as a cook at a juvenile detention center in Hanover County.

"Utter humiliation" is how Wilder now describes the experience, although after his election as lieutenant governor, he got a belated last laugh — his transition office was located in the same office where he had been offered the cook's job thirty-one years before.

But at the time, Wilder was stunned to find the wartime bonds between blacks and whites meant nothing back home. Out of desperation, he decided more education was the answer. He began work on a master's degree in chemistry at Virginia State University, a black college near Petersburg. He also went back to waiting tables. Graduate school was tough — tougher than Wilder had imagined. He remembers one class had only two students in it. His classmate was destined to go on to earn a doctorate, but Wilder was struggling. His classmate, though, had heard about an opening in the state medical examiner's office as a toxicologist. Wilder spent two years there, running blood-alcohol tests, examining lung tissue for autopsies on victims of black lung disease. "I liked the work but I wasn't in love with it," he says.

By now it was 1956 and Wilder had decided he wanted to become a lawyer. The *Brown* decision in 1954 had a profound impact on him — and gave him hope that perhaps the system could be changed from within, without resort to fire and blood. "It did more than just deal with schools," Wilder told the *Post*. "Psychologically it cut the Gordian knot with the past . . . . It made me appreciate that what I thought was visionary and Captain Blood, all in one, well, there was absolutely no place for it."

Virginia's law schools in 1956 were still segregated, though. The state, clinging to its old doctrine, essentially paid black law students to go to school out of state — supplying a $400 stipend as the state's way of keeping their education separate if not equal. Wilder went to Howard University in Washington — and almost flunked out his first semester. He says he was a young man overwhelmed by the big city. "I didn't study. I put things off." Then one day he and four classmates were on their way to lunch. While they discussed classwork, Wilder was suddenly terrified. "I didn't know what they were talking about. We passed a man digging a ditch and I knew 'that's going to be me.' " It was like a crisis to me. That so frightened me I could hardly eat my lunch. When I got back, I studied from then on" — when he wasn't waiting tables.

The hard work paid off. When Wilder took the Virginia Bar exam in 1959, he was the only black to pass. He worked briefly for a black lawyer in Newport News, just long enough to see how things were done. Then he opened up a solo practice three blocks from his parents' home. There were other black lawyers in Richmond then, but Wilder was the first to open an office in the middle of the black neighborhood itself. "People said, 'You're crazy, you'll starve,' " Wilder recalls. He was young, just starting out, on his own. Plus, there was no great demand for black lawyers. The black professionals who succeeded in those days were the ones who could do business without relying on whites — black doctors and morticians, for example, could treat black families unencumbered by segregation. But black lawyers would be up against white lawyers in front of white judges. No, if black citizens were in some difficulty or otherwise needed help "downtown," they knew it was best to hire a white lawyer.

So Wilder had to go out of his way — literally — to keep busy. "For those first years, I would take a case anywhere," he once told the *Virginian-Pilot*. "I practiced in all the courthouses around Richmond. I would drive to Norfolk for a $25 or $50 traffic case and barely break even on it. But I wanted to get myself known. I wanted the experience."

He also had to feed his family. At Howard, he had met Eunice Montgomery, an accounting student from Philadelphia. They were married while he was still in law school. In 1959, their first child, Lynn, was born. Lawrence Jr. followed in 1960 and Loren in 1964.

In those early days when he was struggling to get started, Wilder kept Saturday hours so working folks in the neighborhood could come in when it suited their schedules. Sometimes the Saturday visitors would find a young black man in work clothes cleaning the place. "I'd have a bucket, buffing and waxing the floors," Wilder told the *Washington Times.* "They'd say, 'Is the lawyer here?' I'd say, 'He'll be right with you.' I'd go in, take off the coveralls, and say, 'What can I do for you?' I never lost a client because of that."

He also decided to confront courtroom segregation head on — by ignoring it. There were separate benches for black lawyers and white lawyers. "With my usual degree of arrogance, I sat down at the whites' table," Wilder once told the *Times-Dispatch.* "Nothing happened. I guess they thought I was too crazy to bother with."

With this sort of determination and panache, "his rise was rapid," says William Thornton, a Richmond doctor and long-time leader of the city's dominant black voting group, the Crusade for Voters. "He didn't have a long struggle like some lawyers today."

While the lawyers Wilder admired — the Oliver Hills, the Thurgood Marshalls — were making a name in civil rights cases, Wilder himself was building a practice on the ordinary legal fare. Criminal and personal injury cases became his specialties. "He's one of the best trial lawyers I've ever seen," says state Sen. William Fears. "He's real quick mentally. If you give him a hole, he'll shoot right through it."

Wilder plays to win. He likes bridge, he says, because it gives him the chance to outsmart opponents. He owns Washington Redskins season tickets because he likes the roar of the crowd. Conversely, a lack of interest when there was little hope of victory may have been Wilder's undoing in one legal case that started in 1966. Hired by a New Jersey couple that had been involved in a Richmond traffic accident, Wilder let the case drag on two years before filing suit and later had the suit withdrawn in such a way that prevented filing it again. The couple sued Wilder for $75,000; the case was settled out of court. But they also complained to the State Bar, which gave Wilder a private reprimand — the least severe of the possible punishments. Wilder chose to make the reprimand public by appealing it to the state Supreme Court, where he lost in 1978. Wilder says he wasn't able to locate the other driver in the wreck and says there wasn't much chance of collecting any money from her, anyway. Nevertheless, the court rebuked Wilder for "inexcusable procrastination" and "unprofessional conduct."

But this stain on his record was still far in the future when Wilder started thinking about running for the state Senate in 1969.

The foundations that had held Virginia politics steady for most of the century were starting to crumble in the late 1960s. The Byrd Machine, once the well-oiled engine of the Virginia establishment, was growing rusty and was soon without a leader. U.S. Sen. Harry F. Byrd Sr. resigned in 1965 because of ill health. One of his final public appearances was in Arlington to kick off the gubernatorial campaign. Ira Lechner, a future state legislator, remembers a strange scene that day. Byrd kissed two of his fingers and silently applied them to the cheek of Mills Godwin. "It was very mystical," Lechner recalls.

But it would take more than a silent kiss of approval for the Byrd Machine to carry on its hegemony into the new era that was dawning. The Washington suburbs were pushing out into the old Civil War battlefields of Northern Virginia. Entirely new cities were rising out of the Tidewater scrubland around Norfolk, home to Sunbelt pioneers with no ties to the Old Dominion. In a crescent stretching from the nation's capital to one of the nation's key ports, a new suburban Virginia was rising. The population changes inevitably brought political ones: Byrd's country courthouse clique was fast becoming an anachronism.

The civil rights movement and the activist Democratic administrations in Washington only accelerated the changes going on in Virginia. The Byrd Machine had always kept the state's voting rolls tightly controlled, making Virginia's percentage of registered voters one of the lowest in the South and inspiring historian V.O. Key to snort that "by contrast, Mississippi is a hotbed of democracy." But now the federal Voting Rights Act of 1965 and the abolition of the poll tax opened up the voting booths to everyone. Between the votes of blacks and suburban newcomers, the political rules in Virginia were suddenly being changed.

For black Virginians, the challenge was not merely to vote, but to run. In 1967, Ferguson Reid, a black doctor, won a seat in the House of Delegates, becoming the first black elected to the General Assembly since Reconstruction. That same year, another black doctor from Richmond — William Thornton, longtime head of the city's Crusade for Voters — unsuccessfully challenged state Sen. Ed Willey. Two years later, it looked like Richmond's other state Senate seat was going to come open, giving blacks another chance.

In 1969 Virginians were choosing their first post-Byrd governor. They dramatically broke from tradition by electing Linwood Holton, the state's first Republican governor since the aberration of Reconstruction. But even in that chaotic election year, there was no surprise about who the next lieutenant governor would be — Richmond state Sen. J. Sargeant Reynolds, a Democrat. Speculation on who would succeed him started long before Election Day. Thornton, the city's senior black leader, had first call on making the race. But he declined to run again. On Church Hill, a little-known thirty-eight-year-old black lawyer decided he would.

Just as he would for lieutenant governor fifteen years later, Douglas Wilder made a point of getting into the race before anyone else. Well before the election, he passed the word that he was going to run if Reynolds won.

The special election to fill Reynolds' Senate seat took on more than the usual importance.

Republicans hoped to capitalize on the gubernatorial breakthrough by nominating a popular former mayor — Morrill M. Crowe. Meanwhile, Democrats were split. Outgoing Lt. Gov. Fred Pollard, defeated in the summer's gubernatorial primary, was still looking for a way to stay in politics and announced that he would run for the Democratic nomination for the state Senate. But so had Wilder. What's more, Wilder made it clear that he intended to be on the ballot whether he had the Democratic nomination or not.

Reynolds' Senate district covered the entire city and was predominantly black, although the majority of its registered voters were white. In a one-on-one contest in racially divided Richmond, a Wilder election was unlikely. In a three-way race with two strong white contenders, a Wilder election seemed almost certain.

There was talk among white politicians of maybe arranging a judicial appointment for Wilder to get him out of the way, but he wasn't interested. He really was in the race "all the way." Democrats blanched — and decided not to nominate a candidate at all. Pollard and Wilder were on their own, which suited Wilder just fine.

For white Richmonders getting one of their first good looks at a black politician, Wilder turned out to be an amazing sight. Early in the campaign he came out with an unusual position for a black candidate — he favored the city's plans to annex a big chunk of the white suburbs, provided the expanded city elected council members by wards to ensure some black representation. Wilder cited the same reasons pro-annexation white politicians had — the need to expand the city's tax base. Still, in supporting an annexation that would dilute black voting strength, the *Richmond News Leader* called this "a bold new move for a Richmond Negro politician."

Wilder also found support from a small but influential group of young, white businessmen who saw the need to make some changes in the state's political structure. Financier McLain O'Ferrall was one of them. "I took brochures around in Windsor Hills [an exclusive white neighborhood] and took my life in my own hands," O'Ferrall laughs. "Nobody knew who he was. There weren't any blacks in politics. I guess I was rebel enough to support him." These men were all friends of Lt. Gov.-elect Reynolds and one former state legislator describes them and their motives in supporting Wilder this way: "The Reynolds crowd always fashioned themselves as limousine liberals. They wanted to show how Richmond was cosmopolitan, how they had put the Old South behind them. And it would be good for business. Also, compare Wilder with William Thornton or Henry Marsh [Wilder's law school classmate who later became the city's mayor]. He wasn't confrontational in the way they were. Plus, he was interested in making money." He was someone the rich white boys could identify with.

Dec. 2, 1969 was a cold, rainy Election Day, just like another one sixteen years later would be. Turnout was reasonably strong for a special election. And, thanks to a heavy black turnout and a split among white voters, Wilder won with relative ease:

Wilder, 15,844, 48.4 percent; Crowe, 10,318, 31.5 percent; Pollard, 6,105, 18.6 percent.

A hoarse Wilder took note of the racial divisions in his victory speech that night: "I am very conscious that my margin of victory is a plurality and that the bulk of my support came from black citizens. To these supporters, I pledge to be a long-needed listening post and a vigorous spokesman for their special concerns and needs.

"However, the returns indicate that I also received a gratifying number of white votes. I particularly appreciate this support and I look forward to the time when all men can run as candidate on their qualifications and not as a 'Negro candidate' or a 'white candidate.' "

The editorial reaction in Richmond's two staunchly conservative newspapers was surprisingly warm. The *Times-Dispatch* noted:

"It would be wrong to view Wilder's achievement simply as a victory of blacks over whites. For upon reflection, it will become apparent that the white electorate itself indirectly contributed to Wilder's success.

"Not many years ago, the prospect of a Negro victory in such an election as yesterday's would have brought white voters to the polls in droves to vote against the black candidate. But it didn't happen yesterday. It is believed that the city's white registered voters heavily outnumber Negroes. Even with two strong white candidates in the race to dilute their power, white voters could have overcome Wilder had they chosen to do so. Thus, while yesterday's truant voters obviously didn't give Wilder their ballots, they clearly showed they were not alarmed by the possibility that he would win."

It's remarkable that many of the post-election editorials in 1969 could just have easily been reprinted in 1985, for the circumstances were the same. Wilder's personality reassured people and gave them no cause to oppose him. Commented the *Times-Dispatch:* "An intelligent, articulate lawyer, he conducted a dignified and responsible campaign."

The most exclusive club in Virginia — the forty-member state Senate — now had a black member. What was it going to do with him? By all accounts, Senator Wilder was received cordially. Richmond's other state senator — Ed Willey — phoned him right away to offer congratulations.

Wilder admits that he entered the General Assembly — stepping foot in that hall for the first time in his life — with a tremendous amount of naivete. "I knew absolutely nothing of what was going on," he once told columnist Guy Friddell. "The leaflet about it was as revealing to me as it is to visiting schoolchildren."

Wilder naively expected that since he had replaced Reynolds in the Senate, then he would automatically be appointed to all the committees Reynolds had been on — as important as some of them had been. Apparently the Senate leaders didn't want to offend their new colleague, for Wilder was indeed appointed to all of Reynolds' committees.

Wilder's first deskmate was Bill Rawlings of Southampton County, whose views were somewhat more moderate than those of the Southside voters he represented. Rawlings took Wilder under his wing, taking him to after-hours meetings to which Wilder might otherwise not have gained admittance, teaching him both the written and unwritten rules of the nation's oldest legislature.

"Bill Rawlings explained how it worked," Wilder told Friddell. "He was patient in answering even my simplest questions, carefully explaining bills, saying 'I'm going to vote this way, but you may wish to vote the other way.' " Often Wilder would see Rawlings cast a vote he knew would get him in trouble back home. Rawlings would clamp his teeth down on his pipe and mutter, "That's just the way I voted and the people will have to do what they will." Eventually they did — voting Rawlings out of office. "He was a great role model, I can tell you that," Wilder once said.

But Rawlings did something else. One of the committees Wilder had been appointed to was the committee on Banking, Corporations and Insurance. The money boys around town weren't sure what to make of this black hotshot on their blue-blooded committee. And there were plenty of other, more senior, senators who yearned for the spot. They wanted Wilder off — and went to Rawlings to see what he could diplomatically arrange. Wilder was unhappy with the suggestion and just as unimpressed by the committee Rawlings wanted to put him on instead — Privileges and Elections. It was powerful, to be sure. The Byrd Machine had virtually run the state from this committee by making sure it controlled all the "privileges" in the General Assembly and wrote the election laws for the state. But Wilder wouldn't have any power there. Wouldn't this just be tokenism?

Rawlings was looking years ahead, though. All those old men on P&E would someday be gone, Rawlings explained. Wilder (whose legislative district was redrawn after the 1970 census to make it almost 80 percent black) was virtually guaranteed his seat for as long as he wanted. And if he got on P&E now, someday the seniority would be his.

Wilder recalled the exchange for the *Washington Post:* "Can't you see?" Rawlings asked him, almost devious in his suggestion. "One day you'll be chairman of the committee that handles all government appointments. In a state like Virginia, with a history of denying voting, all the laws relating to elections would come before you." Put that way, Wilder warmed to the idea. Rawlings downplayed Wilder's role to other senators. "He's gonna be a junior member. He can't hurt anything." So the committee switch was made and the Senate establishment was happy. "But when others were resigned or defeated, I stayed on," Wilder told the *Post*. "Stayed on and stayed on! Before you knew it, 'Oh my goodness, he's chairman of the Privileges and Elections committee.'"

That was still far in the future, though, as Wilder began his Senate career. Unlike other freshman legislators, Doug Wilder was never one to be seen and not heard. He was quick to make his mark.

"A lot of people thought he would be militant," says Jay Shropshire, who became Senate clerk in 1975. "He never was. As a result, he moved up. In general, he played his cards right. He got the reputation of being a great orator, a good debater, doing his homework. As the years went by, he became less unique and eventually became one of them, one of the club."

Del. William Robinson Jr., a black legislator from Norfolk whose father was elected to the House of Delegates the same year Wilder was elected to the Senate, remembers things somewhat differently. "I know my father would calm him down. Doug was a firebrand in those days. He and Dad would have long conversations about how to get things done. Most of his advice to Doug stuck."

Regardless, it became apparent early on that Wilder wouldn't hesitate to challenge the Senate establishment. "If you grow up and see a knife fight right in front of you, you're not going to be overawed by some blowhard in the General Assembly," explains state Sen. Buzz Emick.

In one of his first acts, in 1970, Wilder took on not only the Senate leadership but also the traditions of the state itself. This was the celebrated incident in which Wilder and his wife walked out of a reception for legislators when the state song, "Carry Me Back to Ole Virginny," was played. The next day in the General Assembly, Wilder loudly denounced the song for its lyrics extolling the joys of slavery and called for its repeal as state song. Wilder's sudden outburst greatly offended Old Virginia decorum and Wilder's reputation as an unpredictable firebrand was set.

One night not long afterward, Wilder was at another function, this one at the John Marshall. An old lawyer friend who was now in the House of Delegates, Junie Bradshaw, pulled him aside after the event was over.

"I said, 'Doug, why in the world did you do that? Why'd you rip your britches with your Senate colleagues? It just looks like you were trying to be militant.' I was really preaching at him for doing it. He said, if you've got a few minutes, come in the Captain's Grill here. It was after 11. My wife was with me. He said, 'Junie, I'll tell you why I did it. When I was a college student at Virginia Union, working my way through college as a waiter here at the John Marshall, they'd have those conventions there and those conventioneers would have too many drinks at the cocktail party and then at dinner stand up and sing that song and in the next breath, turn to me and say, "Hey boy, give me a cup of coffee." ' Those two were associated in his mind and he had tears rolling down his face. He was just as sincere and humble as he could be. He said, 'Junie, you just don't know how it feels to be black and hear that song.' He said the two were associated like bread and peanut butter. I said, 'Doug, you have taught me a lesson. I've told jokes before that I shouldn't have told.' He said, 'Well, I've told some about honkeys.' He almost had me crying. I said, 'Doug, had you told the senators on the Senate floor the way you just told it to Dee and myself, every senator in the chamber would have voted with you.' "

They didn't — and the effort to repeal the state song was quickly killed. Wilder got partial revenge, though. "It is still the state song," he says. "But they don't play it."

So Wilder did win, in a way. And he learned a lesson. "I didn't have any following to get a bill passed," he once told the *Washington Post*. "So I made it a thing to be able to kill bills." It was a negative power, but it was power nevertheless — something well understood by his Senate colleagues.

Once Wilder took on a bill dealing with tax-exempt status for certain organizations. Wilder noted that one group seeking such tax-exempt status was a country club in an exclusive Richmond subdivision. One of the neighborhood's residents was former pro football star Willie Lanier, who just happened to be black and who just happened to have been denied admission into the neighborhood's country club. Now why would that have been? Wilder wondered aloud. Could it be that Lanier — who stands 6-feet-8 — was simply too big? No doubt club members were afraid he might damage the golf greens, Wilder said, while the chamber chuckled along with him. But, with Wilder's interest aroused, the bill soon died.

Soon other senators were coming to him anytime they wanted to know the "right" way to vote on a bill with potential racial implications or otherwise needed help with their black constituents. And eventually others started coming to him to seek advice on how they, too, could kill certain bills. "That's the way you start building your cadre of support," Wilder later told the *Post*. "Then the lobbyists started paying attention to me. Didn't pay attention at first."

And so, as Wilder gained seniority and support, he eventually gained power, power not only to kill bills but also to pass them. The loud outsider became the consummate insider. "Some senators, if they're there a hundred years, will never understand how to get a bill through," Emick says. "Others — and Wilder is one of them — will watch the place and understand how to get things done."

Wilder gets high marks for learning how the Senate works and making it work for him. He gets low marks from some for a variety of sins, from being lazy to being petty and spiteful. "His positions might be shaped more by opponents on the other side than whether the issue is right or wrong," one "close friend" once told the *Post*.

One former legislator harps on Wilder for not being a hard worker. That doesn't square with Emick's account of Wilder memorizing the rules, but even Emick admits that when a particular issue doesn't interest Wilder very much, he doesn't pay much attention to it — and not having an eye or temperament for detail is often considered one of Wilder's greatest faults.

"He was a lazy legislator," says one former colleague, a liberal Democrat. "He did not really put in a hard day's work. He'd get the press attention and get out. Dr. Robinson [William Robinson Sr., a black delegate from Norfolk] would work five times harder on small issues, milk supplements for mothers with children, school formulas."

Former Lt. Gov. Henry Howell remembers Wilder's early days in the General Assembly this way: "He was rather quiet and blended in," occasional outbursts about the state song to the contrary. "I'd say Doug Wilder was a realist. He didn't try to introduce legislation he knew would have an uphill battle" — except when he tried to get Virginia to recognize Martin Luther King's birthday as a holiday. The result, Howell says, is that by the time Wilder chose to run for statewide office, "I think he arrived without shaking any economic temples, which was good for him. The Main Street group felt comfortable with Doug. The establishment opposed me with a sense of fear. He arrived without many lights twinkling to catch the adverse attention of the business community. He had never put in any bills about banks. The boards of directors of banks were in fear of me." Wilder was certainly a watchdog for black interests but he was no liberal crusader like Howlin' Henry had been.

Whatever his faults, Wilder gained power inside the General Assembly and around the state. But the key question: Did Wilder become powerful because he's black or in spite of it?

"It's a combination," Emick says. "Some senators will jump through a hoop because they don't want him coming into their local black church on Sunday morning and saying something. But for others, the Senate is the white man's territory in the grandest sense, yet he is a black man who is accepted by them. So I would say he did it on his own."

From his Senate seat, Wilder emerged as the state's most prominent black leader for a variety of reasons. For one thing, there was no one else. When Wilder entered the Senate in 1969, there was no one black leader with statewide prominence.

Wilder's personality had much to do with his filling the void. "In a lackluster, leaderless group of people, with no power to speak of other than their vote, he was able, by sleight of hand, force of personality and being state senator, to assert his leadership," says a former Democratic legislator with no love lost for Wilder. "It's no accident that he always showed up [to state conventions] in the ice cream suit. He was a showman. It was the emulation of an old-style Southern politician. Harry Byrd Sr. always used to be in a white suit."

By the early 1970s, Wilder had already established himself as Virginia's only black leader with statewide prominence. Wilder's leadership, though, was symbolic. He did not run a political machine. He was not powerful in the way a local black minister or Crusade for Voters chairman in Richmond might be. His power rested not in the congregations he could command to vote a certain way, but in the connections he had made within the General Assembly, within the coterie of operatives that made up the party establishment — and in the attention the media gave him.

And so Wilder rose in the Senate hierarchy, being re-elected without opposition every four years. By 1976 he had become the first black to become a committee chairman when he took over the Senate Committee on Rehabilitation and Social Services. The chairmanship of the Transportation Committee followed a few years later. By 1984, the vision Bill Rawlings, now long dead, had had more than a decade before was realized when Wilder became chairman of the Privileges and Elections Committee.

In the meantime, much was happening, both personally and politically. In 1978, Wilder was divorced in a bitter proceeding. The records were sealed at his wife's request, making their contents the subject of many rumors. Wilder refuses to discuss the divorce, except to point out that the settlement requires him to pay no alimony. In 1978, he was also reprimanded by the state Supreme Court in the auto accident case that had been dragging on since 1966. Wilder was also graying. The wild Afro of the early seventies gave way to closely cropped salt-and-pepper hair. His children were growing up and going off to college. And Wilder thought about his own political future. A run for Congress? Attorney general? Lieutenant governor?

Another key year in Virginia politics was 1981. Republicans had held the governorship since Linwood Holton's win in 1969. In 1981 the Democratic Party regrouped behind Lt. Gov. Charles Robb and won not just the governorship but all three statewide offices.

Wilder was instrumental in lining up black support for Robb. With a Democrat in the governor's office, Wilder became even more important. Robb appointed more blacks to state office than ever before — and virtually all of them were cleared through Wilder. In the early days of the Robb administration, the governor's staff consulted with Wilder almost daily.

However, the 1982 General Assembly was not a kind one to Wilder. His annual King holiday bill was rudely defeated. Wilder charged that House Speaker A.L. Philpott had stacked the House committee to guarantee its death. Wilder felt the heat from restless black activists who wanted to know why, if he was so powerful, he couldn't get the bill out of committee. Others complained that he was wasting too much time on this symbolic effort and not putting enough effort into reforming the state's election laws.

Did the criticism make Wilder eager to demonstrate his clout? He says no, but many wonder. "After the session in '82, the *Richmond Afro-American* [a weekly black newspaper] climbed all over him," Del. Chip Woodrum recalls. "He may have felt a little threatened within his own constituency. They did a number editorially on both him and Chuck Robb. I think the Pickett thing was his reaction to that, to maintain himself in his own district. Heavens, we all understand that."

It wasn't long after these stinging setbacks that Wilder made the riskiest, most dramatic move of an already risky and dramatic career.

Early in 1982, the opportunity for a quick follow-up to the Democratic sweep of 1981 looked likely. U.S. Sen. Harry F. Byrd Jr., who had left the party in 1970 and had run as an independent ever since, announced his retirement. Republicans were going to nominate First District Rep. Paul Trible, an ambitious young man who unsettled many of the money men on Main Street. If Virginia Democrats could come up with a strong candidate in Robb's moderate-conservative mold, they might win their first Senate seat since 1966.

In line with Virginia tradition, the decision was made privately. Party leaders met throughout the early part of the year, talking over names. Wilder was in some of the meetings, where it was generally agreed that Del. Owen Pickett of Virginia Beach, a tight-lipped, uninspiring moderate, would get the nod. Wilder reportedly went along with this choice, although he wasn't at the final meeting where the decision to go with Pickett was officially made.

Pickett announced his candidacy in mid-March and, right away, made a fatal error. He invoked the name of Harry Byrd, praising the independence which the senator had voiced "so often and so well."

"It was just a matter of making clear on fiscal matters that I was someone who was concerned about fiscal responsibility in government and I used Byrd's name to indicate how I felt about this issue," Pickett recalls. Still, for a 1980s Robb Democrat to wrap himself in the mantle of Byrd was trying to be a little too clever.

Wilder — whether sensing the need to prove himself to his black supporters or voicing genuine outrage — took offense. He declared that Pickett was unacceptable, and that if Pickett was the party's nominee then he, Wilder, would run as an independent.

Suddenly the Democrats' golden opportunity to unite early and pick off the Senate seat was lost while Doug Wilder went eyeball to eyeball with Owen Pickett, Chuck Robb and the whole party establishment. All through the spring of 1982, Doug Wilder, the political terrorist, held his own party hostage.

If Pickett were nominated and Wilder bolted to run as an independent, he'd presumably take with him virtually all the party's black voters. This presumption — never tested but always feared — was what made party regulars tremble. An independent run might be a suicide mission, but Doug Wilder, everyone agreed, was stubborn enough and crazy enough to do it — and take the Democratic nominee down with him. And if the party gave in and Pickett withdrew — oh, the humiliation — who else would they get to run?

Whatever the danger to the party's chances, Wilder was showing all the signs of carrying through with his threat. Petitions were circulated to get Wilder's name on the ballot. Before long, others began grumbling that they had been shut out of the candidate-selection process and that Pickett wasn't a very good candidate anyway. The new governor was put in an awkward spot of having to intervene — and either risk losing black support by sticking with Pickett or risk losing establishment support by going back on his word to support the former party chairman.

Robb's chief fund-raiser, Del. Al Smith of Winchester, went to Wilder to see what could be worked out. Wilder and his ubiquitous companion, Senate clerk Jay Shropshire, were to go out to lunch with Smith. Wilder insisted that Smith take him to the whites-only Commonwealth Club. Smith said he couldn't get reservations for the dining room; Wilder suggested they go to the basement grill. Smith refused, reportedly saying "They don't like blacks up there." Wilder was furious. Tears welled up in his eyes. Friends say they've never seen Wilder so mad as he was that day — and the incident was soon all over the papers. To conservatives, this was all a set-up designed to make Smith (and by implication, the moderate-conservative wing of the Democratic Party) look racist. To Wilder, it was yet another example of how far Virginia had yet to go — and even more reason to insist that Pickett had to go.

Republicans were delighted at the Democratic drama. And Doug Wilder, if nothing else, made a name for himself. "Before that, all people knew was that Richmond had a black senator," says Ross Hart, a Roanoke lawyer and Democratic activist. "After that, by God, people knew who Doug Wilder was." Of course, what kind of name he made for himself was debatable. Many party regulars believed Wilder had done himself grave damage by ruining the party's chances to elect a U.S. senator. But Richmond lobbyist Mark Rubin says the Pickett episode was the key to Wilder getting the Democratic nomination in 1985: "It made all the white people think that Doug Wilder was crazy." Who knew what he might do if provoked? So, once Wilder got into the race, no one was willing to challenge him. "Doug is a brilliant politician," says former Richmond lawyer and Democratic operative Barry Rose. "He just will not blink. That's what makes him so frightening. He doesn't back down."

In the end, it was Robb and Pickett who blinked. Pickett already had a majority of convention delegates pledged to him. But he realized that, without black support in the fall, his would have been an empty nomination. Democrats scrambled to find a replacement, going through a laundry list of odd names before coming up with Lt. Gov. Dick Davis, who had no interest in running. With such a late start in raising money and raising issues, Davis began deep in a hole he couldn't crawl out of. Even though 1982 was a Democratic year nationally, Trible squeaked into office. Says Randy Flood, a Washington lobbyist and former Byrd staffer: "Paul is in the U.S. Senate today because of one man — Doug Wilder."

That might have cost any other Democrat his political career. But it only made Doug Wilder more formidable.

3

Beneath the Portrait of Harry Byrd

July 3, 1984

In his dark, windowless office just off the empty Senate floor, Jay Shropshire was beaming. The Senate clerk was like a little boy at the circus, scarcely able to wait for the show to begin.

Doug Wilder was more fretful. He fussed over his son's tie, making sure it was straight. He made two trips to the men's room to make sure his own tie was straight. His two daughters waited patiently, and quietly, while the men fidgeted with their neckwear.

Shropshire, eagerly looking for ways to help, ducked out to check on whether the TV crews had set up their cameras yet. He came back into his office with his grin even broader than before. "All wired and ready," he announced.

Wilder looked around the room. Shropshire looked back at him. So did his children, as if everyone expected him to say something special before they went out to face the bright lights of history.

"Well, here we go," he said.

Here we go indeed.

The Old Senate Chamber, where the Confederate Congress once met, was crowded. The capital press corps was out in full force. Though no special effort was made to get them there, political curiosity-seekers ringed the back of the room.

Wilder took his place before the lectern bristling with microphones. The official portrait of Harry Byrd Sr. looked over his shoulder. A photographer for the Richmond newspapers maneuvered along the front row to frame the pair for the afternoon *News Leader* and the morning *Times-Dispatch.* Shropshire saw that and smiled even more. Using this room was his idea.

Wilder introduced his children and proudly went over their educational backgrounds in painstaking detail. Loren was not just a student at the University of Virginia, she was a third-year student at the McIntyre School of Business at the University of Virginia. Larry was not just going to law school at U.Va. this fall, he would be attending the School of Law there. Lynn was not simply an architect, she was one for the U.S. Patent Office in Washington.

Standing there beneath the portrait of Harry Byrd, unashamedly pointing out how his children had gone to all the "right" schools, grandly referring to U.Va. as "the university," Wilder sounded just like a thoroughbred Virginia gentleman, wrapping himself in the twin virtues of pride and tradition. The irony was so obvious many would miss it for more than a year. All they could see that day was Harry Byrd, his golden silence, even in oil, tested by what was going on beneath him.

Doug Wilder had come to announce what the papers had been saying for the past two days he would, but few could yet believe: He would seek his party's nomination for lieutenant governor in 1985.

It was almost a year before the party would choose its nominees, almost a year and a half before the election itself. It was even three full weeks before the national party met in San Francisco to nominate Walter Mondale for president. In the sweltering Southern capital this third of July, a Tuesday, state politics should have been on vacation. But Doug Wilder's thoughts were on more distant pursuits.

Once, in a fit of senatorial pique, he had dismissed the lieutenant governorship as a "vacuous" position, its duties of presiding over the state Senate so trivial that they would not tax the abilities of a mere page boy. Now he elevated its importance. "It is a high calling and the opportunity is great," Wilder said. Just as important, it "affords an opportunity in my particular instance to see just how far the horizon is stretching."

The reporters and politicians crowded into the room didn't know quite what to make of it all. Surely he couldn't be serious about this. Why did you choose to announce your candidacy before the portrait of Harry Byrd? the reporters asked. Wilder flashed a big smile. "I've been in this room on any number of occasions and the picture and I get along well." The reporters couldn't help but chuckle.

Reporters asked how his campaign was different from Jesse Jackson's. "His was to strike the conscience of America," Wilder said. "I'm running to be elected."

Why do you think you'll be able to get whites to vote for you? Wilder cited white candidates who had been elected in predominantly black districts. "All I'm saying with my candidacy is turnabout is fair play."

Are you concerned that your campaign might become bogged down on race? "No," Wilder said sternly, "because you and I won't permit that to happen."

Next question?

Race again.

"I don't have to spend a great deal of time telling you that I'm black," Wilder said, pulling on his cheeks. "If you'd have said 'I love you' to a frog, he'd turn into a fairy prince, but there's nothing that can change the color of my skin so there's no need for me to dwell on that. I intend to address the issues."

When did Wilder first start thinking about running for lieutenant governor? "Knowing Doug, it was probably December of 1969," jokes his law partner, Roger Gregory. He's probably not far off. The possibility of running for an office higher than the Richmond state Senate seat was something that Wilder had rolled over in his mind, and sometimes mused about in public, almost from the beginning.

As far back as Jan. 4, 1972, after he'd been in the Senate barely two sessions, Wilder told Channel 6 in Richmond that he was "seriously considering" running for lieutenant governor in 1973. "The time is now that blacks could offer for statewide elective office," Wilder said. "In fact, many are saying that this is what Virginia needs, to show there isn't any denial of public office because of being black."

But nothing came of Wilder in 1973. In July 1975, though, Wilder was again blustering about running for something. Governor, maybe, in 1977, or the U.S. Senate in 1978.

Wilder in the mid-1970s was still very much the Angry Young Black Man, though. "Virginia is leading the way . . . backwards" in the number of black elected officials, he told The Associated Press. That alone made him mad enough to consider running himself, just to make a statement, though he was under no illusions of actually winning. "There are so many deep-seated prejudices that we're not going to get over. Let's not kid ourselves."

The notion of Doug Wilder running someday did not go away, though. The problem was — for what?

Congress? Not when he lived in the Third District, encompassing conservative Richmond and its even more conservative suburbs. "It would be an exercise in futility. I have consigned the district to being so racist that you could just not do it. There are people who just don't believe blacks have any business living, much less aspiring to high office."

Attorney general? "I have no interest at all in it. None. It's not my cup of tea. I don't consider the attorney general's office a steppingstone."

Lieutenant governor? "The lieutenant governor's office is a rather vacuous position. You just rap the gavel and do what a page for the most part could do."

Governor? "Yes, I could see it . . . It's always been put to me lieutenant governor. Why stop there? If people will elect you lieutenant governor, they'll elect you governor . . . I think it would be an interesting test somewhere along the line for a black to run for one of those positions — attorney general, lieutenant governor or governor — so as to put prejudice on the line. Say you can't vote for a guy because he's black. Say it!"

That was the Doug Wilder of 1975, looking at the world in black and white, and quick, almost eager, to draw the racial line and dare people to cross it. So it came as no surprise in December 1976 when Wilder again said he had been "seriously encouraged" by friends to run for the lieutenant governorship he had dismissed only a year before. Still, Wilder's ambitions were bold. "I would not only be interested in the lieutenant governorship, but the governorship," he declared, though he conceded it's "not in the cards yet" for a black to win a governor's race in Virginia.

A few months later, in March 1977, Wilder decided he wouldn't run. But Wilder added an interesting postscript: "My decision not to run this year in no way indicates any disinterest in statewide office." It was a warning that few took notice of. That was just Doug Wilder blowing off steam, they reasoned. Just Doug being Doug.

Four years later, right on schedule, Wilder was again talking about running for higher office, this time for the Third District congressional seat he had once said "cannot be won by a black." Yet on Feb. 19, 1980, Wilder let it be known he was thinking about challenging David Satterfield, the conservative Democrat who had represented the district for eight terms. Meanwhile, Republicans had started making noises about seizing the seat for themselves. Two days later, Satterfield made the surprise announcement that he had decided to retire.

Suddenly things seemed to be breaking Wilder's way. Wilder was out front and now other Democrats had to scramble to catch up — if they wanted to. One by one, three other Democratic legislators in the Richmond delegation declared their non-interest in the congressional seat.

But support for Wilder never materialized. Richmond and its suburbs of Henrico and Chesterfield counties constitute one of the most indomitably conservative congressional districts in Virginia. The political arithmetic seemed plain enough to everyone except Wilder. When the other Democrats decided not to run, none — "not a solitary soul" — called him to offer encouragement.

Wilder sat in his Church Hill office that spring and sulked. There was no point being a candidate if his own party wasn't going to support him. In April he announced that he wouldn't get into the race, but he fired off a few parting shots. "Though I was the first Democrat to express an interest in the seat, I must confess that there has not been the 'clarion call' from the party," he said. "In fact, all that I have read and heard gives rise to the speculation that the party has 'no potential candidate.' It is a 1980 version of Ralph Ellison's 'Invisible Man.' "

Wilder went on to complain that he smelled nothing less than racism at work. "No one can tell me otherwise," he snapped. He ominously suggested that someday there might come "a signal to black voters" that would lead them "in time to support independents and Republicans as well as Democrats, just like white Democrats do." It was classic Wilder — petulant, troublesome, quick to see a racial slight in the political realities of Virginia. Richmond Democrats could only be thankful he didn't do them even more damage by actually insisting on being a candidate.

Two years later came the Pickett episode.

Wilder came close to running statewide in that blustery spring of 1982, closer than he had ever come before, but once again he failed to follow through.

As Virginia Democrats met in a confusing convention in Roanoke that summer to nominate a reluctant Dick Davis for the Senate, many no doubt wished Robb had called Wilder's bluff and thus put him — and his perennial threats — permanently out of commission. But although Wilder was momentarily despised — "I've been *persona non grata*, " he told one interviewer — he came out of the Pickett episode more powerful than ever. The question now was what he would do with that power.

In September 1982, Wilder was interviewed about his political future.

The *Richmond Times-Dispatch* story described him as being "at a crossroads in his career." Wilder seemed to know it, too. "I have always believed that in politics, you either go up or out," he said. So which was it to be? Just as Wilder was mulling over that question, he saw evidence that whites were finally ready to accept blacks in high office.

Davis lost his Senate race that November. He was never able to make up for his late start; he missed by just 33,742 votes — 2.4 percent. Davis wasn't one to look back, though. He went home to Portsmouth, presumably still the front-runner and, as the party's good soldier, at least the sentimental favorite for the Democratic nomination for governor in 1985.

Meanwhile, Trible's Senate campaign had set in motion a game of political musical chairs on the Peninsula that Wilder paid close attention to. State Sen. Herbert Bateman, a Republican, had won Trible's old First District seat in Congress. That meant a December special election for Bateman's General Assembly seat. The Democratic nominee: Del. Bobby Scott, a thirty-five-year-old Newport News lawyer who had gone to Harvard and had once been named the local Jaycees' Outstanding Young Man. Scott's candidacy would not have been unusual, except for one thing. He was black — and Bateman's Senate district was 70 percent white. Yet Scott won, the first time ever in Virginia that a black had won a predominantly white legislative district.

Only four months later came another red-letter day for blacks in Virginia. In April 1983, Governor Robb named the first black to the state Supreme Court.

The appointment of John Charles Thomas won Robb wide praise, even from conservative legislators who, by their own inability to agree on a new justice, had been denied one of their most cherished patronage powers. Virginia editorial writers likewise virtually gushed over Thomas.

For Wilder, the Scott victory and the Thomas appointment were but two signs of the new day he saw dawning. All around him, Wilder saw things he had been told would never happen:

First, in 1982, the General Assembly had given in to an odd coalition of Republicans, blacks, the ACLU, common sense — and ultimately, a court order — to scotch the unwieldy system of multi-member legislative districts that diluted the voting power of minorities (Republicans included) and set up single-member districts instead. That promised to increase black representation in the House of Delegates, at least.

Then in 1983, Congress passed, and President Reagan signed, a Martin Luther King holiday bill. With federal offices now going to be closed on Jan. 15 anyway, it was a foregone conclusion that the General Assembly would reluctantly follow suit and make King's birthday a state holiday.

Virginia had been forced into it, but Wilder would at last claim victory in his long battle.

Those were the most dramatic victories for blacks in Virginia. But quietly, methodically, the Robb administration was appointing blacks to virtually every state agency, board and commission — not simply token appointments designed for maximum PR effect. The head of the powerful Alcohol Beverage Control Board — which runs the state-owned liquor stores and polices Virginia's liquor laws — was black. The chairman of the state Parole Board, and a majority of its members, were now black. And Bobby Scott's election was only the most celebrated of a whole series of elections that blacks were winning in majority-white areas in the 1980s. Across the harbor from Scott's Newport News, Norfolk (65 percent white) elected a black sheriff. Neighboring Portsmouth (55 percent white) elected a black commonwealth's attorney. Roanoke (78 percent white) in the west, Fredericksburg in the east (80 percent white) and Danville (70 percent white) and Martinsville (68 percent white) in the tough heart of Southside had, or once had, black mayors.

No one else saw the pattern the way he did or asked the question. But if blacks could win so many local elections in predominantly white areas from one end of the state to the other, it did not take a terribly big leap of logic for Wilder to suppose that perhaps a black could pull these diverse and far-flung communities all together and win a statewide election.

In his personal as well as political life, Wilder saw Virginia changing. "I've had occasions where the same week I've gotten a racial note I've had a flat tire on the road and a guy, a redneck, driving a pickup not only stops but also helps me change it and then carries me to a service station and they say, 'Oh, no charge.' " A little thing, perhaps, but one that sticks in the memory of a black man who grew up in the forties and fifties.

Wilder also saw the state Senate changing. Once, when Wilder first went there, it was the clubby preserve of craggy, hard-bitten old men not entirely reconciled with the end of Massive Resistance. Now those old men were all but gone, replaced by younger men who shared their elders' sense of fiscal conservatism but whose social views were more enlightened. Indeed, some of Wilder's closest legislative friends — Bill Fears from the truck-farming country of the Eastern Shore and Virgil Goode from Franklin County, where the red clay of Southside rolls up against the moonshining hollows of the Blue Ridge — were from areas that logically should be most hostile to a black candidate. "I knew the areas they represented hadn't produced bigots," Wilder says. Could the people they represented be that much different?

By the late spring of 1983, Wilder had definitely made up his mind to run for something, but, as usual, he wasn't sure what. He announced in May that he might run for the U.S. Senate in 1984 against Sen. John Warner or for attorney general in 1985.

But Wilder was still talking race, not record, as his primary reason for wanting to run. He said it was "high time" Virginia Democrats reward blacks for their party loyalty by putting up a black for statewide office. "No other constituency tends to be ignored this long, and I just don't feel we should be taken for granted forever," Wilder said.

Wilder's May 1983 trial balloon went largely unnoticed. He had talked about running so many times that it had almost ceased to be news. Nothing to worry about, party leaders thought. Little did they know.

Maybe it's the Southern tradition of states' rights, but in Virginia, even with Washington just across the Potomac, presidential politics are distant and inconsequential concerns. So by the summer of 1983, when Democrats across America were starting to focus their attention on the coming presidential election, the political calendar that people in Virginia were looking at was 1985, not 1984. Three Democrats had gubernatorial campaigns up and running.

First there was Dick Davis. As a former party chairman credited with rebuilding the state party after the Howell years, and the leading vote-getter in the Robb sweep of 1981, Davis was the clear front-runner. The lieutenant governor was popular with blacks, liberals and labor. He also was a mortgage banker who, as mayor of Portsmouth, had turned around the aging port city's downtown and made it attractive to business. His profession made it easy for him to deny he was a liberal. He often asked, "How many liberal mortgage bankers have you seen?" But Davis' reluctant 1982 U.S. Senate race refigured the political equation. The only question was how. Would Democrats focus on his loyalty or his loss?

If it was the latter, the beneficiary would likely be Jerry Baliles. The low-key attorney general had barely squeaked through on Robb's coattails in 1981 and was thought to have little chance of moving up to the governorship right away. But Baliles was smooth, sharp, ambitious and meticulous. He was a favorite of the same moderate-conservatives who were so enthralled by Robb. And he was based in Richmond, an advantage not to be overlooked in a state where politics and money have traditionally been centralized.

The dark horse was veteran legislator Dick Bagley of Hampton. Bagley had been traveling around the state sporting a "Statewide in '85" button, and in May 1983 signaled that the office he had in mind was the governorship. Bagley's resume — nearly two decades in the General

Assembly, now the chairman of the House Appropriations Committee —
made Davis and Baliles look like lightweights. And as a businessman, a
proven fiscal conservative with a firm hand on the state's budget, raising
money was something Bagley wouldn't have to worry about. His biggest
problem, though, was that outside the halls of the General Assembly and
his own Tidewater district, few had ever heard of him.

There was a fourth Democratic campaign in progress, too. A junior
delegate from the Blue Ridge Mountains of Patrick County, first elected in
1977 as a protege and political next-door neighbor of House Speaker A.L.
Philpott, was busy traveling around the state, visiting potential contributors and supporters. Governor Robb had taken an unusually keen interest
in the political career of this junior delegate, too, making sure the
back-country lawyer, a one-time assistant county prosecutor, got a hefty
share of the "right" crime bills to co-sponsor.

Her name was Mary Sue Terry and she wanted to be attorney general
in a state that had steadfastly, proudly and repeatedly rejected the Equal
Rights Amendment. But that didn't faze this cautious farmer's daughter.
She had voted against it, too.

Curiously, so far no one had expressed an interest in running for
lieutenant governor — unless Bagley's long-shot gubernatorial bid was
simply a way to attract attention before he dropped down to something
more realistic.

Meanwhile, there were more immediate political problems coming to a
boil. Robb had gotten off to a rocky start with state legislators, who often
see themselves as the real leaders in state government and look on
governors as but passing annoyances. Senate Democrats, in particular,
seemed headed for an open split with Robb. They groused that he didn't
pay them the proper deference. Even worse, they complained that when he
did consult with legislators, Robb favored the House over the Senate. That
was only natural. Two of Robb's closest political allies — his chief
fund-raiser, Al Smith, and his party chairman, Alan Diamonstein — were
delegates.

But that was hardly an explanation to soothe the egos of the prideful
lords of the upper chamber.

The complaints added up and finally, in July 1983, a half-dozen
senators — Wilder among them — met with the governor to air their
concerns. One of the many grievances was that Robb was privately
promoting a 1985 Democratic ticket of Baliles-Bagley-Terry, a ticket that
included only present or former House members. Baliles and Bagley were
big enough to take care of themselves, the senators thought. And the fact
that the image-conscious Robb was doing everything he could to groom

Terry for a historic run for statewide office stuck especially hard in the senatorial craw.

"We were convinced Robb would put together a ticket with Mary Sue as the principal player," Emick says. "We felt other considerations were being ignored, i.e., veteran senators with ambitions." Emick had made an unsuccessful run for the lieutenant governor's nomination against Davis in 1981. Hampton state Sen. Hunter Andrews' desire to someday be governor was well-known. And, of course, Wilder had often talked of running.

One day in the summer of 1983, the three of them — Andrews, Emick and Wilder, accompanied by Jay Shropshire, met at the lunchroom of the Thalhimers department store, a frequent scheming-place for legislators in downtown Richmond. They grumbled about the Robb administration and the inadequacies of the emerging statewide campaigns. As Emick remembers the conversation, it was Wilder who brought up the subject of actually doing something about it.

"I see an interesting ticket here," Wilder said. Why not a ticket of Andrews for governor, himself for lieutenant governor and Emick for attorney general?

Wilder outlined his scenario: At the time, there were only two likely outcomes in the gubernatorial contest. Davis, the popular favorite, might win the nomination outright in the mass meetings to select convention delegates. But if he didn't, then the fight would go all the way to the convention floor. A Baliles, or even Bagley, win in the mass meetings seemed out of the question. Wilder and the others believed that if Davis didn't win outright in the mass meetings, there was plenty of room for other candidates to maneuver. And that's where the Senate ticket of Andrews-Wilder-Emick could come in.

With the election still two years off, this was but idle talk on a summer's day. The three senators agreed to meet again but never did. Emick soon decided that he wasn't really interested in a statewide run, no matter which office. The Andrews trial balloon floated a while longer, then deflated. But Wilder looked on the Thalhimers talk not as mere speculation but as serious strategy.

Indeed, Wilder considered the Thalhimers lunch a real milestone. For the first time, he had been able to talk, in a serious way, with serious politicians, about the prospect of a Wilder candidacy. "I sensed then, the fact that it could be discussed without it being dismissed out of hand opened up possibilities," Wilder says. "So I started thinking about the lieutenant governorship."

That, really, was the only statewide office open to him. Virginians rarely elect governors who haven't previously held some other statewide office. "And he couldn't run for attorney general because of the repri-mand" he had received from the state Supreme Court, says strategist Paul Goldman. "That would have been a heat-seeking missile." The reprimand would be dangerous enough in any race, but maybe in a campaign for presiding officer of the Senate it wouldn't look very relevant.

So Wilder started planning. He spent countless hours in Shropshire's office. "We had been talking about it since the '83 session," Shropshire says. "We had talked about it many times at length. Could he do it? How well would he do in this area or that area?" The Senate clerk had a big map of Virginia on his wall and they often studied that, talking names, numbers, nuance. There in the warm privacy of his friend's office, Wilder was emboldened. "I started thinking early in 1984 that I could run and win," he says. "I wasn't interested in running and coming close. Coming close wouldn't cross any Rubicons. Winning crosses Rubicons."

He also saw clearly the scenario he'd have to rely on to get the nomination: Do it my way or do without black votes in the fall. "I was convinced," he says, "if I pushed it well enough and strong enough, whoever was seeking the nomination for governor would need my support and I hoped to neutralize them so they would not want to pick another candidate." It was essentially Wilder's 1982 Pickett strategy in reverse: Pre-empt the field for lieutenant governor, dare someone to challenge him, make them think if they opposed him they'd forever outrage black voters, then try to bargain with the gubernatorial candidates for a spot on the ticket in return for black support. Of course, he couldn't be quite so blatant about it, but a Wilder candidacy would have a certain implied threat to it.

Wilder occasionally mentioned his plans to his friends. "The people who knew me knew I was not joking," he says. Wilder kept up his talk about running for lieutenant governor throughout the 1984 General Assembly, and the session gave Wilder a chance to add to his resume. The previous November had been legislative election time in Virginia. Wilder had been unopposed; others hadn't — and now the combination of defeats and retirements opened up some choice positions. On the 1984 assembly's opening day, there was the biggest reshuffling of committee chairmen in fifteen years. In the process, the foresight of Wilder's first deskmate, Bill Rawlings, was rewarded.

In January 1984, Wilder became the chairman of the Privileges and Elections Committee — clearly a step up in the Senate's power structure. "There was another signal that Wilder had moved into the inner circle," reported the *Richmond Times-Dispatch* the next day. "He became the Senate pro tem's desk mate, taking the chair on the right hand of Sen. Ed Willey."

Wilder met with Robb that spring and told the governor about his plans to run. Robb reared back his head, allowed himself a "hmmph" and said Wilder's idea was "interesting." "He said keep me posted," Wilder recalls. "I said, 'I'm running.' I told everybody. Some laughed."

Wilder, though, was already looking ahead, way ahead. When he did, he always saw the shadow of Dick Bagley. What was he up to? Despite Bagley's stated interest in the governorship, his "Statewide in '85" slogan was suspiciously non-specific. The widespread assumption was that Bagley was simply running for governor for show and would eventually drop down to No. 2. "I wanted to make sure he didn't step down on me," Wilder says.

By March 1984, Wilder decided the time had come to head Bagley off at the political pass. Wilder released to reporters a letter he had written Bagley, wishing the Hampton delegate well in his gubernatorial campaign and asking Bagley to support him for lieutenant governor. Wilder's aim was both clear and clever — to get Bagley on the record denying any interest in the lieutenant governorship.

Bagley says he was never interested in the lieutenant governorship and that may be true. Still, he didn't take the bait. Wilder couldn't really have expected him to. But it didn't matter. Wilder, with one skillful letter, had claimed the lieutenant governor's race as his own and, strategically, put Bagley on the defensive. If Bagley had changed his mind, he'd have had a lot of explaining to do.

"Nature abhors a vacuum and Wilder got in there and staked out his turf," says Del. Chip Woodrum, D-Roanoke. "Before you know it, if you wanted in there, you had to play King of the Mountain and go in there and knock him off."

It would take another year, though, before the rest of the Democratic Party accepted the inevitability of the Wilder candidacy.

Meanwhile, the first controversy of the 1985 campaign had broken out. Dick Davis had suggested that Jerry Baliles should run for lieutenant governor instead. Davis' intent was innocent enough — he was trying to head off his most serious challenger — but Wilder was furious. "It's obviously suggesting he has a preference that doesn't include me," he objected. This was the beginning of a rift between the Davis and Wilder campaigns that eventually cost Davis the nomination.

On paper, the Davis and Wilder constituencies were much the same — blacks, liberals, labor. As a result, "he felt he didn't need my support to get the nomination," Wilder says. "The Baliles people, realizing that, saw a chink in the armor and moved into the breach" — although it would take almost a year for things to get that desperate.

Instead, Virginia Democrats were soon distracted by another black politician — Jesse Jackson. When it came time to pick delegates for the national convention, Jackson's legions jammed the mass meetings and carried Virginia.

Doug Wilder scrupulously kept his distance. When Jackson came to Virginia on the eve of the caucuses, Wilder attended one of the rallies but filed as an uncommitted delegate. But Wilder saw an opportunity for himself in the black turnout Jackson had inspired. One day that spring Wilder telephoned his friend Jay Shropshire. "That's it," he said. "I'm running." Not long afterward, he had some homemade "Wilder for Lt. Gov." buttons made up to pass out at the state convention.

May 18-July 3, 1984

There were two separate Democratic conventions going on in Norfolk. There was the convention to select national convention delegates and nominate Edythe Harrison, a former Norfolk legislator, for a sacrificial run against U.S. Sen. John Warner. But in the hospitality suites and hallways, the 1985 candidates jockeyed for position. And by far the most visible candidate in Norfolk that weekend was Doug Wilder.

Throughout the spring, Wilder had been becoming more and more open about his anticipated campaign.

By the May convention, Wilder was working the crowd as if the campaign was already in progress. He passed out several dozen of his blue-and-white "Wilder for Lt. Gov." buttons. "People snatched them up and were wearing them," Wilder recalls — whites as well as blacks.

A few days after the convention the *Richmond Times-Dispatch* did a story on what the size of the Jackson delegation at the 1984 convention meant for 1985. The headline said it all: "Wilder support growing."

From here on, the pace quickened.

Wilder was gearing up. It was time for details. Such as money. How much. And from whom. The evening of Monday, June 18, Wilder met with about a dozen friends at his home. Shropshire was there, of course. So were some of the pillars of Richmond's business community, Main Street lawyers and financiers whom Wilder had gotten to know over the years. One of them, financier McLain O'Ferrall, had been Andrew Miller's chief fund-raiser when the former attorney general ran for governor in 1977.

It's sometimes easy to get hung up on the black rhetoric of his public life and forget that Wilder, in his private life, was the millionaire, not the militant. He had made a fortune and invested it in real estate. He belonged to a country club. He knew his way around Main Street. "When he decided to run, he had a lot of political IOUs," says Coy Eaves, a retired insurance executive who was there that night. Now Wilder was calling them in.

The mood that June night was pleasant, cheerful, but not entirely optimistic. "I don't think they thought I could win," Wilder says. But Wilder was convinced he could. He had only to look around his living room that night. "There were only three black people here — Benny Lambert and his brother and Carolyn Moss [a top official in the Robb administration]. My relations [with whites] had been such, if I could get out and get the message out, I thought I could win. I was enthusiastic, knowing I still had to balance Bagley against Davis and Baliles."

Many of the participants admitted their skepticism. "I frankly didn't give Wilder much of a chance," Eaves says. "But if he wanted to give it a whirl, I'd do what I could." Some questioned how much resentment would be left over from the Pickett episode. Others wondered whether Wilder would even have solid support from blacks because he hadn't supported Jackson. "I said I was here before Jackson," Wilder says. "They understood." A ripple of laughter went around the room.

Over in a corner, Lambert was sitting beside a certain white lobbyist for the transportation industry. "He was not very enthusiastic," Lambert says. "He acted like he was not going to get involved." While the others were talking, Lambert whispered something the lobbyist ought to keep in mind. "I very quietly told him, 'Listen, even if Doug loses, he'll still be in the Senate. He'll still be chairman of the same committees. It seems to me like you might want to support him.' " The lobbyist's eyes widened a bit. "He said, 'Oh, I never thought of that.' Then he pulled out his checkbook and wrote a check for a substantial amount."

When the meeting broke up, the Wilder campaign was on "go." Wilder began to psych himself up. "Doug Wilder is the most moderate of moderate drinkers," says Shropshire, "but before he announced he said, 'Jay, when I announce, I will not take a drink anywhere until after I win.' "

That Friday, June 22, the *Times-Dispatch* ran another story about Wilder's plans. Wilder admitted that he "sounds more and more" like a candidate and promised an announcement "one way or another" within three weeks.

The three weeks turned into less than two. Shropshire played political consultant and picked the time and place. Tuesday, July 3 — the day before Independence Day — was likely to be a slow news day so the story would get big play in the holiday papers, when people were sitting at home with plenty of time to read them. Shropshire loved the irony of the first black to make a major run for statewide office announcing his candidacy beneath the portrait of Harry Byrd, the architect of Massive Resistance. Shropshire knew the press would love that, too. So the word was put out: Wilder news conference, July 3, 10 a.m., Old Senate Chamber.

That morning newspapers across the state were abuzz with preview stories. No candidate for lieutenant governor had ever received so much ink — and Wilder wasn't even a candidate yet.

When Larry Framme, the Richmond lawyer who was Third District Democratic chairman, got to his office that morning, he pinned on the "Wilder for Lt. Gov." button he had picked up at the state convention and walked down to the State Capitol. "Seeing Doug Wilder with the picture of Harry Byrd was a sight to behold," Framme says.

When Framme left the Capitol that day, he had one clear thought: "There's no way to deny him the nomination. No white politician who expects to have a political life could step in now and be seen as anything other than a stop-Wilder movement."

July 4-July 11, 1984

On Thursday, July 5, Shropshire was back in his office. And not a moment too soon. From his vantage point as Senate clerk, it seemed like all hell had broken loose. "My phone was hopping that day," he says. "People were calling up saying, 'Hey, what the hell is going on down there? Do you think that so-forth will pull out? What's he want?' " Shropshire leaned back in his big swivel chair and chatted with the senators about the latest news. Over the phone, they couldn't see the mischievous smile on his face.

Jonah Thomas "Jay" Shropshire was the silent partner of the Wilder campaign. How this thirty-eight-year-old good ole Southside boy with a perfect English surname became the leading behind-the-scenes advocate for the state's most prominent black politician makes for a case study of the profound, generational changes going on in Southern politics.

Shropshire came from the red dirt country around Martinsville, a hardscrabble land of tobacco farms, furniture factories and textile mills that hugs the North Carolina line on one side, the Blue Ridge Mountains on the other. Politically, he was a student of A.L. Philpott, the gruff and conservative speaker of the House who hails from nearby Bassett. It was Philpott who brought Shropshire up to Richmond, first as a deputy clerk in the House, later as the chief clerk in the Senate. Along the way, Philpott's protege unexpectedly became best friends with one of his senatorial bosses — Doug Wilder. They talked sports, they talked family, but mostly, they talked politics.

In the days of the Byrd Machine, the clerk of the Senate was Byrd's chief overseer in Richmond, a stern old man ready to crack the whip on any upstart legislators who dared stray out of line. That power was now gone, but the Senate clerkship — at least the way Shropshire practiced it — was still one of considerable prestige. Shropshire also was chairman of the state Compensation Board, the agency that sets salaries for local constitutional officers — sheriffs, county clerks, commissioners of revenue, commonwealth's attorneys — to keep them independent from other local officials. This combination of being both Senate clerk and comp board chairman put Jay Shropshire in constant contact with just about anyone who was anything in Virginia politics.

Shropshire, a cherub-faced fellow with a perpetual grin and hair that was prematurely silver by his late thirties, practiced a modern version of good old boy politics — keeping senatorial secrets, passing on the latest rumors, gossiping with courthouse officials from one end of the state to another, briefing reporters off-the-record, in effect running a one-man political information center. Probably no one else has a better sense of what is going on in official Virginia than Jay Shropshire. And with unique access to characters as diverse as A.L. Philpott and Doug Wilder, Shropshire was also a crucial bridge between the old and the new.

Shropshire's role in the Wilder campaign — always quiet and until now unreported — can't be overestimated. Not many knew that he and Wilder were as close as brothers. Senators coming to Shropshire for advice on how to handle "the Wilder problem" didn't realize they were talking directly to the campaign. And until Paul Goldman arrived in December, Shropshire was, in effect, Wilder's campaign manager. Shropshire sat in on all the early planning sessions. He helped Wilder find a campaign treasurer. He accompanied Wilder on several out-of-town trips into potentially hostile territory. And throughout the campaign, he played a valuable role as Wilder's personal political consultant, a trusted friend whose advice Wilder rarely, if ever, ignored. They talked at least once a day, sometimes twice a day or more toward the end of the campaign.

In the early days of July 1984, Shropshire spent a considerable amount of his time calming down agitated senators who couldn't believe that Wilder had gone and done such a damn fool thing as announcing for statewide office.

Meanwhile, the three gubernatorial campaigns tried to lie low and figure out what a Wilder candidacy meant for them. Robb issued a statement expressing his "high personal regard for Doug" but emphasizing his neutrality. The governor was asked whether he thought a black could win. "I hope we're moving forward on this," he said. "But I am not sure that we are as a state." Robb was simply being truthful, but it was a truth Doug Wilder didn't want to hear. This innocuous little comment was merely the first in a yearlong series of incidents and misunderstandings that finally led to a celebrated blow-up between Robb and Wilder after the election.

Robb's honest assessment of Wilder's chances was almost positive, though, compared to the doom others were prophesying.

The *Virginian-Pilot* in Norfolk quoted an unidentified "conservative former Democratic district chairman" who declared that a Wilder nomination would be "a fiasco." Larry Sabato, the widely quoted University of Virginia political analyst, was just as pessimistic. On the afternoon of Wilder's announcement, Sabato was on the phone with one reporter after another who called for comment. Sabato latched onto the phrase he would make famous in this campaign: "It's too clever by half" for the Democrats to nominate both a woman and a black in 1985, he said.

The overriding angle in all the media coverage was, of course, Wilder's race. "In 1985, 122 years after emancipation and 25 years after the end of Massive Resistance to desegregation, will white Virginians be ready to put a black in the state's second-highest office?" asked the *Richmond Times-Dispatch*.

After the news stories settled down, the editorial reaction kicked in. Even traditionally sympathetic newspapers were harsh in their assessment of Wilder's chances.

The *Virginian-Pilot* predicted that lingering animosity over the 1982 showdown with Pickett would likely do Wilder in. "Moderate-conservatives will have good reason" to deny Wilder support, an editorial said, "and it has nothing to do with Mr. Wilder's color. It has to do with revenge. They probably won't try to deny Mr. Wilder the nomination, knowing that would enrage the Democrats' sizable and growing black constituency, probably dooming the entire ticket in the fall.

"No, the good old boys will simply go fishing, so to speak. When Mr. Wilder journeys to Roanoke or Abingdon or McLean to campaign, the local Democratic chieftains will be busy, unable to accompany him to fish fries or shopping centers. Sorry, Doug. When local Democratic workers operate telephone banks, they may forget to mention Mr. Wilder's name during the calls. Just an oversight, Doug. And when the Wilder campaign goes out raising money, it may come up empty in, say, Virginia Beach, a city which gave generously to Governor Robb in 1981 and to Lieutenant Governor Davis in 1982. Gee, business hasn't been so hot, Doug."

The conservative *Richmond Times-Dispatch* wasn't impressed, either. "Saying that Sen. Wilder's color is all that will matter to white voters is a good way to try to disarm his political opponents, for anyone who dares to criticize him will run the risk of being accused of racism. But the senator has expressed the hope that his color will not obscure the message he intends to take to the voters. That is our hope, too. He will be entitled to gain all he can with that message and his opponents will be entitled to pummel him into political oblivion with it."

September 1984

At Democratic barbecues, local headquarters openings and congressional fund-raising dinners, Doug Wilder quietly got out and started making the rounds during the summer and fall of 1984. Sometimes Shropshire went along.

Wilder — who so far had nothing but himself, Shropshire and a general idea of what he had to do — also made some tentative moves toward getting a campaign organization set up.

Wilder needed a campaign manager. His first choice was an unusual one — Senate colleague Ed Holland of Arlington. One night toward the end of July 1984 Holland got a phone call from Wilder. They chatted for a while, then Wilder dropped his bombshell. Holland was taken aback. Being a campaign manager was a full-time job. He declined, but he did offer to help Wilder in some other capacity. Eventually, this scion of a prominent banking family became Wilder's treasurer, on the condition that he wouldn't be the chief fund-raiser. Wilder agreed, a move that foreshadowed a long dispute with Robb over Wilder's seemingly non-existent fund-raising organization.

Meanwhile, the first big test of the 1985 campaign was in September 1984, when the Democrats' State Central Committee met to decide whether to nominate a 1985 ticket by primary or convention. The Davis supporters — generally the liberals — were philosophically inclined toward a primary. After all, the Democrats had scrapped the primary in 1978 specifically as a way to keep the liberals under control. Similarly, the Baliles supporters — the moderate-conservatives — wanted a convention. But it wasn't as simple as a strictly left-right split.

Wilder, too, wanted a convention. He feared a primary might be too expensive. A primary also would force him to organize a full-fledged campaign on his own. He'd have to persuade whites to vote for a black far sooner than he had planned. Instead, Wilder was hoping that if he could just get the nomination, then a certain amount of white support would come automatically from party loyalists.

Wilder also had seen how blacks had stormed the presidential mass meetings in the spring and ended up with far more delegates at the convention than their percentages in the electorate would have suggested — Virginia is 19 percent black, yet Jackson alone won 26 percent of the delegates to the state convention. Perhaps that might happen again. Indeed, with the winner-take-all system Virginia Democrats use in their gubernatorial caucuses, blacks, if they were lucky, might win even more delegates. Plus, in a primary, Wilder would have no control over how his supporters voted in the other races. In a convention, he could bargain with the gubernatorial candidates, threaten to withhold black support, perhaps set himself up as the tail wagging the Democratic dog.

For the underdog Baliles, a convention seemed the only salvation. Davis had a big following in his native Tidewater and among union members across the state. Baliles' strength was in the conservative suburbs and rural areas. In a primary, a huge Davis turnout in Tidewater, combined with a low turnout in the west, could swamp the state far out of proportion to its population. But a convention, in which each county and city is allotted a precise number of delegates, would put a cap on how many votes Davis could pull out of his base and would guarantee Baliles a certain number of votes. A convention also favored the candidate with the best organization, and Baliles had a reputation of being meticulous almost to a fault.

With similar goals but different constituencies, Wilder and Baliles' campaign manager, Darrel Martin, were natural allies on this issue. They spent a lot of time talking that September, putting together an informal coalition to insist on a convention. It would not be the last time that the unlikely pair of Baliles and Wilder would team up in this campaign.

In the end, the Davis supporters acquiesced and the State Central Committee voted to go with a convention. The Davis campaign was convinced it was ahead and going to stay that way, so why bother changing?

At the time, the convention decision did not seem particularly important. But, in hindsight, Martin calls it "the strategic meltdown of the Davis campaign."

The Davis campaign was overconfident, Wilder was becoming suspicious of the Davis forces, and the Baliles campaign realized that Wilder could not be ignored and might actually be helpful. And now a convention would select the nominee. For Doug Wilder, one by one, the pieces were falling into place.

October 1984

Wilder was optimistic but his friends weren't. He abruptly discovered that in Fredericksburg.

Wilder thought it was time to have a meeting of his closest supporters, the first real get-together he had had since the pre-announcement meeting in his living room back in June. So that some of his friends from Northern Virginia could be there, he decided to have it in Fredericksburg. He reserved a meeting room for all day. The location was ironic. One of the hotel employees told Wilder that former Sen. Harry Byrd Jr. and former Gov. Mills Godwin had been there just the day before, talking politics themselves. Wilder soon found he might have gotten a better reception if he had decided to sit in with Byrd and Godwin. His own meeting, he recalls, "wasn't as uplifting as I had hoped."

He found himself subjected — all day long — to one complaint or criticism after another.

"I was constantly forced to prove myself," Wilder says. "One guy said, 'Now you can't be late.' I said, 'When have I been late?' He said, 'You haven't been.' Then why do you ask? It started getting nit-picky. But I curbed my visual displeasure." (Although not very well, according to some of the participants).

The complaints focused chiefly on what nearly everyone there saw as an utter lack of organization. He didn't have a campaign manager, he wasn't raising money, he didn't even have a fund-raiser, he didn't have a pollster, he didn't have a scheduler, he didn't have a media consultant, he didn't have a press secretary, he didn't have any volunteers, he didn't have any staff at all.

"Some people were very upset," says Del. Benjamin Lambert, D-Richmond. The dozen or so people there — about half black, half white — thought they were part of the campaign's inner circle, yet they knew next to nothing about how Wilder intended to run. In truth, Wilder's inner circle was sometimes only Wilder himself. "It seemed to me Doug had it all in his head and didn't let anybody know except Paul Goldman," says Lambert. And Goldman, at this point, was still in New York.

People started to push their friends to be hired. "They wanted me to hire this person and the other person," Wilder says. "I said, but he lost this election, or he lost that election. I said I'm going to run a tight campaign. I will sign every check." That raised eyebrows.

As McLain O'Ferrall, the Richmond investment broker, looked around the room that day, he saw a bunch of political amateurs fumbling about. "I was the only one who had any experience fund-raising," he says. He didn't claim to be an expert, but he did know one thing. "Dick Davis and Jerry Baliles and Mary Sue Terry had these monstrous staffs and were raising money."

At lunch, O'Ferrall took Wilder aside for a man-to-man talk. "You're a long shot," O'Ferrall told him.

"What do you mean?" asked Wilder, somewhat surprised.

"Your chances are slim and none," O'Ferrall said. "If you raise $400,000 you've done your job and a lot of that has to be from out of state."

Now wait a minute, Wilder said. O'Ferrall had sat in Wilder's living room in June when Wilder and others had talked confidently of raising $750,000 to $1 million and didn't object then. Why was he being so pessimistic now? O'Ferrall said he was just being realistic.

While O'Ferrall had Wilder cornered, he questioned him about some other things, too. "Doug, if you've got any skeletons in your closet, you better think about 'em." Wilder was pleasant enough on that sensitive subject. "Don't worry about that," he said. "Every skeleton I've got has already been printed."

O'Ferrall wasn't the only one who was afraid of some below-the-belt ambush. Back in the meeting, others quizzed Wilder about his personal and professional life. "I told them about the divorce, that the grounds were a year's separation with neither party found at fault," Wilder says. "I told them about the Bar reprimand. I couldn't think of anything else in the closet they'd be embarrassed by." But the participants would have almost rather heard him spill some dark, terrible secret. The denials may have been true, but Wilder's clipped answers didn't breed much confidence.

By the end of the day, Wilder was disgusted. These were supposed to be his friends, the people who said yeah, sure, do it, we're with you all the way. Why were they so down on his chances? He was tired of being around nay-sayers all the time, tired of hearing people say it couldn't be done. He could see now that this would be a long and lonely campaign. But so what? He vowed that this would be the last staff meeting he would have. (And it was.) From here on out, he'd do things his way.

State Sen. Ed Holland sums up what happened at the meeting this way: "Everybody thought he'd have to run in the mold of everybody else, with a big staff, sending out memos a couple times a week." Instead, "Doug up-anchored and sailed off on his odyssey of a person-to-person campaign."

4

Secret Meetings

The November 1984 election returns came crashing down on Virginia Democrats with a sickening thud. The Mondale-Ferraro ticket had been a disaster, losing forty-nine of fifty states. At home, Senate candidate Edie Harrison had done worse than lose in a landslide; she had lost in a landslide of historic proportions. Before the voting had begun, Larry Sabato, the University of Virginia political analyst, checked his records and advised reporters that if Harrison won less than 30 percent of the vote, it would be the worst statewide defeat ever suffered by a Virginia Democrat. When the returns were in, Harrison had won just 29.9 percent of the vote.

The lesson of the 1984 election seemed so obvious. The national Democratic Party had no spine. It had given in to a noisy collection of leftist "special interests." His early endorsement by the AFL-CIO painted Walter Mondale as a labor pawn. Then he was seen caving in to feminists by picking Geraldine Ferraro as his running mate. Ferraro hadn't helped the ticket much. Neither had Edie Harrison.

Now, in November 1984, Virginia Democrats suddenly woke up and, apparently for the first time, realized the madness they were about to commit by nominating a ticket with both a black and a woman. History seemed to be repeating itself. Neither Wilder nor Terry had opposition. Furthermore, in less than two weeks, the Virginia AFL-CIO was set to make its own early endorsement for governor, an endorsement that seemed sure to go to the front-runner, Dick Davis. A Davis-Wilder-Terry ticket, on the heels of a Mondale-Ferraro-Jackson-Harrison disaster?

The drumbeat started.

Virginia Republicans also felt uneasy as they looked toward the 1985 governor's race — the Reagan landslide notwithstanding. They had three likely candidates for governor, but two were losers trying to make comebacks.

One was Marshall Coleman, the former attorney general who had lost to Robb in 1981. All agreed that the young and photogenic Coleman would be a strong general election candidate. Many conservatives loathed him, though, and the appalling debt he ran up during his gubernatorial campaign did little to endear him to the money men of Richmond's Main Street.

The other candidate was Wyatt Durrette, a man who, to put it bluntly, had lost his way to the top. A former state legislator from Northern Virginia, he had lost the nomination for attorney general to Coleman in 1977, then came back to win it without opposition in 1981 only to lose in the general election. He was, in harshly objective terms, an out-of-office politician who hadn't won an election in ten years and whose biggest claim to fame was that he had lost the state's No. 3 office four years ago. It wasn't much on which to base a campaign. But, for conservative Republicans, Wyatt Durrette was all they had and they reluctantly rallied around him.

Hoping to exploit that hesitancy, a third Republican — newly re-elected Northern Virginia Rep. Stan Parris — announced he might soon jump into the governor's race.

In the days after the presidential election, though, the Republicans' inability to find a unifying, inspiring candidate for governor was forgotten as the focus shifted to the hapless Democrats and their "Wilder problem." Standing by the side of the road like some Roman seer, freely pointing out the certain catastrophe that lay ahead, was Larry Sabato.

Who the hell is Larry Sabato?

And why does everyone pay attention to what he says?

That was the question many Virginians may have been asking themselves in the winter of 1984-85, when hardly a political story went by without the U.Va. political science professor, then thirty-two, being quoted as an expert. Indeed, his mere utterances became news stories in their own right: "Wilder's chances 1 in 100 for No. 2 spot, prof says."

Sabato's role in Virginia politics is perhaps unique — an academic analyst who's more prominent, and arguably more powerful, than the politicians he's analyzing. Sabato is the Carl Sagan of Virginia politics — part scholar, part showman, a celebrity scientist in an otherwise anonymous field.

He also is undeniably good at what he does best, which is analyze Virginia election returns. When it comes to finding meanings in actual results, like a medieval astrologer looking for omens in the stars, there's no one in Virginia better than Sabato. Certainly few others have devoted as much time to it. "He has more statistics at the tip of his tongue and on reserve in the back of his mind that anyone else," says Harvey Powers, news director of WWBT-TV in Richmond. "If you ask him who carried Giles County in '62, he'll say, "Oh, such and such." He'll know it. Just pick a county at random. He's the most knowledgeable person on Virginia politics I've run into. He sits there with the knowledge of the universe at his fingertips." That's why Powers hired him as Channel 12's regular Election Night analyst.

Sabato's phone number is engraved in all Virginia political reporters' Rolodexes, if not their memories. No political analysis is complete without calling Sabato for comment. Wilder grumbles about "the Sabato mystique" and why reporters don't call any other academics. The simple fact is there aren't any others who have the same expertise.

Sabato has developed a curious symbiotic relationship with both the press and politicians. Candidates often share their private polls with him and beg him to favor them with a kind word in the press. Some politicians have sent him their statements in advance so, when reporters call for comment, Sabato can have the complete text. In 1984-85, one candidate for governor called Sabato and spent an hour on the phone, explaining why he was his party's best choice. Another cornered Sabato at a dinner and gave a similar pitch, hoping he would give an upbeat analysis. Toward the end of the 1985 campaign, nearly a dozen Republican campaign workers phoned to privately distance themselves from crucial campaign decisions, presumably so Sabato would hold them blameless when reporters called him for comment.

And call they do. "I don't know anyone else in Virginia, except a governor, whose utterances on political entrails are considered news," said George Stoddart, the late press secretary to Governor Robb. "It's the fault of the press. It's gotten too easy."

But Sabato is so outrageously quotable. And more importantly, he's so willing to say publicly what the politicians dare say only privately.

On Edie Harrison: "For her to win, lightning would have to strike five times in the same place."

On Paul Trible: He's "one of the least impressive people ever elected to high office."

On how to predict Virginia elections: The winner will be the candidate "the average suburbanite would most like to have at his cocktail party." Republicans won the 1977 governor's race because "John Dalton might be dull but Henry Howell would spill mustard on his tie."

On Doug Wilder: Well, we'll get to that later. With the Wilder campaign, Sabato "made the fatal error," Stoddart said, "of crossing the boundary between being a commentator and being a participant." On Election Night 1985, the joke was that the big winners were Chuck Robb and Marshall Coleman and the big losers were Mills Godwin and Larry Sabato.

Sabato grew up in Norfolk and worked in Henry Howell's campaigns. But there was an academic streak in this young political operative. One of Sabato's mentors at the University of Virginia had started a series of reports analyzing Virginians' voting habits. When the professor suddenly died, Sabato took on the job of writing the second volume. He was still an undergraduate. After Charlottesville, Sabato won a Rhodes Scholarship to Oxford and wrote a book on the decline of the Byrd Machine, published in 1977. He was only twenty-four, working on his doctorate overseas and already giving interviews back home. The Sabato mystique had begun.

Eventually, Sabato dropped out of partisan politics and became a non-partisan analyst, cranking out his "Virginia Votes" series after each election and writing other books on politics.

Nowadays, during what he calls "the season," the fall elections through the winter post-mortems, Sabato is on the road maybe three days a week, speaking to trade associations, school groups, talk shows. On the subject of political consultants, PACs and political parties, Sabato has a national reputation. But at home, he's known almost exclusively for his role as the chief commentator on and handicapper of Virginia politics.

Sooner or later — and in the winter of 1984-85, it became sooner — the question has to come around to influence: How much does Sabato have? When do his mid-campaign analyses cross the line from clinical observation to unwitting interference, much like a respected Broadway critic whose unfavorable review can close a play?

Sabato emphatically says it doesn't happen, but the politicians just as emphatically disagree. "The problem with all the experts is that what they say becomes a self-fulfilling prophecy," says Edie Harrison. She won't forgive Sabato for dismissing her as "a novelty," a comment she says hurt her fund-raising efforts early in the campaign. Sabato insists he wasn't saying anything that leaders of her own party weren't saying privately. "But who knows" the repercussions, asks Wilder.

In the 1985 campaign, Wilder found out.

"The problem with Larry Sabato was he had a lot of impact on the inner party people," says John Jameson, who ran Mary Sue Terry's campaign. "Clearly, they thought Wilder could not win, but I think Sabato exacerbated it. People could not believe a black liberal could win in a conservative state," but few dared say it. So when Sabato said it, and said it forcefully and repeatedly, that made it respectable to oppose Wilder and emboldened those seeking an alternative candidate.

Sabato, a long-haired hippie who turned into one of the Jaycees' "Outstanding Young Men of America," says his own political views have "drifted" over the years, that he's now an avowed moderate, a "true independent" with no interest in who wins or loses. "You can't find any candidate out there who has so much as paid for a glass of iced tea for me. I may be critical, but I'm not pushing any ideology." In a biting counter-commentary in the *Washington Post* in November 1984, Democratic activist Gus Johnson of Madison County declared that Sabato, the one-time student radical, has now become "the high priest of conventional wisdom."

And that may be the key clue to why Sabato was so wrong on Wilder. In 1985, the conventional wisdom simply didn't work.

Nov. 7-16, 1984

The folly of a Wilder candidacy, and the necessity of Robb to stop it, were recurring Sabato themes.

Sabato was saying nothing publicly that Democrats weren't saying privately. But in fall 1984, Sabato was in all the papers, granting interviews, writing two post-election essays that were published in many Virginia newspapers.

The first ran Nov. 10. In it Sabato argued that a ticket with both Wilder and Terry is "a ticket too clever by half for conservative Virginia and one that ties the state party to the national party's disastrous propensity to play 'constituency quota' games." He urged Robb to take charge, to talk Davis or Baliles or both into seeking re-election and persuading Wilder and Terry to delay their ambitions for the good of the party. "Some Democrats may not like the 'bossism' inherent in gubernatorial slate-making but they will like the loss of their only political stronghold even less."

Sabato was, at least, bipartisan. He warned Republicans that the Religious Right had better keep a low profile or the party couldn't hope to transform the 1984 Reagan Youth into permanent Republican voters.

By now, others had picked up the same refrain. A front-page story in the *Washington Post* Nov. 15 was headlined "Wilder bid worries some Va. Democrats."

Included was this appraisal of Wilder's chances from George Stoddart, Robb's press secretary: "For better or worse, this is still Virginia. That makes it very difficult."

Wilder read that and nearly exploded. "This is still Virginia." What was that supposed to mean? And from the governor's press secretary. What did that mean? Wilder privately demanded an explanation from Robb. "He said that George Stoddart was speaking on his own behalf," Wilder says. "I said, a press secretary for the governor never speaks on his own behalf. I said that it was rather damaging to my candidacy and asked him to have George remain neutral."

Robb says he doesn't remember the specific meeting but says he was used to Wilder's frequent fulminations. "I normally let him get things off his chest," Robb says, in a somewhat patronizing tone. As for the details, "I don't remember every little thing."

In Stoddart's defense, his comment was apparently only an innocent observation. But with the paranoia that prevailed in Wilder's campaign in the winter of 1984-85, Wilder saw Stoddart's comment as a signal that Robb was out to get rid of him. With that kind of suspicious outlook to begin with, Wilder soon saw plenty of "signs" that Robb was egging on a Stop Wilder movement. This misunderstanding was the real beginning of Wilder's celebrated feud with Robb, a dispute that simmered uneasily throughout the campaign — only to rudely erupt in public less than two weeks after the election.

Soon, though, conservative Virginia Democrats had something besides Wilder to worry about. The AFL-CIO had just endorsed Dick Davis for governor.

Nov. 17-23, 1984

An AFL-CIO endorsement has always been, if not the kiss of death in Virginia politics, then at least an embarrassing lipstick stain that needs to be explained away. The state's right-to-work law and opposition to collective bargaining for public employees are the cornerstones of Virginia's pro-business government. Even Democrats must swear fealty to these sacred traditions if they're to have a hope of being taken seriously.

Now, only two weeks after the Mondale debacle, the AFL-CIO was set to make an early endorsement for governor. Some Democrats begged them not to, but labor was determined. It wanted to maximize its leverage in the caucuses.

For Doug Wilder, the labor endorsement was a chance to get a much-needed boost. Even an AFL-CIO endorsement would give his embattled campaign credibility. More importantly, failure to get the endorsement would be a potentially fatal blow. If pro-labor Wilder can't get the labor endorsement, then why should anybody take him seriously? Maybe he really was just running a symbolic campaign.

The courting of the AFL-CIO, though, also revealed one of Wilder's fundamental weaknesses. At this point, there was no such thing as a Wilder campaign, simply Wilder himself — and he seemed to be completely ignorant of how to go about running a statewide race. Davis, Baliles and Bagley had their staffs going all-out to win the union endorsement. (Terry, with her well-publicized corporate support, cautiously stayed away.) But here it was the virtual eve of the meeting and the union hadn't heard a peep out of Wilder. Secretarytreasurer Danny LeBlanc called him to find out what the matter was. "Do you want our endorsement?" LeBlanc asked, somewhat warily. Sure, Wilder said, how do I get it? LeBlanc would have been amused if time hadn't been running so short. LeBlanc mailed Wilder a questionnaire and scheduled an interview for the day before the executive board was to meet.

Wilder came into the AFL-CIO offices in Richmond and still hadn't looked at the questionnaire he'd been sent. He sat down at a table with the labor leaders and filled it out there. "He said, 'I've got to be for this, I patroned the bill. Or, 'I've got to be for this, I voted for the bill,' " LeBlanc remembers. "He had a 100 percent questionnaire."

Nevertheless, a labor endorsement of Wilder was not a foregone conclusion. "To be really candid, there was an element of concern," LeBlanc says. It was such a short time before the executive board met that LeBlanc was fearful he might not be able to muster the two-thirds necessary for an endorsement. "In the Tidewater area, we were concerned there still might be some bitterness over Owen Pickett," LeBlanc says.

Plus, the Davis campaign was quietly putting out suggestions that if the AFL-CIO was really going to endorse Wilder's hopeless candidacy, then labor could do Davis a big favor by not doing it right away. Endorse Davis now, the Davis workers were whispering, and Wilder later. That way it won't come out as a Davis-Wilder endorsement. But LeBlanc — and the other key labor people — weren't buying.

"There was a certain part of the membership that was damned well determined Doug would be endorsed," LeBlanc says.

"To be honest, the blacks had tried to put a little pressure on us," vice president Russ Axsom says. "They made their position known. Here's a candidate with just about a perfect record for working people and he's black. Now what are you going to do? Most of us didn't have any problem." Black leaders weren't taking any chances, though, especially with the Davis campaign trying to head off a Wilder endorsement. The black labor leaders brought in some NAACP people and a black official from AFL-CIO national headquarters to lobby delegates. "It wasn't really necessary, but they thought it was," Axsom says.

The vote for Wilder was unanimous. Labor also endorsed Davis. It made no endorsement for attorney general.

No sooner were the endorsements announced than the Baliles campaign suddenly went on a labor-bashing offensive — accusing Davis of making secret promises to "special interests."

The union endorsement did something besides mark Davis as a special-interest candidate, though. It sharpened the terror of conservative Democrats who dared contemplate the chances of the emerging Davis-Wilder-Terry ticket and forced them to start doing something to stop it.

Doing something about Wilder posed a problem, though.

"If a white with that same kind of super-liberal voting record had run, he would have had six to ten opponents," says one ex-legislator, a liberal Democrat who has a personal distaste for Wilder. "Plus the Bar reprimand! And he's lazy! Just think about this, if Doug Wilder, with the same record, had been white, he'd have been a joke. No one would take him seriously. He made Henry Howell look conservative. It shows we have a strange kind of racism in reverse."

But Wilder was not simply black — he was brazen, and not afraid to shout "racism" whenever it suited him. This was where Wilder's showdown with Pickett become so valuable. All the "experts" had figured Wilder had hurt himself by not being a team player in 1982. Instead, Wilder was now untouchable. Nobody wanted to make him mad.

Wilder and his allies "were walking around with their thumbs in their pockets," Baliles organizer Barry Rose says. "They never threatened anybody. They didn't have to. Everybody was afraid because of the Pickett thing. That was the single most important thing to Doug winning the nomination."

The party's one hope was that Wilder would misfire, that he would say something incendiary and give them an opportunity to oppose him with something other than the fact that a black couldn't win. "But if you didn't take the bait," Goldman says, "you never gave them an opening." Wilder sat back and kept his mouth shut.

"So, in the final analysis, the whole thing was just blackmail," says the ex-legislator. "They all thought it was a suicide run and that made it all the more threatening. Conventional political wisdom would not work. How can you talk him out of it if it's a suicide run? You can't take him to the Commonwealth Club and talk sense to him. What are you going to say, 'Your chances are slim'?"

That didn't stop certain well-connected Democrats from trying, though. Some privately suggested that Wilder might make an excellent party chairman if only he'd drop this silly notion of running for lieutenant governor.

"One man called me and told me he searched his heart and soul and couldn't support me," Wilder says. "The best thing to do was to drop out and become party chairman, campaign for four years, made amends, and run four years from now. He said he would help me, loan me his private plane as well as give me money." The man, a Northern Virginia business-man, was a friend of Robb's, so his call only added to Wilder's suspicions that Robb was up to no good.

"The feeling was universal: 'What does Doug want? What can we do to get him out?'" Sabato says. "These were genuine considerations being discussed on a daily basis in the Democratic Party. You have to admire Doug Wilder for sticking through that period, when there was a universal feeling that he was a sure loser who's going to capsize the whole ticket."

That was a matter of no little concern to the men who wanted to lead the ticket. Bagley was still busy trying to outmaneuver both Davis and Baliles. But those two campaigns were already looking ahead — and both had staff people trying to figure out what to do about Wilder.

The Baliles camp studied a "favorite son" strategy for lieutenant governor that would mute charges of racism with regional pride. Campaign manager Martin was searching for candidates.

One key strategy session with Baliles workers in Northern Virginia was held that November. "At that time, there was a lot of brainstorming about potential candidates" to oppose Wilder, says Barry Rose. "They men-tioned Horan's name [Fairfax County prosecutor Bob Horan], they men-tioned Buzz's name [State Sen. Buzz Emick of Botetourt County]." During a break, Martin whispered to Rose that he was talking to "someone in Tidewater" and asked if Rose thought Don Beyer Jr. — a car dealer who was heading Baliles' campaign in Northern Virginia — might want to run.

72

But Martin let the favorite son idea pass. Baliles, with his moderate-conservative background, couldn't afford to offend blacks.

Wilder, though, was more suspicious of the Davis campaign — and with good reason. "We didn't want him," admits Rhett Walker, Davis' top field organizer. "We were scared about it. We felt Doug would pull down the ticket. We felt he definitely would pull down Dick Davis. Davis had a liberal image from the Senate race and we were victims of conventional thinking."

Davis says he would have welcomed Wilder on the ticket, despite the image problems it would have caused. Wilder was a "superlative" orator, for one thing, Davis says. "At times, on very tough issues, I'd seen him turn the Senate around and I knew because of that he'd be a formidable candidate." But, Davis concedes, "there were people in my campaign who felt otherwise and I was pretty much obliged to follow their advice if I expected them to help me." As a result, says Davis campaign manager Bobby Watson, "some good supporters were doing everything they could" to stop Wilder.

Elsewhere, though, some powerful people believed Davis already had the nomination locked up — and key members of the House of Delegates, who had to run for re-election alongside the statewide ticket, were afraid a Davis-Wilder-Terry ticket would crash so hard they'd lose their seats, too. That instinct for self-preservation led to one of the most bungled enterprises of the whole campaign, the so-called "secret meeting" in the House speaker's office.

Nov. 30, 1984

Never has a "secret meeting" been so well-publicized, nor has such a short conversation generated such controversy. It lasted only thirty minutes or so, produced no decisions and, ironically, didn't concern Wilder as much as it did Davis. But no one believed that.

The meeting began innocently enough, if anything about politics can be called innocent. House Democrats were to meet in Richmond Nov. 30 to discuss filling some judgeships. Del. Alan Diamonstein of Newport News — state Democratic Party chairman and a close friend of Robb's — wanted to get some delegates together to talk about the statewide political picture. A few days before, the word went out to key Democrats to meet in House Speaker A.L. Philpott's sixthfloor office that afternoon after the judgeship caucus was over.

Some legislators suggested that if they were going to talk about Wilder, then the two senior black delegates — William Robinson Jr. of Norfolk and Benjamin Lambert of Richmond — ought to be at the meeting. Diamonstein agreed, but says he was under the impression someone else was going to invite the pair. The "secret meeting" wasn't so organized that there was a formal guest list with one clear-cut host, he says. "We were inviting people that morning. We'd see someone going up the steps and say, 'Hey, come on.'" Whatever the intent, the result was the same. Robinson and Lambert didn't get invitations.

That was public relations mistake No. 1. "A secret meeting of white Democratic legislators" became the standard phrase in the news stories. Holding the meeting in the office of Philpott, the gruff old pol who had once called black delegates "boys," played up that image.

Public relations mistake No. 2: Since it was whites-only, it must have been a stop-Wilder meeting, right?

Actually, according to those who were there, it wasn't. "The thinking was Dick Davis was going to win the nomination and Doug Wilder would be nominated and Doug may not believe this, but most of the talk was about how Dick Davis could not win," says Bernie Cohen of Alexandria.

At one point, someone asked how many of the eighteen delegates present thought Davis really could win the election. Only one — Cohen — raised his hand.

Cohen describes it as "a gloom and doom meeting." He was a Davis supporter and wasn't very comfortable being there. "It seemed like a get-Dick Davis group," he says.

But the concern naturally went beyond Davis. "What everybody was really scared of was a ticket of Davis-Wilder-Terry," Woodrum says, and soon the talk drifted to the other offices. Owen Pickett of Virginia Beach voiced concern about whether Terry could win so soon after Ferraro-Harrison. Few others, though, seemed worried about their conservative colleague.

Chip Woodrum of Roanoke says he threw out the possibility that Wilder might "do OK" but it didn't get very far. The prevailing mood was that Wilder was bad news. "We discussed viable alternatives and frankly there were none," says House Majority Leader Tom Moss of Norfolk. A feeling of resignation began to creep over the delegates. They had let Wilder go unopposed too long. Wilder couldn't be stopped now, not without tearing the party apart. The only hope was if he could be persuaded to withdraw. Cohen, a fellow liberal, volunteered to have a talk with Wilder. And with that, the "secret meeting" broke up.

It didn't stay secret very long. As delegates opened the door and streamed out of Philpott's office, the first person they saw was Benjamin

Lambert sitting outside, waiting to see Philpott on another matter.

"Hey, Benny," Woodrum said.

The second thing they saw was a reporter from the *Richmond Times-Dispatch.*

"He smelled it," Cohen says.

Nov. 30 - Early December 1984

"I've never seen such a quick and dramatic lesson in politics," Cohen says. "We were supposedly knowledgeable Democratic leaders called from various parts of the state because we were supposed to have insight into our areas. It turned out every single one of us was wrong. It was a very powerful lesson in the non-predictability of politics."

But at this point, the lesson was still eleven months off.

The very afternoon of the "secret meeting," long before Cohen came for his talk, Wilder had another visitor, this one also a delegate who had been at the meeting — Al Smith of Winchester. Smith also was one of Robb's biggest fund-raisers and political confidants.

Wilder remembers Smith as distraught over the prospect of his candidacy. "He said, 'We've just got to talk,' " Wilder says. "He wanted an assurance [that] if someone ran, he wouldn't be called a racist." Wilder says he gave it, but also insisted he was in the race to the finish.

When Smith left, Wilder was convinced that a Robb plot was in the works. First, his press secretary had moaned that "this is still Virginia." Then his handpicked party chairman had convened a whites-only meeting. Now Robb's personal fund-raiser had come to strong-arm him. What more proof did Wilder need? "It would surprise me if Robb didn't know" in advance about the "secret meeting" and Smith's visit, Wilder says.

Robb insists he didn't know anything about the meeting until after it became public. "Several of the folks who attended that meeting came in and apologized to me," Robb says. "Especially Alan. He said, 'Hey, boss, what you read is not the case.' " Robb also says Smith was acting on his own — and with good reasons, both politically and personally. "He did have questions about whether [Wilder] could win," Robb says. Certainly Wilder wasn't going to help any ticket in Smith's district. Plus, what incentive did Smith have to encourage Wilder anyway? "He was badly burned by the incident at the Commonwealth Club [during the Pickett episode.] I think he felt set up," Robb says. "Al had considered Doug a friend and thought he had been done in by a friend. It was a long-term hurt and Al is not one to recover quickly."

Cohen got no further with Wilder than Smith did. "I was an old friend and supporter of Doug Wilder," Cohen says. "I went to him and asked him not to do it. I told him it was a big mistake. I really thought it could be damaging to the ticket." Cohen offered to raise money for Wilder if he would set his sights on something more realistic — and less harmful to party fortunes — such as Congress.

Wilder was friendly but, well, firm. "He ended up biting my head off," Cohen says. "He didn't yell. He was a gentleman. He was firm, disappointed and a little angry with me, because I was a friend. That's why I went, because I was a friend. I thought I could say what was being said by others behind his back." Wilder recalls Cohen saying, "As a friend, I can't let you do this. He said the most you can raise is $200,000, $250,000, and you can't win."

Cohen says it was well-known in the General Assembly that he was going to see Wilder about dropping out. "Everybody was holding their breath to see what he told me and after I went, no one else did."

Instead, those worried about Wilder lined up to see David McCloud, the bulldog chief of staff who guarded the governor's door.

"I don't know how many people talked to me," McCloud says, "members of the legislature, members of the business community, members of the Democratic Party, about 'we've got to do something. The governor's got to get Wilder out of the race.' I know a lot of people approached Robb and told Robb the same thing." McCloud says Robb listened to those concerned about a Wilder candidacy but did nothing to pressure Wilder out of the race.

In fact, that soon became the complaint. Commentators started pointing out that while Robb was busy telling national Democrats how to cast aside their special interests and unite around moderates, he wasn't doing a thing to stop the formation of a "special-interest" ticket in his own state.

Rather than discourage Wilder, though, the "secret meeting" actually boosted his confidence. The legislators' fear was proof that his candidacy was making progress. "It showed me there was a great deal of concern that I was on my way," Wilder says. "The scare tactics had already started."

But only four days after delegates at the "secret meeting" had more or less resigned themselves to a Wilder nomination, the landscape of the lieutenant governor's race was completely rearranged — for the worse, from Wilder's perspective.

Dec. 3-6, 1984

December 1984 was a rapid-fire series of one political development after another — almost all of which involved, in one way or another, Doug Wilder.

The first bombshell exploded Monday, Dec. 3. Marshall Coleman ended months of speculation by announcing he would be a candidate for the Republican nomination — for lieutenant governor.

Coleman's move was shrewd. If he ran for governor again, he'd face a tough fight for the nomination with Wyatt Durrette and Stan Parris. If he lost, his political career would certainly be over. But by stepping down to the No. 2 spot — in the guise of "party unity," of course — Coleman became an instant front-runner. He was better known than all his potential rivals put together. No matter who won the gubernatorial nomination, the conservatives would almost have to give Coleman the No. 2 spot. Or so it was thought.

Coleman's decision terrified Democrats all over again. Coleman's candidacy "makes it more imperative than ever that the Democrats do something about the Wilder problem," one unidentified legislator told the *Roanoke Times & World-News.* "The question now is whether we're just going to give the Republicans that seat."

Of course, Coleman didn't have the nomination quite yet. Coleman was a political Gulliver in a field of Lilliputians, but it was a field that was growing more crowded each day. Del. A.R. "Pete" Giesen, the General Assembly's senior Republican, a fellow moderate and an old political neighbor from Augusta County, was going to run. Richard Viguerie, the New Right direct mail wizard from Northern Virginia, was talking about running. So was state Sen. John Chichester of Stafford County, whose biggest claim to fame was that he had once killed the Equal Rights Amendment in a parliamentary maneuver — he abstained on the grounds that he had a conflict of interest because he was married to a woman. The GOP even had a black candidate — Maurice Dawkins, a Northern Virginia lobbyist who ran a symbolic campaign to attract more blacks to the party.

Eventually, Chichester emerged as Coleman's chief opponent. A former Democrat, Chichester was the favorite of Mills Godwin and "the old guard." The Coleman-Chichester campaign became a pitched battle between GOP moderates and old Byrd Democrats. But that was still months in the future. In December 1984, the political scene was changing so fast no one could plan that far ahead.

Coleman announced on a Monday and by that Thursday the Democrats were in even deeper disarray. That was the day the story about the "secret meeting" broke.

Wilder fired back: "Let's get it out on the table now. Let's not kid ourselves. The problem is that I'm black and that is just anathema to some people."

Wilder insisted he was in the race to stay. "There is nothing that anyone could offer me" to get him to drop out, he said.

Dec. 6-9, 1984

The same day the story about the "secret meeting" broke, Wilder called a news conference to announce that, when the General Assembly met in January, he would introduce a "no-cost" bill to crack down on prison escapees. Prisons promised to be a big issue in 1985: One summer night in 1984 six death-row inmates, including Richmond's notorious Briley brothers, had broken out of the maximum-security Mecklenburg Correctional Center. It took three weeks before they were all tracked down and re-captured — two as far away as Vermont, the Brileys in Philadelphia.

Looking tough on crime was Wilder's way of hugging the center. "A lot of people say Doug Wilder's a liberal," he said. "Those people haven't looked at my record." He sidestepped questions about the growing controversy over his candidacy.

He could afford to. Others were saying plenty about it for him. The Democrats' State Central Committee met Friday and Saturday — Dec. 7 and 8 — and party chairman Diamonstein got a beating from blacks over the now-public "secret meeting." Diamonstein vigorously denied it had been a stop-Wilder meeting, but nobody believed him.

The next day, the Republican chairman publicly gave thanks for the dilemma the opposition found itself in.

After all that, with holidays coming on, people were probably expecting the hullabaloo to settle down. But the excitement had just begun. The next Monday was one of the most dramatic and controversial days of the whole campaign.

Dec. 10, 1984

Dick Bagley's staff assembled that Monday morning for a routine staff meeting at the new high-rise Marriott in downtown Richmond. The mood was upbeat. The campaign's field director had stayed up two nights stuffing information packets for the field workers to take back home with them. One guy had just come in from Montana to join the campaign. Everyone was gearing up for the big push after the holidays.

Then the candidate walked into the room and announced he was quitting the race.

The dozen or more staffers sat in stunned silence. Some began to cry softly. Tears welled up in Bagley's eyes, too, as he made a moving speech about how he had come a long way in the polls, but he hadn't come far enough.

When he was done saying goodbye to his staff, Bagley walked the three blocks to the state Capitol to a hastily called news conference to make his decision public.

Larry Sabato was at the Capitol that morning, too — for his annual post-election news conference to go over his analysis of the 1984 returns. He had figured Monday would be a slow news day. Instead, when he got to the Capitol, reporters rushed up to him. You'll have to postpone your news conference, they said excitedly, Dick Bagley's getting ready to drop out of the governor's race!

Sabato crowded into the room to watch. A haggard, despondent Bagley — sick with the flu — fought back tears as he read his statement. He said he had known all along his bid was "an uphill battle." But a poll he had seen just last week was what made the decision for him. "We have not moved forward enough." He simply wasn't well-enough known now. "We hope to correct that over the next four years." So he was getting out now. He said he would try again in 1989.

Then came the questions.

Really, there was only one question, asked many different ways: Would he now run for lieutenant governor?

No, Bagley said, what seemed like a thousand times, no. "I just can't get the lieutenant governor thing to die," he complained. But, to reporters' delight, neither did he make a Shermanesque disavowal. "No politician is going to sit at this table and forever say that something couldn't happen down the road that might interest him." In the back of the room, Sabato was eating it up. "He [Bagley] hemmed and hawed and said 'no' but everyone said 'nudge, nudge, wink, wink,' " Sabato recalls.

By the time Bagley's news conference was over and Sabato got up to give his analysis of the 1984 election returns "no one wanted to talk about 1984. I think I got one question on '84 and then everybody wanted to talk about 1985."

Mostly, they wanted to talk about Wilder.

Sabato said Bagley was the only Democrat who could legitimately challenge Wilder without appearing racist because he's already shown an interest in statewide office. But the racism charge was something the

Democrats were going to have to risk if they weren't going to simply surrender the state's No. 2 office to the Republicans, Sabato argued. Robb was going to have to take charge. "Where has he been to this point?" Sabato asked.

Someone asked what Sabato thought Wilder's chances of winning the election were.

"One in one hundred," he flippantly replied. "But I think the odds are much greater that he would sink the ticket."

After Sabato finished, a reporter from Richmond's Channel 6 came up to him and asked where he thought that one chance in a hundred was going to come from.

100-1.

"The consensus in that room was that I had overestimated Wilder's chances," Sabato says.

But that figure stuck to Sabato like a tattoo.

100-1.

That became the standard background paragraph on Wilder's chances in all the news stories from here on out. It was the headline in the *Virginian-Pilot* in Norfolk.

Between Bagley's withdrawal and Sabato's odds-making, this cold Monday in December 1984 was one of the most eventful days of the whole 1985 campaign. And it wasn't even noon yet.

Dec. 10-12, 1984

Wilder fired back hard and strong even before the afternoon paper had gone to press. Wilder couldn't attack the anonymous "Democratic sources" bad-mouthing him in the newspapers, but he could attack Sabato and so the politician went after the professor with a vengeance.

"It has totally amazed me that Mr. Sabato, all of a sudden, has taken on the role of determining for the Democratic Party what it should or should not do," Wilder told the *Richmond News Leader*. "I thought his job was analyzing what happened in past elections. I have never known of a more blatant, direct and open racist preachment that the Democratic Party should kick blacks in the behind."

The "racist" charge made Sabato bristle. "I kept stressing that Wilder was not a long shot simply because he was black. That could be a part of it, but he was a long shot because of his record and personal problems. I remember making the case that Bobby Scott might have a good chance." But the *Richmond Times-Dispatch* glossed over that distinction more than Sabato would have liked and so, for the first time in his career, he demanded that a newspaper print a correction. Sabato didn't know it, but he was just beginning to feel the heat.

Wilder, meanwhile, kept up the attack the next two days as newspapers scurried to do follow-ups to the double-whammy of the Bagley withdrawal and Sabato's oddsmaking.

Wilder said allowing Sabato to air his views without challenge sets "a dangerous precedent" and he urged fellow Democrats to "call him down."

"Unless Democrats in positions of leadership counter the nonsense issued by the likes of that professor at U.Va., it will do more damage than my candidacy or any future black candidacy can have."

Wilder also moved to quash any talk that he was too "liberal." "That's a code word for racism," he declared.

Wilder further revealed that he had met with Robb on Monday. Wilder wanted to know why Al Smith and other Democrats who might be considered Robb surrogates had begged him to drop out of the race. Robb assured Wilder he wasn't sending them. "He didn't discourage me," an upbeat Wilder told reporters Tuesday. "And not only that, but he said he had no intention of discouraging me." (Stoddart later released a slightly different account of the meeting: Robb "did not indicate support or opposition. Rather, he reiterated his neutrality.")

All this produced a spate of Wilder-under-fire stories the first half of the week: "Wilder turns down suggestions to drop bid." "Wilder perseveres despite opposition." And, more darkly, "Speculation surrounds Bagley for lieutenant governor's bid."

Talk of a "Draft Bagley" movement seemed to materialize out of the very air, even before his news conference was over. "Hallelujah, I'm in favor of it," said Culpeper lawyer John "Butch" Davies, the Seventh District Democratic chairman.

Both publicly and privately, though, Bagley insisted he wasn't interested in challenging Wilder. "We had a conversation a few days after he dropped out," says Bagley staffer Randy Gilliland. "He said that when he planned to run, he said he was going to run for governor and wasn't going to slip into No. 2. He had told Doug that and he was a man of his word."

Bagley's window of opportunity, if it had ever been open, slammed shut. But that didn't stop some desperate Democrats from banging on it.

Dec. 11-17, 1984

December was not a good month for Wilder. Hardly a day went by that some Virginia paper didn't have a sky-is-falling headline: "Wilder defends his bid for office." "Wilder says bid for state post won't hurt party." "Sen. Wilder isn't kidding about running." "'Wilder says critics won't deter him." By contrast, Davis made headlines only once, when he formally announced; Baliles and Terry not at all.

A week after the Bagley-Sabato news conferences, and less than three weeks after the "secret meeting," legislators were back in town for a one-day special session of the General Assembly. The official order of business for Democrats was to elect judges, but the unofficial business was figuring out what to do about Wilder, now that Bernie Cohen's visit — and the whole "secret meeting" — had been such a messy failure.

"Squabble over Wilder candidacy continues," headlined the *Richmond Times-Dispatch.*

Wilder complained that the bad-mouthing from Democratic legislators was having "a chilling effect" on his ability to raise money. Nevertheless, it continued. "In private conversations yesterday," the *Times-Dispatch* reported, "white Democratic legislators again were warning that a Davis-Wilder-Terry ticket would make the party appear to be playing to liberal special interests."

And while Wilder was busy dealing with nervous-Nellie legislators, he was also catching plenty of flak from his supporters.

Up in Northern Virginia, David Temple, the black high school principal who had volunteered to run Wilder's campaign in the D.C. suburbs, and his friend Pat Watt, the white Fairfax County Democratic chairwoman who had agreed to help Temple, were going crazy because here it was mid-December and Wilder *still* didn't have a staff. None. Nobody. For practical purposes, he didn't even have a campaign. He just seemed to spend all his time talking to reporters, slugging it out in the press with Larry Sabato and shadow-boxing with unidentified sources.

To salvage the campaign from imminent self-destruction, Watt put together a six-page campaign outline that mapped out everything that needed to be done — from buttons and bumper stickers to staff meetings — and when it needed to be done. The Watt Plan also called for hiring at least four people to do it all: a fund-raiser, a field coordinator, a press secretary, a scheduler, plus congressional district coordinators, who might or might not be volunteers. If not, that made fourteen paid staffers.

David Temple agreed wholeheartedly and mailed the Watt Plan to Wilder, along with a note penciled in: 'Doug, per our discussions, it is imperative that you structure this thing NOW."

How could he make things any clearer? Temple thought he had been through all this back at the Fredericksburg staff meeting in October. Temple and Watt would be loyal and tireless workers throughout the campaign, but also tireless complainers that Wilder wasn't very well-organized. They wanted to see pollsters, field workers, schedules, position papers, all the things you normally see in a campaign. What they didn't appreciate was that this wasn't a normal campaign.

And although Temple and Watt wouldn't like it very much, by the time Wilder got Watt's master plan, help — of a sort — was already on the way.

Enter Paul Goldman, stage left. Far left.

Dec. 16-17, 1984

The shaggy-haired New York lawyer had come down in May, worked on Edie Harrison's campaign up through her nomination, then conveniently high-tailed it out of town. But throughout the summer and fall, Goldman was on the phone to his friends in Virginia. One of them was Doug Wilder. Goldman started reading all the books he could find on sports figures who had broken the color barrier — Jackie Robinson, Joe Louis, looking for clues on how to break the color line in another field. By December, when Wilder decided he really did need someone to get his campaign going, Goldman, the maverick trouble-shooter (and trouble-maker) loaded up his Honda Civic and came down to see what he could do.

Goldman raced down the New Jersey Turnpike Sunday, Dec. 16, and spent the night in Northern Virginia with his friend Barry Rose — a law student who had signed on with the Baliles campaign.

Goldman was tired from the day's drive but never too tired to talk politics. Rose briefed Goldman on the latest political news and Goldman pored over the old newspapers lying around the apartment. He kept coming across Sabato's essays. "Sabato was eating Doug alive," Rose says.

Goldman rifled through the papers, cursing all the time and working himself up into an indignant frenzy. He had no love lost for Sabato — an old personality clash going back to the last Howell campaign in '77 — and the mere mention of Sabato's name to Goldman was like waving red meat in front of a hungry dog. (The reverse, it must be said, also is true. Sabato has few kind things to say about Goldman. "For two vegetarians, they sure go after each other like carnivores," says Mark Bowles, one of Sabato's former students.)

But Goldman's fury didn't end with that late-night harangue in Rose's apartment. The next morning, Goldman was still muttering about Sabato, except now there was a smile on his face. Now that he had figured out what needed to be done, he seemed almost diabolically at ease. As Goldman drove out of the parking lot, he grinned and shouted to Rose: "Sabato's the grass and I'm the lawn mower."

Goldman was supposed to see Wilder at noon. It was a two-hour drive down Interstate 95 to Richmond, dodging tractor-trailers and speeding tourists on their way to Florida. Goldman had planned to go directly to Wilder's law office, but at the last minute decided to detour through downtown to pick up something. At a stoplight, he eased to a halt and waited for the light to change. For a few moments, he was strangely still; his mind raced forward to everything that needed to be done but everything around him was calm. Downtown Richmond seemed languid compared to the pace up North. Then suddenly . . . a metallic *crunch* . . . and Goldman was thrown forward, jolted back into reality.

The driver behind had just rear-ended him.

It took four hours before Goldman could get the accident straightened out. His rear bumper had been smashed up against the back tire so the tire couldn't turn, not without slicing itself apart. The bumper had to be cut away before the car could even be towed away to be fixed. Damage totaled $800.

What a way to start a campaign.

It was 4 p.m. before Goldman finally got to see Wilder. That was just as well, because Wilder had had a busy day at the one-day special session. The black caucus had blasted Diamonstein for the "secret meeting," Wilder and the party chairman had met to talk things out and reporters had a field day keeping track of who was saying what to whom.

Now the light was failing and Wilder could relax. He and Goldman talked for several hours about what kind of campaign he wanted to run and what needed to be done. "I do believe Doug Wilder had a vague, clear sense of where he wanted that campaign to be when it ended," says David Temple. "As to how to get it done, he didn't have the foggiest idea." Wilder, though, had already started some work. He had gotten a list of party officials around the state and in the evenings he sat by the phone in his den, dialing one after another. "I called them directly at home," Wilder says. "I'd sometimes call twenty to twenty-five at a time. They couldn't say they hadn't heard of me. And everywhere I would go, if you went behind me, things would be a little different. I found the more you got around, the better."

Goldman and Wilder found themselves in agreement on how the campaign should be run. Wilder was going to stress his experience. He wasn't going to get sidetracked into a debate on race. He wanted to keep his critics on the defensive, intimidate any challengers into staying out of the race and play Baliles off against Davis and make them both commit their delegates to vote for him at the convention. But neither was Wilder going to attack his opponents. "The Jackie Robinson model," Goldman calls it.

"Doug had already thought it through," Goldman says. "It was just a matter of tactics and working out the details." By the end of the meeting, Wilder agreed to pay Goldman $1,000 to come down to Richmond 10 days a month to help get the campaign organized.

When the news reached the political writers at the *Virginian-Pilot,* one reporter let out a loud groan.

5

Miracle Worker

After the election, Paul Goldman was hailed as "the unrecognized genius of Virginia politics," perhaps the only man around who could have pulled off the miraculous upset. In the winter of 1984, though, Goldman was recognized, all right, but not necessarily as a genius.

In a state where politicians tend to come in different shades of pale, Goldman is one of the most colorful characters to come down the pike.

The New Jersey Turnpike, in this case.

Goldman — a disheveled, shaggy-haired thirty-five-year-old (in 1985), a fanatic jogger who talks in circles and sometimes runs in them — has hung around on the fringes of Democratic politics in Virginia since the seventies. Technically a New York lawyer, he has made Virginia his second home, inexplicably migrating South every few years to, as one Democrat ruefully put it, "comfort the afflicted and afflict the comfortable."

A former VISTA volunteer on the Southside of Chicago, Goldman seemed to see Virginia as the political ghetto of Democratic politics, a state where even Democrats, the successful ones anyway, acted like Republicans. If Goldman had been around in the sixties he might have been registering voters and planning boycotts in Mississippi; in the seventies and eighties he was running liberal Democratic campaigns in Virginia. Both were about as popular with the local ruling class.

Goldman's one big success came in his first Virginia campaign, when he managed Henry Howell's last-time-around crusade for governor in the 1977 primary. Howell's nomination was hailed as "the biggest political upset in this century in Virginia" and so alarmed Democratic conservatives that they vowed never again to hold a primary, lest that kind of dreadful "mistake" repeat itself. For Howell partisans, Goldman was the Yankee guru who had performed the miracle, yet less than a week later he was forced out — and he's been on the outs in Virginia ever since.

"When I see now he's recognized as a genius, it's unbelievable," says Chuck Colgan Jr., the Manassas telephone company worker who led the effort to draft Dick Bagley for lieutenant governor in 1985. "He was always Dr. Disaster in the party. Everything he touched turned to shit."

Not quite. The pros — national political consultants such as Bob Squier, state guys such as Darrel Martin — came to respect Goldman's insight and intellect. "If he's on your side, he's a good one to have," says Randy Gilliland, who worked for Bagley and Baliles in 1984-85 and then went off to work gubernatorial campaigns in Alabama and Louisiana. "If he's against you, look out."

The people Goldman really infuriated were those in the Democratic establishment — staid, cautious types who thought they had things under control and wanted to keep them that way. David McCloud, Robb's chief of staff, calls Goldman "a loose cannon" and "a gnat on an elephant's ass." Other Democrats have even stronger feelings. "They don't just hate him," says Goldman's lawyer friend Barry Rose, who worked in the Baliles campaign. "He's like an itch they can't reach. They can't get rid of him. He keeps popping up."

Part of it is politics. Goldman is unquestionably liberal in a state where even Democrats go out of their way to cling to the label "conservative." Goldman made his political career in Virginia backing all the "wrong" candidates, candidates who were challenging the established order. And if he wasn't egging on liberal outsiders, then he was meddling in party affairs. In 1981 he filed a formal complaint against the Virginia Democratic Party with the U.S. Justice Department, a move that nearly forced the postponement of a convention that was set to crown Robb for the governorship.

"He was always seen as a gadfly," says former state legislator Ira Lechner, "a troublemaker, a guy outside the process."

Goldman never wanted office. If he did, maybe the establishment could understand him better, and maybe it could have bought him off long ago, dispatching him to some far-flung do-gooder office where he'd be out of the way. Nor was Goldman interested in money. If so, he could have cashed in long ago as a political consultant. In a jungle full of mercenaries, Goldman is more of a missionary, a crusading zealot in the game for a higher purpose. He only signs on with candidates he believes in, then pushes their cause with a single-minded fanaticism as unnerving as his ragtag personal style.

After the 1985 election, Dick Bagley introduced Goldman to the Democrats' State Central Committee this way: "Never has there been a campaign manager more arbitrary, more slovenly, more unorthodox — and never one more brilliant and spectacularly successful."

But that hardly begins to paint an adequate picture.

"Paul is one of the most unreal political characters I have ever seen," says Senate clerk Jay Shropshire, shaking his head in disbelief.

"He's like someone you'd write to *Reader's Digest* about as your most unforgettable character," says Marian Tucker, a legislative aide from Norfolk.

"He's kind of a gonzo politician," says Del. Chip Woodrum of Roanoke. "There's something scary about him to a conventional politician like myself. At the same time, he's also kind of endearing."

Goldman is like a live Raggedy Andy doll. His personal appearance makes people either want to hug him like they would a lost, wet puppy or scream in horror at what the cat dragged in. He comes across like a walking disaster area — hair uncombed, clothes wrinkled, eyeglasses falling apart, munching on some unidentifiable food he pulls out of his pocket, mumbling about some far-fetched political scenario. His car is crammed full of old newspapers and dirty laundry. His New York license plates have been taped to the back window ever since the December 1984 fender-bender on the way to Wilder's office ripped off his back bumper. Barry Rose tried to persuade him to get some Virginia tags so it wouldn't look like a carpetbagger was running Wilder's campaign; Goldman refused as a matter of principle.

Despite his law degree, Goldman has no real job. Certainly he doesn't have a law practice in the normal sense of the term. He says he has lawyer friends in New York and New Jersey that he sometimes does research for — legal theory is his specialty. But don't look for him arguing motions before some local judge. Goldman, as he does so many other things, shrugs off his employment status. "A lot of lawyers never go to court," he says.

What he does do is come down to Virginia for days, weeks, months at a time to meddle in state politics, then disappear, only to turn up again in a late-night telephone call from who knows where. Sometimes not even

Wilder's office knew where to find him. The rumor in Howell days was that Goldman lived off a trust fund. Nowadays his wanderings are so commonplace that no one bothers to ask anymore. Goldman himself is typically vague about how he supports himself. He apparently has money somewhere. He reads the *Wall Street Journal* religiously and plays the stock market. He's been known to interrupt interviews every fifteen minutes or so to check on the price of certain stock. After the 1977 campaign, Goldman was involved in some business deals with Bill Wiley, later state treasurer, who praises Goldman's business acumen. "Paul has a really good analytical mind, no matter what he brings it to," Wiley says. "He's not nuts and bolts. He's more of a thinker, and a brilliant thinker, too."

Goldman also has tried his hand at writing mystery novels. "He's a good writer," says Baliles campaign manager Darrel Martin, who holds a master's in English and once taught at the University of Richmond. "I believe he's publishable. [So far publishers haven't agreed.] He's an exceptional writer."

The real mystery, though, has always been Goldman himself.

Ira Lechner was one of Goldman's close friends and political confidants until the former Northern Virginia legislator removed him as manager of his 1982 congressional campaign. Yet not even Lechner knows much about Goldman. "No one was ever sure how Paul lived. He lived essentially out of his car."

Goldman eats virtually nothing yet runs constantly. "I can't conceive of where he gets enough calories to run ten miles a day," Lechner says. "His metabolism is always teetering on the brink of him falling asleep. He has no visible means of support. He drives a car jammed with stuff. He sacks out at people's houses. He's almost like a vagabond. Nobody knows where Paul came from. He just always shows up in different campaigns."

Pinning Goldman down on just how he lives, or pinning him down on just about any subject he doesn't want to talk about, is a lost cause from the beginning. "Paul's evasive," says Danny LeBlanc, the AFL-CIO secretary-treasurer. "That's his style."

To the uninitiated, the appearance of Paul Goldman is like something out of the spirit world suddenly materializing in their midst. "I'm sure we're as strange to him as he was to us," says Glenn Craft, the Democratic chairman from Wise County in the Appalachian coalfields. "He comes on like he just crawled out from under a rock. You talk to him and he mumbles and jumbles, but all the time his mind is turning."

Goldman's five passions are politics, health food, the stock market, pinball and running — and he pursues them all with relentless determination. "I've seen that SOB run in the damn snow," Gilliland says. Linda

When Hell Froze Over

Moore, a Baliles organizer from Roanoke, was in Richmond once on campaign business and spotted Goldman jogging down the street. She pulled her car over to the curb so she could talk to him. Goldman saw her but didn't stop. Instead, he kept jogging in circles around her car, talking whenever he passed by the window. "I wanted to grab hold of him and make him stop," Moore says.

Jim Gibbs, now the registrar in Stafford County, worked in the Howell campaigns and got to know Goldman during the '77 primary. "We were always helping him get his clothes together and driving him places. He was non-functional on a personal level. We were all like Paul's mother and father," Gibbs says. "He just looked so incompetent." Goldman's laundry was a constant crisis in the Howell campaign. "It would pile up in the office and not get done," Gibbs says. In the Wilder campaign, Goldman started bringing his clothes in to wash in the sink in the kitchen of Wilder's law office. The candidate reportedly didn't think much of that.

Goldman haircuts were infrequent, usually under duress (generally by direct order of the candidate) and almost always coincided with some major and unavoidable public event — the convention or Election Night, for instance. David Temple and Pat Watt, Wilder's organizers in Northern Virginia, were so appalled by Goldman's sloppy appearance that during the convention they wanted to keep him sequestered in a room backstage so no one would see him with the candidate. When Goldman finally got cleaned up for Election Night, it took awhile before anyone backstage at the Democrats' victory party recognized him.

Food is a constant reference point when Goldman's name comes up. Even in Howell days, his diet was infamous — not so much because he was a vegetarian but because he was so picky and unorthodox about it. "He never ate three meals," says Gibbs. "He carried around a bag of nuts and ate all the time." His favorite snack during the Wilder campaign was bland little Cheerio-looking grain puffs called Oatos, which often ended up scattered around whatever office or car he was in. He also left his grape stems lying about. Michael Brown had two nicknames for Goldman. One was "the Doctor," out of respect for his professorial intelligence. The other was "the Great Grape Gobbler."

"Paul Goldman is the most single-minded political operative I have ever seen," says Darrel Martin. "He lives, breathes and sleeps politics seven days a week. I don't know how he does it. He came over to headquarters in the spring. He had this Styrofoam cup. He opens it up and it's rice. They had boiled it. He said, 'They were supposed to steam it. Let's go back.' It took over an hour to drive across town and change the rice.' " But Martin knew it had to be done or the meeting would never take place.

Goldman's peculiar dietary demands caused all kinds of problems once he left Richmond and accompanied Wilder on the candidate's two-month station-wagon trip around the state — the fabled "tour."

Shropshire remembers once when Wilder called, belly-laughing over the phone. "You'll never believe what Paul did tonight, Jay." What's that? Shropshire asked. Goldman, it seems, had walked into a Southwest Virginia diner and, seeking to avoid a delay, ordered two raw potatoes, a requirement that apparently horrified the waitress. Goldman couldn't seem to understand her problem. "Paul eats 'em like they're apples," Shropshire says.

If one image of Goldman on the tour was showing up at a Democratic dinner chewing on a banana, the other was his arriving at a reception at someone's home, excusing himself and then appropriating the phone for the rest of the evening. If it was a cordless phone, so he could wander aimlessly around the house while spinning his scenarios, all the better.

For Goldman, the telephone is the most marvelous invention since the wheel. It is the key not only to his managing the campaign while out on the tour but also his peripatetic lifestyle. Even when Goldman was in New York, he'd spend hours on the phone to contacts in Virginia, keeping up with the latest political nuance, perhaps better than many Virginia insiders.

Back when they were on speaking terms during the Howell campaign, Larry Sabato was one of Goldman's sounding boards, sometimes unwillingly so. "I remember my parents coming in once, I was still in school then, and I couldn't get him off the phone," says Sabato, now a University of Virginia professor. "He had been on for two hours. I tried to get him off, but telling him you had to go wasn't good enough. You ended up having to hang up on him."

Another time, Goldman called Sabato from a phone booth and talked for forty-five minutes. "He talked and talked and I kept hearing this horn in the background," Sabato says. "I didn't think anything. I knew he was at a phone booth. Then he didn't even say goodbye or hang up. He dropped the phone and ran off. He had been riding with someone and made them stop so he could use the phone and they got tired of waiting for him so they started to drive off. I heard all this. I heard him yelling 'Wait!' and heard the car door slam."

Goldman, for all his talkativeness, is also a master of silence. Goldman's buddy Darrel Martin is also given to the same trait. "Conversations with him are frequently filled with one long pause and then an outpouring," Martin says. He remembers one late-night phone call in the spring of 1985 when the mutual pause went on much longer than normal. Martin asked if Goldman was still there but got no answer. After a couple unanswered inquiries, Martin began to get worried. "I could hear the TV going in the background. Finally I had to call the desk clerk and get someone to check to make sure Paul was OK. He had just become enthralled in something on TV. He assured me he was quite all right. He's an interesting fellow to run a campaign with."

For all his enemies and eccentricities, Goldman is tolerated for one simple reason: He's good at what he does, sometimes very good. He can tear apart a set of voting returns as good as anyone this side of Larry Sabato. He loves to play with numbers and run computations in his head, putting together different political equations.

"Paul is the type of guy who, if you put him in a room and said come up with ten new ideas a day, he would," says Richmond lawyer Larry Framme.

Goldman has an uncanny ability to leap ahead and size up a political situation, figure out where events are headed and come up with a list of options to problems others haven't even realized lay ahead.

"He's like a good chess player," says Barry Rose. "He can look ahead ten moves. I don't think there's anyone else in the state who can do this. The shot at Chuck [Robb] after the election? No one knew what that was about. That was about '89." By disowning Robb's coattails early and insisting Wilder won on his own merit, Goldman apparently figures he'll be able to trade short-term fallout against Wilder for long-term credibility. Make sense? Time will tell. But that's a good example of how Goldman thinks. Less than two weeks after winning the upset of the century, he was already plotting almost four years ahead.

Goldman's ability to discern the future so clearly — or at least what he is convinced is clearly — also sometimes makes it difficult for him to get along with the poor, confused souls still plodding along in the present.

"I know of ten people I work with, at least nine say Paul Goldman's an asshole, that he's the contrariest, hardest-headed guy they've ever seen," says Russ Axsom, the state AFL-CIO vice president.

Indeed, says Gibbs, "Paul has worked for a lot of candidates but he didn't get along with any except Doug Wilder."

The supreme irony is that Goldman is actually a native Southerner, if birth is the only requirement. He was born in West Palm Beach, Fla., but lived there less than a year. He grew up in Queens and studied political science in the late 1960s at a big-name Northern university he's since fallen out with and doesn't want named. His first campaign was the chaotic presidential year of 1968, when the eager undergraduate signed on as an advance man for Bobby Kennedy. He was in Los Angeles the day of the California primary, setting up events. By the time Goldman got back to New York, Kennedy had been assassinated.

After graduation in 1970, Goldman spent a year as a VISTA volunteer on the Southside of Chicago, living and working in a public housing project. His ugly memories of the Chicago ghetto gave the Wilder campaign a special meaning. After VISTA came law school, and campaigns in which Goldman served as a low-level strategist and researcher — Dan Walker for governor of Illinois in 1972, Brendan Byrne for governor of New Jersey in 1973, Hugh Carey for governor of New York in 1974. He also found time to squeeze in a master's degree in public administration from Princeton. Contacts from the Byrne campaign paid off and Goldman landed a job as counsel for the New Jersey Division of Consumer Affairs in 1975. He stayed only about a year. In the summer of 1976, he quit to move to Virginia to work for Henry Howell.

Goldman first met Howell only a week or so after Howell's razor-thin loss to Democrat-turned-Republican Mills Godwin in the 1973 gubernatorial race. A friend who had worked in Howell's campaign introduced the pair. Goldman was fascinated with the twangy Southern populist. During the next few years, Goldman made several trips to Norfolk to visit a growing circle of friends, most of whom had worked in Howell's '73 campaign and hoped to be around for one last run at the governorship. In the summer of 1976, with the next governor's race coming up in a year, Howell invited Goldman to Virginia for a strategy session — and eventually hired him as campaign manager.

"I was impressed by his political savvy," Howell recalls.

He was in the process of applying to the University of Michigan to work on his doctorate. But the idea of running a campaign was appealing. The Ph.D. fell by the wayside. Goldman was on board by the Fourth of July weekend, 1976.

Almost immediately, things went sour. Two weeks after he arrived his pay was cut. And he found even Howell's strongest supporters were pessimistic about the candidate's chances.

The problem was that by 1977, Henry Howell — now in his third try for the governorship and his fourth statewide race in eight years (five if you count the '69 runoff) — was used goods. Liberal Democrats loved Howlin' Henry for his crusading convictions, but they were getting tired of losing. Some were beginning to look at Andrew Miller, the two-term attorney general, a moderate-conservative with close ties to the business community, as the best way for Democrats to get back into office.

That's where Goldman came in. He changed Howell's image. Howell's biggest problem was that he was seen by critics as a rabble-rouser, definitely not gubernatorial material in the aristocratic Virginia tradition. "What Paul did for Henry Howell was he made him acceptable," Gibbs says. "If you look at a poster of the '77 campaign, you won't even recognize Henry. He had new glasses. He had changed his hairstyle, new clothes. Paul created a distinguished Henry Howell out of a most undistinguished candidate and I say that in a positive sense, and he beat Mr. Democrat. Paul created a whole new person out of Henry Howell and, politically speaking, it was brilliant."

The other half of the strategy was for Howell to stay cool and calm, to do nothing that would scare conservatives and send them flocking to the polls to "save the commonwealth." It was a calculated attempt to depress the turn-out. "The Miller people expected a 600,000-vote turnout and if 600,000 people voted, then Miller would win," says Bill Wiley, who worked in the Howell campaign. "Paul was not in disagreement with that presumption but he disagreed with that turnout."

By 1977, many of the old-line conservative Democrats had voted Republican so often that they weren't really comfortable voting in a Democratic primary if they didn't have to. So Howell's small vote was hard and Miller's potentially big vote was very soft, Goldman reasoned. If Howell could run a low-key campaign that didn't stir up a big anti-Howell vote, then all his campaign had to do was find its own supporters and quietly get them to the polls.

Howell's was almost an invisible campaign, conducted by telephone through a massive phone bank operation. The public perception, though, was that the campaign was all but over. All the polls gave Miller a huge lead, so huge many people figured they didn't need to vote.

When the returns came in on the night of June 14, Miller was the loser. "It really was a Truman-Dewey thing," says Marian Tucker of Norfolk, who worked in the Miller campaign. "The only one [Miller staffer] before the primary to say, 'Uh, wait a minute, we might lose this' " was a soft-spoken field coordinator named Darrel Martin.

The *Richmond Times-Dispatch* broke out the war type for a huge headline that screamed: "HOWELL WINS."

For a few heady days, Goldman was the miracle man. "He was *the* guru," says Bill Wiley. What really made a name for Goldman was "the interview," published in the *Richmond News Leader* two days after the primary. Several months before the election, Goldman had sat down with three reporters and, off the record, laid out congressional district by congressional district the predicted turnout and Howell's winning margin.

When the embargoed predictions were finally compared with the actual returns — and they were off only by a few thousand votes here or there — Goldman looked like a political Nostradamus.

Goldman says the numbers weren't that big a deal. "If it was going to happen, that was the way it had to happen," he says. Still, when the numbers hit print, Goldman looked like a genius. "The press recognized Paul as the person who did it," Gibbs says. "Paul never gave anybody any credit, but it was a group effort. The press established a tremendous reputation for Paul. I think he got a little too much credit."

But less than two weeks after what was then the upset of the century, Goldman was out.

Howell wanted someone more organized to run his fall campaign. "I wanted Paul to stay on [as a strategist], but he considered that a demotion," Howell says. "Paul was a great thinker and strategist, but we needed someone to head up fund-raising and finding volunteers. If you had an army, Paul would be head of the intelligence section, but you wouldn't put him in charge of the motor pool."

Howell and Goldman also had problems getting along. "Goldman was constantly spinning these Machiavellian tales and intrigue," says U.Va.'s Sabato, then a Howell adviser. "Henry Howell did not like that. He's a very uncomplicated person. He knows what he thinks is right and that's it. It was like oil and water."

Goldman slunk home up North. That fall, at the suggestion of Bill Wiley, he returned to Virginia to work in Ed Lane's campaign for attorney general. Sabato remembers that when Goldman came back, he was "the most forlorn creature you've ever seen." He would come around Howell headquarters only when he had to, but wouldn't come in. Sabato and others had to go out into the hall to talk with him. And the Lane campaign was a sorry come-down from the high of the Howell upset.

As it turned out, lieutenant governor candidate Chuck Robb was the only Democrat to win that fall, and Goldman went back to New York. Thanks to a friend in the Carey administration, Goldman was eventually named the chief lawyer for New York's consumer protection board, a post he held from 1979 to 1980.

By then, however, Goldman was inexplicably back in Virginia. This time he was trying to elect an old Howell ally, H.R. "Peck" Humphries of Kilmarnock, as state party chairman. Humphries lost to Owen Pickett, the favorite of the moderate-conservatives who were now pushing themselves back into power, but Goldman lingered, eventually signing on with first Shad Solomon and later Ira Lechner, the heirs to the Howell tradition.

Both were also Jewish, and Goldman says he was taken by the idea of electing a Jewish candidate in a Southern state. Gibbs has another theory. "One reason Paul came to Virginia is that he thrives on challenges, impossible challenges. I think he looked around the country and saw Virginia as the worst state for a Democrat. It was the most intransigent political nut to crack and he saw Henry Howell as his vehicle to do the impossible." Even after Howell, Goldman always signed on with political mavericks who never stood a chance in tradition-bound Virginia. "Paul looks for those kind of candidates," Gibbs says. "He wanted to perform the miracle." But no matter how hard he tried, he always ended up on the outs even with the outsiders.

Goldman soon had differences with Solomon, who in 1981 was seeking the Democratic nomination for attorney general against a well-connected Richmond legislator named Jerry Baliles — and was let go.

Goldman hung around, brooding about the changes taking place in the Democratic Party. The moderate-conservatives were taking charge, trying to rid the party of its Howell connections and nominate a safe ticket with Robb at its head. In the process, they had done away with the primary and set up a convention. "One day I decided, this should be covered by the Voting Rights Act," Goldman says. He spent a weekend in early February typing up a legal complaint to file with the U.S. Justice Department.

Goldman's complaint stirred up a minor crisis. A collection of liberal groups — the NAACP, the ACLU, the Southern Christian Leadership Conference — joined in the complaint and put the Democratic establishment on the defensive.

Meanwhile, Democratic leaders went to Wilder, who brokered a deal: The party would be allowed to nominate its candidates by convention, so long as the delegate formula wouldn't dilute the black vote. That satisfied the Justice Department but cut the legs out from under Goldman's argument. Nevertheless, some liberals continued to press the case and even on the day of the convention, Virginia Democrats were in court fighting a motion to enjoin the party from nominating its candidates.

Not long after the '81 convention, Robb campaign manager David Doak asked Goldman to work for Robb as a liaison to all the disgruntled liberal groups he had been stirring up all spring. Goldman agreed. Bob Squier, who was Robb's media adviser, says Goldman played a key role in the Robb coalition. "I don't think he got enough credit for what he did in Robb's race. He was an effective spokesman for Robb from the center to the left. He sat there day after day saying, 'He's OK, he's OK,' which protected Robb on the left and allowed Robb to run right down the middle."

Goldman ended up writing a chapter for Robb's transition book. The fifty-seven-page treatise dealt with Robb's style of administration and potential political problems he'd encounter, especially the 1982 Senate race and the 1985 governor's race. "He did exactly what I told him to do," Goldman says gleefully. "Not that he wouldn't have anyway [Goldman did tailor his advice to Robb's personal style], but the point is they'll have a hard time explaining I'm crazy. Urging Robb to go slow, not be too partisan, appoint conservatives to his Cabinet. This is the work of a wild man? With this transition chapter, they have a lot to answer for, some vague charge that I'm hard to get along with."

In fact, Robb once invited Goldman to his office to talk politics during the Pickett crisis and mentioned the transition chapter. "I've read your stuff," Robb told him. "I didn't realize our minds were in sync." Goldman relayed that comment to Doak afterward and Doak chortled: "Don't tell anyone that. It'll ruin both of your reputations."

Soon, though, Goldman was on the outs again. In 1982, Ira Lechner, having twice failed to win the nomination for lieutenant governor, decided to run for Congress and hired Goldman as his campaign manager. Goldman accompanied Lechner to a campaign meeting at the home of a key supporter. "He put his feet on the coffee table and she just freaked out," says Barry Rose, who also worked in the campaign. "Then he started messing with Owen Pickett. Ira was trying to make peace and Paul was stirring it up." So once again Goldman had to go.

"Paul had a terrible antipathy against Pickett," Lechner remembers. Pickett stood for everything Goldman stood against — a cautious Democratic establishment that looked on liberals as troublemakers. Even after Pickett dropped out, Goldman formed a group called Committee to Save the Democratic Party, which attracted some attention.

Shortly before the convention met, Wilder asked Goldman to put together a group of liberals and labor activists to talk to about why he did to Pickett what he did. And before Goldman went back to New York, he told Wilder that if he ever thought about running for statewide office and needed any help, to give him a call. They talked in an offhand way that the lieutenant governor's race in 1985 might be a good campaign to try.

Two years after Pickett, Goldman resurfaced in Virginia, this time with with yet another liberal, Jewish underdog — Edie Harrison. Goldman had told her that if she got close to winning the Democratic nomination, he'd come down and work for her. Goldman more or less ran the campaign in the month before the convention, then got out of town while the getting was good.

Once back in New York, though, Goldman stayed on the phone, talking to Wilder and his other contacts in Virginia.

When Hell Froze Over

Wilder had come to respect Goldman's political acumen. "I don't know of anyone more analytical and who can make more of meager resources," Wilder says. "I knew in controlled circumstances Paul could be as effective as anyone." Controlled circumstances? "Well, you just can't let everything be said to the press," Wilder laughs. That's one reason why Goldman never got the title of campaign manager. Wilder wanted no mistake about who was really in charge — he was.

This time something unusual happened, though. The partnership clicked; the two got along. "It takes a rare person to get along with Paul," Sabato says. "It tells you a lot about Doug Wilder that he gets along with him. I don't know what, but it tells you a lot." Whatever it says, the thing that matters here is this: For perhaps the first time, Goldman had a candidate willing to go along with his strategy. And the combination worked wonders. "Politics is timing and luck," Gibbs says. With Wilder in 1985, "those two came together for Paul in his long quest for a miracle — and it became a national miracle."

At first glance, Doug Wilder and Paul Goldman are a most unlikely political odd couple — the polished, immaculate Southern black with the soaring cadence of a Baptist preacher, whose hopes of winning depended on how well he courted the state's conservative establishment, and the ill-kempt New York Jew who mumbled vague nonsense and had made a political career out of attacking the establishment.

Nevertheless, Goldman says, "We're a lot alike. We're very different in a lot of ways, but we're on the same wavelength."

The differences, though, provided some laughs for Michael Brown, a Wilder nephew and former NAACP official who joined the campaign in January and had a front-row seat at the daily Doug & Paul Show.

"You could tell the senator the house was falling down — no problem," Brown says. Wilder was unflappable. "Paul's hair needs to be cut and tie put on? That's a serious problem. Paper on the floor? A serious problem. Feet on the furniture? A serious problem."

Wilder had to keep after Goldman like an errant son. "I remember times he'd say "I'm sitting in the car until you comb your hair,'" Brown says.

Meanwhile, the secretaries and lawyers in Wilder's office fought a running battle with Goldman over his crude housekeeping. "He might have three or four cartons of milk in the refrigerator," Brown says. "He'd buy one, use part of it, then figure it had all gone bad and buy another. He'd leave his spoons [for his wheat germ and milk] all around and people would get upset." But, no matter how much he fretted about Goldman's appearance, Wilder was eventually able to overlook these transgressions. Wilder didn't hire Goldman for looks. He hired him for his mind. Goldman was just the sort of scheming character Wilder needed to make his long-shot, high-risk campaign work. ("I'm not crazy," Goldman once laughed, "but I am devious.") And scheme Goldman did.

"The senator would get a big kick out of Paul's handling of certain people," Brown says. "He'd sit in the chair and die laughing about the way Paul would handle whomever, whether in terms of getting money from someone or the press or a party person. With the press, they'd try to pin him down and Paul would fence with 'em. They could never pin him down. The senator would walk out of the office and fall halfway down on his knees laughing sometimes."

Goldman was perfect for playing the "inside game" of mass meeting politics, where he was fighting other Democrats, the whole campaign was being played out behind-the-scenes and Richmond was rife with rumor and intrigue.

Perhaps the biggest surprise was that Goldman really did know how to run a "traditional" Virginia campaign. The Wilder campaign may have been frighteningly untraditional in its organization and day-to-day management, but to the public, Wilder came off as a dark-skinned Virginia gentleman, the type of candidate they had long been accustomed to voting for — war hero, tough on crime, respectful of the commonwealth's fiscal conservatism, no disturber of the business peace. In many ways, Paul Goldman, as an outsider, has a keener understanding of the Virginia mind than do many Virginia political operatives. He may understand it only as a caricature, a stereotype, but the voting public only pays attention to the broad outlines anyway. Significantly, Goldman's two successes have come with taking men perceived as liberal hell-raisers and remaking them into distinguished middle-of-the-roaders.

And this time Goldman got away with the one thing that has haunted him in every other campaign — his disdain for organization. "He was perfect for the Wilder campaign because it never had any organization and never pretended to have any, so all he had to do was strategy and press," Lechner says. "Ironically, it was the Baliles organization that made sure the black voters got to the polls."

6

The J-J Day Massacre

Dec. 18, 1984

Governor Robb was becoming increasingly worried. The only political news in December 1984, it seemed, dealt with Doug Wilder and how his candidacy would drag down the whole ticket. The color of Wilder's skin "had become an obsession," Robb says. "The whole feeling needed to be lanced and I took it upon myself to lance it."

His attempt, though, only worsened relations with Wilder.

Wilder was already upset with Robb because the governor, in his public comments, seemed to be questioning whether Wilder could win. Robb says his choice of words was intentional. Had he openly declared Virginia ready to elect a black, that would have been akin to drawing a line in the sand and daring people to cross, he believes. "You can't do it in a confrontational way," Robb says. "That's why I always said 'I don't know but I hope so.' Rather than stick my chin out and create waves, you do it in a positive sense."

Robb says an all-out push for Wilder before the nomination would have been counterproductive because it would look as if Wilder had been forced on the party. "I was careful not to look like I was a crusader," he says. "That would have killed it." But, behind the scenes, Robb says he was doing all he could to make things easier for Wilder. "The number of people who came to me [to get him to talk Wilder out of the race] was just enormous. I talked to them and they went on neutral."

The governor "did more early on to legitimize Doug's candidacy than anyone," said his press secretary, George Stoddart. "He, more than anyone, save Doug, believed Doug could win. It was like carrying the whole team on his shoulders. Anytime he heard about any hare-brained idea to deny Doug the nomination, he was just adamant about it."

Others confirm Robb's account that he was actively talking up Wilder's chances. "Privately, Robb was saying a year beforehand that Wilder could win," says Baliles campaign manager Darrel Martin. Indeed, says one key Baliles aide: "There was a lot of frustration from some people that Robb was sending that message to him."

But that's not the way Wilder saw things at all.

He wanted Robb out publicly promoting his candidacy well before the nomination. Instead, he believed he saw four clear signs that Robb was trying to get him out of the race. They came not from Robb personally but from people close enough to the governor that Wilder was convinced Robb had a hand in them. The first had been Stoddart's comment that "this is still Virginia." The second was Diamonstein's "secret meeting." The third was Al Smith's private plea that he drop out. The fourth was the offer from a Northern Virginia businessman, a friend of Robb's, that if Wilder would withdraw, he could have the party chairmanship and a private plane to use.

Robb snorts at Wilder's suggestion that those four events should have been seen as an orchestrated stop-Wilder movement. "If there were only four of them, and some of them were just meetings, not people actually talking to him, he should have seen that as an open invitation to run," Robb says. "I had a lot more than that try to talk me out of running in both 1977 and 1981." Robb suggests, none too charitably, that Wilder is unnecessarily paranoid. "If you see shadows behind every tree, you can paint that picture," he says, but in this case it's simply not true. "I have a well-deserved reputation for discouraging people from running but I never tried to discourage Doug or Mary Sue in the slightest."

With that in mind, Robb tried on Dec. 18 to help Wilder. The governor called a news conference — on what turned out to be Paul Goldman's first full day on the job running Wilder's campaign — to tell Wilder's critics to, in effect, put up or shut up.

In his news conference, Robb blamed the media for focusing exclusively on Wilder's race and Terry's gender. "Everybody's had their turn at writing the stories that relate to race and gender. I think that's been pretty fully explored. Now let's move on to other qualifications."

Robb said the race-oriented media coverage had intimidated some "qualified candidates" from getting into the campaign. Robb contended that, contrary to some news accounts, a challenge to either candidate would not necessarily be based on prejudice. "I think anyone who would suggest that the challenge to Doug Wilder is racist or a challenge to Mary Sue Terry is sexist is just way off base."

The governor then invited challenges to both Wilder and Terry and said he would defend challengers against accusations of racism or sexism. "I don't want to have a continued dialogue that simply suggests that we ought to get people out of the race. Let's get somebody else into the race, if anybody wants to challenge . . . I'm not recruiting but I'm not discouraging anyone from running. If somebody wants to get in, I'm saying 'go to it' and I'm saying I'll stand up and say 'it's not racist to challenge Doug Wilder.'"

In the lieutenant governor's race especially, "I think [a challenge] would be healthy and I think it would be healthy for Senator Wilder, particularly given the doubts that have been raised."

Robb also tried to neutralize Larry Sabato. The U.Va. analyst, he suggested, should be called "Dr. Dial-A-Quote."

To hear Robb and Wilder talk about the "put up or shut up" news conference, you'd think they were talking about two entirely different events.

Robb calls it "the greatest individual service I did" for Wilder.

Goldman calls it "the low point of the campaign" and proof of Robb's alleged perfidy. "If the greatest service you perform for a candidate running in November is in December the year before, I rest my case, your honor. He takes credit for something I thought was dangerous. Most people I talked to at the time thought he was setting the stage for someone to come in against us."

Robb says he wanted to make sure that, even if Wilder won the nomination unopposed, he was seen as winning it on merit. "I did it in a positive way, to make the nomination worth something . . . That cleared the air. That did lance the boil that would have made the nomination almost worthless. The point I made was the party did not go out to field a black and a woman for those positions, but was responding to legitimate candidacies."

Wilder, however, was furious.

If Robb's news conference had been to say put up or shut up, "all I heard was put up," Wilder says.

He was absolutely convinced now that Robb was against him. Wilder categorically rejects Robb's contention that the news conference was called "to clear the air." Robb was "calling people in against me," Wilder says, "saying he would personally defend people. He had given carte blanche amnesty to people who would run, then threw in Mary Sue" just for appearances.

Wilder met with Robb to air his grievances. "He said it was his way of endorsing me," Wilder says. "I said the way it came out, you issued a call."

Dec. 19, 1984

Paul Goldman liked to envision himself as a gunfighter riding into town as a one-man posse, threatening to shoot up the saloon, firing off a few stray rounds every now and then just to see the townspeople run for cover.

The Wild West analogy — with himself as the hired gun single-handedly bringing frontier justice — was one Goldman called on frequently during the Wilder campaign.

It didn't take Goldman long — one night in Barry Rose's Falls Church apartment — to figure out what needed to be done first for Wilder. Gunfighter Paul would have to fire off a few warning shots to shut up all the people who were saying Wilder would drag down the ticket. Goldman couldn't attack them directly. And Wilder certainly couldn't. Wilder, at all times, had to be cheerful, pleasant, non-threatening. Besides, at this point, Wilder's critics were hiding behind the anonymity of "unidentified sources." But there *was* Larry Sabato, leaning against the water trough, prophesying doom. Sabato made an easy target. Goldman took dead aim.

Goldman and Sabato had first met in the Howell campaign. "There never was a falling out because I'm not sure there was ever a falling in," Goldman says. Jealousy probably had a lot to do with it. Both began as left-wing election analysts — but it was Sabato who was adopted by the establishment and given respectability. Now, at long last, Goldman's personal enmity was reinforced with a professional rationale to go after him. "He was out there and it was affecting the public debate," Goldman says, confirming Democrats' worst fears about Wilder on the ticket.

Goldman spent the afternoon of Dec. 18 — his first full day with Wilder and the day of Robb's "put up or shut up" news conference — mulling over possible attack lines. "I wanted to think up something that would be memorable, something that would stick."

When he had it, Goldman wandered into Wilder's office and outlined his case for going after Sabato. "We've got to get the debate off the race question and on to qualifications," Goldman argued. He went over his quip about "Dr. Shockley," a reference to the Nobel laureate who has suggested whites are genetically superior to blacks, with Wilder. He liked it. Wilder, like Goldman, had a keen dislike for Sabato. "He's a very dangerous man," Wilder says of Sabato. "Suppose I was John Doe and was white and running for office and he made those comments. He couldn't have raised funds. He couldn't have run at all."

With Wilder's blessing, Goldman called the *Richmond Times-Dispatch.* What Goldman said was this: By arguing that Wilder can't win, Sabato is "in danger of becoming the Dr. Shockley of Virginia." He said Sabato was doing such "a terrible disservice to the people of Virginia" by implying they're too racist to vote for a black candidate.

"It was a risky shot," Goldman admits, "a carom shot. But you've got to have some smoke coming from the gun to let people know it's loaded and you're willing to use it." But Sabato was an easy target. He was an academic, so he had no political allies to rush to his defense.

Sabato was blindsided. "I was pretty outraged by the use of the phrase "Dr. Shockley." I've never been much of one for name-calling. I didn't appreciate it because I've had a pretty good record on civil rights in my personal life. I felt Goldman was pursuing a personal vendetta against me."

In the *Times-Dispatch,* Sabato defended his analysis of Wilder's chances. "It's not my personal preference," he said, but "what I want, and what my analysis leads to has to be different."

The story got little attention, but among the Richmond insiders Goldman's well-aimed bullet exploded like a nuclear warhead. For most, this was how they learned that Goldman was back in town. "I know a lot of people were upset," he says. "I know I got calls from friends. They didn't understand the strategy." But, Goldman says, it did keep Sabato quiet.

A few days later, though, one of Sabato's friends sent the professor this homespun piece of doggerel:

A pox on Paul Goldman, that race-baiting scum
To drag through the dirt the good name of our chum;
In the coming year, we must confess;
We hope Doug does worse than Edie — 30 percent or less.

January 1985

Goldman's next official duty as Wilder's "consultant" was to hire a campaign manager. It seemed every time Wilder met with Robb, the governor was after him to hire both a campaign manager and fund-raising director.

Goldman says he made an honest effort to hire both but couldn't find either. "There was a lot of pressure being put on Doug to drop out," he says. "Anybody who wanted to be a campaign manager would make a few calls" and find out how futile this campaign really was. "I probably talked to twelve people, probably closer to two dozen. They all said we didn't have a chance, 'don't know if it will help my career.' By mid-January, it was clear we couldn't find a campaign manager." By then, the mass meetings were just over two months away — March 30 and April 1. Goldman decided he would have to act as campaign manager (though he never had that title) through the caucuses at least. But with Goldman in charge, the pressure on Wilder only increased. Virtually every time the two met from now until September, Robb begged Wilder to hire a "real" campaign manager.

Meanwhile, the campaign staff doubled. Michael Brown joined Jan. 5.

Brown, a stocky, scowling man whose Mephistophelian goatee masks a surprisingly gentle personality, was always identified in the press as Wilder's nephew. That description played up the bootstrap, familial aspect of the campaign, but does Brown a disservice. Brown, in his late thirties, had worked statewide campaigns in 1977 and 1978 and, until joining the campaign, was field coordinator for the state NAACP.

But the blood-tie did play a part. Wilder wanted a lean campaign, run by people he could trust.

Although it was Goldman who got the credit afterward, "Michael actually played a pivotal role in the campaign," Goldman says. "A lot of what I did was do-able because of Michael." To get right to the nub of it, a lot of blacks weren't happy about Wilder having a white campaign consultant, especially some Jewish guy from New York. Nor did they understand why Wilder wasn't being more visible in the black community, why he wasn't speaking out on black issues, why he wasn't striking back at critics who said a black couldn't win. "You talk to people about broad-based strategy and it sounds logical but they have no feel for it, they've never been through it," Goldman says. As the stop-Wilder crowd "kept pounding on race, a lot of blacks wanted to do more, to draw the line," to provoke a confrontation. Brown could talk to them, keep them quiet. He had credibility. When Michael Brown — ex-NAACP, Wilder nephew — assured worried blacks that everything was OK, they had to believe it.

Brown played a key role in the Wilder campaign in another way. He was the nuts-and-bolts man. The Wilder campaign was just a two-man outfit. Goldman was strategist, speech writer, press secretary, media consultant, campaign manager. In short, he did all the thinking and talking. Brown did everything else. Everything.

He knew how to organize precincts. Now he just had to do it on a grander scale. "I was calling people left and right, party officials, teachers, labor, ministers, activists," Brown says. "Some were open. What's Doug Wilder want me to do? I'll do it. Others hinged support on certain things; some were non-committal."

Brown also was Wilder's driver. From January to July, if Wilder moved, Brown moved. More often than not, Goldman went along too, so the entire campaign — as small as it was — was on the road. (With the phones back in headquarters ringing unanswered, critics complained.)

Conspicuously missing from this division of labor was a fund-raiser. There was none, a point that irritated Robb and other party officials to no end. It's remarkable then that the Wilder campaign had any money at all. Goldman says the campaign was kept afloat early on by Avetus Stone, a black businessman from Northern Virginia. He and his STIA Systems and Associates, a computer firm in Oakton, contributed about $12,000 — almost half the cash Wilder took in by the first reporting period.

For now, fortunately, the campaign didn't need much money. The first campaign finance report was coming up Jan. 15, though, and there was an abnormal amount of curiosity to see how much money Wilder had raised. Goldman was determined that Wilder come in over $50,000. "I did a lot of creative accounting to get that," Goldman admits. "I counted everything not nailed down" as an in-kind contribution. Since the campaign was being run out of the basement of Wilder's well-appointed law offices, Goldman had a lot of furnishings to choose from. Brown got on the phone to relatives around the country, saying if they were ever going to give money, now was the time.

Goldman finally got the numbers to add up to $50,287. It wasn't exactly impressive. But, much to Goldman's delight (and relief), Wilder was doing better than some of the Republicans running for lieutenant governor. Marshall Coleman, as expected, was pulling down big bucks — $257,823. But Pete Giesen reported only $28,159 and John Chichester came in at only $27,009.

In reality, though, the Wilder campaign was so poor it probably qualified for political food stamps. At this point, there was still no campaign literature. Once Wilder did get some brochures printed, one of Brown's duties was to go around the room after meetings and pick up whatever had been left. If they had been crumpled, he'd smooth them out and use them again.

"The senator, if he saw paper being Xeroxed, he'd say, 'What's this cost?' " Brown says. "He was very mindful of money. That's natural if you come from humble beginnings and amass a fortune, and he used to tell us, 'This is other people's money, people like to see it used wisely.' "

Organizationally, the Wilder campaign was pathetic, too. Goldman never had any interest in putting together an army of precinct volunteers across the state and Brown didn't have the time. The only place there was a hint of formal organization was in Northern Virginia, with David Temple and Pat Watt. They soon became exasperated with Goldman. "It became very discouraging when we're organizing in the Eighth and Tenth [congressional districts] and ask how are we doing in the First and the answer came back, 'Well, I think we'll ask,' " Temple says.

Goldman spent most of his time fencing with the campaign insiders in Richmond. He figured a field organization was a waste of time. The people who would go to the mass meetings would be drawn by one of the two gubernatorial candidates, not those for the lower ballot offices. Goldman's strategy was to force both Davis and Baliles to file their people as Wilder delegates and have Wilder simply piggyback his way to the nomination, no matter which gubernatorial candidate won.

So Goldman stayed on the phone night and day, calling his contacts in both the Baliles and Davis campaigns, hoping to plant dark inferences about what unspeakable evil would befall them if they didn't file their people as Wilder delegates. It was the old "Pickett factor" at work again, this time augmented by Goldman's fresh shot at Sabato. "I never threatened anybody," Goldman says. "I never had to. They were thinking the worst."

In January 1985, though, it was tough to see the two gubernatorial campaigns helping out by filing their delegates for Davis-Wilder or Baliles-Wilder. Almost daily there were new rumors that someone was about to oppose Wilder. "It's fair to say as late as January, there was activity on all sides to get Doug out," says Barry Rose, who worked in the Baliles campaign. "Nobody would talk about it but it was wild."

Goldman and Brown had joined a campaign under siege. The windowless basement where they worked — Goldman didn't even have an office, his desk was out in the hall — only contributed to the bunker mentality. The Wilder camp felt surrounded, with shadowy figures all around them lobbing in a few rounds every day. With no way to fight their way out, Wilder, Goldman and Brown resolved to just hunker down inside their fortress and bluff everyone into thinking the Wilder campaign was stronger than it really was. "The way they won the nomination was just brilliant," Rose says. "It just was smoke and mirrors, yet they got what they wanted."

They even named the gubernatorial candidate of their choice.

"The best thing we had going for us was mystery," Goldman says. He was perfect for the role. But Brown was even worse than Goldman. "I felt like everybody was trying to get us," Brown says. "It didn't matter if you were black, white, pink, purple, we wouldn't let you in. They'd stop you at the top of the steps and we'd go up. We were paranoid. We didn't want people to know our weaknesses."

Despite being so short-handed, though, Goldman even rejected one offer of help because he feared the volunteer would be a "mole."

The AFL-CIO sent over a black organizer but Goldman made it clear he didn't want any outside help. His official excuse: No room. "See, even my desk is out in the hall." But the truth is Goldman was suspicious of organized labor. Even though the AFL-CIO had endorsed Davis-Wilder, Davis was naturally the union's top priority. The Davis and Wilder campaigns were on the outs and Goldman knew the time was fast coming when Wilder might have to sabotage Davis to save himself. If that happened, Goldman didn't need a labor "spy" looking over his shoulder.

For now, Wilder seemed to be winning the Siege of Church Hill. Always, it was assumed that someone would come in to oppose Wilder. But here it was January and time was getting short.

"I don't think anyone ever factored in that no one would take that first step," Rose says. "In January, all of a sudden, they started realizing it. I remember telling Paul in January, if no one announces in the next thirty days, you've got it."

January 1985

The General Assembly convened in January and, among Democratic legislators, Doug Wilder was the talk of the town.

For House Democrats, in particular, the makeup of the statewide ticket was a matter of some immediate concern — the entire House of Delegates was up for re-election in the fall.

Del. William Robinson Jr., D-Norfolk, puts it bluntly: "The Democrats were all scared shitless that a black and a woman on the ticket spelled doom for members of the House. Tom [Moss] was worried as hell we'd lose our majority and he'd no longer be majority leader and the speaker was worried he'd no longer be the speaker and committee chairmen down the line — so you had some vested interest being expressed."

Moss took it upon himself to talk to Wilder and persuade him to withdraw. "I could do that," Moss says. "My record on black issues couldn't be better, if I do say so." But Moss got no further than Al Smith and Bernie Cohen and all the others before him.

The only thing left to do was for someone to actually get in the race against him. But the stop-Wilder talk remained just a whispering campaign in the cloakrooms.

"Nobody wanted to get the rap of being out front," Robinson says. "It was just this amorphous body of people. Nobody wanted to be branded a racist. I had a number of one-on-one, or two-on-one, or three-on-one discussions that always began, 'It's not that we don't want a black on the ticket but we don't think Doug can do it.' I said, if you go around spreading doom, that is what will happen."

·To counter that kind of talk, Robinson and Benjamin Lambert of Richmond — the two senior black delegates — mounted a two-pronged offensive.

First they went to the House leadership and laid down the law. They made it clear they would regard any challenge to Wilder as racially inspired. Whites feared any challenge would be seen that way; Robinson, Lambert and Co. came out and said it. "Anyone who [ran against Wilder] would have been dead in politics," Robinson told them, "because black office-holders around the state, from county supervisors to members of the General Assembly, would take that real personally."

Next, Robinson and Lambert held a series of breakfast meetings to stiffen the spines of junior legislators worried about re-election. "It was very informal," Robinson says. "Their principal concern was, how do I try to sell this back home? I just told 'em, in my view, I do not believe this state is as sexist or as racist as many people believe."

Over on the Senate side of the Capitol, political survival was not a major issue. The senators weren't up for re-election. They also had to deal with Doug Wilder on a daily basis. Nevertheless, the Senate was hardly a Wilder campaign headquarters. Wilder's supporters were pointedly shunned.

"There was a lot of coolness in the chamber," says Arlington's Sen. Ed Holland. "Ed told me he had never been so coolly treated," Wilder says. "He was upset."

Roanoke's Sen. Granger Macfarlane remembers something else, too. "I thought Doug worked hard during the session, especially on business-related bills. I remember one bill on insurance that was very important to the business community. He cast the deciding vote on that."

In favor of business, of course.

With the General Assembly in session, Wilder was out of commission as a candidate from early January through mid-March, just a scant two weeks before the mass meetings. This was a campaign without a full-time candidate. But that didn't faze Goldman a bit. Scheduling was a pain, anyway. He set out to wage the real campaign, to pester the two gubernatorial campaigns into filing their delegates for Wilder.

In early January, Goldman and Brown met with Bobby Watson at Davis headquarters. Watson loved to bluff and bluster as much as Goldman did. The meeting was like two wild animals in the first stages of a territorial dispute. The claws were still sheathed, but they circled each other warily. They wouldn't tangle today, but a clash was inevitable.

"I don't have anything against Doug," Goldman remembers Watson saying. "But look, Paul, I have a poll." Watson tapped his desk menacingly, as if threatening to produce the awful evidence. "It says if Doug does everything right, gets every break in the book, everything, he might get 40 percent. Absolute tops."

Goldman just grinned his annoying grin. "Well, I hope you didn't pay the guy."

But Watson kept coming back to the 40 percent figure. "And you could see 'em really saying 35 percent," Goldman says. "Forty percent was the top number."

The meeting ended with both Watson and Goldman choosing to temporarily withdraw to their lairs, but now the battle lines were drawn. As they were leaving, Goldman turned to Brown and said: "Well, that confirms it. Davis is trying to dump us. It makes sense. Would you want to run with a guy you didn't think could get 40 percent? Of course not."

Wilder was already suspicious of the Davis campaign, had been for almost a year now.

"Davis never called me one time, from the time I announced until after the nomination," Wilder says. "They didn't ask me to do anything to help them. In politics, you never do anything for free. If they were not doing that [asking Wilder for help], what were they doing for me?"

For now, neither gubernatorial campaign wanted Wilder on the ticket. Baliles' moderate-conservative supporters naturally weren't Wilder fans. Ironically, though, it was Davis and his liberal supporters who were far more dangerous to Wilder. Because he had such strong liberal support, Davis was theoretically more immune to criticism if he moved to jettison Wilder. Furthermore, Davis was so far ahead — he figured to sweep Tidewater and Northern Virginia; those two areas alone might give him nearly enough delegates to win the nomination — that his staff was already starting to worry about the general election and how much Wilder would hurt. Davis needed a more conservative-looking running mate to moderate his own image. "They bought the Sabato line hook, line and sinker," Wilder grumbles.

Both Davis and his campaign manager wanted to leave Wilder alone, says Chris Spanos, a Washington lawyer and Davis organizer. "The problem was Ron Dozoretz [and other major contributors] felt differently." They didn't understand the dangers in opposing Wilder, he says. Certainly some of the field workers did. "We were scared to death of it [opposing Wilder]," says Mark Bowles. "It was so volatile. We wanted to stay away from it. We had our hands full."

But a campaign, like an octopus, is a sprawling creature with lots of tentacles and sometimes the brain can't always control what all its arms are doing. In the case of the Davis campaign, the big contributors, especially, weren't in a mood to see their investment in Davis go bad because of Wilder's insistence on being on the ticket.

"Some of these people are not professional politicians," Watson says. "It's like the National Guard. They're weekend warriors. They saw the problem and they made up their mind they didn't want to see it happen."

The problem was how to oppose Wilder without getting caught.

"It was people mostly in the Davis campaign saying we've got to have someone else to run," says Richmond lawyer Larry Framme, a Baliles supporter. "They were convinced they could not win with Wilder on the ticket. It was becoming very serious to the Davis people. They were scared as hell, but they couldn't figure out what to do about it except [for] underground encouragement of Dick Bagley, which was all they could muster, because if they ever got their fingers caught in that cookie jar, they'd get their fingers cut off and their head lopped off, too."

Pinning down exactly what the Davis campaign did to oppose Wilder is extremely difficult. The participants are reluctant to talk. Dozoretz, by most accounts one of the ringleaders in the movement, says only that whatever he did was designed simply to help his friend Dick Davis.

But the efforts apparently took at least two forms:

• Dozoretz opened back-door negotiations with Goldman in February to see what it would take for Wilder to withdraw.

• Davis supporters also apparently tried to persuade some key black leaders to publicly oppose Wilder's bid.

One was Henry Marsh, a Richmond city councilman and former mayor. Marsh had been Wilder's roommate in law school but had since become a political rival.

In 1985, Marsh, a Davis supporter, remained publicly neutral on Wilder's bid, but was reportedly "very active" behind the scenes in trying to solve the Wilder problem. "They were hoping to put together a number of prominent blacks to endorse another candidate or say publicly that Wilder wouldn't win," says one Baliles campaign staffer. "Henry Marsh played a very big role in this." Wilder suggests he knows at least part of what Marsh was up to. "Marsh may have been one of those to call on the bishop," Wilder says with a knowing wink, referring to Norfolk churchman L.E. Willis, a key force in Tidewater's black precincts.

One call Marsh definitely made was to Framme, apparently in hopes he could get the moderate-conservatives supporting Baliles to join him in doing something about Wilder.

"He said 'you-all have got to stop him,' " Framme recalls. "I said, wait a minute, no one in the white community will do it. If you think Doug Wilder is a problem, you'll have to stop him in the black community. The only way to stop Doug Wilder is for you, one or two other first-tier black leaders to call a press conference at the Capitol with the TV cameras on and say 'Doug Wilder, we love you, but you can't win.' "

One problem the Davis campaign faced in finding blacks to oppose Wilder was simply numbers. Who would be credible black spokesmen? "The only possibilities were Henry and Willis," Framme says. "Henry refused. He said it would look too much like a personal vendetta. Bullshit. Henry didn't want his balls cut off."

Marsh stayed neutral.

Eventually, though, it was the moderate-conservatives who were starting to get worried, not that Wilder wouldn't be opposed, but that he would be. The Baliles campaign was especially worried that Davis might start giving signals he'd prefer a more conservative running mate. "Our concern was that moderates would assume Davis had the nomination, then form an alliance between Davis and moderates to get Doug off the ticket," says one Baliles strategist.

Meanwhile, Framme went to see Dick Bagley "trying to get a feel for what he was going to do. I said, 'Dick, you can't win it. If you want to stop Doug, it has to be in the black community.' If a white politician previously not interested in running for lieutenant governor had announced, Sherman's march to the sea would have seemed calm to the hell that would have been raised."

None of this was reported at the time. For all people out in the precincts knew, the Davis campaign was all for Wilder and it was the moderateconservative Baliles supporters who were giving Wilder the devil. But the insiders in Richmond knew the truth. "It was a classic case of overconfidence," one Baliles adviser says of the Davis campaign. "They played right into our hands. We didn't have to allege they were trying to get Doug off the ticket. They were."

Of course, at this point, Baliles staffers were, too, but their fear of running on a ticket with Wilder was slowly being replaced by the fear that, at the rate the Davis-Baliles race was going, their man wouldn't be running on any ticket at all.

The key for Wilder was winning delegates to the state convention. Most of the Davis delegates could be counted on to also file as Wilder delegates no matter what the big contributors wanted them to do. But even if most of the Davis delegates did instinctively file for Wilder, that likely wouldn't be enough. The scenario Goldman was haunted by was this: The mass meetings are over. Wilder comes in with fewer than 50 percent of the delegates committed to him — maybe only 45 or even 40 percent. But you were unopposed, critics say. Why were so many delegates unwilling to support you? The media report the delegate count as a vote of no-confidence in Wilder. When examined closely, it becomes evident that Wilder's delegates come almost exclusively from the cities, almost none from the suburbs or rural areas. Clearly, he has only a narrow base of support — a geographic truth but a demographic euphemism. The media now portray Wilder as a "special interest" candidate who can't even win votes from white, middle-of-the-road Democrats. Then someone releases a new poll showing how Wilder will drag down the ticket. Rumors are put out about alleged skeletons in Wilder's closet. If Davis has a majority, his liberal delegates are persuaded to offer an olive branch to the defeated Baliles camp by nominating a more conservative running mate, perhaps Baliles himself. If Baliles has a majority, his moderate-conservative delegates want to get rid of Wilder anyway. Either way, the dump-Wilder momentum builds — and a Draft Bagley movement starts almost by spontaneous combustion.

The only way to avoid such a scenario was for Wilder to win at least 50 percent of the delegates in the mass meetings — and, to make sure the media put a positive spin on the story, they had to come from throughout the state to show how broad-based Wilder's candidacy was. To accomplish that, Goldman would have to get both gubernatorial campaigns to file delegates for Wilder. More to the point, the key to Wilder amassing broad-based support was the moderate-conservative Baliles — with his base in the Richmond suburbs and the rural west.

But how could Wilder get those conservative delegates to file for him? What leverage did Wilder have over Baliles to force a deal? The answer was Richmond.

Davis — if he swept Northern Virginia and Tidewater — would be so close to 50 percent Baliles would be in a position of having to win almost everywhere else if he was going to even stand a chance. Certainly it was imperative that he carry his adopted hometown of Richmond. But Richmond was Wilder's hometown, too. What if Wilder decided to file his own, uncommitted, slates in Richmond and really crank out his black supporters to push them through? What if Wilder teamed up with Davis? Either way, Baliles was out of luck — and the race.

Richmond was complicated for another reason, too. Baliles had to have all of it. Yet there was a good chance he might have to settle for a split decision in Richmond. And that wouldn't be good enough.

In most Virginia cities and counties, Democrats elect convention delegates on a winner-take-all basis. In some places, though, delegates are elected by precincts or wards to make sure blacks aren't shut out by a white majority.

Richmond's Democratic committee would decide Feb. 27 which method the capital city would use. That meeting became all-important. With Richmond so racially divided, precinct mass meetings would guarantee both Davis and Baliles a certain number of delegates. Depending on how well Davis did elsewhere, splitting Richmond might be enough for him to win the nomination.

A citywide mass meeting — still winner-take-all — upped the ante considerably more. The result might depend on which way Wilder went. But then again, it might not. Baliles-Uncommitted could very well shut out Davis-Wilder or Uncommitted-Wilder. It all depended on who showed up. Baliles and Wilder were looking at playing a very dangerous game of Richmond Roulette.

Perhaps the two could come to some understanding, such as an unlikely Baliles-Wilder citywide slate in Richmond. That would satisfy Baliles, but it wasn't good enough for Wilder. So what if Wilder helped Baliles by not giving him any trouble in Richmond? What did Wilder get out of it that he couldn't get if Davis-Wilder or Uncommitted-Wilder swept Richmond? What Wilder needed was to get some of Baliles' delegates around the state to file for him. Would Baliles give him those? Was Baliles so desperate that he'd trade Wilder "free" delegates in the west in return for peace in Richmond? A Baliles-Wilder slate there at least kept him in the game. A Davis-Wilder win in Baliles' own Richmond, though, would wrap up the nomination for Davis.

Already both the Davis and Baliles campaigns were calling Goldman, asking what sort of deal could be worked out in Richmond. So there it was. For the next two months, Paul Goldman spent his time bargaining for delegates, horse-trading with the two campaigns to see just how much Richmond, and Doug Wilder's support there, was worth.

Four key meetings in January moved the process along.

First, Wilder made a weekend trip to Tidewater to visit Bishop L.E. Willis and find out whether Willis was going to lead a stop-Wilder movement. The two went horseback riding at Willis' farm in Chesapeake. One pictures a surreal Western scene, with two black cowboys riding the range, both powerful lords of their respective spreads, each sizing the other up to figure out whether one's territorial claim was a threat to the other's.

They talked about the pressure Willis was getting to endorse Bagley. "There were those who pushed him for it," Wilder says. "He told me, "I'm with you 100 percent." The two agreed to keep in touch. "We'd get calls, 'The bishop is acting this way or that.' I knew he had all kinds of pressure on him" from the Davis campaign.

Next, Wilder invited Baliles and Martin to meet with him and Goldman one morning at his home. They talked politics for about an hour and a half. Ostensibly, Wilder and Goldman wanted to let Baliles know they weren't working against him.

None of the participants say much about what exactly happened at this meetings Certainly no deals were struck just yet. This much, however, is known:

They talked about the Richmond mass meetings and who Wilder's black supporters were going to back there. "Richmond was like a test," Goldman says. "I said, 'Look, we're not going to embarrass you in your hometown. We don't want to be embarrassed in our hometown.' We let Baliles know there was no reason to fight in Richmond." Now, how much could Wilder get for that? Baliles, in turn, wanted to know how much he could get from Wilder.

Baliles apparently sounded Wilder out about what it would take for some key blacks to endorse his candidacy. Wilder, for his part, made it clear he'd like to win over some of Baliles' conservative supporters for, as one participant puts it, "as little price as possible." Apparently Baliles and Martin made some tentative assurances about certain people who might find it possible to endorse Wilder — but no real promises. "I would call these more exploratory talks, than anything conclusive," Baliles says.

Wilder and Goldman began to see their bargaining power over Richmond was still rather limited. Neither gubernatorial candidate was desperate enough yet to make the statewide deal — we give you Richmond, you give us everything else — that Wilder wanted. "At that point," Goldman says, "Baliles needed us in Richmond and nothing more. Davis needed us in Richmond and nothing more." It would take a few more weeks yet, and some apparent Goldman treachery, before that desperation set in.

But one result was clear. This Baliles-Wilder summit was the beginning of the end of the Baliles campaign's effort to get Wilder off the ticket. The urgency to stop Wilder with a favorite son candidate was replaced by an urgency to stop Davis, even if it meant joining up with Wilder.

The third meeting was one Wilder and Goldman held with Davis and Watson. This one wasn't nearly so interesting.

Davis said he had nothing against Wilder. But neither did he offer to help him. The meeting did nothing to change Wilder's and Goldman's minds: The Davis campaign was out to dump Wilder. Baliles, however — now there was a man they could do business with.

The final meeting only reinforced Goldman's distrust of the Davis campaign. Goldman went to Norfolk to see Willis himself. They met in the office of one of the bishop's radio stations. Willis apparently had access to Davis polling data, and several times cited figures from it. Specifically, Goldman claims Willis told him that Wilder was a sure loser. If Wilder runs against Marshall Coleman, he won't even get all the black vote, Willis said. Goldman tried to pin Willis down on what he was going to do. The bishop seemed evasive. "What I do will be based on what I feel is best for the black people," Goldman says Willis told him. Goldman left convinced Willis eventually would come out against Wilder.

Finally, Davis' treasurer, Ron Dozoretz, had started calling Goldman every few days to see if Wilder could be persuaded to drop out.

Goldman didn't need anyone to spell it out for him.

Willis eventually endorsed Wilder and the crisis — real or imagined — passed. But by now something far more interesting was happening. Baliles was visiting Wilder. He'd come by Wilder's home at night, after the General Assembly had adjourned for the day, and sit in the den and talk politics, about how his campaign was going and what he hoped to do if he was elected governor. Just when Goldman thought he'd have to get rough with Davis and Baliles to get the delegates he needed, Baliles, of all people, had started courting Wilder.

This was the axis on which the whole campaign turned.

Feb. 2 was the date circled on all the campaign calendars.

The Democrats' State Central Committee would meet that morning to set the rules for the convention.

That night the party's Jefferson-Jackson Day Dinner would be held at the new Richmond Marriott. A thousand Democrats from throughout the state would be there.

Between the committee meeting and the dinner, J-J Day was the major political event before the mass meetings themselves. It was crucial that

Wilder make a good impression.

One day in mid-January Wilder and Goldman sat down to talk about what they were going to do for J-J. They had been putting off ordering literature, but now they definitely needed something to pass out. "I wanted something to go against what people thought," Goldman says.

While he thought about what to do, Goldman wandered around the office. Wilder had a wall full of awards, plaques, honorary degrees. Goldman started reading some of them when suddenly his jaw dropped.

He turned to Wilder, incredulous. "I didn't know you won a Bronze Star."

Wilder shrugged. "That was in Korea. That was a long time ago. I don't talk about it much."

"What did you do to get it?" Goldman asked.

Wilder waved him off. He didn't want to talk about it. "It's on the wall."

Goldman didn't have glasses on so he had to stick his face up close to the plaque and squint:

"TO Corporal Lawrence D. Wilder, US52137240 Infantry FOR HEROISM IN GROUND COMBAT, Korea, 18 April 1953 . . . "

Goldman was ecstatic. "This sounds like Rambo," he shouted. "This is John Wayne." The more he read, the more excited he became. This was it. This was his campaign literature. Doug Wilder — war hero. He looked over at Wilder. The senator was very sternly shaking his head no.

Two of the most stubborn men in Virginia now went head to head.

"We went through a long period of negotiation," Goldman says. "Doug understood it was important, but he didn't want to make it sound like he was trying to profit from it. 'Yes, Paul, I understand it's an important thing in Virginia. Yes, I know Robb ran TV footage of Vietnam.' "

Finally, Wilder relented — slightly. Goldman could use the Bronze Star citation on the literature, but there could be no references to Wilder's campaign on the same brochure. Goldman went off and sulked. He was determined to figure out a way to run the citation. One night Goldman was alone in the basement, stewing over Wilder's decision. Then it hit him. Why not just print the whole citation, verbatim? Put a picture of Wilder on it and it would be self-explanatory. Wilder would be happy. Goldman would get his war hero message out. Bingo. Goldman knew he was a genius now.

Goldman went to Norfolk to personally supervise the printing. He watched his red-white-and-blue war cards roll over the press and drove back to Richmond with a carload full, grinning as if he had enough ammunition in the back seat to wipe out the whole Virginia Democratic Party, and half the North Korean army to boot.

Goldman also had some posters printed up — in full color. He believed it was essential for a black candidate to show he had a first-class campaign. The expensive, full-color campaign materials would make an excellent first impression.

Michael Brown found the glossy, full-color posters were big hits at Democratic gatherings. Perhaps too big. "The poster was too good for a campaign," he complains. It became a collector's item. Wilder wanted to sell them but Brown wouldn't let him. "But we had people come up, ready to put up $2, $5 for posters. The senator always said, 'See, I told you we could have sold them.' " But the worst thing was when people inevitably asked Wilder to autograph the posters. He couldn't refuse. "But I knew each one he signed wouldn't be in a window," Brown says. "It would be framed on somebody's wall."

By now, both gubernatorial campaigns were pestering Goldman about Richmond. Goldman loved it. This was high political intrigue and he was at the center of it. "Martin calls up and says, 'You know, Davis wants to dump you.' I said, 'Yeah, thank God you don't.' Then Watson calls up, 'You know, Baliles wants to dump you.' I say, 'Yeah, thank God you guys aren't.' "

But the way Goldman saw things, it was still too early to make the deal he needed to make:

"As we approached Feb. 2, both sides were telling you the other side is trying to scare you, so I felt no leverage to put on either side. Baliles is not going to make a move until he has to. Davis is not going to make a move because he thought he was winning already."

The way Goldman saw it, Wilder had to go with Baliles in Richmond. For one thing, it would be impolitic to challenge Baliles on his home turf. For another, a Davis-Wilder sweep in Richmond could wind up killing Wilder in another way. "Davis probably thinks if he could beat Baliles in Richmond, Baliles would be out, then the conservatives would revolt against Wilder," Goldman says.

For now, though, Baliles knew Wilder had little choice but to help him in Richmond, Goldman says, so "he doesn't have to pay us anything." What Wilder needed was to find some other incentive, besides simply peace in Richmond, for Baliles to file all of his delegates around the state as Baliles-Wilder. But the Baliles campaign wasn't interested. It wasn't desperate yet.

All that changed Feb. 2.

Goldman was eagerly waiting for the State Central Committee meeting. "I knew the count backwards and forwards. I knew Davis would take it."

The J-J Day massacre — the political equivalent of the St. Valentine's Day massacre — was about to begin. And in the Davis campaign's organizational ambush of the Baliles campaign, Wilder found the key to his own nomination.

Feb. 2, 1985

The night before, Rhett Walker, the top Davis organizer, was scared. The forecast for Richmond called for snow. Most of the Davis people were from Tidewater and Northern Virginia, where even a light dusting constitutes a blizzard. He was afraid many of them would stay at home, while the hardy Baliles delegates from rural Southside and the western hills — not to mention hometown Richmond — would roll in like pioneers and the whole plan would be ruined.

But Walker awoke to find no snow had fallen. The sky was still a dingy gray but the immediate crisis had passed. With his troops assembling secretly, Walker could get on with the assault.

Officials from the four campaigns met that morning. They were supposed to agree on the five at-large members which the State Central Committee would elect to a temporary credentials committee and a temporary rules committee that would start the convention. The remainder of the temporary committee members would be elected at the congressional district level — many of them, in fact, already had been.

One of the purposes of these at-large delegates was to help balance the committee by race and gender. Party headquarters wanted the four statewide campaigns to come up with a "unity" slate for the five at-large seats. Otherwise, if the campaigns fought things out seat-by-seat, they might never come up with the right balance. The at-large members weren't supposed to be elected until spring, but if the four campaigns agreed on a unity slate, they could get it over with today.

The negotiators had met that morning, went over convention rules, then were supposed to meet again at 11 a.m. to work out the unity slate.

But the Davis rep never showed up.

Darrel Martin caught wind of what was up about an hour before the meeting. To hell with the unity slate; Davis was going for all five at-large seats.

Martin knew right away that Baliles was in trouble. Even though it was a Saturday, the General Assembly was in session. That meant party Chairman Alan Diamonstein, a delegate from Newport News, wouldn't be there to run the meeting. Diamonstein could have ruled the election of the temporary credentials and rules committees out of order. But without Diamonstein there, that meant party Vice Chairman Jessie Rattley, a Davis supporter, would be the presiding officer.

Martin twice called Baliles, warning him that if he didn't get Diamonstein to come get the gavel out of Rattley's hands, the Davis campaign was going to try something very unpleasant. Martin even dispatched a car to pick Diamonstein up. But the chairman reportedly had been warned by Robb's staff that the meeting would be "too hot to handle" and he'd best stay clear of the whole thing. Diamonstein refused to come.

Barry Rose first smelled trouble when he saw the signs — red and yellow signs, the red ones with a big "N" for no and the yellow ones with a big "Y" for yes — stacked in the corner of the meeting room. He knew the Baliles campaign didn't have any signs to show people how to vote.

The Baliles staff had met the night before but had been decidedly disorganized. Rose didn't realize just how disorganized until now. He was at the door, handing out Baliles stickers, but had alarmingly few takers. Lots of people were wearing Davis stickers, though. And there were those Davis signs stacked in the corner. "We knew it was all over," he says.

Before the central committee meeting, the Davis staff caucused upstairs with its supporters to go over what was about to happen. The Baliles supporters straggled in completely unaware. It was like one of those medieval legends where two rival families are invited to a banquet and then the hosts rise up and slay their guests.

Except the Davis campaign wasn't even going to wait until dinner.

The Davis staff rolled into the committee meeting like a well-oiled machine. Its objective: Ram through as many pro-Davis and anti-Baliles rules as possible and seize control of the temporary rules and credentials committee. Election of the at-large members wasn't on the agenda, but as long as Davis had a majority on the central committee, it didn't matter. The Davis supporters could simply vote to put the election on the agenda as new business and be done with it.

Davis consultant Tom King came up to Martin before the meeting began and announced: "I've got the votes and I'm going for it."

The Davis ambush was heavy-handed but shrewd. In a mass meeting campaign, especially one where the caucuses are winner-take-all, polls are nearly meaningless. One voter in the school gym can make the difference between shutting out your opponent and getting shut out yourself. Without polls, though, there are few road marks for political observers to judge how well the candidates are doing. Thus the signs that do exist — fund-raising, for instance, or endorsements — take on incredible significance. Even a win for Davis on some obscure rule changes at an otherwise routine committee meeting would be reported as a major victory.

The ambush served a more practical purpose, too.

"We wanted to make sure our interests were protected," Watson says. "We felt some party people did not want us to be the nominee and would stack [the convention] with automatic delegates." Seizing the commanding heights of the temporary credentials and rules committees would enable Davis to cut that off at the pass. Those five at-large members just might make the difference.

The recurring military analogies are appropriate. "They just came in and massacred us," moans Rose. Says Watson bitterly: "That was the day we won a major battle and lost the war."

The Davis supporters were running the meeting like it was the convention itself. They had signs, floor leaders, the works. Two Davis whips sat in the front row with their signs. Whenever it was time for a vote, they signaled their supporters.

"Their people were cheering and were all pumped up," says Rose. "It was disgusting. Darrel got up and made an impassioned plea that [the election of the temporary committees] is not on the agenda, that it's unfair." But Martin's appeals to fair play counted for little with the Davis campaign. Martin pleaded with Goldman to join him in calling for a "unity" slate. But Goldman refused.

Martin then did the only thing he could to forestall the inevitable defeat — he told the Baliles supporters to walk out and then called for a quorum count.

Chaos ensued.

"Getting people to walk out is difficult," says Karl Bren, a Baliles organizer. "They don't want to do that." The most trouble the Baliles staff had was with its handful of black supporters. They wouldn't leave. It was one thing to be for Baliles when most of their friends were backing Davis. It was quite another to get up and walk out. Some simply wouldn't do it.

Rose confronted a black supporter from Northern Virginia. "He wouldn't move," Rose says. "I said we need you off and he wouldn't move." Rose was practically shouting at the man. Rose angrily suspected a Wilder double-cross.

Martin begged Goldman to help him get people off the floor. It's in your interest, too, Martin told him. If Davis gets Baliles here, Wilder will be next. But Goldman refused. Three committee members asked Goldman if the Wilder campaign wanted them to leave. Goldman left them hanging. "We're neutral," he said. All three stayed put.

With Baliles' supporters cowering out in the hall, the Davis supporters hooting at them as they fled, anxious field workers for both sides running around buttonholing the doubters that remained, the quorum count began.

It was a disaster.

The Democrats couldn't figure out how many people constituted a quorum. They couldn't even figure out how many people were supposed to be on the committee; the final count was off by an incredible seventeen. "If they had counted correctly, there would not have been a quorum," Martin says. Using the wrong figures, Davis had his quorum.

The Davis supporters let out a war whoop — and then proceeded to ram through what they came for:

• They voted to elect the five at-large members of the convention's temporary rules and credentials committees that day and filled them with Davis supporters.

• They defeated a plan to add two hundred "automatic" delegates — mostly local and state party officials who would likely have been for the more conservative Baliles.

• They stripped Richmond Democrats of their traditional city convention, a unique two-tier procedure that gave white conservatives a second chance to outmaneuver the black delegates elected in the mass meetings. In effect, the State Central Committee simply required Richmond to elect its delegates like any other city — and made the Feb. 27 city committee meeting even more important.

Paul Goldman, mysterious as ever, for some reason seemed enormously pleased with the outcome.

"I remember looking at Paul," Walker says. "I nodded and he did the same and then he walked out of the room."

It didn't take much imagination for the Baliles campaign to see what would happen next. If Baliles stayed in the race and posed a threat, the Davis people would simply go into the mass meetings Baliles was likely to win, disrupt them with some parliamentary tactics, both sides would get angry and elect their own slates, then the Davis-stacked temporary credentials committee would rule on the disputed delegations.

This was intraparty politics at its meanest. But the most treacherous political operative that day was Paul Goldman, who could have helped Martin get some of Baliles' black supporters off the floor.

"I knew Paul was grinning a lot that day," Watson says, but he

:ouldn't quite figure out why and didn't have time to worry about it. Maybe he should have.

"My feeling was the Baliles people wouldn't move until they had to," Goldman says. But maybe now the Baliles campaign was desperate enough :o cut a deal even with Doug Wilder.

Paul Goldman was in rare form. He showed up at the dinner wearing a :uxedo — with a bright red T-shirt poking out from underneath at the :ollar. "And he had that hair of his slicked down. He looked like a gangster," says Karl Bren. "I thought, 'Who is this man?' He looked so different."

Democrats that night may have asked the same thing about Doug Wilder when they saw Goldman's treasured "war card."

Goldman was delighted with the response. Once again, he had turned the Virginia Democratic Party upside down. All the liberals were in an uproar. Doug Wilder — war hero? All the conservatives were taken aback. Some were even nodding approvingly. Doug Wilder — war hero?

The discontent was greatest in Northern Virginia, home to Virginia's most liberal Democrats. David Temple, Wilder's organizer there, was just short of furious. He didn't care if it was the only piece of literature, he refused to distribute it back home. "There was no way I was going to let that card be unleashed prior to the convention in Northern Virginia. After the convention, with a lot of moderates and conservatives and military people, it worked well." But Goldman didn't give a hoot about the liberals in Northern Virginia. He figured they would support Wilder out of liberal guilt even if Wilder came out in favor of chucking the cease-fire and making a quick run for the Yalu. The people Goldman was playing for were the good ole boys down in Southside, up in the Valley, out in the Southwest. And they were eating it up.

"Toward the end of the campaign, that's all they wanted," Goldman says. "They realized by going with a war hero image, it's not popular in Virginia to attack a war hero."

With all the excitement of the afternoon, the speech-making that night didn't seem very important, except for one wry comment from Baliles: "Don't stick your fork in this nomination — it isn't done yet."

Wilder, though, whispered to Goldman: "Everybody in the Senate thinks Jerry is dead and Davis has it easy." Goldman loved it. He went up to Baliles and told him: "Best thing that ever happened to your campaign. Worst thing to happen to Davis."

Another candidate might have punched him then and there. But Baliles saw what Goldman was driving at. "You're absolutely right," he said. "We're gonna get moving. Don't count us out."

Feb. 3, 1985

Before the Democrats left Richmond, David Temple and Pat Watt organized a Sunday breakfast meeting between Wilder and two dozen or so Northern Virginians.

The meeting seemed to be going OK, Wilder thought. Then Chris Spanos spoke up. He was a Davis coordinator in Northern Virginia, which right away made him suspect in Wilder's eyes.

Spanos said he recently received an unmarked white envelope in the mail. So had five or six of his friends. Inside each was a copy of the state Supreme Court's decision upholding Wilder's reprimand by the State Bar. Would Wilder care to explain what exactly the problem was in that case?

After the Davis ambush of Baliles the day before, Spanos' question sounded to Wilder like the other shoe starting to drop. "It put a chill on the meeting," Wilder says, still angry long after the incident. "I got the distinct impression from Chris, 'This guy here, we may have to go along with him, but we don't like it.'"

Spanos insists it was a perfectly innocent — and legitimate — question. "I brought it up because if I was getting it [anonymous copies], I was sure others were. I thought he got it out of the way very well."

Across town, Larry Framme held a brunch for visiting Democrats. The topic of the day was the State Central Committee vote. If that was any indication of Davis' true strength, things sure looked bad for Baliles, didn't they?

Wilder, never known for his punctuality, showed up late. After Wilder had time to circulate, Framme took him aside to talk privately. Framme had something on his mind but first he needed answers to some questions.

For several weeks now Framme had been talking with the Terry campaign, trying to form an alliance with Baliles in the mass meetings. "I was telling them it would be much more difficult to win with Davis on top of the ticket," Framme says. But the Terry people wanted nothing to do with it. They figured they were in — and with all the money Terry was raising, it might not matter who she ran on the ticket with.

Now, after the beating Baliles had taken at the central committee meeting, the need for Baliles to form an alliance with someone was urgent. The options were limited, though. Baliles-Wilder?

Framme quizzed Wilder about what he wanted and what sort of campaign he'd run if nominated. "We're in this race to win, not just the nomination, but the general election," Wilder told him. "If you believe that, you'll know how we'll run."

Framme let Wilder go back to working the crowd and mulled over his answer.

Before long, the brunch was breaking up. Finally there was just Goldman, Framme and Brown. For two hours Framme and Goldman jousted back and forth, Framme pleading, cajoling, exhorting, Goldman circumspect, vague, evasive. Brown stood back and watched.

"If you seriously want to win the election, you know you can't win with Davis on the ticket," Framme said, over and over again. Why doesn't Wilder team up with Baliles in Richmond? Framme asked. Surely Wilder must see it's not in his interest to help nominate Davis.

Goldman, as always, was cryptic. "Hey, we're not against anybody," Goldman said whenever the talk turned to the Richmond mass meeting. Neither would Goldman say what kind of fall campaign Wilder was planning. He did, however, repeat the same magic line Wilder had — Wilder really was in the race to win. "If you believe that, then you know how we'll run," Goldman said.

Goldman was sitting on a church pew Framme had picked up as an antique. "I knew he couldn't be lying," he jokes. "From then on, I was convinced. I never thought it would be a Jesse Jackson-style campaign. If Doug was to have any chance, he had to run to the right. The Northern Virginia types would always vote for him. Doug Wilder could have run stark naked down Broad Street drunk and they'd have supported him. Ideologically, that's the way they are. Paul knew that. He could do damn near anything and they'd still support him. He had to get the conservatives."

Wilder's bill cracking down on prison escapees. The war card. Framme could see it all falling together now. Wilder really *was* serious about this. "My only fear," Framme says, "was at some point, it may get so bad that he would conclude he had no chance and then all bets were off."

But at this point Framme wasn't worrying about November, he was worrying about whether Jerry Baliles was even going to make it to the convention. Baliles needed help, badly, and he needed it from blacks, liberals, Northern Virginians, the very groups Wilder had for the asking. And as long as Wilder just *thought* he had a chance in the fall, then maybe he'd behave himself and not be the big liability so many thought he would be . . .

Doug Wilder finally had Jerry Baliles just where he wanted him. Now it was time to deal.

7

Baliles Plays the Wilder Card

Feb. 10, 1985

Barry Rose was calling from a pay phone at the Cascades Inn in Williamsburg. He had more bad news for the Baliles campaign. The First District Black Caucus had just adjourned without endorsing either candidate for governor.

The Baliles campaign had gone all-out to win the group's backing. Baliles desperately needed a major breakthrough in the black community — after the previous weekend's State Central Committee meeting he needed a breakthrough anywhere — and this was thought to be the place. Davis hadn't spent much time working the caucus and didn't have the votes. But instead of supporting the eager Baliles, the caucus put off its endorsement until the next month and went home. Rose was deflated. He had to wonder: Would Baliles *ever* break through in the black community?

"That was the point we were starting to see Davis' black support rolling," Rose says. "They had the bishop and it was really scary. We were spiraling."

Rose dejectedly called in the bitter result to campaign manager Darrel Martin.

But on the other end of the phone back in Richmond, Martin seemed distant and unconcerned. His mind seemed to be on other things.

Martin mulled over what Rose told him with one of his trademark long pauses. Then he asked, in a somewhat hushed, conspiratorial tone: What would you think about Baliles endorsing Wilder?

Rose nearly dropped the phone. "It really blew me away," he says. "I didn't think we'd do that."

The idea of a joint ticket came reluctantly to the Baliles campaign, but it had been gaining momentum for several weeks now — ever since that morning meeting at Wilder's home and the subsequent evening chats Baliles and Wilder had in the latter's den. Jefferson-Jackson Day highlighted the urgency. "Jerry was gone at that point and he knew it," Wilder says, "just gone."

After the Davis ambush, the Baliles campaign braced itself. "We were waiting for the other shoe to drop," says Baliles organizer Karl Bren. "What endorsements are they going to come out with? Who are they going to get to turn on us? But they didn't have a follow-up. Nothing happened. They didn't come in for the coup de grace and we kept organizing."

The next two months wouldn't be pretty ones.

Bren, a veteran of both Vietnam and previous Virginia campaigns, says organizing the Baliles campaign for the March 30 and April 1 mass meetings "was the hardest single thing I've ever done. That was hand-to-hand combat."

The Baliles campaign had two goals, now more imperative than ever — reach outside the party to bring in new people to the mass meetings and cut into Davis' nearly unanimous black support — if Baliles was going to hope to be competitive in the cities and some Southside counties.

There was never any serious question of Baliles being unacceptable to blacks. He was a moderate-conservative in the mold of Chuck Robb — conservative enough on fiscal matters to satisfy the big money boys, but "progressive" on social issues. His problem was that Dick Davis simply had black support locked up first.

Joining up with Wilder was Baliles' key to unlocking it.

Over in Davis headquarters, Watson had feared from the beginning that if Baliles were pushed far enough, he might take the risk of forming an alliance with Wilder. "We felt all along that was his ace to play," Watson says, "and we felt confident that Jerry was so cautious, he wouldn't play it."

University of Virginia political analyst Larry Sabato got a feel for some of the subterfuge going on when he paid a courtesy call on Wilder in February to explain the basis for his now infamous "100-1" quip back in December. Sabato and Wilder sparred a bit over both that and Paul Goldman, but mainly Wilder wanted to complain about fellow Democrats. It was a rare, illuminating glimpse of the angry and temperamental Doug Wilder that the candidate kept so well hidden during the campaign. "He was fulminating about Chuck Robb, complaining that Robb was trying to undercut him and find another candidate," Sabato recalls. "He was cussing up a blue streak about Chuck Robb. In Doug Wilder's character, there is a 'let's-get-even streak.' " Wilder complained that Robb was getting a lot of credit he didn't deserve and that someday Robb's people would get tripped up by their own plotting and scheming, Sabato says. Wilder also complained that Davis was trying to push him out of the race and said Sabato shouldn't be surprised if Baliles and Wilder started working together soon.

Wilder and Goldman were obsessed by the alleged villainy of the Davis campaign. Once more, they saw signs of a Davis double-cross in the works.

The focus on the Richmond mass meeting — and the city committee's decision Feb. 27 on whether to elect delegates citywide or by precinct — was now getting intense. But while Davis consultant Tom King was calling a couple of times a week, trying to get Goldman to cut a deal for Richmond, Davis treasurer Ron Dozoretz was trying to get Goldman to persuade Wilder to drop out.

From late January until early March, Dozoretz and Goldman talked regularly — maybe two or three times a week, always on same subject: What would it take for Wilder to pull out? "Would Doug consider it? How about if we did a poll to show he couldn't win," were some of the questions Goldman recalls. "He really felt Doug didn't have a chance, that Virginia was not ready. He said Doug had an obligation not to run, that he'd wreck the party, that Doug should get out and become party chairman and help the next generation of blacks."

Goldman was worried by what he saw as Dozoretz's back-channel negotiations. It looked like the Davis campaign was getting ready to disown Wilder. And since he didn't have a deal yet with Baliles, Goldman still had no way to get Baliles to file his rural and suburban delegates for Wilder. Now the Wilder campaign's other fears were being realized. A Draft Bagley movement had started. Short of an outright announcement by Bagley, how much worse could things get?

The Draft Bagley movement began with only four guys from the edge of Northern Virginia, none of whom was a big name in the party — Walter

Sheffield, a lawyer from Fredericksburg, Randy Flood, a Washington lobbyist from Manassas, Chuck Colgan Jr., a phone company worker and state senator's son from Manassas, and Norborn Beville, the Democratic chairman in Prince William County. "The truth is the active party people pushing Draft Bagley were small in number, but among Democrats the hope was almost universal," Sabato says.

However, Flood and Co. soon found many of the Democrats they needed weren't about to go public with their opposition to Doug Wilder. "They didn't need Paul Goldman to tell them Wilder would remember every slight, that to make an enemy of Doug Wilder was to make a serious enemy," Sabato says. "These were people who would have been making headlines if Wilder had been a white liberal. In private they were saying, 'What can we do about Wilder? Oh, my God!' and in public they were saying, 'Senator Wilder is a fine candidate. He'd be good for the party.'"

So Draft Bagley began with four guys from Manassas and Fredericksburg and ended the same way. In between, it's difficult to gauge how close they came. Bobby Watson and Darrel Martin, who presumably know something about Democratic politics in 1985, both dismiss the Draft Bagley movement as a lot of talk and not much action. Flood and Colgan say they had some "major" political figures lined up and ready to go public if the draft movement had taken off, but few were willing to help them get to that point. "We got some calls from some pretty big shots within the Democratic Party," Flood says. But then, when Flood would call them back for specific help, "They said, 'Oh, we better not do this, you go your way, we'll go ours.' That's when I knew we were truly on our own."

Significantly, though, Bagley refused to flatly rule out any interest in challenging Wilder. "I want to think about it carefully," he said. "If there were a consensus [for him] that would make it simpler." For those reading between the lines, Bagley's statement seemed clear enough.

Wilder — trying to head off a draft — spent a lot of time talking to Bagley during the General Assembly session, bluntly pointing out the consequences if Bagley challenged him: "I talked to him quite enough to let him know it would be nothing other than a knock-down, drag-out fight. I wasn't going anywhere. I told him it was to his advantage to coalesce behind my candidacy if he wanted to have a future in the party.

"He said, 'If I decide to do anything different, you'll be the first to know. These people have gone right far for me, I don't want to shut the door on them unceremoniously,'" Wilder says, not especially pleased by Bagley's assurance that if he changed his mind, he'd let Wilder know. "He never told me publicly or privately" that he definitely would not run.

Bagley says the Wilder camp was overreacting. "I was never a potential impediment," he says. Behind the scenes, though, there were a lot of frantic phone calls. "There was considerable enticement" for getting into the race, Bagley says, "both in numbers and money . . . But it would not have been in my character to get into that race and have been perceived in a certain way."

Feb. 17, 1985

Two weeks had passed since the State Central Committee meeting, exactly one week since Darrel Martin first suggested to Barry Rose that Baliles might endorse Wilder. In that time, Larry Framme had been lobbying the campaign to do something with Wilder — offering himself as the front man for a Baliles-Wilder alliance — and Martin had been mulling over the options.

Martin says Baliles was never in as bad shape as everyone thought. But the perception that he was way behind was potentially fatal and was starting to have an effect. "By building an alliance with Wilder, we were able to scramble the press perceptions," Martin says. "I believed the Wilder card was a card to be played."

That night, Martin convened a meeting in Baliles' headquarters to discuss the proposed endorsement. But many staffers objected. They worried that an outright endorsement would alienate too many of Baliles' conservative supporters — especially in Owen Pickett's hometown of Virginia Beach, where Baliles had hoped to score an upset in Davis' Tidewater back yard.

So the endorsement was scratched. Still, Baliles had to do something with Wilder. What was it going to be? A frustrated Martin told Rose to see what he could work out with Goldman.

That night Rose went to dinner with Linda Moore, a Baliles organizer from Roanoke. They talked over what the obvious alternative was — getting some prominent moderate-conservatives and some prominent blacks together to lead a Baliles-Wilder group ostensibly independent of the two campaigns. "He'll never get credit for it," Moore says, "but it was Barry Rose's idea and Darrel Martin was strong enough to buy it."

Feb. 18 - March 3, 1985

The next two weeks were perhaps the most intense of the whole nomination campaign. Wilder was still tied up in the General Assembly; Paul Goldman, meanwhile, fended off more speculation about Dick

Bagley, and worked out a deal with Baliles for Richmond, all the while negotiating with Barry Rose and Darrel Martin for the biggest campaign surprise of them all.

The easy ones first.

On Feb. 25, the Virginia News Network — a statewide radio network — released a poll of Democratic city and county chairmen. They favored Bagley over Wilder by a margin of 65 percent to 13 percent.

But Wilder sent nothing. He never had any issue paper of any kind until the fall, when Robb's staff insisted on writing some for him.

Meanwhile, it was becoming clear that something was up between Baliles and Wilder. "We had the idea Goldman was living in Baliles headquarters," Watson says. "There was an epidemic of paranoia. Two weeks out, we knew it was coming. It was just a matter of how and when."

With that backdrop, the outcome of the Richmond city committee meeting on Feb. 27 was no surprise.

The Baliles and Wilder supporters joined together to vote to elect the capital's delegates citywide, guaranteeing that Baliles would carry Richmond. Officially, the slate would be filed as Baliles-Uncommitted, but it was "understood" that almost all of those uncommitted delegates would vote for Wilder. To cement the pledge, the Baliles campaign saw to it that key Wilder supporters were included on the Baliles slate.

What's more, by now the all-encompassing deal Goldman had been looking for was in the works.

After the aborted Wilder endorsement at the Baliles staff meeting Feb. 17, Barry Rose got together with Goldman to see what sort of deal could be worked out. Sometimes Darrel Martin called, too, but most of the plotting was done in late-night meetings in the basement of Wilder's law office and the upstairs dining room of the Grace Place, a vegetarian restaurant in the Fan.

The immediate solution was to put together a group of moderate-conservative Democrats — all identified with Baliles — to endorse a Baliles-Wilder slate, a clear enough signal that the Baliles campaign thought Wilder was acceptable. Later, Wilder hoped to get Baliles' help in rounding up delegates in rural, white counties in which he'd otherwise be shut out, and Baliles hoped to get Wilder's help in finding some key blacks to endorse him.

Officially, the Baliles-Wilder committee was a spontaneous movement independent of either campaign. In fact, campaign manager Martin made most of the initial calls to line up Baliles supporters.

Framme had already volunteered to do something with a Baliles-Wilder alliance, so he was an obvious choice to lead the coalition. A year later, when he was elected state party chairman, Framme was credited in several newspaper stories with "masterminding" the Baliles-Wilder alliance. Nothing could be further from the truth. Not until fairly late in the game did he get a call from Rose outlining what the campaigns needed him to do. And to show how well choreographed the whole thing was, even among the participants, not even Framme was sure exactly what was going on.

"I was very careful not to talk with high people in either campaign," Framme says. "I didn't want to say I was asked to do it. I wound up talking with Barry Rose. I assume he was talking to Goldman. It was one of those deals where I know you're talking to someone but I don't know who. If you're really talking high-level, wink twice, that sort of thing. Finally, I got a call from Barry one night, 'Let's do it.' "

The news conference was scheduled for Monday, March 4.

But now Framme's fearlessness started to wear off. "Jerry knows about this, doesn't he?" he asked Rose, somewhat nervously. But Rose wasn't sure.

Now even *he* began to wonder.

March 4, 1985

Larry Framme stood alone before the TV cameras and announced the formation of "Virginians for Baliles and Wilder."

"The Democratic Party needs to get behind this ticket now," he said. Other Democrats have had plenty of time to get into the lieutenant governor's race "but now their time has passed. It's too late for somebody else to jump in. Doug Wilder should and is going to be the lieutenant governor nominee and this party ought to get behind it and recognize that."

Framme also promised to come back within two weeks and produce a list of people supporting Baliles-Wilder "that will knock your socks off."

The reaction from the Davis campaign was predictable. Bobby Watson dismissed the Baliles-Wilder committee as "a last-minute, thrown-together attempt to use Doug Wilder's campaign to benefit Jerry Baliles."

Privately, though, Watson was envious. "It was a brilliant stroke," he says. Now it was just a question of what it would all amount to — how much support would Baliles pick up, how much would he lose, how would Davis respond, how many Baliles delegates really would file for Wilder?

It took a while to measure the full impact of the Baliles-Wilder alliance — until the mass meetings, to be exact. The immediate reaction, though, was silence — from all quarters.

The Davis camp figured it didn't have to respond.

"There was a lot of thinking that Dick was going to win the nomination" regardless, says Dozoretz. "You're thinking you're going to win, so why do something to disturb the balance?"

The AFL-CIO was furious at Wilder, for siding with Baliles and undercutting Davis. "There was just about mutiny," says vice president Russ Axsom. But what could labor do? It couldn't disown Wilder.

The Baliles-Wilder alliance also made for more difficult times between the Baliles campaign and its supporters. There weren't many complainers, but enough to give Darrel Martin and Larry Framme some anxious moments — especially since many of them were in Virginia Beach.

Most Baliles supporters, though, saw the necessity of cutting a deal with Wilder. And the Davis supporters grudgingly recognized it, too. AFL-CIO secretary-treasurer Danny LeBlanc remembered a prophetic conversation he had had with former Del. Ira Lechner the year before. "Ira was the first person to tell me that Wilder would run and win the nomination and win the election," LeBlanc recalls. "And he said whoever is able to get Doug Wilder to run with them in the caucuses will get the gubernatorial nomination."

March 6, 1985

So Davis did nothing. Labor complained but did nothing. Baliles' conservatives complained privately but did nothing. But, so far, the blacks Baliles was after had done nothing, either.

Baliles-Wilder threw the whole campaign into suspended animation. It halted Davis' momentum, especially among blacks. But it had not yet transferred that momentum to Baliles. Instead, everyone seemed to stop, take two steps back and look to see what was happening. But, if Democrats decided Framme's committee was just a front with nothing behind it, the campaign could easily resume just the way it was.

Down in Newport News, Barry Rose was working frantically to pull off the next surprise. On this one, he had a deadline. Framme had promised to come back in two weeks with a list that would "knock your socks off." And this time he would need some genuine surprises.

"We knew to stop the Davis momentum, we had to have a significant black [endorse Baliles]," Framme says. That was essential to complete the symmetry of Baliles-Wilder — conservatives endorsing Wilder, blacks endorsing Baliles.

But who?

Goldman says there was one man Darrel Martin was "fixated" by: Bobby Scott, the only other black state senator. He was in Davis' back yard. But, surprisingly, he still hadn't committed.

Martin felt Wilder now owed Baliles help in getting Scott to endorse him. Goldman did give Martin tips on how to woo Scott — and passed Martin's interest on to the Newport News senator. But actually pulling off the deal was a tall order. Dick Davis had been good to Bobby Scott. When Scott ran for the state Senate in the December 1982 special election, Davis had dispatched Bobby Watson to Newport News to run Scott's abbreviated campaign. Davis had campaigned heavily for Scott. Everyone just assumed he had to be for Davis. And that was part of the problem.

"Davis could not believe Scott was not on board," Framme says. "But Scott got the feeling Davis was coming in and organizing Newport News around him. He came to the conclusion in his own mind, Davis couldn't win and whoever was nominated, Bobby would be the one to deal with."

Rose was dispatched to Newport News to get Scott on board with Baliles. "I basically went down and talked to Bobby Scott for two weeks," Rose says. He vividly remembers the first meeting he had with Scott, before the Baliles-Wilder committee was even announced. "He said, 'The Davis people are neglecting me.' I said, 'You're very important to us. I'll visit you every day until you decide,' and I did."

While Rose courted Scott, other Baliles supporters kept Scott's telephone line busy, some promising money if he ever wanted to run for Congress. "We had everybody in the world calling Bobby," Rose says. "He loved it."

Late in the evening of March 6, Rose was once again back in Scott's office. Davis and Baliles were scheduled to meet that night in Virginia Beach, in the first of a series of debates. "I could see he was leaning," Rose says. He asked Scott if he'd like Baliles to stop by on his way back to Richmond that night. No, Scott said, don't bother. Baliles will be too tired. Rose saw his chance. "I thought 'great.' We'll get Jerry to come by. That will really impress him." A few minutes later, Rose was on the phone to Martin, explaining what needed to be done.

The debate that Wednesday night was between Davis and Baliles, but, at times, it was mostly about Doug Wilder.

The debate "exposed few substantive differences," reported the *Richmond Times-Dispatch*. "But there was a marked difference in tone as they confronted the ticklish question of whether [Wilder] would help or hurt their prospects in November."

Baliles "sounded positively more eager than Davis to run on such a ticket," the paper wrote. Baliles repeatedly suggested that opposing Wilder at this late date would hurt the party. "Davis, meanwhile, said that while any contest is divisive, 'We can patch whatever comes up.'"

The Strawberry Banks Motel and Restaurant sits off Interstate 64 just as the interstate emerges from the Hampton Roads Bridge-Tunnel on the Newport News side. Its big red neon sign glowed in a gaudy come-on against the night sky above and the dark water behind it. The lights of Norfolk were low on the horizon across the harbor, like a string of little stars stretched across the water's surface, broken now and then by the silhouette of an ocean vessel riding the tide.

Here's where Barry Rose and Bobby Scott were waiting when the Baliles caravan came through on its way home from Virginia Beach.

Rose's plan had worked perfectly. When he told Scott that Baliles wanted to stop by that night to see him, "I tell you he was very, very flattered."

But Scott still wasn't ready to endorse.

March 8-10, 1985

Moses Riddick is a cagey and cantankerous old man who for years has been the key black leader in Suffolk, the peanut city on the western edge of Tidewater, where the coastal suburbia disappears abruptly into the hard, dense forests of Southside. Riddick sometimes was every bit as impenetrable as the pine woods around him, but it was well known in Democratic circles, if you wanted to carry the black vote in Suffolk, Moses Riddick was the man you needed to deal with. He had been city councilman, vice mayor. In 1969 he sought the Democratic nomination for lieutenant governor, finishing a dismal fourth in a four-way field, an experience that weighed heavy in Riddick's mind as he pondered Doug Wilder's chances sixteen years later. "A lot of the white people were surprised and looked at me like I was an animal," Riddick remembers.

In 1985 he was a paid organizer for Dick Davis. And at a Davis rally March 8, a reporter sought Riddick out to ask what he thought about Wilder. Riddick spoke his mind. Lord, did he speak it.

Wilder's candidacy, he declared, "is going to hurt the whole Democratic Party. If we come in with a woman and a black, that ticket is a dead duck. I hate it, but it's a fact of life."

When Riddick's comments hit print they ricocheted around Virginia like the sudden blast from a loose cannon; here was a key Davis organizer, a week before the filing deadline, urging Davis to drop both of his potential running mates; here was perfect ammunition for Baliles-Wilder to use against Davis with black voters.

Bobby Watson called Riddick and sternly warned him that if he said anything like that again, he'd be fired. "I nearly killed him," Watson says. "He was a loose cannon and he shot off." Riddick snapped back: "Nobody buys me."

Watson asked Riddick to apologize and get the Davis campaign off the hook; he refused. And the "dead duck" comment was hung around Davis' neck like an albatross.

March 8-10, 1985

Goldman hadn't spoken to Rose in nearly a week. Two nights after Strawberry Banks, he called. It was well after midnight, but Goldman rarely noticed the late hour. If he did this time, it was only to heighten the drama. Goldman said he had something very important to tell Rose. But it was so secret Rose had to promise not to tell anybody else. 'If anybody finds out, it's off," Goldman warned. Rose was accustomed to Goldman's secretiveness, but he had never heard Goldman that adamant before. Rose had no choice but to agree.

Goldman almost whispered his news: "Bobby's going to do it."

Rose shouted for joy. Baliles-Wilder was going to pay off after all.

Scott was the knockout blow of a one-two Baliles-Wilder punch. With Framme's original announcement, the Baliles campaign signaled its willingness to run with Wilder. With Scott's endorsement, the Baliles campaign got what it really wanted in return — a major black politician witnessing that Baliles was acceptable to black voters; his endorsement quieted any conservative grumbling that Baliles had gone too far in allowing his people to endorse Wilder. And Wilder, in doing his part to "deliver" Scott, had now repaid Baliles for those conservative delegates out in the suburbs and rural west.

Scott conveniently was more than just a big black name. "Without me, Baliles would not have had a district chairman or legislator from Tidewater," Scott says, "so I covered a lot of bases. There would have been a serious problem if he had not had a name out of Tidewater to pick from."

Officially, the Wilder campaign had done nothing to encourage Scott's endorsement. Behind the scenes, though, Goldman was quite busy in arranging the Scott endorsement. Goldman and Scott talked frequently. Scott also talked to Wilder himself. Did Wilder encourage Scott to endorse Baliles? Scott smiles and jokingly rustles some papers on his desk as if looking for a prepared statement on the subject. "He was aware of the fact I was going to do it and didn't tell me not to," Scott finally says.

And it was Paul Goldman who wrote Scott's speech.

March 10, 1985

Bobby Watson was asleep that Sunday night when Bobby Scott called. Watson wasn't surprised by what Scott told him he was going to do. "I had met with him the previous week and he was acting really strange. Plus, we had started to pick up rumors from Newport News that 'Bobby's endorsing Baliles.' "

Still, it was an awkward late-night conversation between Scott and his one-time campaign manager. "He said he hadn't been included in things," Watson says. "That wasn't true. He was in the first meeting we ever had. Bobby had a lot of reasons that were really just excuses. It was very painful for us, very painful for Dick Davis. It was very painful because Bobby didn't call Dick. He did it through me."

Scott dismisses that. "I assumed Dick Davis would find out."

After Scott hung up, Watson couldn't get back to sleep. He was furious at Scott's defection. "I might have thrown a few things," he says. He woke up his wife to tell her. She just mumbled and went back to sleep. Then he started calling other Davis staffers, waking them up in the middle of the night to break the news.

March 11, 1985

Scott was nervous when he got to the Capitol in Richmond. This kind of high political drama — which Goldman and Wilder both reveled in — went against his own cautious instincts. "I don't like to surprise people," he says. 'When you call a news conference, it ought not even be newsworthy. I remember showing up at the press conference and meeting Margie Fisher [of the *Roanoke Times & World-News*] at the elevator going up to the Capitol. She looked at me like, 'What are you doing here?' "

Exactly a week before, Larry Framme had been nervous like Scott. But now Framme was grinning.

"We promised you [last week] that we would be back with a list that would knock your socks off," Framme said. "We keep our promises. Tighten your garters."

March 14, 1985

Ten days after Baliles-Wilder was announced, the *Times-Dispatch* had its first editorial comment on the prospective ticket: "Baliles and Wilder, Maybe."

The editorial acknowledged the shrewdness of the alliance but warned that Baliles risked losing some of his conservative support. Larry Framme read the editorial and breathed a deep sigh. "When I read that I thought we just might pull it off," he says. "They didn't like it, but there were worse things they could have said."

And by this point, it was becoming increasingly apparent that the long-awaited conservative backlash to Baliles-Wilder was not going to develop. Instead, "Doug could step back and watch Davis and Baliles bid against each other to see who was the strongest supporter," Scott says.

In Suffolk, Moses Riddick was amazed at what he saw happening. "Whoever saw a man tie up the Democratic Party like this?" he asks. "Baliles said I'll run with him. Davis said I will too. Didn't nobody want to alienate him. Each one would get up and make glowing speeches about him. I thought, 'Well, I'll be doggoned. Something's gonna happen.' "

Something was gonna happen, indeed.

Baliles-Wilder "stopped any stop-Wilder movement in its tracks," says Chip Woodrum, the state legislator from Roanoke. "It was kind of like a sledgehammer right in the forehead."

Too bad Chuck Colgan and Randy Flood had just sent out their first big Draft Bagley mailing. "There was a narrow period of time when the momentum was with us," Flood says. "Sometimes you miss it. Sometimes you hit it."

The Draft Bagley committee missed it.

The morning Bobby Scott endorsed Baliles, a furious Bobby Watson called up Paul Goldman and chewed him out.

The Scott endorsement struck the Davis campaign like a knife in the back. "It was more a personal blow to me and Dick Davis more than anything," Watson says.

And that was the problem.

"The Davis people reacted with absolute outrage to Bobby," Framme says. "They let that stop 'em . . . But they were just too mad to react."

In fact, the Davis campaign did react, but in what were, in retrospect, all the wrong ways.

Watson ordered an all-out offensive on the Peninsula to prevent other defections. "I told Rhett Walker, who was my best organizer, 'Do what is necessary. Move to Newport News.' I went down and put it together. I put radio on. I had wanted Rhett to go to Roanoke [where it looked like Davis had a decent shot of scoring a major upset in Baliles territory], but if we lost the Peninsula, Roanoke wouldn't have made any difference. I went down there and did mailings. I dropped everything and made that my cause. If mailing out $1 bills to every voter in Newport News would have made the difference, I'd have done it."

Here comes the real value of the Baliles-Wilder deal:

• It helped clinch the nomination for Wilder, certainly.

• It answered in advance any questions about whether Baliles and Wilder would work for each other in the fall.

• It moderated Wilder's image. "Baliles-Wilder gave Doug conservative credibility," Framme explains.

• Finally, it cemented the personal relationship Baliles and Wilder had been building through Baliles' nighttime visits to Wilder's home. After Framme's announcement, Baliles and Wilder met at least once a week until the convention in late May.

For Baliles, the alliance was even more valuable:

• It helped crack open previously inaccessible Northern Virginia.

• It helped Baliles pick up some black support.

• And perhaps most importantly, it forced Davis to divert critical organizational resources to protect his Tidewater base, both in Scott's hometown of Newport News and the region's black neighborhoods in general. "As a result, we got our ass kicked in the western part of the state," says Davis organizer Mark Bowles.

Elsewhere, too.

The unofficial connection between Baliles and Wilder was one of the main selling points for Baliles organizers among black voters. Although Wilder professed his neutrality, some blacks started to buy the argument that the Baliles-Wilder committee proved Baliles was more willing than Davis to accept Wilder on his ticket.

Officially, neither Baliles nor Wilder had endorsed the other. Behind the scenes, though, the Wilder campaign was actively helping the Baliles campaign line up black supporters. "The beauty of Baliles-Wilder was it was cover," Rose says. "It was paper thin, but it was cover."

Down in Southside, Davis hoped to carry some conservative counties with big black populations. But Baliles organizer Randy Gilliland was putting together "a strange coalition" of blacks and conservatives. Whenever Gilliland ran into trouble lining up black support, he called Paul Goldman for help. "Paul would make sure someone of influence would call and make the case why they should be for a Baliles-Wilder candidacy," Gilliland says.

Likewise in Richmond, Baliles organizer Debbie Oswalt often called on Michael Brown. "We'd call Michael and say I need two people here or ten people there. Or check these people out. Are they reliable? If they say they can turn out ten people, can I believe them? He played a lot of games for a while. He had to pretend to be neutral with both sides but help us and do it in a way that the Davis people couldn't point to and use to incite people. We wondered, by him not being blatant, whether he was double-dealing, but he came up with the names when I needed them."

In Northern Virginia, Baliles-Wilder made Baliles look more appealing to liberals. "All of a sudden, it started moving lots of people," says Falls Church car dealer Don Beyer Jr. "We went to liberals and said, Doug can win with Jerry."

Thanks to Wilder, the momentum started to roll for Baliles. And thanks to Baliles, the momentum started to roll for Wilder, too.

March 15-29, 1985

By now the question of whether Wilder would be on the ticket was rapidly becoming moot: With just a week to go before the mass meetings, both the Davis and Baliles campaigns were filing their delegates for Wilder.

In some places, in fact, the Baliles campaign wouldn't let its supporters be delegates unless they officially backed Wilder. "We were really hard-line," says Baliles organizer Barry Rose, who was working Tidewater. "Without Baliles-Wilder, all our people would have filed uncommitted. I had to sit on people to file for Doug. I was up the night before calling people, pleading with them to change their filing to Baliles-Wilder."

The same thing happened all over Virginia. In Manassas, Chuck Colgan Jr. and Randy Flood saw the conditions for a Bagley draft eluding them. "We had some groups of forty or fifty ready to go Bagley but the Baliles people put in a phone call and they switched. If it hadn't been for Baliles-Wilder, we could have held him to 40-45 percent."

But now, as the lists of pre-filed delegate candidates rolled in, Goldman saw the possibility of Wilder getting more than 50 percent of the delegates. "In places it didn't matter who won, I'd get delegates either way," he says.

So Wilder was in, even before the mass meetings began. Former GOP state legislator Ray Garland wrote in his weekly newspaper column: "The riskiest high-stakes gamble in the annals of modern Virginia politics is within an ace of being tried.

"The Democrats know the awful risk they are taking and it scares them to death; but the prospect of confronting Doug Wilder and trying to deny him the nomination scares them even more.

"Doug Wilder knew exactly the hand he was holding and played it like a master. He cocked his pistol and laid it on the table. There wasn't a Democrat of standing who had the guts to say no."

March 30, 1985

The mass meetings were in two parts. Davis was expected to win big on Saturday, when 2,386 delegates, mostly in urban areas, were elected. The question was what would happen Monday night, when the remaining 1,114, mostly in rural areas, would be chosen. (There would be 104 automatic delegates, for a total of 3,604.) Would Baliles be able to stay close enough on Saturday and score big on Monday night to go over 1,802? Or would Davis get so close to 50 percent on Saturday that he could win Monday even by losing?

When Barry Rose got to the school where the Hampton mass meeting was being held, he found practically the entire Davis campaign out front, shaking hands — Davis himself, and seemingly all the top Davis staffers.

The Davis people must be worried, Rose thought. They were.

After Baliles-Wilder, Davis invested considerable effort into protecting his Tidewater base. On Saturday, the work paid off.

Davis swept every Tidewater city — coming out of Tidewater with a whopping 633 delegates. Baliles, meanwhile, with support from Wilder, swept Richmond and its suburbs — 422 delegates in all — plus another 78 in Roanoke. That gave him 500.

With each man winning his home base, all the campaigns waited Saturday night for the results to trickle in from smaller cities — and from Northern Virginia, where the counting went on into the night.

Rhett Walker and Mark Bowles, fresh off the big Davis win in Tidewater, were driving out U.S. 460 to Roanoke that night, on their way to organize Southwest Virginia Monday night. All the way through Southside, Walker and Bowles stopped every forty-five minutes or so, wherever they could find a pay phone, to check in with headquarters. What about Northern Virginia? It seemed to be taking forever to get the results. They called and called. Finally some results were in — and they weren't good. Baliles had carried Springfield and Annandale, picking up 92 delegates in all. Both had been expected to be Davis strongholds.

Walker and Bowles were stunned. "If that was true, we'd lost two of our strongest areas and the weakest were yet to come," Walker says. It was a long, dark drive to the next pay phone. When the pair finally got to Roanoke late that night, they solemnly checked in with headquarters again. This time there was jubilant shouting on the other end of the phone.

"We won! We won!" the headquarters staffers said.

"Won what?" Walker asked.

"We've won the nomination."

But Walker couldn't believe it. How could Davis have won the nomination when he had lost a big chunk of Northern Virginia?

Back in Richmond, Paul Goldman was in the Democrats' "count room" at the Hotel John Marshall while the results were coming in. Things looked good for Wilder, very good. Goldman called Wilder at home. "We're going gangbusters," he said. "We got it. We're cleaning up. We'll get 2,330," more than enough to lock up the nomination.

Then he paused. "I think Jerry can do it, too."

March 31, 1985

It took until Sunday morning to get a fix on what had actually happened. The official count gave Davis almost a 400-delegate lead, just 445 short of the 1,803 he'd need to win the nomination:

Davis	1,358
Baliles	964
Uncommitted	63

"We have won," a Davis consultant declared. He then proceeded to brief reporters on how the Davis forces planned to wrap up the nomination Monday night. But few outside his own campaign were buying the inevitability of a Davis victory.

Now it was a matter of who you believed was in the toughest position Monday night, Davis for having to win about one-third of the delegates from lukewarm rural areas, or Baliles for having to win two-thirds of them. And, of course, there was always the possibility that neither man would come out of Monday night with an absolute majority and the 104 "super delegates," mostly state legislators, would tip the balance.

April 1, 1985

It wasn't even close. In the Shenandoah Valley, in Southside, in

Southwest Virginia, Baliles won just about everywhere Monday night. He didn't win enough delegates to win the nomination outright — leaving the nomination in the hands of 200 uncommitted delegates and those state legislators who were automatic delegates. But in a bit of psychological warfare, Baliles went ahead and declared victory anyway.

April 2, 1985

"The Davis people were stunned after Monday," Rose says. "For forty-eight hours, they couldn't do a thing. But Baliles was awesome."

First thing Tuesday, Baliles was on the phone to uncommitted delegates and he stayed there for virtually two days straight. Campaign workers shuffled in and out, dialing the numbers for him. "We had two phones," Rose says. "When he'd see one call was winding down, he'd signal with his finger and the other person would start calling the next one. It was awesome. We got first crack at everybody because Davis wasn't calling."

The Davis campaign had counted on knocking Baliles out in mass meetings. No one had really thought about what to do if that didn't happen. Now suddenly Davis was behind — while Doug Wilder and Mary Sue Terry, of all people, were the only Democrats securely in place on the ticket. Wilder had won about 60 percent of the delegates and he called a news conference on Tuesday to declare his victory. "A landslide endorsement by the standards of the political science profession," he proclaimed.

April 1-26, 1985

Davis vowed to fight on, and for nearly a month the two gubernatorial candidates appeared to be taking a collision course toward the convention. There were the expected credentials challenges and for a while the temporary committees that the Davis forces had seized on J-J Day took delegates and gave the lead back to Davis. The Baliles campaign howled that Davis was trying to steal the nomination and protested that the Davis-dominated credentials committees were illegal. Robb declined to get involved, at least publicly. But behind the scenes, his chief of staff, David McCloud, negotiated not only a cease-fire but a surrender. It would be a Baliles-Wilder-Terry ticket, after all. Davis? He would become party chairman for the second time.

So what happened? How did Dick Davis let the sure thing elude his grasp? There are many theories.

Maybe the Davis campaign shouldn't have gotten so worked up over Bobby Scott and the prospect of losing in Tidewater and spent more time trying to pull off an upset in Roanoke and Southwest Virginia. Maybe the Davis campaign should have paid more attention to rural areas in general. Maybe the Davis campaign shouldn't have agreed to a convention back in 1984.

But there's also the matter of Doug Wilder. Darrel Martin says Baliles lost only one locality — Virginia Beach — because of the informal alliance with Wilder. Where he won because of him is harder to say. A black minister in Southside here, a "realistic" liberal in Northern Virginia there. All in all, the alliance with Wilder mostly was a matter of rearranging the dynamics of the campaign. But rearrange them it did.

Scott Reynolds, who organized the Seventh District for Davis, reflects on it this way: "The supreme irony with the Davis campaign is that we were absolutely, fundamentally convinced it wasn't the AFL-CIO endorsement that would bring us down, not money, but Doug Wilder. And that's what happened. But it wasn't because we were linked to him but because we weren't. That is the irony."

8

The Poor Boys of Summer

April 8-10, 1985

Michael Brown lay crumpled up in the back seat of the car, moaning whenever Paul Goldman hit a rough spot in the road, which seemed entirely too frequently on the long ride out to Roanoke. For three hours plus, Goldman chattered away about politics, Wilder chided him about his lead-foot driving and every so often a low groan came up from the back seat.

Welcome to the Wilder campaign.

Doug Wilder had performed a double political miracle — he had not only locked up the nomination, but he had done it without really campaigning. From January through February, he was tied up in the General Assembly. During March he got out some, but then mostly in the eastern part of the state. Now, a week after the mass meetings, Wilder made his first real campaign trip out west, a three-day drive to Bristol and back.

Goldman had been pressing Wilder to go out to the Southwest for some time now — the region figured prominently in the campaign plan

Goldman was starting to mull over — and he insisted on going along.

Michael Brown woke up that morning with a terrible throbbing in his neck. The pain was excruciating, as if someone had put his neck in a vise and twisted it. This was a crisis. With Brown out of commission, Goldman would have to drive. Goldman didn't mind but everybody else did. Wilder, who kept a close eye on the speedometer regardless of who was driving, was especially nervous whenever Goldman was behind the wheel, practicing his New York driving habits on the roads of Virginia.

Nevertheless, the threesome got to Roanoke intact by midmorning. Brown went off to look for a heating pad while Wilder and Goldman went to a news conference.

The *Virginian-Pilot* in Norfolk had just released a poll showing 59 percent of Virginians didn't think a black could be elected to a statewide office, and at his news conference, Wilder was peppered with questions about the results.

Afterward, Wilder spent the rest of the day calling on Roanoke politicians. Not until well after dark did the Wilder campaign set off down Interstate 81, with Goldman still behind the wheel. No one really counted on Abingdon being almost three hours away. To them, Roanoke was on the western edge of the state. The idea that, geographically, a good third of the state lay beyond it hadn't really sunk in yet. And certainly no one counted on the snowstorm.

About 15 miles outside of Abingdon, the snow started to fall. The flakes were huge and they splattered on the windshield like snowballs. Goldman turned on the wipers, but they soon got loaded down with snow and groaned under its weight. Goldman turned on the defroster, but the windshield started fogging up faster than the defroster could steam it off.

By now, there was almost an inch of snow on the ground. There were no reflectors on the highway. Headlights did no good; they lit up only a thick, impenetrable wall of snow. Goldman slowed to a crawl but still had only a vague notion of where the road had gone. He was weaving back and forth between the guard rail and the shoulder on the other side looking for it. "I can't see a thing out there," he muttered.

Someone suggested they pull over and wait for the storm to pass. "No way," Wilder said. He had visions of being buried in a snowbank by the side of the road. "I'll drive." He motioned for Goldman to change seats with him. Wilder settled in behind the wheel and rolled down his window. "You put your head out the window and tell me when I'm getting off the road," he instructed Goldman. And so for the last 12 miles into Abingdon, the candidate drove down the interstate, his head sticking out one window, the campaign manager's head sticking out the other. Brown peered out the back window, letting Wilder know if anything was coming.

Wilder crept along at 25-30 miles an hour, almost feeling his way down the interstate. Suddenly, out of the darkness behind him, an angry horn blasted in his ear — and a tractor-trailer materialized out of the snow. It barreled by at what seemed 100 miles per hour, splashing everyone with a wave of slush and just missing Wilder's car — not to mention his snow-covered head — by two feet. Wilder swerved to the right to miss it, but by then the phantom truck had disappeared into the night as quickly as it had appeared.

The close call with the truck scared everybody and Wilder slowed even more. It took half an hour to go the final eight miles. "It was just brutal," Goldman recalls. The trio didn't get to Abingdon until 1 a.m.

By Wednesday, Wilder was working his way back up I-81 toward home. At a breakfast with Montgomery County Democrats, an elderly black man came up to Brown with something weighing on his mind. He motioned toward Goldman. "Is that white fellow there with y'all?" he asked.

Brown said he was. The black man seemed greatly troubled. "Listen, uh, what's his role?"

"He's the campaign manager," Brown said.

Now the man really looked worried. "Man, you can't have anybody like that," the old black man warned Brown. "He's got hair down all over his face." He looked back at Goldman and grimaced. "Where's he from?"

"New York," Brown said.

"Uh-huh," the old man grunted knowingly and then wandered away. Brown had to force himself to keep from laughing.

For Wilder, the April trip into Southwest Virginia was a brief get-acquainted venture into foreign country. These mountains and valleys, their communities nearly as pure white as the dogwoods that were just now bursting into bloom in the woods, promised to be hard country for a black Democrat from Richmond. But Wilder was surprised. The people he had met seemed genuinely glad to have Wilder come see them, wished him well and said they'd work for him. The clear air of the open country west of the Blue Ridge was a refreshing change from the oppressive, doomsday political atmosphere that hung over the capital.

Minds started to turn on the ride back to Richmond.

"I found that was fertile territory and we'd better come back," Wilder says. "I found that area did not belong to anybody and we'd better work it. And I knew next time we'd have to get off the interstate."

Would he ever.

May 1, 1985

Less than a week after Dick Davis had dropped out of the Democratic race for governor, Stan Parris quit the GOP contest. That night a beaming Wyatt Durrette was interviewed on WWBT-TV in Richmond about how he viewed the rematch with Baliles, this time for governor, and why he thought he could win.

Running with Robb and Davis, Baliles "had excellent assistance from his running mates in 1981 and I didn't," Durrette said. "This time he's likely to have more controversial running mates than I will."

How will they be controversial? the interviewer asked.

"What will make it controversial I think is the fact that one of his nominees is one of the most liberal individuals — the candidate for lieutenant governor — ever to seek statewide office in Virginia."

Paul Goldman was getting into his motel room from a night on the town just as the 11 o'clock news was coming on. He plopped down in front of the TV with an orange and a cup of yogurt and called his friend Barry Rose, the Baliles worker who had helped organize the Baliles-Wilder alliance.

Rose was watching the Channel 12 news; Goldman was flipping channels. He got to Channel 12 just as the excitable Rose shouted into the phone: "Did he say the *most* liberal?"

May 2, 1985

First thing in the morning, Goldman and Rose went to the station to see a tape of the evening news the night before and scribbled down a transcript.

Durrette's comments were honest enough and would have disappeared into the air if Goldman hadn't gotten hold of them. But Goldman knew he had something useful. He sat down with Wilder and went over the interview. It looked to Goldman like Durrette was telling fellow Republicans, hey, don't saddle me with a controversial running mate — such as Marshall Coleman. It also looked like Republicans were previewing their fall attack — call Wilder a "liberal," a "controversial" one, at that, then link him to Baliles. And notice Durrette had spoken in the plural of Baliles' "controversial running mates," meaning he was going after Terry, too.

"This is a hell of a thing," Goldman said. "Here's a man trashing

Coleman, his potential running mate, and also Mary Sue. Let's get some others in the line of fire."

Wilder's eyes lit up. He had practiced restraint all winter long while anonymous Democrats sniped at him in the newspapers. He knew he couldn't attack then. But now he had a Republican out in the clear. "He said, 'Yeah, let's go real quick, let's hit 'em on the liberal thing before they're ready for it,'" Goldman recalls.

Goldman holed up in the basement of Wilder's law office for a day and a half, researching Durrette's voting record. The plan was to list fifty issues (Goldman could only come up with forty-nine) on which Durrette and Wilder either had the same position or on which Wilder had a more conservative position, then challenge Durrette to explain how and why Wilder was so liberal. The next question was implicit: Was it because he was black? And what made the conservative Mary Sue Terry so controversial? Was it because she was a woman?

Goldman the gunfighter was about to fire off another round, except this was no warning shot. Poor Wyatt Durrette didn't even know what hit him.

May 3, 1985

The news conference was set for 2:30 p.m. Friday. At 1 p.m., Goldman was still furiously typing away on the computer. When he finished, he tried to make copies for all the reporters, but Wilder's new high-speed copier broke and Goldman had trouble coaxing more copies out of it. Goldman gave Wilder one good copy and sent him on to the news conference with instructions to read the whole six pages and read it very slowly, stalling for time until Goldman could figure out how to get some more copies.

The news conference was vintage Wilder, full of self-righteous indignation.

Wilder noted Durrette's Channel 12 comments and challenged the Republican candidate for governor to meet him at the Capitol on Monday to explain himself. Wilder went over the forty-nine issues — mostly generalities such as "continuation of our good business climate in Virginia"— and railed against Durrette for apparently deciding he couldn't beat Baliles again, so he was going to pick on "little Douglas."

The statement never mentioned race and only briefly mentioned the alleged liberalism.

But that, of course, was what the reporters questioned Wilder about and he talked about race rather freely — freely enough to make even

Goldman increasingly nervous as he listened from the back of the room.

When Durrette said Wilder was one of the most liberal candidates ever nominated for statewide office, was he using "liberal" as a "code word" for black? one reporter asked. Wilder quickly responded in the affirmative. "I don't think there's any question some people have used it in just that way. Some people may have gotten a message he didn't intend. If I'm some obnoxious liberal, what makes me so? . . . The message got over to some people. The point is: Does he intend that? . . . I don't believe he is a racist and I wouldn't call him one. The only thing he has to do is come and tell the people of Virginia he didn't mean to say those mean and nasty things."

Wilder was asked if he thought Durrette was appealing to racism by suggesting that he was controversial.

He noted that Durrette had indirectly included the ever-cautious Terry in his comments even though the only thing controversial about her was her gender. So as for the racism, "it sort of gets in the air."

May 3-4, 1985

Durrette had long since forgotten about what he had said about Baliles having controversial running mates or Wilder being the most liberal man ever nominated for statewide office. "I didn't view it as any more controversial than saying I had bacon and eggs for breakfast," he says. "I said it casually, with no forethought. It was a casual comment that was so obviously true. If I had said that about Henry Howell or [state Sens.] Joe Gartlan or Charlie Waddell who had the same record, it wouldn't have made the news."

But on the morning of May 4, his offhand comments a few nights before suddenly exploded into headlines — ugly, damning headlines — all across the state:

"Wilder says Durrette attacks may appeal to racial prejudices."

"Wilder accuses Durrette of race-related remark."

"Wilder says Durrette uses racism: Democrat claims code words draw attention to his color."

Robb's press secretary, George Stoddart, called to say the governor was upset that Wilder had gone on the attack, especially on such a sensitive subject. Other Democrats were furious — and terrified. Suddenly, all their worst fears were being realized — Wilder careening out of control, pointing his finger and shouting racism at the top of his lungs. And it was only May. What would he be like come October?

"Everybody was nervous because it was race," Goldman says. "It was like a brush-back pitch. It looked like we were out of control, but we knew exactly where we were throwing it."

The initial reaction around the state was outrage — toward Wilder. The Durrette campaign thought it had turned the attack around on Wilder. "This is a blatant attempt by Senator Wilder to inject race into this campaign," declared Durrette's press secretary. "To say that Doug Wilder is a liberal is no more of a racial code word than to say that Walter Mondale or Henry Howell . . . is liberal," Durrette said.

Don Huffman, the GOP party chairman, called on Democrats to muzzle the out-of-control Wilder: "They know that this is standard operating procedure for Doug Wilder . . . Doug Wilder's vintage brand of intimidation politics may be fine for the Democratic Party, but the people of Virginia deserve better."

The editorial reaction was equally harsh, even from normally sympathetic newspapers. "If this is the nature of political debate in Virginia this year, it's going to be a long, weary trip to the November election," wrote the *Virginian-Pilot*. "Never has L. Douglas Wilder been so artless as he's been in his exchange with Mr. Durrette."

Only a few people glimpsed the brilliance of the attack at the time.

Looking back, Don Harrison, Durrette's press secretary, can pinpoint the beginning of the end: The day Wilder went after Durrette. "I think that's when our trouble really started," Harrison says. "We had to go on the defensive and explain what Wyatt meant. And it stuck when it shouldn't have stuck."

It is difficult to overstate the impact Wilder's attack had. Wilder came out the loser in the short run. But incredibly, with one simple news conference, he made it virtually impossible for Republicans to do to him what Republicans do best — accuse Democrats of being liberals.

Wilder's unexpected outburst terrified Virginia Republicans. The foul stench of being called racists — even when it was clearly untrue — was too much for the Republicans to bear. Instead of holding their noses and flailing away at Wilder's voting record, from then on they went out of their way to avoid upsetting Wilder so he wouldn't call them that awful name.

But the Republicans didn't just back off for a few days or a few weeks, they backed off for the whole campaign. "From then on, whenever his name was mentioned, whatever the issue, we decided no, we can't afford it," Harrison says. "We just had to hope he strangled himself."

Durrette blames the media. Wilder "played the racial card early and the media let him do that with impunity," Durrette says.

In any event, Wilder's attack did more than disarm the Republicans on the liberal charge, though that was considerable enough.

Wilder, in taking a sledgehammer to swat Durrette's fly of a statement, had knocked a sizable cornerstone out of the foundation of the Republicans' campaign strategy. Durrette had wanted his running mate — whoever he may be — to attack Wilder, to "soften him up" by calling him a liberal all summer long. Then Durrette could put Baliles on the spot by challenging him to defend his controversial running mate or repudiate him. Either way, Durrette would come out the winner.

But after May 3, there were few Republicans around who wanted any part of saying anything bad about Wilder. If they couldn't call him a liberal, then they wouldn't call him anything. They just wanted to ignore him, in hopes he'd go away.

With that, Doug Wilder was already halfway home.

March 16, 1985

One Saturday night in March, Wilder went to Waynesboro to speak at an NAACP banquet in the Shenandoah Valley city. It was only a few weeks before the mass meetings and, on the way back to Richmond that night, Wilder allowed himself to think about the fall campaign beyond. Who would he rather see the Republicans nominate?

Goldman, riding with him, thought about the question a bit. "Coleman would give us a lot to shoot at," he said. Coleman was so controversial he might take the heat off Wilder. Then Goldman thought aloud some more. "[New Right activist Richard] Viguerie would be great, but he's not going to get it," He went back to his first choice. "Coleman presents an attractive target."

Wilder listened to Goldman's ruminations, then shook his head. "No," he said finally. "Chichester. Take my word for it. I'll beat Chichester."

May 31, 1985

As Republicans gathered in Norfolk to begin their two-day convention, the campaign for lieutenant governor was the only race still going on. But it was conducted with all the intensity of a political jihad — and all the subtlety of a Soviet purge.

"It was a wide-open and unabashed effort to stop Coleman," says John Alderson, a Botetourt County insurance agent and GOP activist. "You had

Giesen, Viguerie and Dawkins holding him down while Chichester beat up on him."

Down on the convention floor, up in the hospitality suites, the campaign was fought with strong drink, dark whispers and vicious fliers, many of them from the Chichester campaign. The debt Coleman ran up in his 1981 governor's race was a sore subject with many Republicans and Chichester made sure the old wound stayed raw.

But the real complaints against Coleman had little to do with money or past defeats. They were purely personal and political, the worst kind of grudges to take into the hot, close quarters of a contested convention. With Doug Wilder as the Democratic nominee, revenge-minded Republicans felt perfectly free to exact their pound of political flesh from Marshall Coleman in full public view.

"There was a feeling he was not a true Reagan Republican, that he's a Rockefeller Republican, and some felt the need to expurgate that stain out of the party," explains former GOP legislator Ray Garland.

Compared with Coleman, Chichester brought no discernible strengths to the general election ticket — he was a small-town legislator with little name recognition, no statewide following and no access to major money.

But in Norfolk, Chichester was the vehicle for a lot of Republicans to vent their frustrations, held back now in some cases for eight years. Chichester's attraction was as easy as ABC — anybody but Coleman.

June 1-2, 1985

Coleman boasted he would win a first-ballot victory.

He didn't.

He didn't even have the lead. Instead, Chichester held a 10-vote edge, while the other candidates trailed far behind. It was all over. Chichester's lead ballooned as the voting continued; he finally clinched the nomination on the fourth ballot.

By comparison, the attorney general's contest was a breeze; Virginia Beach Del. W.R. "Buster" O'Brien was nominated over token opposition.

Republicans who were scared of calling their Democratic opponent a liberal for fear they'd be called racists had now nominated a little-known legislator known mostly for being the chosen candidate of Mills Godwin, the one-time leader of Massive Resistance.

To run against a black man with more legislative experience than the last four lieutenant governors combined.

One by one, the pieces to what would be the most spectacular upset in

Virginia history were starting to fall into place.

Durrette's media adviser Ed DeBolt had pushed for Republicans to nominate just about any other candidate than Chichester. Nothing personal, but he thought a former Democrat was a dangerous symbol to add to the GOP ticket in a campaign against a black candidate. "I know what a race-baiting person Doug Wilder can be," DeBolt says. "The last person you want to run against someone as adept as that is someone who is seen as part of the Byrd Machine."

But while only a few lonely voices in the Republican Party expressed fear that the campaign would be painted as a stark choice between Virginia's past and future, Democrats relished the possibility.

The contrast was one the Baliles campaign "not only anticipated but planned for," Baliles says. His campaign had picked a campaign slogan of the "New Dominion" — a play on Virginia's traditional nickname of the "Old Dominion" that nicely capsulized both the futuristic thrust of his platform as well as the prospect of having a black and a woman as running mates.

Baliles says capturing the high ground of the future was one of the keys the 1985 campaign. "One of the characteristics of this country is the optimistic nature of the people, that we look to the future and anticipate change," Baliles says. "The three of us represented that kind of change symbolically as well as substantively."

Baliles' belief that the Democrats could successfully run a future-oriented campaign in tradition-minded Virginia also made him more optimistic about Wilder's chances than many others were. "I felt he could hold his own in the campaign," Baliles says. "He was an effective legislator. He had an engaging personality. He was politically cautious." Just as important, though, "there have been significant demographic changes in Virginia in the last 10 years or so," Baliles says, "and I was aware of those." The Republicans didn't seem to be.

June 8, 1985

The convention that nominated the barrier-breaking Baliles-Wilder-Terry ticket was remarkably boring. Democrats, for once, put their internal fights behind them.

State Sen. Virgil Goode, D-Rocky Mount, got a few roars with his nominating speech for Wilder that poked fun at Chichester's ties with Godwin: "Our candidate for lieutenant governor is not going to be a lackey for the overseer from Chuckatuck."

And Wilder's acceptance speech brought the lackadaisical convention to its feet. "Just a mile from this very site, I was a young boy growing up and playing on the cobblestone streets of Church Hill. Back then, who would have thought that someday he would rise to head the Senate Transportation Committee and be responsible for all the roads, highways and mass transit facilities in the commonwealth of Virginia?

"Back in the 1950s, when I served my country, I was unable to participate in the affairs of my state government. When I wanted to become a lawyer, I was forced to go to school outside of the state because the laws didn't permit me to attend a Virginia law school.

"Who would have thought that in the lifetime of that young soldier he would rise to become chairman of the Senate Privileges and Elections Committee, responsible for writing all the election laws in Virginia?

"When I entered the Senate in 1970, I was ranked forty out of forty. Who would have believed that in the career of that freshman legislator, he would rise in the judgment of his peers, both Republicans and Democrats, to become ranked as one of the five most effective lawmakers?

"And who would have thought that all that has occasioned in these past years would occur in my lifetime, to where today in this great coliseum, in a hall filled with the party that has controlled the General Assembly during this century, that I would be standing here as the Democratic nominee for the office of lieutenant governor of the common-wealth of Virginia?"

For a moment, you could almost hear a tear drop.

"God, he could wave the flag," says lawyer Bill Parks, the Bath County Democratic chairman. "He had the best speech at the convention." Parks remembers sitting out on the convention floor with his friend Charlie Holbert, a biology teacher from Alleghany County. Holbert was shaking his head, whispering that Wilder didn't have a chance. Parks wasn't so sure. "I said, 'Listen to that speech, Charlie, listen to that speech.'"

June 9, 1985

The post-convention affair at Richmond financier McLain O'Ferrall's home was something of an oddity for the ragtag Wilder campaign: a fund-raiser and a high-dollar one at that. Of course, all things are relative. The $1,000-per-person fund-raiser brought in $42,000, the biggest one-night haul of the whole Wilder campaign. Meanwhile, Baliles and Durrette, each looking at raising and spending $3 million, were hitting contributors who could write checks for that much at one time.

Jordan Goldman, Governor Robb's senior counsel and no relation to Paul Goldman, remembers the O'Ferrall fund-raiser as a typical Wilder campaign production. This Goldman was baffled, not to mention hurt and outraged, at the charges the other Goldman later made about how Robb's staff did little to help Wilder, especially when it came to fund-raising. "The Robb people bent over backwards [to help Wilder] at the expense of the other two," Jordan Goldman says. "I spent at least ten times as much time on the Doug Wilder campaign as I devoted to Jerry Baliles and Mary Sue together."

Jordan Goldman's work started in earnest with the O'Ferrall fund-raiser. He takes credit for personally calling about twenty people to see if they could contribute; about eight did. "Was it difficult? The answer is yes. No one thought he had a chance. It had nothing to do with where he was on the political spectrum or the color of his skin, but as a political investment, it wasn't there. My pitch was a moral pitch, a strong appeal to people's sense of history."

Jordan Goldman got to O'Ferrall's home on time, promptly at 6:30 p.m., so he could thank the people he had badgered into coming. It was one of those viciously hot days so common to Richmond in June. "Nobody wanted to be there," he recalls. "I walked in and Paul Goldman was on the couch reading a newspaper. A couple of people I had called walked in. I talked to them. Paul kept reading his newspaper. The senator wasn't there yet. People were standing around sweltering. Someone said, "Should we give him a call?" He was at home. He had gotten delayed somehow. But people were there forty-five minutes standing around without the senator and the whole thing was about only an hour. That characterizes the disorganization and disarray that followed. You don't get people back with that kind of performance."

Summer 1985

The Wilder-Chichester race was on. One anonymous Republican gloated at his convention: "If Chichester's alive on Election Day, he's in." Many Democrats feared the same thing. "I can't remember anyone outside the Wilder campaign in midsummer telling me they thought Wilder had a prayer," says John Jameson, Terry's campaign manager. "Wilder scared a lot of Democrats."

One day in early summer, in the coalfield town of Wise, Mayor Glenn Craft was down at the local garage. So was an old man he knew. They got to talking about what all good Southwest Virginia Democrats talk about when they get together — politics. The old man looked Craft squarely in the eyes. "I've been a Democrat all my life," he said. "My father and grandfather were Democrats before me. But I'll be damned if I'm going to vote for a nigger."

"Why not?" Craft asked.

The old man hemmed and hawed. It's like this, he finally explained. His father had often been accused of being such a partisan Democrat "that he'd even vote for a nigger if he ran as a Democrat." The old man had always taken that as the supreme insult. Now, indeed, he was confronted with that awful reality — a black man running on the Democratic ticket — and he just couldn't bring himself to pull the lever. "I know it's not right," he said, "but that's the way I feel."

When even the yellow-dog Democrats of the Southwest — so-called because it was said they'd vote for an old yellow-dog as long as it was a Democrat — felt that strongly about the subject, Wilder's odds seemed long indeed.

Scott Reynolds, an AFL-CIO staffer, saw the coming campaign this way: "I was convinced if John Chichester had his name on the ballot and spent $150 on bumper stickers, as long as folks knew his name, the racists down in the Fifth [Southside] would elect him. I thought the sophisticates in Northern Virginia wouldn't get it because they're not interested in state races and I thought Democrats in Tidewater wouldn't turn out" because they were still mad over what Wilder had done to Pickett and Davis. "I figured the most he could get was 45 percent and he could claim that as a victory." And at 45 percent, Reynolds was being pretty generous compared to other Democrats.

Robb says even Wilder himself was unsure about his chances. "Doug never gave me the impression that he could win the general election until way late in the game," Robb says. He's convinced that Goldman's plan was just to win the nomination, "then go out and be a martyr in the general [election], so he could blame the loss on Virginia's backward ways." Wilder and Goldman say that's not so.

Questions of race and record aside, Democrats had two good reasons to believe the Wilder campaign was doomed.

One was Paul Goldman. He refused to hire even the most elementary campaign help — a scheduler, for instance. The other reason followed closely behind. Money. Wilder had little of it and wasn't expected to get much more. Further, he had no fund-raising staff and repeatedly ignored pleas to hire one.

Both subjects came to dominate Wilder's summer, as Robb tried repeatedly to get Wilder to hire a new campaign manager and pay more attention to fund-raising.

Two weeks after the convention, Chuck Colgan Jr., one of the Draft Bagley leaders, met with Wilder to let him know there were no hard feelings. Wilder was friendly enough. "We kinda laughed it off," Colgan says. But Wilder's campaign organization also seemed comical.

Colgan picked up a Wilder bumper sticker. It broke apart in his hand. The campaign had gotten a bad batch. Other materials were non-existent and sometimes it seemed the Wilder campaign was that way, too. "We couldn't get phone calls returned," Colgan says. "Or signs. We had to go through an extraordinary effort to get signs. We kept calling for signs and couldn't get any. I think they only had nine hundred for all of Northern Virginia. Hell, we could use nine hundred in Manassas alone."

Tommy Jordan, a railroad union man in Roanoke, was in Richmond for a labor meeting in the summer and tried to schedule Wilder to speak at a union dinner in the fall. Jordan asked Goldman who kept the candidate's schedule. Goldman said he did, then proceeded to open a file folder stuffed with loose sheets of legal paper, some of which fluttered to the floor. "That was his schedule," Jordan says, still aghast. "We're not spending money on staff," Goldman explained. Jordan could see that. "Who's helping you?" he asked hesitantly. "You're looking at him," Goldman said with a big grin.

If outsiders came away with the impression that the Wilder campaign was a catastrophe in the making, imagine what the Democratic insiders in Richmond were thinking.

Goldman's personal style irritated many people. Often he was mysteriously unavailable during regular working hours when the other campaigns had questions for him. Then, says Sandy Bowen, Baliles' deputy campaign manager, "he'd show up at 11:30 p.m. Just when we were dragging ourselves home, here comes Paul Goldman, looking like someone put him in a paper bag and shook him up, and he wants to have a grand philosophical discussion."

This did little to inspire confidence in the Wilder campaign among the other Democratic camps. The governor, most of all, was concerned. "There was no campaign," Robb says. "There never was a campaign." At least not in the usual sense of the word.

Goldman had made a conscious decision to simply ignore certain parts of traditional campaigning. He didn't bother to set up a field organization. He figured the Baliles people would take care of their running mate, too.

Wilder and Goldman, however, took the bare-bones campaign to even greater extremes:

• They did next to nothing to energize and mobilize Wilder's base. Goldman simply assumed blacks, labor and liberals would figure out what was going on and be motivated enough to vote without anyone having to encourage them (a strategy that nearly backfired). He made no effort to contact black ministers, union organizers, liberal activists, the whole network that normally would be working on Wilder's behalf.

• They had no one researching issues. If Wilder, after sixteen years in the state Senate, didn't know about it, then it must not be much of an issue, Goldman reasoned. And Wilder wasn't going to be running on the issues, anyway.

• They had no media consultant, no pollster, no professional help of any kind. Goldman said he would handle the campaign's media, even though he had no experience producing TV commercials.

• Finally, they had no formal fund-raising organization. They simply counted on the other two campaigns and Robb to raise money for them and spent much of their own time complaining that the governor wasn't doing enough.

"Paul worked on a limited part of the campaign, the exciting parts — media and strategy — while the rest of the campaign he basically ignored, including fund-raising," Robb says. "I got very exasperated. He's a creative thinker, but you have to have someone to manage the campaign. Paul is a brilliant strategist but as a campaign manager, he's a disaster."

Money was the other big concern fellow Democrats had. How in the world was Wilder going to raise enough money to finance a credible-looking campaign?

Incredibly, Wilder steadfastly refused to hire a fund-raiser and, not so incredibly, Goldman seemed not the least bit interested in the subject. Actually, Goldman says, "I used to talk to Doug about money a lot. He'd say, 'Don't worry. We'll have it.' He'd say, 'How much do you need? Don't worry. It'll be there.' "

During the campaign for the nomination, Wilder didn't need much money. But even after the nomination, his campaign was a pitiful sight. Organizing even a simple reception was a major ordeal. "Others seemed to be able to get their liquor free but I went to the ABC store," says Michael Brown, who drew that assignment quite frequently.

Goldman assumed Robb would "take care" of Wilder's fund-raising, putting out the word among the big contributors to unlock the bank. Just how much Robb helped Wilder raise money, like almost everything else involving the two men, is an area of some dispute. Goldman accuses Robb and his staff of "sitting on their hands" and producing only a meager amount of money for Wilder. That accusation sends most Robb staffers into a fury. "To say we sat on our hands is about the most preposterous statement you could make," says Jordan Goldman, a Robb staffer. "It has no basis in fact or reality. We did everything possible."

Robb says from the beginning the Wilder campaign was one of his priorities, for obvious political reasons. And as the summer went along, Robb became increasingly frustrated.

"I made calls around the country, especially to influential black leaders," soliciting money, Robb says. Many times they wanted to speak to Wilder directly and he passed their names and numbers on to his office, but the calls never got returned and the contributions never got solicited.

"I had many calls from friends who were not getting letters answered or phone calls returned," Robb says. "They were getting turned off and a significant source of money was going untapped. Political money is funny. It has to be courted. Even PACs have to be courted. I'm sure any campaign loses a few, but this campaign lost all these folks."

Robb and his staffers say they were quite creative in trying to find ways to raise money for Wilder. Lynda Robb was on the phone to people as far away as California, hoping to use the old Johnson arm-twisting magic. When Jordan Goldman was in Norfolk for the naming of his sister's son, at a ceremony with upward of seventy people present, "I basically turned that into a rally for Doug. I had little groups talking about Doug. Those are things Paul Goldman doesn't know. Hell, at a family gathering that personal, if I make a conscientious decision to inject politics into it, because you think it's that important, that speaks to a strong commitment. And that's not radically different from what [press secretary] George Stoddart was doing or [chief-of-staff] David McCloud was doing or [staffers] Phil Abraham or Carolyn Moss. We had no responsibility to do anything. If any of those fellows think we did, then they have a misunderstanding of being in the public employ."

Meanwhile, the Baliles campaign also was trying to get Wilder into the fund-raising business.

In June, Baliles fund-raiser Bill Wiley took a friend of his to see Goldman about the possibility of hiring his friend's Washington fund-raising firm. Goldman didn't seem to think it was necessary and kept talking about a fund-raiser Wilder had coming up in Washington as proof that he was raising money. Wiley pressed him on the details, but Goldman just shrugged his shoulders and said the hosts were taking care of everything. Wiley came away suspicious. "My friend went back and snooped around for me and found out nothing had been done."

After that, Wiley tried repeatedly to get the Wilder campaign to hire his friend's company. But Goldman was adamant. He said the pros charged too much money. The only thing left for Wiley to do was to put out the word among Baliles contributors that any money they could see fit to pass on to Wilder would be appreciated by both campaigns. How many did, he doesn't know. "They could have raised twice as much money as they did raise, but there was no apparatus whatsoever," Wiley says.

In the fall of 1984, Wilder had been the keynote speaker at the state NAACP convention. John Edwards, a white Roanoke lawyer who was then city Democratic chairman, remembers that Wilder spoke about his campaign and concerns that he wouldn't be able to raise money from the "traditional sources."

"Well, black people have money too," Wilder said, smiling.

Edwards remembers thinking to himself, "Hmm, I hadn't really thought about it that way."

Apparently no one else had, either.

One of the great untold stories of the Wilder campaign — and one with political implications well beyond Virginia — is how much money he raised from blacks. In tapping a heretofore untapped source of campaign money, Wilder showed that he and other black candidates need not be held back by the fear of not being able to raise money from the "traditional sources." Wilder's campaign was funded largely by contributors who sent in their money in chunks of $200 or less. More specifically, Wilder demonstrated for perhaps the first time the financial clout of a new social group in America — the emerging black middle class.

Goldman estimates (and bookkeeper Chuck Nichollson confirms) that about 60 percent of Wilder's contributors were black. With collection plates being passed at black churches on Sunday morning, that figure isn't necessarily surprising. The more significant figure, however, is this: About 40 percent of Wilder's money — approximately $275,000 — came from black contributors. And as we shall see, that was easily only a fraction of what Wilder could have raised from Virginia blacks if he had had the full-time fund-raiser Robb wanted.

In funding his campaign with contributions from blacks, Wilder was simply doing what other candidates have always done — soliciting money from his base.

But contributing money to a black candidate was "a new idea," even for blacks, says Roger Gregory, Wilder's law partner. "Normally the solicitation is for the black vote, not money. Sometimes candidates might even pay groups to help get you to the polls." For blacks to contribute financially "is a phenomenon," he says.

The first surprise in studying Wilder's financial reports and interviewing his unofficial fund-raisers is how much money came from blacks. The second surprise is how little he received.

When Hell Froze Over

One need only skim the reports to think of many other Virginia blacks who might have contributed to the Wilder campaign had they been asked. There was no organized fund-raising campaign among black churches, for instance. And the fund-raisers that Jackie Epps and her friends organized focused almost entirely on Richmond and Petersburg and neighboring counties; only a haphazard attempt was made to raise money among the sizable black population of Tidewater, none at all, really, among blacks in other parts of the state. Epps and her three helpers all worked full-time jobs; none had any experience in fund-raising. If Wilder had had four professional fund-raisers working full-time, even if they only worked the black community, it is not hard at all to imagine him raising several times again as much money as he did.

It was at the epicenter of Virginia's new black middle class — black lawyers and other professionals on Richmond's Main Street — where Wilder's "secret" fund-raising campaign started.

Jacqueline "Jackie" Epps had been an assistant commonwealth's attorney in Newport News; later she landed a job in the attorney general's office under Jerry Baliles, where she was senior assistant attorney general for criminal affairs. During the early winter of 1985, Epps began to wonder why she didn't see anyone out organizing for Wilder. "I just started calling people, mostly lawyers," she says. "I'd call people and they'd want to help but they didn't know how. I'd say, 'We need money.' But no one on the staff had time to do it." One day she began badgering a lawyer friend about why he wasn't organizing fund-raising events for Wilder. It was important, she argued, for Wilder to run a well-funded campaign and where else was money going to come from but other black professionals like him? But her friend shrugged and gave some excuse about being too busy.

Epps, though, kept after him so much that one day he turned the argument around on her. If she was so concerned about Wilder not having enough money, why didn't she raise some herself?

That's how Epps one day found herself in Wilder's law office, directed by the candidate to the basement to find Paul Goldman. But he didn't seem terribly interested in talking about raising money. Instead, he was scurrying back and forth around the office, absorbed in some other project he kept muttering about. Epps had to practically run after Goldman, peppering him with questions, just to keep him in sight.

How do you organize a fund-raiser? she asked. Goldman waved her off with brusque, one-sentence answers. You need some sponsors first.

What are sponsors? How do you get them?

Goldman seemed exasperated at having to stop what he was doing and explain such an elementary fund-raising concept to this woman who had barged into his basement unannounced. You need some people to pledge money in advance, so you'll know the event will be a success before it starts, he said wearily.

Epps gamely decided to give it a try. She and some friends sat down and drew up a list of 135 people they knew. Then they started calling. "We decided to make it $100 a person. We thought that was high," Epps says. Looking back, maybe it wasn't high enough. Epps and her friends were startled at how easy it was. Nearly half the people they called — fifty-four — agreed to be sponsors at $100 apiece. Some volunteered to give even more money. Epps was delirious with excitement. "We hadn't even had it yet and here we have more than $6,000 already," she says. She and her friends sat down and made another list of people they knew. This time they came up with five hundred names. Each one was mailed an invitation to a $100-per-person fund-raiser in late March. Then the phones started ringing. Regrets? No — people wanting to know why they hadn't been invited. Next thing she knew, Epps was mailing off another four hundred invitations.

The fund-raiser was a smashing success. A jazz band played, young black professionals sipped wine and nibbled cheese. And Doug Wilder, after circulating through the crowd, took home close to $15,000, the biggest one-night amount of the campaign up to that time.

"The candidate was so pleased that the next thing I knew, he was referring people to me to talk about fund-raising," Epps says. "I guess it was by default. It just happened. He'd say, 'You're in charge of fund-raising.' I'd say, 'Don't say that. You need someone recognized in the business community,' and he said, 'No, I need workers.' "

And so as spring moved into summer, Epps found herself setting up other fund-raisers — in Richmond, in Petersburg, in Tidewater. Helping her were three other black women, none of whom had any experience in raising money, either. Dot Powell and Margaret Spencer were both assistant attorneys general. Jackie Frazier, an old college classmate (Howard '68), was the only non-lawyer of the bunch. She worked for the city of Richmond, coordinating some of the city's federal programs. As a group, they were familiar with a fair amount of territory within an hour or so drive of the capital: Powell was a native of Dinwiddie County outside Petersburg; Spencer grew up in King and Queen County between Richmond and Tappahannock; Epps came from Newport News; Frazier was a native Richmonder.

These four women, who worked their regular jobs by day and organized fund-raising receptions by night, were the unheralded cogs of Wilder's fund-raising machine.

Theirs was gritty, unglamorous work. They came up with mailing lists out of their heads. "I had a little note pad, always jotting down names," Frazier says. They addressed invitations themselves. "They began to call me Mrs. ZIP code after a while," Frazier says, because she came to know them all by heart. They even set up many of the receptions themselves. "I used to laugh that I was lugging so much liquor around in the trunk of my car that if I was hit, it would go up in smoke," Frazier says.

They had to cajole, persuade and otherwise sweet-talk time and money out of reluctant blacks who had never given money to a candidate before and weren't sure this was the time to start, even if a black man was running. "I had people tell me, 'It's a waste of money, he can't win,'" Epps says. "I'd say, 'He can win and you ought to be a part of it. Even if he doesn't win, you ought to be a part of it.'"

For this, Epps, Frazier, Powell and Spencer received no recognition for the key role they played in a historic campaign except the private thanks of the candidate. Not even the other Democratic campaigns, to this day, know the full story of what Epps and her friends did. "I know she organized some events for them," says Bill Wiley. "I don't know what specifically she was doing."

Of course, Wiley and Epps were working on such entirely different monetary scales as to be almost laughable. "With Jerry, our cutoff was $5,000," Wiley says. "If someone could give that, they'd get a personal visit" from the candidate. If they were only going to give less than that, it wasn't worth the candidate's time.

Wilder, meanwhile, received $5,000 or more from only ten contributors — the largest being $13,125 from the state AFL-CIO; the others were business friends of his from Richmond or such traditional big givers as United Coal of Bristol ($5,000) and Tidewater psychiatrist Ron Dozoretz ($6,000). Instead of graciously calling on board chairmen and developers and financiers to pocket big checks, Wilder spent his time bouncing from one $100-per-person fund-raiser to the next — and Epps often had to struggle just to get the price that high.

Many people Epps sought as potential hosts for fund-raising receptions seemed horrified at the prospect of asking their friends to give $100. "I kept telling people, they will respond, but people would say 'no, not in Petersburg' [or wherever]. It was a learning experience for a lot of them. They said, "How about $10?' But you can go into Newport News and Norfolk and ask for $100." And get it.

Instead of targeting one person for $5,000 the way the Baliles campaign would, Wilder's fund-raisers had to fill up an entire room with people just to get that much.

"We'd sit down and say this group should give $5,000 and wouldn't turn 'em loose," says Frazier. "It was very thrilling to see what you could do. In the beginning, when we started talking about $100, people would say that's a lot of money. Then as time went on and we got all the good press, it wasn't as difficult. In the end, we were talking $250. I guess it is a phenomenon how it was done. It all adds up, all those nickels and dimes and fives and tens."

June-July 1985

One flashpoint for Wilder's fund-raising was the Democrats' joint campaign committee, chaired by Richmond lawyer Larry Framme.

The committee's major role was to run an unprecedented get-out-the-vote campaign with an equally unprecedented $110,000 contribution from the Democratic National Committee.

The Democrats' expensive GOTV drive was kept well-hidden until it was unleashed on the streets Nov. 5. But it may well have tipped the balance in one race — Wilder's. It also provoked repeated complaints from the Wilder campaign.

The GOTV drive targeted precincts where Democrats usually got 70 percent or more of the vote. In practice, that meant the "targeted" precincts were mostly black and the get-out-the-vote campaign became synonymous with a get-out-the-black-vote campaign.

But Paul Goldman didn't like the plan. He didn't like it one bit.

He saw all that money the joint campaign was getting and wanted it for himself — for a Wilder TV blitz aimed at white swing voters.

Goldman also didn't like all the emphasis on black voters. He contended that Democrats didn't need to make a special effort to go after blacks, that as long as Wilder was seen as a strong candidate, then blacks would turn out in unprecedented numbers. He turned out to be dead wrong, but no one knew that yet.

In an attempt to get the money for his own campaign's use, Goldman waged a guerrilla war at the joint campaign committee's weekly meetings. "Paul would either not show up or send Michael Brown, who would either complain or not say anything," says Bobby Watson, the former Davis campaign manager who now had become the party's executive director. And when Goldman did show, "we had some heated meetings, in which Paul made some veiled threats and tempers flared," says Terry campaign manager John Jameson.

Goldman the gunfighter played his favorite role to the hilt. "I never threatened anybody," he says, "but there were a lot of meetings when I took my gun out and cleaned it, spun the chamber around, let them see the bulge in my pocket."

As a result, there were a lot of people out there who thought Goldman was the last thing Wilder needed running his campaign and set out to have him removed.

The governor, for one.

Talk of replacing Goldman was almost an everyday topic of conversation among Democratic "insiders" in Richmond. "There was a feeling of 'OK, Doug, you really fooled all of them and got the nomination. Now it's time to get serious and hire yourself a real staff,' " Barry Rose says. Goldman would be allowed to stay, of course, as long as he wasn't in charge.

Goldman recognized the advantages of having someone else publicly responsible. His concern, though, was mostly one of image. "Paul was looking for someone to be the front man," Rose says. "They wanted a white, male conservative, preferably one who looked like a member of the Richmond establishment." Lots of names were kicked around, though that was as far as the notion got.

The real push to replace Goldman as campaign chief, though, came in June and July from Robb and his chief of staff, David McCloud.

"They were chopping on his neck for months," says Baliles campaign manager Darrel Martin. "They wanted someone they could control and they were seeking a more orthodox campaign structure."

"They said he was abrasive and offensive," Wilder says of the complaints lodged against Goldman. "I told them I would handle it," which was Wilder's way of doing nothing. But the pressure stayed on.

Robb was becoming increasingly irritated because he was referring potential contributors to Wilder and their calls weren't getting returned. "I had to call Vernon Jordan a couple of times [because Wilder didn't]. I said, 'Doug, you can't do this. My credibility is at stake. You've got to call these people.' I ended up making excuses for him. 'Well, he has to spend all his time on the road.' Even the best campaigns have weak spots, but this one simply wasn't a campaign. I kept saying you can't have an unmanned office. He said, 'You're right, you're right. I'll do it. I'll take care of it.' I'm sure he felt defensive."

But no matter how much Robb reminded Wilder that he needed to pay attention to simple things like returning phone calls and Wilder assured him he'd do a better job, Wilder never seemed to pay any heed. "It was a source of enormous frustration," Robb says. "I counted to ten any number of times."

Finally Robb became so exasperated that one day he sat Wilder down in the governor's office and, like a stern father to a lackadaisical teen-age son, explained the political facts of life. "I told him in a straightforward fashion that he needed a campaign manager and a fund-raising director. I told him Paul was a brilliant strategist but he needed someone to manage the campaign organizationally. There was no campaign. Never. . . . I'm sure he felt I was heavy-handed with him."

Wilder's response, Robb says, was " 'anybody I want I can't get.' I suggested people, places he could go to." In 1985, only Virginia and New Jersey were having statewide races. "All the political junkies around the country would just love to come in and manage this campaign," Robb says. "I think he just assumed, 'I can't get who I want.'"

Eventually Robb, seeing he was getting nowhere with Wilder, deputized McCloud to talk some sense into the recalcitrant candidate.

McCloud and Wilder had lunch on July 9. "I talked to him at some length about getting someone to manage the thing," McCloud says. "He basically told me he was going to do it and agreed with it. He understood he had a problem."

McCloud came back to the governor's office and thought, at long last, Wilder would do something. In reality, Wilder had simply conned McCloud into thinking he would.

"Doug said, 'They're trying to drive a wedge between you and me,' " Goldman says. "Doug would say, 'they're after your scalp, we'll play 'em along.' " But Wilder never felt any urgency to change his lineup. Keeping the staff small so he could save money — in hopes of having enough for a big TV blitz in the fall — was the focal point of the Wilder campaign from the beginning. And everything they were doing worked, so there was no real crisis to change, Goldman says. "Some people were coming in saying, 'You need more staff.' They were like Chicken Little. They'd say you need someone to do TV. I'd say we've got someone to do TV. They'd say you need someone to raise money. We raised half a million. You need someone to write speeches. I wrote the speeches. I didn't even have a secretary. I typed everything myself in the computer and ran it off myself. I'm probably the only campaign manager who didn't have a secretary."

As for the Robb-McCloud charges that Goldman wasn't very well organized, Goldman responds testily: "This is what I had to deal with. The worst kind of character assassination. If you don't kiss their ass, they say the worst possible things about you. It's personal. It's totally personal to them. If you show any independence, they don't want you. I wanted to get Doug

Wilder elected but all they cared about was perfume and looking good on TV.

"And this is what they're admitting to. You're scratching the surface of the character assassination of the Robb administration. I worked for the guy and never asked for a damn thing. I took a hell of a lot of abuse for him. I've run two campaigns in Virginia — Howell and Wilder — and both won. What more do I have to do?"

Those comments give a clue to the depth of feeling in the Wilder and Robb camps. From Wilder's perspective, Robb hadn't helped a damn bit during the campaign for the nomination. In fact, Wilder thought Robb had purposely tried to hurt them with his call for challenges. Now he saw Robb moving in, apparently trying to seize control of the campaign, in effect setting up a self-serving rationale for a Wilder defeat: Well, we tried to get someone in there to manage the campaign, but he wouldn't listen. If Robb really wanted to help Wilder, why didn't he start calling up all his business buddies and make them put checks for $25,000 each in the mail?

From Robb's point of view, the governor, despite the required public vows of neutrality, had been privately helpful to Wilder during his quest for the nomination, telling people quietly that Wilder could win, declining to lead any anti-Wilder charge, talking others out of doing so. Robb saw his "put up or shut up" challenge to Wilder's anonymous opponents in the shadows as just what the beleaguered Wilder campaign needed. Now he saw how disastrously ragtag Wilder's campaign was and tried to be helpful, though the candidate was ungrateful and the campaign manager was downright hostile.

Wilder didn't realize how difficult it was to raise money for him, Robb says. The governor couldn't ask his chief fund-raiser to help, for instance, not after the embarrassing incident during the Pickett crisis when Wilder asked Al Smith to take him to the all-white Commonwealth Club and Smith refused. "I never asked Al for help with Doug," Robb says. "I know I kept getting little hints from Doug and Paul that Al was not raising enough money for him, but we were lucky to keep him on board after that incident. Al had considered Doug a friend and thought he had been done in by a friend. It was a long-term hurt and Al is not one to recover quickly. He was badly burned by the incident at the Commonwealth Club. I think he felt set up."

Robb also says Wilder was frequently complaining about various political figures who he said weren't doing enough for him. "It was a fairly standard occurrence for him to have a litmus test of potential offenses and I'd hold his hand and say that's not what it means, or if there was a problem, I'd take care of it," Robb says.

Goldman, however, cites the July 9 lunch between McCloud and Wilder as proof of Robb's perfidy. Tuesday, July 9, was three days after Goldman had announced the Wilder campaign was desperately short of cash — the crucial "poor-boy" strategy, which he purposely never explained to fellow Democrats — and a day after Wilder had announced his plans to visit every city and county in the state by station wagon. "The guy has gotten through the convention. The strategy is being set, the tour's announced, the guy's got a three-man campaign, the guy's going on the road in a month and they're trying to get the campaign manager fired. Robb didn't play a harmonious influence. They didn't say they'd raise the money. This was after the tour was announced, after the poor-boy strategy. Obviously they didn't like it. They saw it would be an independent show."

Goldman's answer hints at another reason why Wilder didn't hire additional staff. Control.

A small, secretive staff had advantages beyond economy. It meant Wilder and Goldman could run the campaign the way they wanted, without interference from the many self-appointed Democratic wise men who now rushed to give them advice.

Wilder ran a closed shop, in which Goldman was the only real outsider. When volunteers were needed for a particular project, he called in family members to help. He'd already hired one nephew, Michael Brown. In April, he hired another, Chuck Nichollson, to keep the books. When Nichollson, a former bank vice president and now a partner in his own accounting firm, set down to go through the records, he discovered something unusual. Wilder had set up a unique accounting system all his own, an incredibly complex system of checks and balances that meant no one person had control over the money from the time it came in until the time it was deposited in the bank. Nichollson was impressed because it meant Wilder never had to depend on just one person for everything. He was always in control. Indeed, only one person besides the bookkeeper had complete access to the financial figures, and that was Wilder. He even wrote all the checks himself. Goldman had only a vague notion of how much money was in the bank at any given moment. This was Wilder's campaign in more ways than one.

Summer is a quiet time in politics, a time for raising money and recruiting volunteers, a time for making the rounds at countless smoky barbeques and blue-ribboned country fairs across the rural heartland of Virginia.

Michael Brown drove Wilder most of the time and watched his uncle, the fearless power-broker who had stared down Owen Pickett and an entire party, suddenly turn timid. The truth was Wilder was a masterful politician, but a rusty campaigner. He hadn't had opposition since his first race in December 1969. He might be quite at home bluffing and blustering with his white colleagues in the halls of the General Assembly, but venturing into an all-white crowd at a barbecue in Southside Virginia was something else entirely.

"Although he's extroverted, in the beginning of this campaign, it was a little difficult to get him to extend his hand," Brown recalls, "especially in what might be considered hostile groups. But he grew into it during the campaign until he didn't care where he went. In the beginning he would be a little stand-offish. The crowd looked like a big sea and he was a little afraid to step into it. He would feel good if he was in the company of a friend so he would spend a lot of time with that one friend," and, unless someone came up to him, Wilder was hesitant to go up to them.

Once in early summer, Wilder went to a fish fry in Suffolk. Brown remembers Wilder standing at the edge of the white crowd, tentatively looking it over. "What do you think?," he asked Brown. "I said 'go ahead, just start walking around.' I tried to get a couple people to come up and give them literature. But as time wore on, he'd pull up his sleeves, loosen his tie," and wade in. By the time Wilder got to the mountains of Southwest Virginia in early August, he was being hailed as a natural campaigner, the best rural barnstormer Virginia has seen since Henry Howell.

What to do during the summer was a big question for the Wilder campaign. Wilder was such an underdog he had to do something to generate some positive — and free — publicity during the summer. He had to first show that he enjoyed broad support within his own party and win over the Democratic conservatives who were all for Baliles and Terry but were quite skeptical of this black fellow they'd heard was so liberal. Wilder also had to begin demonstrating that he could represent all Virginians, not just blacks. Yet he had to do it in a way that neutralized the racial factor instead of heightening it. That alone was a tall order. And Goldman had his own requirements. Every time he added up Wilder's numbers, conservative rural Virginia was the killer. Even though most of Virginia's vote was now in metro areas, any winning margin Wilder would get there wouldn't be enough to offset the thundering defeat he could expect in one rural county after another. But how to do all those things? Goldman sat in his windowless basement and began thinking.

Wilder had gotten a warm reception on his brief trip out to Southwest Virginia in April. He needed to go back and spend more time there. Plus there was such extraordinary media interest in Wilder that just about anything he said or did would be broadcast from one end of the state to another . . .

Just before the convention, Goldman went to Wilder with a plan: The tour.

Goldman wanted Wilder to get in a car and visit every city and county in Virginia. For maximum media coverage, he should do it in the summer, when nothing else would be happening. And he should start in Southwest Virginia. The mountain folk in those coalfield counties felt so overlooked by the rest of Virginia that they'd likely embrace any candidate who took the time to visit them, Goldman argued.

The tour would be the major pitch to not only Southwest but rural areas throughout Virginia. Also, Goldman says, "I wanted to make some non-ideological TV commercials that would appeal to conservatives." Tour footage of Wilder slapping backs and shaking hands at country stores would be perfect.

But Wilder was skeptical. He was imagining all the things that could go wrong. Campaigning by car for two months? It didn't seem very dignified to him. But Goldman was insistent, tossing out one argument after another why Wilder should get in the car right now.

Finally, Wilder agreed to at least think about it. He told Goldman to go ahead and work up a schedule and he'd look at it. But he was making no promises. Goldman spent two days in the basement with a Magic Marker and a state highway map, playing connect-the-dots. "Paul would be at his desk muttering, 'Now if we go through here . . . no, can't do that,' " says Larry Wilder. "My father joked that Paul made up most of these towns."

The more Goldman worked on it, the better he thought his idea was. Goldman got the idea that Wilder could call on rural weekly newspapers along the way. When he saw how many little towns in the Southwest had weeklies, Goldman began to mutter. If he wanted Wilder to go to every town with a newspaper, no matter how small, damn, he'd have to stop in almost every town he went through. *That's it!* Goldman had just had another brainstorm. Why not announce in advance that Wilder was going to stop in every town he went through, no matter how small?

Goldman, meanwhile, was running a personal campaign to get Wilder to say "yes" to the tour. Goldman tagged along on a mid-June trip to the annual chicken festival in Crewe, a small town in Southside, and brought along the map he had drawn the tour route on. He spotted Edgar Bacon — a former Lee County legislator — showed him the map and asked him what he thought. Goldman had planned to start at the Cumberland Gap, the westernmost tip of Virginia. That just happened to be in Bacon's home county. Bacon was ecstatic. He went up to Wilder and started strong-arming him into doing it.

Wilder gave in.

The next day the *Virginian-Pilot* and a string of smaller papers published the first Mason-Dixon poll. The governor's race and attorney general's race were dead heats.

But Chichester led Wilder by 13 percent, 42-29.

From the outside looking in, it looked like the Republicans had it made. Sure, the Democrats had nominated Jerry Baliles, a Robb-style moderate-conservative, for governor, but they had put him at the head of a vulnerable rainbow ticket. The Republican ticket of Durrette-Chichester-O'Brien might not have been sexy — some complained that the GOP had nominated "three dull white guys" — but it was at least consistent and conservative, two good Virginia traits.

Behind the scenes, though, the Republicans started off woefully divided — and things only got worse.

While the Davis supporters generally signed on for Baliles without question, many Parris people left the Republican convention as bitter as ever. The Chichester-Coleman campaign had only widened the breach between the moderates and the conservatives, between the old Byrd Democrats and the "real" Republicans.

But no matter what problems the party had, Chichester was always seen as the Republicans' one sure winner.

If Doug Wilder was blazing new territory, though, so was John Chichester. In a state as race-conscious as Virginia, running against the state's most prominent black politician had its own set of problems. Several times, Chichester had to stop himself from using one of his favorite expressions — "things are as clear as black and white."

Chichester found himself in a difficult position in another way. Suddenly it seemed every Republican in the state had advice for him on how he ought to run his campaign. Moderates warned him never to mention Wilder's name, lest any attack be construed as a racial appeal. Conservatives, though, wanted Chichester to be the ticket's chief hatchet-man.

This put Chichester in a bind.

Chichester is, by nature, a nice guy. He was a small-town insurance agent who often did his own radio commercials because he liked the personal touch. He had won his state Senate races the same way, by running personal campaigns, emphasizing his record as a businessman, community worker, a dependable conservative. He did not like the slicing, prosecutorial attacks of many lawyer-politicians and he didn't want to start here. He wanted to run his campaign much like he sold insurance. His main pitch even had a touch of salesmanship in it — he wanted to take the largely ceremonial office of lieutenant governor and use it as a platform from which to recruit new industries to Virginia.

Chichester's reluctance to go on the attack put him on a collision course with not only the Durrette campaign but also his own campaign manager, Dennis Peterson. They would battle throughout the fall.

The Chichester campaign had other troubles besides pressure from the Durrette campaign and a reluctant warrior for a candidate. Money was a big one. The campaign had gone into debt to win the nomination. "Unfortunately, it never got any better," says Mike Thomas, No. 2 man in the campaign. "People had said we'd get truckloads of money because we were running against Doug Wilder." Instead, contributors decided since Chichester was going to win anyway, he didn't need the money.

Neither could the Chichester campaign recruit many volunteers; Republicans just couldn't seem to get excited about any of their candidates. As summer went on, the campaign seemed to be stuck in the mud, unable to raise enough money or recruit enough volunteers to really get things moving. "We told people in the late part of summer that come September, there would be polls showing Doug Wilder ahead and people would wonder what was going on," Thomas says.

Indeed, the Republicans' first poll in late June gave Wilder a three-point lead. A Republican National Committee poll in August gave Wilder a five-point lead. Neither was really alarming; the polls simply showed both candidates had the rock-bottom party support and little else. "It's something I'm not sure we got people to understand, that John would not be automatically elected," Thomas says. "I haven't seen a campaign yet run on reality and this one was less than most."

As the summer began, Republicans in the other two campaigns began to hear stories that the Chichester campaign wasn't quite as well-oiled as the plane the candidate flew himself around in.

"I don't want to overplay it, but probably a day didn't go by that we didn't hear some horror story about scheduling, that John had canceled an appearance or canceled a whole day of events," says a staffer in one of the other Republican campaigns.

There also were repeated stories of Chichester, fed up with the schedule the staff had put together for him, simply flying off on his own. "This is a true story," the staffer says. "There's a businessman's club in Virginia Beach called the Red, White and Blue Club. Buster O'Brien helped start it.

O'Brien was scheduled to speak one day in the summer. Lo and behold, who shows up virtually unannounced but John Chichester. He'd been scheduled into Southside but he canceled it, said, 'I'm going to Virginia Beach, find me something to do.' "

Inside Chichester's headquarters, the confusion was even worse than anyone knew. The contrasts between the Wilder campaign and the Chichester campaign couldn't be starker. Wilder kept his staff small and closely held; the people who worked for him were either his relatives or personal friends. Chichester had a fourteen-person staff of people he'd never met before. At the same time Doug Wilder was loyal to his campaign manager, defending him against criticism and refusing entreaties to replace him, John Chichester was trying to fire his.

Wilder and Goldman were the perfect political couple. Chichester and Dennis Peterson were a disastrous mismatch.

Peterson says his disagreements with Chichester began immediately. "The day I should have left was my first day on the job," says Peterson, a former Richmond TV reporter who has worked in Virginia politics for more than a decade. "He vetoed my first decision, which was to rent a headquarters. Do you know where he wanted to have the headquarters? In a motel room." A supporter who owned a motel in Richmond had offered to give Chichester some free rooms. Peterson wanted a formal headquarters like everyone else for appearance's sake. Chichester said no. "We ended up piddling around for a month before we got a headquarters," Peterson says. "By the convention, I was thoroughly disgusted. By the end of the campaign, I felt like a hostage. I wanted out of there and couldn't leave."

Peterson says that Chichester had difficulty accepting the relationship between candidate and campaign manager. Peterson wanted Chichester to go out and campaign and let him run the show in headquarters. But Chichester insisted on day-to-day control, just as if he were going off to sell insurance but still expected to be in charge of the office when he got back. Peterson and Chichester were constantly bickering over who was in charge of what.

"He didn't want us to open any mail unless it was in a BRE [business reply envelope]," Peterson says, aghast. "A campaign gets tons of mail. It got us into some embarrassing situations when the mail wasn't opened up." Chichester says of course he wanted to read all the mail — it was his campaign and he'd be the one to suffer politically if someone important got miffed because the candidate's staff refused to send him to this Ruritan barbecue or that Rotary luncheon.

When Chichester's scheduler found herself caught in the middle, she simply quit, adding to the turmoil. One result: The Chichester campaign is now cited in Republican campaign manager schools as a textbook example of how a meddling, interfering candidate screws up the works.

By the convention, Peterson was fed up and wanted out. In July, he and consultant Bob Weed came up with an idea for Weed to run the campaign, freeing Peterson to work on media and advertising — without having to deal with the candidate.

Weed went to Chichester's house to outline the plan. Chichester said he'd think about it. The more he did, the less he liked it.

"I recognized Dennis' shortcomings," Chichester says, "but I thought with a short rein on him, we could work together." The next day Chichester went to Richmond and turned on his insurance-selling charm, a trait voters saw all too little of. "John took me out to lunch and asked me to stay," Peterson recalls. "He said, 'Golly, Dennis, we've been in this from the beginning.' I made some specifications about the communication level, really reiterating the agreement we had from the beginning, that I'd have authority to make decisions. It was pretty good for a month and then he violated it again. I should have left then."

But Peterson was stuck in a campaign that became more dreadful with each passing day. "I was a trouper," Peterson says. "I'm not saying this just to pat Dennis on the back. I put up with more stuff. I dedicated the most difficult, unhappy year of my life to getting him elected. It may be self-serving, but it's the truth."

The internal problems plaguing the Chichester campaign weren't the only family feud within the GOP. The estrangement of the mountain-valley Republicans from the 1985 ticket became painfully clear to Wyatt Durrette not long after the convention, when he paid a visit to former Gov. Linwood Holton — the state's first Republican governor and one of the last remaining symbols of the party's mountain-valley heritage — at his Washington, D.C., law office.

Durrette wanted Holton to serve on one of his campaign committees as a public show of support from the party's moderate wing. Holton listened politely but said no. For a former Republican governor to turn down a Republican gubernatorial candidate's request to serve on a harmless little committee was astounding. But Holton had his reasons.

"I told him I appreciated the offer and knew he needed a broad base but I was afraid this would be a Mills Godwin ticket that would be racist and far more conservative than I was comfortable with. Therefore, I had to decline," Holton says.

But then Holton delivered a pointed warning to Durrette: "If the Republicans in any way tried to take advantage of Wilder because of race, I would come out publicly for him. Wyatt accurately and truthfully said to me, 'I'm not a racist. There's not a racist bone in my body.' And that's true. When he was in the legislature, he and Wilder got along very well."

But Durrette couldn't control his fellow Republicans. And Holton knew it.

Holton didn't want to go through the ordeal of publicly betraying the party he once led to power. "I guess there never really was any serious risk that I would endorse the Democratic candidate for lieutenant governor, although I remain fond of him," Holton says. "He has been helpful to me in the past. He cast the deciding vote on the [bill to set up a] Cabinet in 1971. But I was very serious about my injunction to the Republican candidate for governor that I would be monitoring very carefully any effort to inject race into that campaign."

For Linwood Holton, the Wilder-Chichester campaign was more than a political contest, it was the embodiment of everything he had fought for — and against — all his life. Holton had grown up in a time when it was the Republicans who were the progressives on racial issues and the Democrats were the ones urging Massive Resistance to court-ordered integration. In 1965, Holton ran for governor against Mills Godwin — the Byrd lieutenant who had been the legislative floor leader for Massive Resistance — and lost. Four years later, Holton led the Republican breakthrough in Virginia by putting together an unlikely coalition of then-moderate Republicans with blacks, labor and disgruntled liberal Democrats. Racial harmony was the hallmark of Holton's administration.

Before long, though, conservatives — both the Byrd Democrats and a new crop of home-grown Republicans — took over the Virginia GOP, elbowing Holton's moderates out of the way. By 1978, when Holton sought the U.S. Senate nomination, he could muster only a poor third; by 1985 he was virtually a man without a party. Now he took the extraordinary step of threatening to endorse Democrat Wilder. It was the only way he knew how to make sure his fellow Republicans ran a race-neutral campaign against Wilder.

Holton's concern was not Durrette personally or even Chichester but more the faceless old conservatives along Richmond's Main Street. "I knew people in the background, people who helped finance his campaign, who would have used race against that Democratic ticket," Holton says. "I wanted to hold that to a minimum and the threat of my endorsement may have held it to a minimum. I know my role for the Republicans, or my possible role for one of the Democrats, was discussed inside the Republican campaign. They were worried about what I would do or might not do."

And they had good reason to be. Durrette left his meeting with Holton plainly worried about what might happen if Holton carried out his threat. "I took it seriously, yes," Durrette says. "It was irrelevant because a racist campaign would not have been run. I was worried, though, that he'd wake up one morning and see a headline that misrepresented something and call a reporter. He can be impetuous."

July 3, 1985

Chichester wasn't the only Republican having problems with his campaign. Before long, Durrette fired his campaign manager. Michael Conlin, from Michigan, was out. Bruce Miller, a former Godwin aide, was in. The Main Street money crowd regarded this as very much "their" campaign. They would tolerate nothing less than complete control. In demanding Conlin's ouster and having him replaced by Miller, they were ensuring just that.

It proved to be a key event for Wilder's campaign as well. The Conlin firing was the first spark in a slow-moving chain reaction of seemingly unconnected political events that eventually exploded, nearly blowing Wyatt Durrette and John Chichester right out of the race.

July 3-6, 1985

Doug Wilder and Paul Goldman paid little heed to the goings-on in the Durrette campaign that would later prove so crucial.

They had their own problems. Money, for one. Too much of it. At least more than they'd like to admit. For the Wilder campaign, it was a bizarre situation to be in.

The first set of financial disclosures for the fall campaign was due a month after the conventions — the Republicans' were due July 2, the Democrats' a week later.

The GOP financial reports were quite interesting. They showed none of the three candidates doing very well at opening Republican wallets.

Reporters tend to focus more on the bottom line — how much money has the candidate raised in all? — and use it as a running score of which candidate had the strongest campaign. Just as important — but often overlooked — was how much each candidate had in the bank. And that's where Goldman was worried.

Wilder wasn't raising much money either — but neither was he spending much of it. With no campaign to speak of he'd managed to save virtually everything he'd raised. Chichester, by contrast, had to go in debt to win the nomination. But Wilder's report would show he had an impressive $131,000 in the bank. Chichester had less than $20,000.

For Wilder, it was an embarrassment of riches — he had more money in the bank than Baliles had. More importantly, Goldman says, Wilder's $131,000 already was enough to mount a modest TV campaign in every media market except ultra-expensive Northern Virginia.

Other Democrats would have loudly broadcast the astonishing surplus as proof that Wilder was a credible candidate. Goldman, though, wanted to keep it quiet. He felt it would be easier to pressure and shame fellow Democrats into giving money if they thought Wilder was nearly broke. Plus, it might lull the Republicans into a false sense of security.

So how could he divert attention from this incredible mismatch of cash on hand and keep reporters' eyes focused on the total raised — Wilder's $204,000 to Chichester's $238,000? Further, how could he get reporters to play up the widely held notion that Wilder was such an underdog that Republicans need not even bother with him? Plus, Goldman was sitting on the station-wagon tour. He'd have to announce it soon. Was there some way he could fit the two together, make it look like Wilder was forced to take the tour because he didn't have enough money for a "real" campaign?

Goldman was in the basement reading through the Fredericksburg newspaper, the *Free Lance-Star,* on the Fourth of July when he came across a quote from Dennis Peterson, casually predicting Chichester would raise $1 million.

Goldman knew he had found the perfect foil.

What Goldman had in mind was what he fondly calls the "poorboy" strategy. He wanted to plant the easily planted idea that Wilder was having trouble raising money.

"Poor-boy gets the focus off our money in the bank," Goldman says. "I was really worried about that. Chichester would come and say, 'Look at them, they have $200,000,' and get people nervous. So we calculated we'd be outspent 2-1" and pointed to that figure with great fear and trepidation.

Timing was a key part of the poor-boy ploy. Goldman planned to "leak" Wilder's professed poverty on Friday. Then on Monday, he'd announce the tour, in hopes of overshadowing the financial reports due out the next day.

It was media manipulation and it worked like a charm.

Goldman went to the office Friday morning and started casually calling reporters, letting them know Wilder was scaling back his fund-raising goals from the $1 million he had (foolishly) set last summer to $500,000. He'd be outspent 2-1, Goldman moaned to the state's political reporters. "With friends like Mills Godwin, I'm sure Chichester can raise $1 million. We can't," he griped.

Goldman knew he had scored when Bill Byrd of the *Virginian-Pilot* in Norfolk called him back, pressing for more details. "He had quotes from everybody around the state," Goldman says. "He said there was a lot of interest in the story in Norfolk. They were planning it for the front page and he needed some more information." Goldman acted wary but played right along.

"Shortage of funds hampers Wilder's campaign," was the headline.

Every major newspaper in the state ran a "Wilder running low on money" story. And even the governor got suckered in.

"I took Paul at his word," Robb says. So when the film crews came in to film some TV spots for Baliles, the governor "borrowed" them to film his own commercial for Wilder — a commercial he never told Wilder about until after the election, when Robb felt forced to write Wilder an angry letter detailing all the ways he helped the candidate.

If Wilder really had been unable to afford TV commercials, then the governor would have insisted the joint campaign committee use some of its money to put the spots on the air, he says.

Goldman asks why, if Robb was so concerned about Wilder not being able to afford TV commercials, he didn't go out and raise money for him instead. Robb says he was trying to but Wilder wouldn't return the calls and had no one else on the staff to do it for him.

And the finger-pointing goes on.

But the real point is that the poor-boy strategy worked. "I think that was the real key to the campaign," says Phil Abraham, a Robb (and later Baliles) staffer. "He claimed he was unable to raise money and that tied up the Chichester campaign."

July 8, 1985

Backed by a map of Virginia outlining his intended journey in a spaghetti-bowl squiggle of lines, Doug Wilder announced "the tour."

Starting Aug. 1 — "whether by pickup truck or van or four-wheel of some sort," the transportation hadn't been worked out — at the Cumberland Gap in the westernmost tip of the state, Wilder declared he would ride some three thousand miles — "longer than a family car trip across America" — from one end of the state to another, stopping in more than three hundred cities, towns, villages and assorted wide places in the road.

"I will stop at every town I enter, no matter how many voters may live there," Wilder said.

It was a nice little speech, full of hokey rural sentimentality. But, reporters asked, money's the real reason you're doing this, isn't it?

"Obviously, we can't fly around in airplanes that cost $200 an hour," said Goldman, trying his best to sound defensive.

"Wilder going to the people: Short on television money, he plans to touch all bases," was the headline in the *Roanoke Times & World-News*.

The day after Wilder announced the tour, David McCloud took him out to lunch to talk about the dire need to find someone besides Goldman to run the campaign.

With the tour announcement coming just two days after the "poor-boy" stories, Democrats had another chance to get mad at Wilder and Goldman all over again. Most thought the same thing about the tour that Terry campaign manager John Jameson did. "I thought it was the most ridiculous thing I'd ever heard."

Larry Framme was one of the few people who thought the tour was a good idea. "That shows you how naive I was," he laughs. "Then I talked to some of the pros and they said it was nutty." Alan Albert, a Baliles adviser, is even more blunt: "Some people thought it was absolutely insane."

The reaction wasn't limited to those on high. "Your local activists thought it was the death knell," says Jim Gibbs, the Stafford County Democratic chairman. "Someone up here called it Paul Goldman's invisible campaign," says Don Beyer Jr., who was heading the Baliles campaign in Northern Virginia. "Let's take the candidate and hide him in the smallest town we can find out of the way of TV cameras so no one will know he's black."

For the media, though, the tour promised to become a social event — how would a black man be received in Virginia? How, especially, would he be received out in the hollows of Southwest Virginia? The *Virginian-Pilot* seized Wilder's tour and editorialized about it as "A Virginia Odyssey."

"The pilgrimage will be a testing time for both candidate and electorate, and a learning time for those who watch from beyond the state's borders, curious to see how Virginia has progressed in its race relations . . . The electorate will be measured by its reaction to Mr. Wilder's candidacy. Will attention be paid? . . . Make no mistake: Far more is at stake in the lieutenant governor's election than whether Mr. Wilder or his Republican opponent . . . holds the state's part-time, No. 2 elective post. Once concluded, the 1985 lieutenant governor election will tell a tale of Virginia itself."

This editorial goes a long way toward explaining the whole campaign. Elevating the campaign to some grand referendum on Virginia's racial progress was the absolute worst thing that could happen to the Chichester campaign, but that's exactly what the state's major newspapers now proceeded to do. The editorial writers had already done it. Now the reporters, correctly or not, looked on Wilder's tour as the perfect way to measure firsthand just how much racism was still left in Virginia. Wilder's tour became *the* political story of the summer.

July 9, 1985

The Democrats filed their finance reports. The news accounts focused on Baliles. No one really picked up on how large Wilder's surplus was — except maybe Chichester campaign manager Dennis Peterson and Terry consultant Tom King.

Peterson accused the Wilder campaign of "dripping in hyprocrisy" for pleading poverty; but few reporters paid attention to his complaints. "They had a preconceived notion," Peterson says, and were suckered in.

Meanwhile, not long after the reports came out Goldman called King to pester him about whether the Terry campaign was going to help raise money for Wilder. King just laughed.

"Don't even talk to me about money," King said. "I've read your reports. You've got more money than Baliles."

There was a long silence on the other end of the phone.

"Is that so?" Goldman finally asked. "I haven't read Jerry's report."

"You'll have more TV than we will if you keep this up," King said.

Goldman vigorously disputed that. "You have more money."

"Yeah, but we're spending it," King said. "You've got $113,000. Assume you just double it. That's close to $250,000. How much TV do you want?"

Goldman, knowing he was caught, tried to weasel out of it. "That's just a temporary accounting blip," he said.

"Bullshit," King said. "I've read your reports."

"You've read our reports, huh?"

Yeah, King said. "Mary Sue has money. You have money. Nobody else has any money."

"Ssshh," Goldman whispered. "Don't tell anybody about it."

King agreed and hung up, laughing.

He still marvels at how many people missed Wilder's wealth. "I'd say honestly there were only a few people who figured out what they were up to. Ninety-nine percent of the time I'd say 'you're crazy, Paul.' " But this time he saw Goldman was right to plead poverty. If Democrats thought Wilder had enough money, they might quit giving, because they didn't yet think he had a chance to win — they just wanted to keep him close.

"Everybody was saying 'Jesus, we don't know if Doug can raise money,'" King says. "That talk was going on all summer. I kept my mouth shut."

July 13, 1985

It didn't take the Baliles campaign long to figure out what the change of commanders in the Durrette campaign meant. It was a sure sign that the conservatives had seized control, that the positive, upbeat campaign urged by moderates was going to be ignored in favor of a full-fanged assault on Baliles.

The question for the Baliles campaign was how to respond — and contrast the Old Guard's takeover of the Durrette campaign with the Democrats' own theme of a "New Dominion." The first Baliles-Durrette debate was coming up before the Virginia Press Association at the Wintergreen resort, high in the Blue Ridge mountains of Nelson County south of Charlottesville. "Chris Bridge [Baliles' press secretary] and I sat up the night before that debate, rewriting the opening and closing statements," Baliles issues adviser Alan Albert says. "We stayed up until 6 a.m. It was clear what to do."

Durrette was going to argue that Baliles' education plans cost too much; Baliles was ready with a counter-punch that Durrette didn't really care about education, including a brutal recitation of selected Durrette votes in the General Assembly. Baliles stole the headlines the next day, and with them the education issue as well. "Durrette was never able to re-establish his credibility as the education candidate," Albert gloats.

And things didn't get much better for the Durrette campaign, at least not right away. Four days later, President Reagan, citing his recent cancer surgery, canceled his trip to Richmond. Instead, he sent Vice President George Bush. But the vice president didn't draw quite the crowd to the July 30 fund-raiser that the president might have. As a result, the Republicans didn't raise nearly as much money as they had counted on. Plans for an early TV blitz, paid for with cash from the president's visit, were scratched.

By the time the Durrette campaign did get on the air in mid-September, Baliles had already been on for three weeks, cutting up Durrette as a flip-flopper on the issues and portraying himself as the pro-education candidate. Durrette's campaign was sagging so badly then that he had to make a swing through Southside with Mills Godwin at his side just to rally the conservative troops. It was at the end of that Southside tour that the long line of dominoes, which first started toppling in early July with the firing of Durrette's campaign manager, tumbled directly into the path of the Wilder-Chichester campaign.

Late July 1985

In Terry headquarters, the consultants were studying their first poll. Campaign manager John Jameson looked at the numbers and shook his head sadly. "I think we just wasted $20,000," he said. Look at these numbers. The ones for Baliles and Terry seemed about right. Baliles had about a seven-point lead and Terry had about a five-point lead. But these numbers on Wilder — can they possibly be right? The poll showed Wilder up 36-26 — a ten-point lead! And when the "leaners," those who said they were leaning to one candidate or another, were added to the definites, Wilder's lead ballooned to 14 percent: 44-30. Could this possibly be right?

The poll dumbfounded the Democrats who saw it.

"After a while, we became convinced he [Wilder] was ahead mainly because of name ID, but when people found out he's black, he wouldn't get above the mid-40s," Jameson says. But not long after, a Baliles poll confirmed the Terry poll. It gave all three Democrats comfortable leads: Baliles 34-29, Wilder 33-26 and Terry 32-22.

July 28, 1985

With three days left before Wilder's trip to the Southwest, Michael Brown had a problem. A big problem. The other campaigns were flying their candidates around in private planes and Brown couldn't even find someone to lend Wilder a car.

"I called I'll bet thirteen different companies, agencies, people, whatever to get people to assist us," Brown says, "and you'd be surprised at the kind of responses I'd get. 'Oh, give me a call back on Tuesday.' Or, 'Let me think about it.' They'd been reading all the newspapers. 'You're going to drive to every town, every hamlet, every knothole?' The senator had given me the names of personal friends who had access to cars but it didn't materialize."

Brown called his friends in Baliles and Terry headquarters. "The other campaigns couldn't help us. I talked to [Baliles fund-raisers] Curry Roberts and Bill Wiley. 'Where do you get your cars from? People tell me they can't loan out cars. They have a hundred different reasons.' I called Mary Sue's people. 'Oh, that car dealer is a personal friend of Mary Sue's.' 'Well, can't he be a personal friend of ours, too?' It was like, 'Hey, you got your campaign, we've got ours.' "

Finally Brown, running out of names on his official list and running out of time, called the man he had bought his first car from years ago, now in semi-retirement. "Listen, I need help," Brown said and explained his problem. The man listened. "Call me the next day," he said. Brown had heard that line before. But the next day when he called back, the man had come through. "You got it," he said. "I've got you a brand new 1985 station wagon. Y'all are going to love it. It's got AM, FM, air conditioning, power steering, cruise control."

Brown was overjoyed. But now he had another problem. Goldman had given him precise instructions — he wanted an *old* station wagon. Brown didn't quite think this luxury vehicle fit the poorboy image.

Brown went to break the news — in the presence of both Goldman and Wilder. Goldman was adamant. No. This won't do. He was ready to turn it down. Wilder was amused but a bit fearful. "Well, I would like some modern conveniences," he said. "I'd like to have air conditioning." Goldman remained insistent. Find another one.

Now it was Brown's turn to be just as hard-headed. "Look," he said, "I have gone through hell trying to get a station wagon. Now we've got one." If Goldman wanted another one, he could go find it.

Goldman shrugged his shoulders. Wilder had his car. "A borrowed station wagon" was the quaint phrase in the news stories.

Perhaps the calmest person in the midst of all this was Wilder. He had overcome his initial reluctance and now was looking forward to this little jaunt over the back roads of Virginia, jawing with the good ol' boys at the country stores along the way.

Not long before Wilder left, his neighbors had given him a present — a NASCAR driver's jumpsuit. On the back they had written "Good Ole Boy." Wear this when you go to see House Speaker A.L. Philpott, they told him.

Wilder got such a kick out of his "good ole boy" race car driver's suit that a year later he was still wearing it around the house.

July 31, 1985

For Doug Wilder, this last day of July was spent on the practice of law.

He was in court that morning, seeking to continue one case and turn it over to his law partner. The afternoon he spent in his office, straightening up the loose ends of a law practice he wouldn't return to until after the election.

While Goldman and Larry Wilder drove ahead with the station wagon full of reporters, Wilder flew out to Southwest Virginia that night. By the time he got to the Cumberland Gap Holiday Inn — just over the state line — it was past 9 p.m. and Wilder hadn't eaten dinner yet.

The candidate carried in his own luggage. From the front desk, he spotted Goldman, Larry and a half-dozen reporters in the restaurant. Wilder dropped his suit bag to the floor and, in a characteristically flamboyant gesture, raised both hands in a touchdown salute.

He had arrived.

But the question was: Would he finish? Or would the tour finish him? Would the tour, and Wilder's determination to see it through, earn him the grudging admiration of enough voters to keep the final margin respectable?

Or would the tour show the Old Dominion simply wasn't ready for Doug Wilder in the flesh and turn into a pitiful, pathetic slog across a pointedly disinterested Virginia — in the full glare of the media?

The third prospect, that the tour would find white Virginians genuinely enthusiastic about Wilder's personal approach, steadily build momentum and turn Wilder into the recognized front-runner by the time he reached the Eastern Shore was so laughable it wasn't mentioned, not even in jest.

Before long, just Wilder, his son and Goldman were left in the hotel's empty dining room. The last waitress on duty scurried around, setting up tables for breakfast and waiting for this final party to leave. Wilder and Goldman talked quietly, ignoring the rattle of silverware behind them.

Everything was set. They had their captive audience of reporters. They had a dramatic backdrop of the most rugged country, certainly geographically and maybe politically as well, in the state. Election Day was still three months away but Wilder's campaign had come down to the first three days of August. Whatever happened Thursday, Friday and Saturday would be splashed all over the Sunday papers. No other part of the tour was likely to receive such extensive coverage. That was Goldman's great gamble, that Wilder's reception in the three westernmost counties — Lee, Scott and Wise — would be so warm that coverage would spark the momentum the campaign so desperately needed.

But as the last night of July wound its way down, perhaps the only people in Virginia who thought it would work were sitting in a deserted restaurant in Tennessee with an impatient waitress hovering behind them, wishing they'd hurry up and leave.

9

The Fightin' Ninth

Aug. 1, 1985

The first day of August was off to a miserable start and it wasn't even breakfast yet. Overnight, clouds had moved into the coalfields. Heavy with moisture, they sank into the valleys and refused to budge.

At the visitors center, shirt-sleeved tourists who drove all this way expecting to play Daniel Boone and look through the Cumberland Gap into the Kentucky wilderness instead found themselves staring into a thick, chilling mist.

Further up on the Virginia side, the craggy peaks of the Cumberlands snagged the clouds and they began spilling a cold, hard rain on the countryside. Farmers had been trying all week through intermittent showers to get up the hay they'd cut. Now it would rot in the fields for sure. All across Lee County, Democratic precinct workers woke up to the leaden sound of rain beating on the roof, all the excuse they needed to stay inside and skip that Doug Wilder breakfast down at the Gap.

At the Cumberland Gap Holiday Inn, the five reporters who had come to chronicle the inevitable disaster could see that political forecast clearer than anything else. The ones who had gotten in late the night before peered out the restaurant windows and debated where the Gap was and how long it would be before the rain started here.

Wilder came down from his room to find the lobby empty except for former state legislator Edgar Bacon and a clump of reporters. Evelyn Bacon was at the door, straining to see through the mist.

"I hope they'll be here," she said. "I called everybody."

Wilder tried to be optimistic. "Well, it is raining."

"It rains all the time," she said solemnly, still searching for signs of headlights cutting through the fog.

"Well, if you called them, they'll come," Wilder said.

Southwest Virginia juts into Appalachia like a wedge driven deep into the mountains, with the Cumberland Gap — the pioneers' gateway to the West — at its point.

It is easy to picture what Southwest Virginia looks like — dark mountain hollows where the sun seldom shines, gritty company towns where coal dust hangs in the air, toothless old hillbillies peering out the screen door at a world they don't understand — even if many of those images are half a century or more out of date.

But it is almost impossible to grasp just how far away Southwest Virginia is from the rest of the state.

Most Virginians, most eastern Virginians anyway, grow up with the impression that Richmond is the center of the state (if not the universe) and that Roanoke is somewhere on the western frontier. Yet even from Roanoke it's quicker to drive to the beach than it is to reach some of the coalfield communities. Roanoke likes to think of itself as the commercial hub of Southwest Virginia, but even from Roanoke, far Southwest Virginia is more a concept than an actual place people are directly familiar with.

Move west and Virginia's mental border moves, too. "A lot of people think Virginia ends at Abingdon," says Sue Poteto, a social worker from Pennington Gap. Yet even from Abingdon, the Cumberland Gap is still a hard two-hour drive over narrow mountain roads. It's so far west that the mountains start to peter out and the narrow valleys begin to broaden into wide fields of rolling hills again. Virginia's western tip farther west than Detroit. In fact, the county seat of Jonesville is closer to seven other state capitals than it is to Richmond, a bitter fact Lee County residents are quick to point out to visitors from the east. "I daresay 90 percent of the people out here have never been to Richmond or Norfolk," says Tom Geisler, a retired miner from Dryden. "We've really got a different state out here."

No matter which way they look, Southwest Virginians find themselves outsiders — proud Virginians surrounded by out-of-state neighbors, yet ignored by their in-state cousins, or patronized when they are noticed. Not surprisingly, then, Southwest Virginians often seem as resentful of eastern Virginians as they are eager to earn their respect and acceptance. They are quick to embrace a stranger as a friend and make him welcome, but just as quick to take offense at any slight, real or imagined, especially if it has to do with the coalfields somehow being backward or otherwise behind the times.

Come election time, both parties woo the big-money coal barons, but ordinary voters are lucky to get more than a glimpse of statewide candidates when they make a quick, obligatory tour of the Southwest. "When Linwood Holton [a Big Stone Gap native] ran for governor, we felt close to him," Geisler told Wilder when they met at the Pay-less Supermarket in Dryden, "and John Dalton [from Radford] was a fine fellow, but most of the rest of 'em, you might say, are foreigners in a way."

Doug Wilder — eastern, urban and black — was the ultimate outsider. The conventional wisdom back east was that Southwest Virginia was the absolute worst place for Wilder to start his tour because Appalachia was bound to be so damned prejudiced. Friends in Richmond whispered to Wilder that he might not want to go "out there, with those people." Wilder joked about the warnings afterward, but the fear about how this black Richmonder might go over in deepest Southwest Virginia was quite real, on all sides of the mountain. Glenn Craft, the Democratic chairman in Wise County, one of Wilder's first stops, got anxious calls from chairmen in later counties. "They were a little apprehensive about how things would go," Craft says. "They wanted to know how things went here." One of Wilder's supporters back in Richmond was apprehensive, too. "We thought it could get really ugly, with a lot of name-calling," she says. "We were really worried."

But it turned out that the veins of Southwest pride and party ran deeper and stronger than the old veins of prejudice that apparently had been mined out years ago. When Doug Wilder announced that he not only was going to take time to visit dozens of coalfield communities, but he was also going to start his tour here, the response was exactly as Goldman had hoped: Southwest Virginians, these cranky, contrary, unpredictable, stubborn old white mountaineers, embraced Doug Wilder like a long-lost son.

The reporters were picking through the morning newspapers when suddenly they looked up and noticed the lobby was filling up with people. And Edgar Bacon seemed to know them all. He scurried about, helping the ladies with their raincoats, pumping hands with the men as if he himself were the candidate.

At first, it seemed just a coincidence. This was, after all, a small community and Bacon was, after all, a prominent figure, so it made sense that at any public place he would meet a lot of people he knew.

But something still seemed out of place. Bacon acted as if he was expecting everyone. He positioned himself at the door so he could look out into the parking lot to see who else was coming. And inside, the crowd milled around the lobby, as if waiting for orders.

Reporters warily began looking at one another for clues. Who were all these people and why were they here?

"Oh, we're here for the breakfast," one woman answered.

"What breakfast?"

"The Doug Wilder breakfast."

What was going on here? Hadn't anyone told these people Wilder didn't have a prayer, that they were wasting their time? Were they so far west, so far out of touch, that they hadn't heard the state party wasn't behind Wilder, so they didn't have to be either? Yes, he is a Democrat, and yes, this is partisan territory, but hadn't anyone told these people that Wilder is, well, you know, *black?*

Evidently not, because still they kept coming: old women chattering about their canning, weather-beaten farmers grumbling about the rain, government officials whispering courthouse intrigue. And not just one or two token office-holders either, but a whole slate of local Democratic chieftains.

In the days when the Byrd Machine ran Virginia, the clerk of the court — with an eight-year term, a virtual political immortal — was often the key fixer, the leader of the Democratic courthouse ring. In more recent times, the clerk's political influence has diminished, but not in Southwest Virginia where voters take politics so seriously: Lee County clerk Charles Calton gives away matchbooks with his name and home phone, just in case citizens need a reminder of who can help them out. It would be difficult to imagine someone who better personified the establishment in Lee County. Yet here Calton was, openly supporting Wilder. He had driven 40 miles from his home in Dryden to be here at the Gap for breakfast. Later he would escort Wilder around the courthouse, join him for lunch and attend a reception in his honor that evening.

In all, thirty Democrats braved slick mountain roads and midsummer indifference to eat breakfast with Wilder. Goldman was off somewhere in a corner grinning. He'd just led his captive audience of reporters into the first trap.

In retrospect, no one should have been surprised. Still, the mistaken picture of Southwest Virginia as a hard-bitten land of tight-lipped mountaineers, quick to take their rifle down from the mantel at the first sign of a black man (or any stranger, for that matter), was so overwhelming that everyone overlooked the political lay of the land. In Southwest Virginia, politics run as strong as blood and religion, perhaps stronger. In Dickenson County, there really are Democratic funeral homes and Republican funeral homes.

In a state where political independence had been raised to a saintly virtue by Harry Byrd Sr. and his "golden silence" in presidential years, Southwest Virginians still cling to a fierce party loyalty they defend in such bitter blood-feuds that the congressional district long ago earned the nickname "The Fightin' Ninth." The coal counties along the Kentucky border are overwhelmingly Democratic; the valleys to the east, with their small farms, are notoriously Republican. With that general division, elections here are always fought with an evangelistic zeal. Sometimes they've been fought with fists, too — or even more deadly weapons.

It was this rigid allegiance to party that the pundits overlooked when they trembled with fear at the prospect of Wilder going "out there with those people" to commence his tour. But those who knew the Fightin' Ninth best knew Wilder was going into a country almost tailor-made for a black Democrat seeking to prove he could win support from white party loyalists.

At the inauguration in January 1986, former Gov. Linwood Holton, a son of Wise County, took Wilder aside and told him he hoped he could tell him a joke without Wilder being offended. "When you went down to Southwest Virginia, I know what you were doing," Holton said. "You told those old boys up in the hollows, 'All your lives, you've been saying you were such a strong Democrat you'd even vote for a nigger if he'd run as a Democrat. Well, here's your chance.'"

Wilder, Holton reports, nearly doubled over with laughter.

That first day in Lee County was hard to figure. Everything went right. Bacon led Wilder all over the county, dropping in on surprised voters from the bank at Ewing to the garage at Rose Hill to a road crew at St. Charles. Yet at every stop Wilder was greeted not only politely, but even warmly, enthusiastically. It was hard to figure.

At breakfast, Edgar Bacon gave a booming speech on Wilder's behalf, reciting his resume from Korea through the General Assembly. "He's the most qualified candidate for lieutenant governor I've ever seen and I've seen a few," Bacon declared.

After breakfast the crowd recessed to Cudjo Cave — a collection of gas stations and mini-marts that mark the last place to gas up before crossing through the Gap into Kentucky. The rocky ledges beside the road were draped with kudzu vines. Wilder's tour began there, in the parking lot of Mike Thompson's souvenir stand. Wilder faced east and made a little speech about why he was making his tour. A small knot of supporters clustered around him but few could hear him over the traffic on U.S. 58 — tractor-trailers growling their way up the steep grade, others hissing as they rode their air brakes down the mountain. The Eastern Shore had to seem a long way away. When he was done, Wilder shook hands with everyone again, press and politicians piled into four cars, someone got out into the road to stop traffic and the tour was off.

The first stop was supposed to be Ewing, a one-street farm town. But halfway there, Bacon unexpectedly turned down a rutted gravel road. Someone joked that Bacon, a state highway commissioner, was purposely taking Wilder, the senior member of the Senate Transportation Committee, down the worst roads he could find. Weaving back and forth to avoid potholes, the procession eased past the True Gospel Wilderness Church — the paint was peeling off, so it was hard to tell if any preaching was still done there — and into the muddy parking lot of an abandoned quarry. Bacon got out and waved his hand at the rusting equipment. "I wanted you to see what's happening," he said. "They used to grind stone here for road construction but the highway business falling off is killing us." The old orator Bacon began painting a sorry picture of a dying county — its population has dropped by one-third since the end of World War II — its families torn apart simply because the county couldn't afford to build better roads to attract industry.

His plug for more road money duly noted, Bacon finally got everyone to Ewing for Wilder's first foray among the voters. Bacon led the way, bursting into the People's Bank, calling the tellers by name. The women started to say hello, then stopped in mid-syllable as they saw the entourage jamming into the bank's tiny lobby after him. Bacon pulled the candidate through the crush to shake hands. Wilder seemed almost easy to miss alongside the effervescent Bacon, who clearly was enjoying the show. Wilder spotted a blond receptionist named Virginia Wilder. "Now look a-here, we've got a cousin," he announced, picking up her nameplate for everyone to see. "Now you know Edgar knew what he was doing." The receptionist blushed, the other tellers giggled and then the whole crowd squeezed through the door to hit the Western Building Supply and Ewing Farm Supply before moving out. Back in the bank, the twenty-two-year-old Virginia Wilder confessed she'd never heard of the candidate before. "I'm really uninformed." In ten minutes, Wilder shook hands with maybe ten voters. One town down, three hundred and some more to go.

The next stop was a medical supplies factory at Rose Hill. An assistant manager was found to take Wilder around, but it wasn't a break, so he wouldn't be able to talk with any workers. Most of them didn't bother to look up from their machines anyway.

Back in the stockroom Wilder was finally able to buttonhole some stray workers. "Uh, well, I think I've heard of him," said D.C. Hounshell, "but if he's with Edgar there, I'll vote for him." Hounshell said his father was a Democrat so he reckoned that made him one, too.

The reporters peppered him with questions about race. "No, I don't really think it makes a difference," he answered. "We don't have many blacks out here, so it's not a major factor. Oh, you've got some that wouldn't vote for him if he was their brother but in this day and time, in this part of the country, the younger generation accepts it more than the older generation." Hounshell was more interested in Wilder's visit than his race. "That'll make one difference, I think. Usually they come to Bristol and don't come to this end of the state."

Outside, the rain had finally come, slashing the ground in great white sheets. Everyone was soaked by the time they got to the cars.

On to Bacon's Garage, run by one of Edgar's cousins. Ann Bales Middleton was waiting for a mechanic to tell her what was wrong with her car. She was delighted to meet Wilder — and proudly showed off his campaign literature to the reporters tagging along after him. Did she think being black would hurt him? "Oh Lord no, I hadn't even noticed."

At Grabeel's Supermarket, Wilder and Bacon roamed up and down the narrow aisles, surprising shoppers as they pondered the canned goods. Middle-age housewives looked up from their lists to find themselves surrounded by men who wanted to shake hands and stuff literature into their carts. A toothless old man, the stubble of a neglected beard on his sunken cheeks, was backed up against the shelves when the procession trooped by. What did he think of Wilder, someone asked him. The old man took a long look at Wilder's picture on the one flier, but was still confused. "Which one was he?"

The Wilder caravan rolled on to Jonesville. Wilder bounced up the steps of the county courthouse and introduced himself to a stranger. "Oh, I'll do you right in November," the man said. "I'm a damn good Democrat." County clerk Calton was waiting for him inside with a half-dozen more supporters and took him around to meet the other county officials. Porter Greer, a retired miner, wore a Wilder baseball cap. He leaned against a sign for the Rebel Bonding Co. and offered his impressions of how his neighbors would respond to a black candidate. "I tell you. I've talked to a whole lot of people and it'll make no difference. He's a Democrat and that's what people care about."

This was starting to sound ridiculous.

It seemed like the whole county courthouse showed up at lunch to eat with Wilder at the Lazy Susan restaurant in Jonesville. A Bristol TV crew came by and taped the crowd. Then it was back on the road.

The afternoon schedule began at the grandly named little community of Ben Hur, where Wilder visited the Lee Vocational School. The candidate breezed through the teachers' lounge shaking hands, then disappeared down the hallway. The teachers, sitting around eating their bag lunches, barely had time to swallow their sandwiches. "We didn't get a chance to ask him any questions," one protested. A reporter obligingly went after Wilder and pulled him back in so the teachers could pepper the candidate with questions about merit pay.

A bearded man sat in the corner, arms folded across his chest, watching with detached amusement. Like the class smart aleck, he finally raised his hand and asked Wilder a long, involved question about what he thought of new state regulations that were "encouraging" handicapped students to move out of institutions and into private homes. Dr. Allen Miller didn't tell Wilder he was the director of a private institution for handicapped students near Charlottesville that was being threatened by those very regulations.

Wilder nodded as he took in the whole question and then smiled like Hank Aaron watching a home run pitch come across the plate. "Earlier this year I had a girl write me about that very problem," he said. "She was the victim of cerebral palsy. She types with a helmet. I think it took her a whole day to write the letter. She's nineteen, a registered voter. I had lunch with her just last week at her institution. There's no way she could receive treatment in a private home like she could in the Children's Home."

And then Wilder proceeded to smack Miller's question right out of the park. He stood there a solid five minutes, reciting the law, explaining why it was written the way it was and pointing out in detail why it was wrong. Miller was so stunned all he could say was, "I'm really happy to hear you're aware of the situation." But Wilder wasn't finished. He launched into a discourse on how private group homes for the handicapped are hard to find because they often run up against local zoning restrictions. He pointed out that the problem isn't limited to group homes for handicapped adults but also affects day-care centers and homes for the elderly.

Miller was flabbergasted. He had expected to catch this politician off-guard. Instead, "he knew about the situation and was right on target. That was impressive. Most people in the legislature don't know much about it. He was the first person that hit the nail on the head."

Wilder probably won Miller's vote right there. But in a state with 5.5 million people, it takes a long time to win elections when you have to do it one vote at a time.

Bill Markham leaned on his idle jackhammer and studied all the commotion that had suddenly broken out in St. Charles.

One minute he and his road crew had been working on the bridge in this run-down coal town, one that had fallen on such hard times that even the United Mine Workers office had closed.

The next minute a caravan of shiny new cars rolled by, pulled off the road and out jumped almost a dozen men in suits and ties.

What on earth now?

A black man in a gray banker's suit seemed to be in charge. He walked right up to the work crew, which had no choice but to cut off its machinery and see what was going on. The black man flashed a smile and offered a hand to shake. "Doug Wilder's my name. I'm the Democratic nominee for lieutenant governor. I'll be on the ballot in November. I hope you can support me."

No sooner had he moved on to the next worker than two more men followed in his wake, pressing literature into every available hand. A handsome young black man passed out slick cards with the older black man's picture on one side and an official-looking war citation on the back. The other man — a sort of scraggly haired white fellow whose baseball cap nearly came down over his eyes — waved a sheet of paper with some kind of chart, part of it highlighted, and kept repeating the black man's name in a nasal Yankee accent, like a medicine show man talking up his act.

The rest of the crowd hung back while all this was going on. But as soon as the two men handing out literature passed, the others, too, zeroed in on the befuddled workers, asking all kinds of questions and scribbling down the answers. What's your name, sir? What did you think of the candidate? Are you a Democrat of a Republican? Do you think you'll vote for him?

Markham pushed the hard hat back on his head and tried to make sense of all this confusion before he said anything. "Well, what's he stand for? More money or what?"

"He's a Democrat."

Markham thought on that a little bit. "Well," he said slowly, "I've been a Democrat all my life and I reckon I'll vote for him."

That out of the way, the reporters tried to ease around to the question they really wanted to ask. They'd sort of whisper it, like it was some big secret: "The fact that he's, uh, you know, black, how much of a difference is that going to make around here?" But they kept asking it over and over, in every possible way. It was so frustrating for them because everywhere they went the answers were always the same and just not very believable ones, at that.

Markham had the same answer as all the rest. "Oh, I don't think so," he said. "You don't find much of that up here."

Then, as quickly as it appeared, the crowd suddenly was gone. The black man was getting back in his car and the reporters dropped their questions in mid-sentence and shouted thanks as they ran after him. The road workers were left standing by the bridge, thumbing through the literature they'd been given, still in a daze about what it was all about. Was he really that guy running for lieutenant governor? What in the world was he doing way out here? When the men got home tonight, they'd sure have something to tell their wives and neighbors: The damndest thing happened today. We were working on the bridge over at St. Charles when all of a sudden these cars pulled up . . .

A fat, red sun was sinking behind the mountains. Shadows rolled down across Jonesville and back up the hills on the other side of town; only the church steeples were tall enough to catch the last of the light. The rain clouds had finally passed and now stars were starting to blink in the purpling sky. From Edgar Bacon's hilltop home, you could look down the valley and see the mist moving up from the creek bottoms, curling around the farms — and the headlights on the long line of cars still coming up the road.

Bacon had promised "a little reception" to close Wilder's day in Lee County, but it was turning into more of a full-scale garden party. Evelyn Bacon set out a lavish spread on her fine china and nearly one hundred people — most of them over fifty, all but three of them white — milled around on the damp grass, waiting for a chance to shake Doug Wilder's hand. Larry Wilder manned the back of the station wagon, doing a brisk business selling Wilder baseball caps for $3 a shot.

Charles Couk seemed to know as much about Lee County as anyone. The owl-faced little man of seventy-nine had been mayor of Jonesville for twenty-four years. He was asked how Wilder would do in the Southwest.

"The Democrats will support him," he declared, as if that was all that mattered. In Lee County, maybe it was. What about race? How will that affect things? "Oh, there may be a few old people who are prejudiced," he said, accenting the word "old" as if he really didn't count himself as a senior citizen. "But the young people, it doesn't really matter to them." Couk seemed truly surprised to hear that some Democrats back east might not be supporting Wilder. Couk pursed his lips and shook his head angrily. "That's just not right."

Edgar Bacon chaperoned Wilder around the crowd and introduced him to all his neighbors. Things seemed to be going very well. People seemed eager to meet Wilder and this big-city black politician was doing an amazing job at holding up his end of conversations on farming and coal mining. And something else was happening. The evening was growing old but no one seemed to be leaving. Finally a couple of old-timers came up to Bacon and pulled him aside. "Is Wilder going to make a speech?" they asked cautiously. Bacon said he hadn't planned on it, that they could leave whenever they wanted. The old-timers were disappointed. "We'd kinda like to hear what he has to say."

Bacon called everyone around to the back porch so Wilder could say a few words. The candidate got up on the steps to the kitchen, talked about his determination to visit every city and county and thanked everyone for such a wonderful day. "If the other fifty-nine days come anywhere close to matching this day, there is no way I will not win in November," he declared. That was certainly true enough. The old folks, many of whom were the same ones who had been at breakfast, cheered. Eighty-year-old Bashie Kincaid pushed through the crowd, pinned a rhinestone donkey on Wilder's lapel beside his Bronze Star — "this is just something I picked up; I want you to have it" — and hugged him. A photographer had shown up and the old lady hugged Wilder again so she could get her picture taken with him.

Only after that did the crowd begin drifting home. Wilder saw them off, then went inside to find his host. He stuck his head into the basement — and spotted about a dozen county officials lounging around the smoky rec room. Lloyd Davis, a county school official, noticed that Wilder's eye seemed to leap immediately to the pool table in the middle of the room. The candidate went over to the rack of pool sticks. "He eyed them like he was no stranger to a pool stick," Davis recalls. "He took one down and eyed it. If you know pool, you can tell if someone knows anything about pool. He rolled the stick on the table. I could tell he was no novice. As soon as he got a stick out, I could tell he wanted to exercise his ability."

Dub Hines, the county registrar, recognized it, too. He offered to take

Wilder on. "We'll see how you spent your youth," someone laughed.

Wilder grinned. It wasn't long before all the men were lining up to take him on. They were laughing and joking, kidding Wilder whenever he made a good shot. "We can see your youth was misspent." "We know how you worked your way through school." The mood was warm and clubby, as if Wilder was one of the boys and always had been. "It was as though you'd known him all your life," Davis says. "I'll bet throughout the rest of the tour he never felt the closeness he did that night. It wasn't like he was a candidate for lieutenant governor. Everyone wanted to beat him. I wanted to. I knew he would respect the challenge. He didn't want anything given to him." And it wasn't. But one by one, Wilder beat the local hot-shots, coolly taking aim, pocketing his balls exactly as he wanted. Davis waited on the side until he could see Wilder was tiring and then took him on. He was the only pool shark to beat Wilder that night.

"I could see they weren't just being polite," Wilder says. "They were saying, 'He's our nominee, we'll do all we can to get him elected.' " It was the wives who finally broke up the party. "They came down and said, 'Really, we must be going,' " Bacon recalls. "Otherwise they'd have been there until two o'clock." Before he left, Calton pressed a $100 bill into Wilder's hand. "We'll be with you," he said.

"We went upstairs after the pool-shooters left," Bacon recalls, "and I told him, 'Now Doug, I think it's gone over well today. If you can do this throughout the state, it's really going to be a worthwhile tour.' He had an uncertainty in his mind. But when he saw in our county, how these guys were treating him as any other successful legislator, he knew he was going over well. He told us how much he appreciated the way people received him, shaking his hand, swapping stories with him. I think that first day came to him as a great relief."

Wilder went to sleep in Bacon's guest room at 1 a.m. He was ecstatic. "I thought, not bad for a first day," he says. The reporters, on the other hand, went to sleep in the Jonesville Motor Lodge skeptical and confused. Certainly everyone Wilder had met seemed glad to see him. Maybe that neighborliness should have been expected here in the down-home Southwest. And certainly he had been welcomed warmly by the local party machinery, which had put on an impressive show three times in one day. But how much of that was the old warhorse Bacon's doings and how much of it was genuine support for Wilder? His comments from the back porch steps couldn't be disputed. If he did this well all the way across the state, maybe he could win. But Lee County was just one county out of almost one hundred. And what would happen in all those others when Edgar

Bacon wasn't around to lead the way? That would be the true test.

Aug. 2, 1985

The second day of the tour was a disaster. There's no other way to put it. Wilder knew it, Goldman knew it and worst of all, the reporters saw it.

Joe Gatins of the *Richmond Times-Dispatch* sent back a story that began: "L. Douglas Wilder ran into political hardpan in Scott County yesterday after plowing more fertile campaign ground in neighboring Lee and Wise counties."

Rex Springston of the *Richmond News Leader* filed a disaster story, too, which made the front page of the capital's evening paper: "Everyone has had one of those days. L. Douglas Wilder, the Democratic candidate for lieutenant governor of Virginia, had his yesterday."

There may be some truth in the show business adage about bad publicity being better than no publicity at all — at least the word got out that Wilder was on tour — although it didn't seem that way at the time.

Even the day before, there were signs the second day of the tour wasn't going to go well. Wilder was scheduled to spend the morning going underground in a Westmoreland Co. coal mine between Appalachia and Big Stone Gap. But the company sent word it wouldn't allow reporters on its property.

So on the second day of his tour, Wilder spent all morning making a dramatic visual pitch to the working class voters of Southwest Virginia he so desperately needed — while a TV crew from Roanoke waited in the parking lot of a closed-down restaurant nearby, looking through a fence, unable to even get on the property.

Once he got out of the mine, the trouble only got worse. Time was tight. He needed to move on to Abie's Tackle and Gun Shop, the first public stop of the day. Instead he got his first real introduction to road problems in Southwest Virginia, Edgar Bacon's detours notwithstanding. The only road to Westmoreland's Bullit mine crosses a railroad track. And for a full half hour, Wilder sat there, watching a coal train rumble past.

It was check day in Appalachia. "This place around here, there's just three kind of checks — coal mining, railroading and welfare," said retired miner Ott Stanley. And this was the day they all came in.

The town of Appalachia was immobilized. A long line of horn-honking pickup trucks tied up Main Street from one end of this grimy little town to the other, as old miners came down out of the hills to pick up their Social Security checks and black lung checks. Drivers leaned out of their windows to shout at friends on the sidewalk; they leaned on their horns if shouting didn't work. They tried to make impossible left turns across traffic and wound up sitting catty-corner in the middle of the street. Sometimes they simply stopped where they were and their buddies came up to talk with them right there. One wife carried her grocery bags out to her husband's pickup and loaded up the truck in the middle of the street. On check day, the whole town ground to a noisy halt.

Luther Anderson, a retired deputy, stood outside Abie's Tackle and Gun Shop watching the mess get worse. "It's really turning out to be a bad day," he said. Abe Isaac — the Abe in Abie's — was apologetic. He had promised to turn out a big crowd of Democrats to meet their candidate for lieutenant governor. Only two or three showed up. "Everybody's waiting on their check. But we won't let him down at the polls, though. No sir, he won't have to worry about Appalachey."

It was nearly noon before Wilder got to Abie's. He came down the street shaking hands, still dressed in his miner's suit — a searchlight on his helmet, dirty boots over his dress shoes. Shoppers across the street saw the TV cameras, came over to see what all the commotion was about and a crowd began to gather. Wilder waded into it with obvious enthusiasm.

Ott Stanley would have been here anyway. He's hung out at Abie's ever since he retired from forty-five years in the mines. "This is my corner for the last six years." Stanley shook Wilder's hand, then stepped back to look him over. Stanley was a regular sidewalk philosopher. "I vote Democratic, I reckon," Stanley told the reporters who clustered around him. "I vote for the man I think is for me. If he's a good man, I don't care what he is. I read about a feller and size him up. If I think he's for the laborin' class of people, I vote for him."

What about Wilder? "From all I can read about him, he seems a pretty smart fellow." Does that mean you'll vote for Wilder? Stanley thought a bit. "I think so." What about race? Stanley seemed surprised by the question. "We've got colored people around here," he said. "We've got some colored people who was raised here, raised in the coal camps. They've been here all their lives. They're respected. It's not like up around Richmond. Color don't make too much difference around here." He looked over at Wilder again. "He seems an awful shrewd fellow. They say around here, if you find a shrewd colored fellow, you got a smart one."

The traffic out of Appalachia was as bad as the traffic in. Wilder was more than an hour late getting to Big Stone Gap, but six people were still waiting to eat lunch with him at the Italian Restaurant and Carry-Out. After that, it was downhill all the way to Weber City.

The afternoon unraveled like thread. After lunch, Wilder was supposed to stop at the *Big Stone Gap Post* for an interview, but the editor wasn't there and no one knew when he was going to be back.

The tour was running behind anyway, so Goldman decided Wilder should go on to Duffield, where a group of Scott County Democrats was supposed to be waiting at the Ramada Inn.

But when Wilder got to Duffield no one was there. Goldman searched through all the Ramada's meeting rooms and found them empty. The desk clerk pleaded ignorance. Everyone stood around waiting for orders until it was finally decided that as long as he was here, Wilder should go to the Big A Warehouse supermarket next door.

The Big A should have been a sign to stay away from supermarkets the rest of the day. Wilder didn't meet more than a half-dozen voters and those he did meet looked at him as if he were some sort of apparition. A few stammered "thank you" to his literature but that was about all. It was embarrassing to watch this proud man wandering up and down the aisles of the empty store looking for someone to shake hands with.

But the worst was yet to come.

It was four o'clock on a Friday afternoon when Wilder arrived in Gate City and, outside of the Democratic loyalists at Abie's and at lunch, he hadn't met two dozen voters all day. Cecil McClelland, a slow-moving bookbinder who was county Democratic chairman, was waiting for him at the county courthouse. "I understand you'd like to do some interviews," McClelland said. "Why don't we go over to the radio station?" The entourage crossed the street and filed upstairs into WGAT. No one was in the lobby. McClelland poked around, found a youthful disc jockey in the studio and announced that he had Doug Wilder here for his interview.

The DJ had no idea what was going on. "I'm just part-time," he said. "Everybody took half a day off."

"Can't you just ask him some questions?" McClelland asked.

"No, I'm not qualified to do that," he said.

McClelland tried to persuade him that all he had to do was give Wilder a mike and just let him start talking but the DJ would have nothing of it. "He says he's not qualified, let's get going," Wilder said.

McClelland took Wilder down the street to Del. Ford Quillen's law office. Quillen was out of town on business. His law partners weren't in, either. Wilder shook hands with the secretaries and left. The sheriff wasn't in his office, either. Wilder found some prisoners hosing down a patrol car out back, but didn't offer to shake hands.

The editor of the local paper, the *Virginia Star,* was in, however. McClelland had arranged that much — his wife was the paper's editor, writer and photographer. She interviewed Wilder in the newspaper's cramped basement office while her husband lamented the lack of preparation for the candidate's visit. "I work every day and didn't have time to do it," he said. "If he had gotten down here about nine this morning, he'd have met a lot of people down at the flea market."

By now it was close to five o'clock and Wilder still hadn't met any ordinary voters in Scott County. So when McClelland suggested they go to some of the supermarkets on the edge of town, it seemed like a great idea. Judith Pierson was cleaning the sliding glass doors at the new Food Lion when Wilder came by and introduced himself. "Oh, I saw you on TV," an excited Pierson said. "I thought I recognized you." It was the last thing to go right in Gate City.

A few minutes later Wilder was kicked out of the store.

Wilder had worked his way through most of the supermarket when the store manager zeroed in on him. Wilder saw the man coming, extended his hand in greeting and introduced himself. The manager listened blankly while Wilder reeled off his standard spiel about how he was traveling to every city and county in Virginia. Then the manager told him he had to leave, the store didn't allow solicitations. A reporter asked about his politics. He wasn't amused. "I don't want to discuss it," he snapped and hustled the candidate and his crowd out the front door.

McClelland suggested they try the new Oakwood Market in adjacent Weber City. Wilder sent Goldman in first to check if it was all right. The owners of this supermarket were delighted. It was their grand opening and were looking for all the publicity they could get. The two owners met Wilder at the door and ushered him in like a celebrity. Wilder met maybe two dozen voters here, more than he'd met all day.

Buoyed by the success at the Oakwood, the campaign moved on to the Food City. Goldman had barely gone in to get permission when he came back out again. The store's manager was right behind him, looking as angry as if he had just caught the competition snooping on prices. No campaigning here.

The reporters waited at the front of the store while Goldman and Wilder went to use the pay phone by the manager's office to check in with Michael Brown in the Richmond office. That seemed to infuriate the manager even more. He demanded that the reporters leave at once. Can't, someone said. We're riding with them. Then go outside and wait there, the manager ordered. "I don't want you bothering any shoppers, do you hear?" The reporters shuffled out the door and stood on the sidewalk while the manager stood at the checkout line, arms folded, feet apart, glaring at these strangers who had dared invade his supermarket. In the parking lot, a bag boy went up to Larry Wilder and asked: "Are you all Hare Krishnas?"

The signs of doom were unmistakable. Maybe Lee County had been a one-day wonder. Edgar Bacon wouldn't have been thrown out of a supermarket. He'd have probably had a cousin or nephew or niece working at all of them anyway. Yet even while the traveling pundits of the press were pronouncing the tour a bad idea from the start, so many Democrats were trying to get into the Mountain Empire's tiny banquet room that the waitresses had to open the partition and let some sit in the dining room.

When it came time to speak, Wilder was fired up, as if trying to make up for the disaster of the afternoon. Until now he had been low-key, purposely so, delivering a simple message about how his campaign was based on his faith in the people of Virginia to choose the most qualified candidate. In Weber City, he lit a barn-burner of a speech about why he was the most qualified. Many of the lines would be repeated as the campaign wore on, but never with this passion.

Wilder talked about his bill to require mandatory sentences for escaped felons. "If you're a lifer, you'd better keep running because if you're caught, you won't get out again. I didn't talk about that. I did it," he said, stabbing the air with his finger. "I didn't just talk about education. I put in a compulsory school education bill so we wouldn't have young people out willy-nilly on the street when they ought to be in school. People ask when I became interested in crime. I say as soon as I got there in the Senate, I put in a drug paraphernalia bill. That was back in 1971. I'm not a Johnny-come-lately to the political scene."

It was a masterful performance, one that showcased Wilder's strongest suits: his resume and his power as a speaker. One of the women was so moved she pulled Goldman's baseball cap off his head, passed it around and collected $132.50. Why hadn't Wilder's poverty-stricken campaign done that before, he was asked. Goldman gave his usual sheepish grin. "It hadn't dawned on me. Maybe we'll start doing that."

In Bristol, lawyer Kurt Pomrenke, city Democratic chairman, whisked Wilder away for the night. The reporters hustled Goldman into the Holiday Inn's bar and grilled him about the debacle in Scott County.

Outside of the set-piece party functions, Wilder probably didn't meet twenty-five honest-to-goodness voters all day, reporters complained.

"So?" Goldman answered. "If you go into a town of 2,500 people and meet twenty-five people, by proportion, if you went into Richmond you'd have to meet 2,500 people. No candidate ever meets 2,500 people in a day." Word will get around, he insisted. "When was the last time a candidate spent two solid weeks in the Ninth District? People will start paying attention."

A word-of-mouth campaign? Come on, Paul, the reporters pestered, here you have one of the best orators in the state. He was brilliant tonight except nobody heard him. Why not have him speak more often instead of just shaking hands? Instead of taking him into a small town and having the local Democratic chairman introduce him to all his friends, why not put him in front of civic groups — the Ruritans, Rotary, the Farm Bureau, the VFW?

Goldman mumbled something about groups like that being hard to set up when the tour needed them. Besides, he said, reporters were missing the point. Look at the party support Wilder was getting in Southwest Virginia. "Four or five months ago they said you'll never get a vote out here, but Democrats are rallying to Doug as much as any of the candidates. They're identifying with him. They're identifying with him as a man who worked his way up. And his Korean War experience, that's a big thing out here."

Yes, but you need more than Democratic voters, the reporters countered. Trying to reason with Paul Goldman, though, was like trying to reason with a brick wall. After two days, it was obvious the tour wasn't going to work. Why wasn't Wilder out raising money? That's what he'd need in October, not clippings from local newspapers. If he really wanted to make this tour, why didn't he do it right after the convention? Now he's committed to staying on the road through September, leaving only October — one month — free for real campaigning. By then it surely would be too little, too late, as if it really mattered at all.

At least with Mike Musick helping out, maybe Wilder won't have a repeat of what happened in Scott County. Musick, a University of Virginia student from Russell County who was a former campaign worker for Rep. Rick Boucher, had been signed up to advance the rest of Wilder's tour through Southwest Virginia. He seemed to be on the ball. But what difference would it make? After today, all the reporters were going home to write their stories for Sunday. Campaigns are media events, yet Wilder would be campaigning in a vacuum. Suppose Wilder did get big crowds in some of these other towns — if a tree falls in a forest and no one's there to hear it, does it make a sound?

Aug. 3, 1985

Kurt Pomrenke was worried. A month ago Mary Sue Terry had been in

Bristol for a Saturday morning breakfast and only twenty-five people showed up. The Bristol Democratic chairman had spent the week calling everyone he knew, just hoping enough people would show up to meet Wilder so neither he nor the candidate would be embarrassed too badly. He hesitantly told the Holiday Inn to expect twenty people.

He got fifty-two instead.

Waitresses had to bring in extra tables — in the same room where the night before Goldman had been questioned so unmercifully. Even then some people had to sit in the dining room.

After the missed signals in Scott County, the big Bristol crowd looked awfully good to Wilder. "It pumps the adrenalin more so than you can imagine," he told the Democrats. "It makes my job easier. I'm horsed up, pumped up and ready to go for the next several hundred miles. All we've got to do is put our shoulders to the wheel and push, push, push. And pay no attention to the naysayers that say it can't be done."

After breakfast, Pomrenke took Wilder to a bluegrass festival on State Street, mostly to kill time. He wondered whether it was a good idea to take the state's most prominent black politician into the crowd. But Wilder eagerly waded in, sometimes shouting to make himself heard over the twang of the banjos. He spotted a man with a VFW cap and started swapping war stories. Pomrenke was astounded at how well the crowd took to Wilder. "When he first went up to them, I could see they were hesitant but as he talked to them, you could just see them warm up to him. He could always find something to talk with somebody about." Wilder spent almost an hour working his way around the edge of the festival crowd. Eventually he wound up near the stage, where he shook hands with a burly old bluegrass musician. A few minutes later the man grabbed the microphone and introduced Wilder. Applause rippled through the crowd. Pomrenke began to doubt what he was seeing. He had long since given up on the lieutenant governor's race. Now he began to wonder. "I still didn't think he could win but I began to think he might run a respectable race after all."

Aug. 4, 1985

The reviews were in and they were cautiously favorable.

The media coverage of the first three days of the tour "could have been the death knell of the campaign," Wilder says. Instead, the state's major newspapers uniformly expressed surprise at the big crowds at party functions and emphasized the comments from ordinary voters who said race didn't matter to them.

The *Richmond Times-Dispatch* played up quotes from voters who were undecided, but: "Their doubts, their indecision, seemingly had nothing to do with race. Indeed, time after time last week, Southwest Virginia voters said that race would have little bearing on the Election Day outcome in their isolated corner of the Appalachians."

All the papers focused on the mechanics of the tour and overlooked its mystique. "The key question as Wilder's tour continues is whether a country store campaign suited to running for county sheriff can work in a statewide race," said the *Times & World-News*. "Wilder's long march seems sure to stretch the candidate's already anemic campaign organization even thinner by the time the sixty-day trek is over," said the *Times-Dispatch*.

Still, considering the things the reporters were saying privately, it was kind treatment. The only thing that sent Goldman into a tirade was the description of him in the *Times-Dispatch* as a "grape-gobbling, banana-munching vegetarian."

Only the *Richmond News Leader* came close to stumbling upon the truth that would ultimately make the difference in the campaign: "Throughout the day, person after person said he hadn't heard of Wilder. However, few had heard of Chichester [either]."

When Doug Wilder turned in the long driveway, he saw the biggest Confederate flag he'd ever seen. The pole was as tall as a street light, planted squarely in the front lawn of the estate. A scruffy-looking white man in work clothes was sitting on the front porch of the mansion.

This was the man Wilder had been told to be sure to see while he was in Southwest Virginia?

Mike Musick eased the car to a stop and cut off the engine. Well, here we are.

Benjamin Lambert, the black optometrist/legislator back in Richmond, and Bob Lambert, white quarry owner in Abingdon, share the same last name, the same wide girth and the same politics. Once at a Democratic convention, each spied the other's name tag and joked how they must be cousins. The two Lamberts became unlikely fast friends. Benny Lambert liked to introduce Bob at state conventions to friends by saying, "This is my white cousin." The friendship was so firm that in the summer of 1985 Bob Lambert had even rung up Benny Lambert and invited him to a family gathering he was planning out in Abingdon. "I said 'No, I can't make it, but when my friend Doug Wilder is out there, you take care of him,' " Benny Lambert says. And he reminded Wilder that his buddy Bob, owner of the the Acme Stone quarry outside Abingdon, was a man with plenty of money to spend on candidates who struck his fancy.

But now, after the pleasant cruise up the interstate and a less-pleasant ride down the dirt road to the house, Wilder was having some second thoughts. Lambert's country drawl had sounded friendly enough on the phone, but Wilder didn't know what to make of this rebel flag business. Or, for that matter, what to make of Lambert himself — a slow-talking man whose big jowls seemed even bigger with the thick wad of chewing tobacco he kept inside his cheeks. Every now and then he'd lean over, part his lips and let a long, vile stream of tobacco juice drip out onto the ground.

But too late to turn back now.

Wilder went up to introduce himself. Lambert squeezed his meaty hand around Wilder's and invited him to sit a spell.

The pair sat on the porch talking. Lambert was bragging about his house. "I reckon we got the prettiest little house and farm in Southwest Virginia," he said. One of the oldest, too. Got the date on the cornerstone to prove it. It's under the porch. Come on, Lambert said, I'll show it to you.

Lambert bounded down the steps, got down on hands and knees and crawled under the porch. Wilder, minus a coat but still in his dress clothes, cautiously followed him.

After Lambert was satisfied Wilder had gotten a good look at the cornerstone, they crawled out, dusted themselves off and went to look at the barns. Lambert breeds horses and he wasn't going to pass up a chance to show off his stables. Wilder mentioned he liked horses, too. Lambert flashed a big, proud grin. "OK. I just might arrange for you to get one."

Lambert led Wilder back around to the house, which had certainly changed a lot since the eighteenth century. Lambert had a swimming pool outside, a hot tub inside.

In the hall Wilder spotted a bucket of mountain trout and commented on how he'd had some tasty fish at the Village Inn in Dryden last week.

"You are staying for supper, aren't you?" Lambert asked.

Wilder was hesitant. "I was still looking at that flag," he recalls. But Lambert was insistent. Come on, have some supper with us.

Those trout did look mighty good.

"Oh, those won't be enough," Lambert said. "The boys will be eating with us."

Boys?

Lambert meant his cousin and another fellow. One had a big chaw of Red Man the size of a man's fist jammed in his cheek. The other was dipping snuff.

"You mind going with the boys to get some more fish?" Lambert asked.

"Now?" Wilder asked.

"Sure."

Now this was something to think about. Lambert seemed a nice enough fellow but he was flying that Confederate flag, and a damn big one, too. And what was this talk about sending Wilder off with the "boys"? He'd never even met these people before, and they were dressed like some kinds of rednecks out of "Deliverance." But there wasn't time to think it all through. In a jiffy, Lambert gathered up some fishing poles and tossed them in the back of his pickup. Wilder gingerly crawled in with "the boys" and off they went, the state's most prominent black politician riding off into the Southern woods with some burly white strangers who flew a rebel flag in their front yard.

They must have made a sight when they stopped at Jimbo's Market — two white men clumping in wearing boots and overalls, looking for some worms to go fishing with, while a black man in his Sunday clothes tagged along behind them, asking for razor blades. Nobody said anything, but Wilder felt that everybody in the store was looking at him and wondering what he was doing with those guys.

The fishing didn't last long. They went up to one of Lambert's quarries. The water was dark limestone blue and icy cold. The fish were almost leaping out. In a half hour, they caught about two dozen, mostly mountain trout, a couple of catfish. Lambert took them back to the house, fried some and smoked the rest. "Doug helped out. He turned 'em once," Musick recalls, "but Bob was definitely the master chef." Then everybody sat down to a country supper. Afterward, some of Lambert's buddies came over to meet Wilder.

By the time they left, Wilder said he'd better be going, too. Lambert said he hated to see him go and wanted Wilder to see his TV first. Lambert escorted Wilder into the living room, where there was a big-screen set. The threesome that remained — Lambert, Wilder and Musick — watched TV a spell. "As I remember, Bob kinda reached out," Musick says. "He had the check already drawn. He gave it to Doug and said 'I guess we made it out the right way.' " Wilder looked at the amount: $1,000. Pocket change for Baliles, that was big money for Wilder. "I'll get you another $1,000 before long," Lambert said. And he did.

The story of Wilder's visit with Bob Lambert was one the candidate told throughout the campaign whenever he was before a black audience and needed to illustrate the type of support he was getting from white voters. Often there were loud gasps when Wilder spoke about going to see a man flying "the biggest Confederate flag I have ever seen."

But the flag story was more than a good campaign tale. In a way, it shows how much the South has changed — and also how much some blacks remain skeptical of the changes that most whites now take for granted. "All these rebel flags flying on license plates — that is hate," said the Rev. M.O. Brown, a black Bristol preacher, when asked about the racial climate there. And months after the election, Bob Lambert's Confederate flag still stuck in Wilder's mind, a haunting, troubling image he couldn't quite resolve with the well-meaning man who flew it. Lambert, on the other hand, hadn't given much thought to it during Wilder's visit. "I noticed he kept taking his eye to that flag, but I didn't think much about that," Lambert says. "I fly the flag all the time. We've been flying it for years. We're old Southerners, you know." The irony of a man who proudly flies the Stars and Bars also proudly supporting a black candidate for office hadn't occurred to him. "Times have changed, you know," he says laconically. For him, Southern pride no longer has anything to do with race. "I was with Doug all the way," says Lambert, "even before I met him."

And not long after his visit with Bob Lambert, Wilder phoned Benny Lambert back in Richmond. "You got any more cousins like that in Southwest Virginia?"

Aug. 5, 1985

Wilder was on his own now. The reporters were gone. A few showed up here and there for specific events, but the intense media interest in the tour was over. Wilder had only been on the road four days.

The Wilder campaign had passed the test of media scrutiny in Lee, Wise and Scott counties. But now it entered another, equally risky phase — making the tour work the rest of the way.

Chichester had two months to fly around the state, raise money and monopolize the major media markets — while Wilder was stuck driving down back roads, stopping at country stores in search of voters to shake hands with. It was the campaign equivalent of simply disappearing from the face of the earth for two months.

The idea that Chichester would intentionally pass up free publicity — as he would — was inconceivable. And the prospect of Wilder becoming a folk hero, a *cause celebre* whose arrival was anticipated by grizzled old farmers sitting around country stores, was so fantastic that only someone seriously out of touch with Virginia reality could possibly imagine it.

The first full week of the tour began with a breakfast in Russell County. There were thirty-five Democrats at the Bonanza restaurant in Lebanon, remarkably enthusiastic for a Monday morning. "It was sort of like a tent-revival atmosphere," says Musick. The county chairman suggested taking up a collection. Someone found a sausage box, crossed out the brand name, scrawled in "Wilder" and passed it around. When it came back, there was $202 inside.

Then it was on to Cleveland and Dante, lunch with United Mine Workers officials at Castlewood, then into St. Paul, Coeburn, Tacoma and Norton. In each town Wilder was greeted by the local Democratic organizer, who would take him around and introduce him to other Democrats — lawyers, town officials, shop owners. At the Cleveland Town Hall, Wilder spotted a sign on the wall from an old coal company that used to work the area: "Wilder Coal Co." "Doug saw the banner and laughed uproariously," Musick remembers. At Coeburn, car dealer Bill Hunsaker showed up with a robin's egg blue '63 Thunderbird convertible and had Wilder test drive it around the parking lot. Wilder loved it and even inspected the engine. Sometimes Wilder and his tour guide would stop by a grocery store, such as the Piggly-Wiggly in St. Paul, to meet a few ordinary voters. And sometimes they'd visit the local weekly newspaper for an interview.

While Wilder was at the newspaper in St. Paul, Musick went up the street to talk to a lawyer — and came back with a check for $200.

These were signs of genuine encouragement. But how much did they really mean? Mostly the tour was a long, slow haul over the mountains, interrupted by raw little towns where Wilder met maybe a dozen voters before moving on.

Wilder got to Norton, a gray city of rail yards, late in the afternoon. Stores were closing, people were going home, but Ninth District Chairman Jack Kennedy was there with a few other Democratic regulars to show Wilder around anyway. They were walking down the street when a middle-aged man in greasy olive-drab overalls got out of his pickup and shouted at Wilder.

"What are you running for?" the man yelled.

Wilder went over and introduced himself.

"How'd you get here?" the man demanded to know.

Wilder started telling him about the tour and how he started in Lee County last Thursday.

"No," the man said, "how'd you get here?"

Wilder asked what he meant.

"We need some new roads," said Hoge Horne, a fifty-five-year-old mechanic. "Every day I lose up to an hour and fifty-seven minutes at one stop on account of the trains going down the road and I can't get home."

The main road from Coeburn crosses railroad tracks four times between the Norton city limits and downtown, Horne said. When the trains shift cars, they sometimes tie up traffic for more than a mile. The state was supposed to build a fancy bypass, "but you can look over there and see nothing's been done," Horne complained, pointing toward a hill on the edge of town.

By now he had an audience as local Democrats gathered around to see what was going on.

"I know you don't have time to come and look," Horne said, "but if you did, you'd see what I mean."

Wilder, with an eye on the local reporters clustered around him, wasted no time in responding: "Well, why not?" he said. "Let's go have a look."

Horne was suddenly thrown off-balance. "You sure?"

"Sure, let's go," Wilder said, already opening the door to Horne's pickup and crawling in.

"This won't take long," Horne said, and the truck lurched into gear.

Larry Wilder had already led the way into a bank Wilder's local escort had wanted him to visit. Then he turned around and noticed no one was behind him. "All I could see was a truck about to pull out, reporters leaping onto the truck. I looked at Paul [who had jumped onto the truckbed]. He's as wide-eyed as anyone. Then I saw my father in the middle of the pickup." Ninth District Chairman Jack Kennedy threw up his hands to stop the truck but it was too late. Horne was already out on Main Street headed for the first crossing. "Do you know where your father went?" Kennedy asked Larry Wilder. No, he answered. "Do you know whose truck that is?" Kennedy asked. No, Larry Wilder answered again. Now everyone was really confused. Why had the candidate just jumped into a stranger's pickup truck and ridden away?

Horne took Wilder out to the city limits and back, across all four tracks twice. Sure enough, there was a train at one crossing. It was a short one but it came grinding to a halt right at the crossing, blocking traffic for almost a minute. Horne was delighted to catch one in the act. "There's not much traffic now, but imagine this at rush hour." Wilder agreed the problem was a bad one.

Horne spent half an hour chauffering Wilder around Norton, then returned him downtown. Wilder thanked him for the tour and promised to look into what was holding up the bypass.

Horne was tickled. "My wife'll never believe it when I get home," he said.

Wilder asked what his wife's name was — and while Horne was busy posing for pictures for the local paper, Wilder wrote him a thank-you note to give her as evidence.

That night some three hundred people jammed into the Brass Lantern Restaurant at Wise to hear Wilder, and the candidate responded by delivering one of the best speeches of the campaign. "There were people who said we were crazy to start a cross-state campaign in Lee County," Wilder said. "They said, 'You're going way out there? Way out there in the Southwest?' They said, 'We may never see you again.' I said, 'Bye, y'all.' " The Southwest Virginians loved it. This was a man they could identify with — and one who clearly identified with them.

Afterward, a dozen people followed the candidate to Glenn Craft's home and kept Wilder up past midnight until the Wise County party chairman finally had to tell them the candidate needed his sleep.

The next morning, Craft reminded Wilder how at the convention the candidate had promised him to come down to Wise County "and take my whipping."

"I hope we didn't whip you too bad," Craft said.

Wilder's smile was as bright as the dawn.

Aug. 6, 1985

The mountains became steeper, the roads narrower, the country grimmer. Dickenson County, hard by the Kentucky border, is a county without a single four-lane road or stoplight. At the county seat of Clintwood, Commonwealth's Attorney Gerald Gray was the host of a noontime reception for Wilder. When it came time to pass the hat, the chosen headgear was a miner's hard hat.

By late afternoon, the Wilder station wagon had found its way to Haysi, another little coal town near the Kentucky line. "The streets were just black," Larry Wilder remembers, with more coal trucks rumbling through, spilling their loads and giving the streets another dark dusting.

While Paul Goldman went off to find a telephone, the two Wilders headed for the Moose Lodge, where a small crowd was said to be waiting for the candidate's arrival. While the senior Wilder chatted with some old fellows about coal mining, Larry spotted a big bearded miner with a chew of tobacco in his jaw and a frown on his face. "There was this big fat guy, with a huge stomach and mutton chop sideburns," he remembers. "He looked like the stereotyped Southwest Virginian. He was not saying a whole lot. He was real quiet, putting chaw in his mouth. I looked at him and I said to my father, something to the effect of he appears like he may or may not be one of my father's most ardent supporters, and you can guess what an understatement that was."

Just a few moments later, the mean miner suddenly grabbed Wilder by the arm and pulled him into a corner. "Let's go back here," he said. "I want to talk to you." There he whipped out a roll of bills and peeled off $100. "We'll get you some more. We'll get some of the boys here to support you. We don't talk much but we vote around here." Larry Wilder came up to see what was going on and Wilder introduced him. "You've got a good daddy, boy," the miner said. "Stick with him."

From Haysi, it was on to Vansant and Grundy by sundown. The Buchanan County line was looming ahead. If Wilder knew its reputation, he didn't let on. He was still thinking about the burly red-shirted miner back in Haysi.

"I think he was genuinely surprised," says Larry Wilder. "He'd been told not to go out there. Not that he believed it, but still the thought was there and as we'd go places, he'd make that his theme."

By now, the big media pressure of the first few days was off and the tour was starting to develop its own private rhythm. The station wagon campaign would roll into one little town after another, and the threesome would go into their routine with a precision that would do both con men and crusaders proud — Goldman searching for a pay phone while Wilder hit the nearest country store, feed store, post office, or whatever seemed the likeliest meeting place. "My father would invariably wind up giving a speech or discussion," Larry Wilder says. "Paul was always scurrying about, lining up the next stop, and then eventually someone would pass the hat." Larry would be behind his father, passing out the "war cards" and tour post cards.

Then it was back into the car to check the map, figure out what the next town was and get ready to do it all over again.

As amazing as the scene was when Wilder and Co. would descend upon some unsuspecting little burg like a tornado out of the clear summer sky, the scene in the car between stops was even more so.

Wilder was always admonishing Goldman to keep the car neat, a near impossibility whenever Goldman was involved. "My father got tired of seeing little Oatos all around the car," Larry Wilder says. The candidate also seemed to have a constant fear that Goldman would get into some unspecified trouble along the way. "He always told me, 'Look after Paul,'" Larry Wilder says. Then there was the constant tug of war over the maps. "My father had a map and Paul had 'our' map," Larry says. "Our copy, before it was lost, was ripped into sheets. Every time Paul asked my father for his map, he said, 'No, this is mine.' " Wilder, in fact, kept his map and his copy of the tour schedule locked in his briefcase — the one with the lock only he knew the combination to.

There was always a certain air of seriousness in the car — emanating from the candidate. "He wouldn't even mention [Chichester's] name among us," Larry says. "It was always 'my opponent.' "

Mike Musick had spent the day on the road on to Tazewell, lining up places for Wilder to stop on Wednesday. But he kept looking at his watch, making sure the time didn't slip away from him. He wanted to make sure he had plenty of time to get back to meet Wilder at the Buchanan County Courthouse at 6 p.m.

"I was scared to death about Grundy," Musick says. "I took off to the courthouse to make sure at least someone would be there to meet him. I figured if the tour would bomb anywhere in the state, it would bomb in Grundy."

Grundy. The town's very name has a disparaging sound, low and guttural like the painful grunt of some wild animal, or at best absurdly comical, like the schoolmarmish Miss Grundy in the "Archie" comic strip. Either way, the ugly sound is not far off from the ugly picture many Virginians have of Buchanan County and its county seat. Buchanan is perhaps the most reliably Democratic county in Virginia. It also is reputed to be one of the most racist.

It's tough to say how much of Buchanan County's reputation is deserved. It really doesn't matter, probably, because the stories have such widespread currency that the mere mention of Buchanan County in connection with race serves as a convenient, and readily understood, metaphor.

Buchanan County has only twenty-one blacks out of a population of 37,989. But even that figure exceeds expectations. "They have no blacks in Buchanan County," says Washington County Democratic Chairman Fred Parker. "The last one they had they hung in the 1940s sometime and ran the rest out of town. The story goes that back in the days of the civil rights movement, the civil rights workers would come down and they'd escort 'em right to the county line."

Others tell stories of the infamous sign that was posted at the train station (or county line, depending on who's telling the story) and read something to the effect of "Nigger Be Gone by Sundown" or "Nigger Don't Let Sundown Catch You in This County." Either way, the sign story is apparently true. "I've seen those signs," says House Speaker A.L.

Philpott, though he won't repeat the exact wording, not even in private. "They were crude."

With all this in mind, Musick cut his advance work short and raced back over the mountains to Grundy. But when Musick got to the courthouse, he found cars parked everywhere — and a big crowd waiting for the candidate. "I was standing there in a corner with my mouth hanging open," Musick says. Maybe some thirty Democrats squeezed into the Board of Supervisors' meeting room for coffee and donuts. "And Doug charmed them all," Musick says.

County officials came up to Wilder, slapped him on the back and assured him they'd round up all the support for him they could. Musick was practically in shock. "I remember people patting him on the back saying, 'Don't worry, people say you won't do well in Buchanan County but we know you will.' " For another candidate that might have been an insult; for Wilder, the people seemed absolutely sincere.

By the end of the day, Wilder was bushed. All that riding, all that handshaking could take its toll. And there was still work to be done. Wilder's briefcase was stuffed with cash and checks, collected at all the pass-the-hat sessions along the way. He didn't like the thought of carrying so much cash around. He wanted to go to a bank in the morning and trade in all the bills for a cashier's check they could take back to Richmond over the weekend. He was also more than a little curious to know just how much he had raised.

So, as midnight approached in their motel, the candidate, his son and campaign consultant sat on one of the beds, counting out the cash, piling it up in neat little stacks. Larry Wilder found the scene unreal. "Even though people realized my father's campaign was necessarily small, I don't think anybody would picture him and Paul in charge of everything. Yet here they were counting the day's haul. I took the ones and fives and they took the tens and twenties." Wilder regaled his traveling companions with some story about the movie "The Treasure of the Sierra Madre," and how its plot related to this campaign. Larry Wilder couldn't help but shake his head as he counted out the money. "I thought, this has got to be wrong. There ought to be a different way to do this."

Aug. 7, 1985

Back in Richmond, Vice President George Bush was in town for a fund-raiser that netted $200,000 for the GOP. Unfortunately, that was only about half of what the Republicans had expected to make when they had originally booked Reagan, now recuperating from cancer surgery.

The shortfall came at a bad time for the GOP. The Democrats' latest finance reports came out the same day — and showed both Baliles and Terry raising more money than their Republican opponents. Even Wilder seemed to be holding his own. Chichester had raised $306,240, but Wilder wasn't far behind, with $301,410. Significantly, Chichester's fund-raising total included what he had raised to get him through the convention, so of that $306,240, he now had only $84,360 in the bank, plus $96,100 in debts. But Wilder had no debts and a little more than $175,000 in the bank — an edge of more than 2-1.

Aug. 9, 1985

Madison Marye was sitting on the hood of his car in the little courthouse town of Independence, waiting for Wilder to show up. He checked his watch. Wilder was late.

Two men came by and asked Marye — the state senator for the rural district running from Grayson County to Montgomery County — what he was doing in town. When Marye told them Wilder was about to arrive, they shook their heads. "Well," they said, "he's certainly nice but he doesn't have a chance. We don't know if we can support him or not."

Marye himself wondered how Wilder would go over in his district. It was mostly highland country, where the lovely Blue Ridge spread out into a hilly plateau. These were mountaineers of a different sort from the kind that welcomed Wilder to the coalfields. They shared the same pride and same prejudices of other Southwest Virginians. But they were farmers, not miners, men and women with an innate distrust of government. Marye was a farmer, too, from up in Montgomery County, and that was one reason for his success in what otherwise would be politically barren territory. Even in the days when Democrats ruled Virginia, the Republicans thrived here, the mountain in the original mountain-valley Republicans.

But Marye's doubts soon began to ease. While Marye sat on the hood of his car in Independence, Wilder was being chased down U.S. 21 by a man honking his horn and waving at him to pull over.

Elk Creek is easy to miss. There never was much there and nowadays there's even less. The old Elk Creek Shell used to be the main landmark, but it's closed now. Still, Elk Creek is the first community you come to coming down the mountain from Wythe County and it was on the state highway map, so Goldman was determined Wilder would stop there.

Farmer Ralph Delp had been told to do what he could to round up some people to meet Wilder when he came through. Delp had outdone himself — maybe forty people showed up. But now Wilder was way overdue and the crowd began to drift away, pleading chores to do at home. Still, some two dozen folks remained, curious to meet this black fellow who's traveling all around the state, stopping in tiny places like Elk Creek.

Three or four blacks were in the crowd. One of them was talking to Lasco Simms, a local forestry worker, about Wilder's campaign. "Him being black, I don't know if he'll have a chance or not," the black man said. Some of the whites tried to cheer him up. "Oh, you can't tell," one of them said. "He's got a good record. That means a lot."

The men were busy talking, looking up the road every now and then to see if any cars were coming, when a station wagon whizzed past them. Was that him? It looked like a black fellow riding in there and another black fellow driving, someone said. Usually not too many blacks go through here. And he's supposed to be driving a station wagon. Maybe he's going to skip Elk Creek since he's running behind. "Catch him, catch him," a couple of the men shouted. Cliff Simms, the retired county treasurer, looked at his brother Lasco. "Well, I reckon I'll go get him," Lasco said.

Simms got in his car and went barreling down the road.

Coming down the mountain on Virginia 21, Larry Wilder spotted some construction workers working on the highway, so he pulled over so his father could get out and talk to them. A sign for the Elk Creek dragstrip was nearby. So much for Elk Creek, they thought. The station-wagon campaign rolled on.

A little farther down the mountain, the car whizzed past a little country store. "I had my eyes on the road," Larry Wilder says. "Paul noticed some people. "Hey, there's some people." I briefly let my foot off the gas, but my father said go on. Paul said, "I don't know, Douglas, people are starting to get wind that we're coming through."

Wilder was unconvinced. He'd spotted the people, too, standing around a store back there but hadn't paid much attention to it. "I don't think my father appreciated that people were anticipating him," Larry Wilder says. "Paul was always trying to build things up but Dad discounted it."

All of a sudden a car zoomed up over the hill, doing 60 or 65 on the mountain road. Larry eyed it in the rear-view mirror. "You're doing the speed limit," his father advised him, "Don't worry about it, let him pass you." But the car stayed right on their bumper.

The way the story was embellished later on, it had a nervous Larry Wilder frantically checking his rear-view mirror to report on the progress of the speeding car gaining on his tail:

"It's getting closer, daddy." "Better keep going." "He's right on our bumper, daddy." "Better keep going." "He's waving at me to pull over, daddy." Then Wilder would stop and deadpan: "Well, this was Southwest Virginia, so we didn't know what to expect," a line that invariably brought guffaws to Southwest Virginia audiences that liked a politician who could poke fun at himself.

Larry Wilder tells the story this way: "I looked into the mirror and there's a guy coming up on me. Finally he's right behind me. He's gesturing. I don't know what to make of it. Then he passed us, got in front of us and slowed down, still gesturing."

However the story was told, Simms finally caught up with Wilder about two miles down the road. Simms honked his horn, pulled up beside the station wagon in the passing lane and motioned for Larry Wilder to pull over. "Better stop and see what he wants," Wilder said.

A middle-age man wearing a hunting cap and camouflage pants got out of the car and ambled back toward the station wagon. The air conditioning was on. Wilder told his son to cut it off and roll down the window.

"You Senator Wilder?" the man said.

Wilder said he was.

"Aren't you looking for us? Elk Creek? You passed it back there."

Larry Wilder looked over at Goldman, who had to bury his face in his hands to keep from laughing out loud.

Doug Wilder jumped out of the car, shook Simms' hand and they all had a good laugh. Wilder rode back to Elk Creek in Simms' car and stayed about twenty minutes. Goldman spied a pay phone, called The Associated Press in Richmond and put Lasco Simms on the line. Who would have thought two weeks ago that people would be coming after us, wanting us to stop in their town, Goldman kept telling the AP in his rapid-fire Veg-a-matic sales pitch.

When Wilder finally left Elk Creek, he had the good ole boys there firmly in his pocket. "I didn't think he had a chance," confessed Lasco Simms, "but after I met him, and talked to him, saw his personality, it changed my mind. I heard other people talking about it, too. He just changed everybody's mind. There were twenty-five of us there and we talk, to different people, so you know word gets around."

Just as Paul Goldman said it would.

When Wilder told him what had happened back at Elk Creek, Marye could scarcely believe it. He knew those people. "I thought to myself, that's a good sign. He's catching on."

Marye would see a lot more signs in the three days he squired Wilder around his district.

In Dublin that Saturday, Wilder stopped by a barbershop. The man cutting hair mumbled, "How you? Glad you're in town" and nothing else. Wilder left, thinking he had gotten a chilly reception. The next Monday, at the courthouse in Radford, Wilder spotted the same man. The barber went up to Wilder and mumbled again, "How you? Remember seeing me?" Wilder said he did. "Where?" the barber asked. "At the barbershop." The barber nodded silently, looking Wilder over. "We got a VFW lodge down the street," he finally said. "Like for you to go down and take a picture with the fellows. I'd like to introduce you around."

Michael Brown was in his basement command post working the phones when out of the corner of his eye he saw a black man he didn't know come down the steps, an alarming breech of security at the front desk.

The phones were almost hopping that morning and it took almost fifteen minutes before Brown could get them quieted down enough to see what this stranger wanted.

The man introduced himself as Mallverse Nichollson, an administrator at Norfolk State University. He said he was in town for the day and wanted to drop a little something off at Wilder headquarters. Nichollson said he'd been off on vacation and decided to call a few friends to see if they could help out the Wilder campaign and here was the result. He handed Brown a thick wad of checks. Most were for $25 or so each, but they totaled more than $1,185. For once, even the inscrutable Michael Brown let his emotions show. "He was somewhat stunned," was the understated way Nichollson recalls the encounter.

But Nichollson wasn't done. In the weeks to come, he continued to forward checks to the Wilder campaign, by mail this time. In all, he raised about $4,000 from his impromptu one-man fund-raising campaign. Like Jackie Epps and Paul Goldman, Nichollson sees "black money" as a key source of contributions for black candidates in the future. "I'm talking about a whole clientele that's not on anybody's mailing list," he says. "It's almost a gold mine out here that's just never been worked before."

Another sign of the financial role the black middle-class played in the campaign came the second weekend in August, when Wilder took a break from the tour to attend a fund-raiser that Dot Powell — the assistant attorney general who was part of Jackie Epps' fund-raising team — had helped organize. It was at the home of Larry Elder, the white common-wealth's attorney in rural Dinwiddie County, just outside Petersburg. Elder had cautioned the eager Powell not to expect much of a crowd — but the hundred people who showed up (about half black, half white) exceeded even her expectations. So did the $5,000 they left behind. "It was the most successful fund-raiser he'd ever had," Powell says.

Aug. 12, 1985

Back to the Fightin' Ninth.

Madison Marye met Wilder in Radford on Monday morning for the second of the candidate's three days in Marye's sprawling district. Whenever he was with the farmer Marye, Wilder could count on putting in a full day's work. "Madison wore me out today," Wilder told his son one night.

After hitting businesses downtown, Marye took Wilder up to Giles County on the West Virginia line. This was Republican country and might be a tough county for Wilder to crack. Marye was in for another surprise.

"Doug just came out here and charmed the socks off everybody," Marye said. "He conducted an excellent country store campaign. He took advice, which most candidates don't do. One thing I mentioned, when you go into a country store, do it with the smallest possible entourage possible. Usually there's one guy taking notes, one taking pictures, a couple handing out literature, people don't know who the candidate is. He thought it was good advice and began leaving off some of the people, telling 'em to stay in the car. Very frankly, I thought Paul should stay in the background more and he did. Paul didn't look like a Southwest Virginian. He tried to fit in by wearing his baseball cap but try as he might to fit in with the country store, he couldn't fit in.

"Usually it was just Doug and myself who went in. Sometimes his son came along and he was a great asset. He was quiet, inoffensive, created the impression of a nice, clean-cut young man. And it didn't hurt for Doug to be able to say, 'This is my son, he's a law student at the University of Virginia.'

"When you go into a country store, I feel you ought to buy something. Well, don't you know, up in Giles, the store owners wouldn't accept money for anything. That indicated to me, here's a fellow who's really being accepted. We didn't pass up anyone. You know how Southwest Virginians sit. Never know what they're thinking. They may have a scowl on their face and you say, 'How are you?' and may turn out to be pleasant. Well, Doug shook hands with everyone and no one refused his hand. He campaigned as if he didn't have a care in the world. He could see the momentum was picking up."

In the county seat of Pearisburg, two teen-age girls — both white — ran up to Wilder and asked for his autograph.

And that night in Marye's impressive hilltop home, Marye and Wilder sat in the living room, talking softly about how it was such a great thing that the grandson of a Confederate officer and the grandson of a slave could find themselves in such a situation.

Aug. 13, 1985

The next morning at Hale's Restaurant in Shawsville, several men came up to the table where Wilder and Marye were eating breakfast, introduced themselves and said they hoped he won.

What was happening here?

The big crowds at party functions in the coalfields were easy enough to explain. Party loyalists were eager to give Wilder a good welcome.

Community pride had something to do with the big turnout, too. Never before had a statewide candidate spent so much time in such small communities. Wilder's race also played a part — a positive one. If there was a poor turnout for Wilder in Southwest Virginia, it likely would be construed by the media as hillbilly racism. "We wanted to show we weren't what some people thought we were," says Jack Kennedy, the district's Democratic chairman.

But that hardly explained the reaction of ordinary voters, the miner in Haysi who pulled Wilder aside and gave him $100, the barber in Dublin who took Wilder to meet his VFW buddies, the country store owners in Giles County who refused to let him pay for his Coca-Cola.

"I still think the strangest phenomenon is how well he did out in Southwest Virginia," says A.L. Philpott. "Obviously he struck a responsive chord with those people, but I don't know how he did it. I thought the hostility would be so strong he couldn't overcome it."

It turns out that the political experts were remarkably out of touch with what the voters were really thinking. Not even the old warhorse Edgar Bacon was prepared for the response Wilder got when he went store-to-store in Lee County. "To be truthful, I had some reservations about the color situation," he says. "I didn't how know much people would be affected. I thought it was absolutely crucial that we got that tour started off properly. If it flopped the first day, what a terrible crash it would have been. But we didn't know. We just didn't know what the reaction would be. We thought our people would be tolerant and not pay any attention to race."

But they turned out to be not simply tolerant but enthusiastic. They not only shook hands with Wilder, they took him by the arm to introduce him to their friends.

Curiosity was certainly one powerful factor in Wilder's favor. Just who was this black man — war hero, powerful state senator — who had the state party in such a tizzy? Wilder was a celebrity. Of sorts.

"People wanted to meet him," Marye recalls. "People ran across the street to meet him. He wasn't the stereotype people thought he would be and as soon as they found that out, that helped to ease their minds."

Wilder had always discounted those who warned him he would stumble into a snakepit of racism in the Southwest mountains. "We had a lot of friends out there and we just couldn't believe they could be that much different from the people around them," he said later.

He had the legacy of history on his side, too.

This was the South, all right, but it was the Appalachian South: Southwest Virginians are the descendants of pioneers, not plantation owners. The antebellum mountaineers generally were poor, family farmers. They owned no slaves, were often indifferent to the Civil War and indignant at being forced to fight to defend a slaveholders' confederacy. West Virginia is the most obvious example of Appalachian estrangement, but Unionism also flourished in pockets throughout the Southern mountains.

Old patterns linger: In Lee County, blacks account for less than 1 percent of the population; the whole Ninth District is only 2 percent black. The result is that Western Virginia — from Southwest Virginia up through the Shenandoah Valley — simply does not have that history of racial tension the rest of Virginia does. "There isn't a lot of racism here," explains Louise Callahan of Lee County, "because there isn't a lot of race." So Doug Wilder evoked more curiosity than controversy west of the Blue Ridge.

Wilder had another thing going for him in Southwest Virginia — that traditional mountaineer independence. The Southwest has never had the same reverential respect for the monied interests of Richmond's Main Street that John Chichester, an ex-Democrat with a good English surname, inadvertently represented. "There's just none of that old plantation mentality in Southwest Virginia," says Fincastle's state Sen. Buzz Emick.

Southwest Virginians looked at Wilder, who may be from Richmond but had done battle with the state establishment often enough to prove himself, and saw him as one of their own in a most peculiar way. They, too, feel discriminated against.

So Southwest Virginia turned out to be the perfect place for Wilder to start his station wagon campaign. Where else could he go and run less of a chance of encountering overt racism in full view of the state's media? The Southwest was a picture-perfect starting point. It was rural. It looked conservative — and helped Wilder build an image of an old-time Virginia politician barnstorming the state. Southwest Virginia was to Wilder what the West Virginia primary was to John Kennedy in 1960. The terrain is similar and both candidates had perceived handicaps to overcome. Kennedy needed to show a Catholic would win Protestant votes and backwoods West Virginia was the unlikely spot he chose to make his stand. Wilder needed to confront the dual issues of racism and party support.

Southwest Virginia gave Wilder exactly the kind of support he needed. The press saw enough in Lee, Scott and Wise counties to get out the bare outlines of the story — and put pressure on other counties down the line to at least match the Southwest welcome.

The initial flurry of stories focused on the official response from the party leaders and precinct workers in Lee, Scott, Wise and Bristol. For the most part, however, the media missed the story of the spontaneous, populist-style reception Wilder got the rest of the way.

Marye saw part of it. By the time he and Wilder parted company at the country store at Copper Hill in Floyd County on Aug. 13 and Wilder headed down Bent Mountain to Roanoke, Marye was convinced Wilder had a real chance of winning. "I was ecstatic by the time he left," Marye recalls. "The ball started rolling here and he just swept through the state gathering momentum."

But no one knew it was coming, so no one bothered to look — until it was too late.

10

Breakfast with the Speaker

Aug. 14, 1985

U.S. 220, the four-lane highway from Roanoke to Rocky Mount, winds through a set of mountains so unimpressive the gap doesn't even have a specific name. Nevertheless, it marks a significant cultural passageway from the valleys of Western Virginia into the red clay country of Southside.

First stop: Franklin County, a hardscrabble, moonshine-drinking, gun-totin' county where the hottest attraction is the local dragstrip (where the promoter once invited the county supervisors to judge his wet T-shirt contests) and even zoning regulations have been considered an infringement on a man's way of life. After two weeks in the Appalachian mountains and valleys, Franklin County was the first place on his tour where Doug Wilder would run into the Deep South — or at least as deep as the South gets in Virginia. The line between Roanoke County and Franklin County is marked not only by the required state highway sign, but also a gun shop flying a tattered rebel flag.

When Hell Froze Over

It was late one afternoon when Wilder arrived at Boones Mill, a classic Southern town with kudzu running rampant on the hillsides and one little combination souvenir stand/fruit stand after another. At the Exxon, the gas pumps were almost lost in the confusion of pottery, yard ornaments, and big bushel baskets of plump red tomatoes, fresh out of the fields.

While Wilder jawboned with the good ole boys at the station, Nancy Cook of the *Daily Press* of Newport News raised her camera and snapped the perfect picture of the campaign: Wilder, in his white shirt with the French cuffs, tie loosened, waving a greeting to someone off in the distance. Behind him, perfectly framed, was the sign "Boones Mill Exxon: Virginia apples, cold cider." And a faded Confederate flag.

Evening fell. By the time Wilder and state Sen. Virgil Goode, D-Rocky Mount, got to Sydnorsville, the lone store there had closed. Wilder took out one of his post cards, penned a brief note and left it sticking in the door. Then they headed on back to Rocky Mount and a supper with Franklin County Democrats.

State Sen. Granger Macfarlane had come down from Roanoke; he was curious to see how Wilder would go over with his first real Southside audience. Senate clerk Jay Shropshire from nearby Martinsville was curious, too.

What they found amazed them both. There were maybe 150 people that night, about half white, half black. But instead of clumping up in little segregated groups, they seemed to mingle easily, laughing and slapping one another on the back.

"That opened my eyes," Macfarlane says. "There was a harmony in that room between whites and blacks that enthused me. People came through the line and sat where they wanted. They weren't divided up into little groups. I thought I sensed a genuineness of interest in Doug's campaign."

Folks just couldn't wait for Wilder to circulate among the crowd. Instead, a long line of people formed to go up to him, a down-home receiving line for the celebrity-in-the-making.

Goode saw something else happening as folks filed out. "We left a hat at the door and there were several hundred dollars in it," he says. "We raised $500-$600, almost all in $10 and $20 contributions."

That night, Wilder and Shropshire went back to Goode's home. "We sat there in the living room," Shropshire recalls. "Doug was reciting where he was last week. He'd say, 'Virgil, you wouldn't believe the response we got in this county, that county.' Virgil would say, 'Did you see so-and-so there?' and he'd say yes."

Goode and Shropshire sat there in amazement. Wilder was meeting all the right people, all right.

Tomorrow morning, he'd meet one more.

Aug. 15, 1985

The beauty and danger of the tour were the same. Wilder had pledged to visit every county and city in the state. In each one, reporters would be looking to see who was there and who wasn't. The intense media focus on Wilder made even the most reasonable absence seem suspect. And politicians knew it, too.

In Southwest Virginia, Wilder had no trouble commanding big crowds from the yellow-dog Democrats of the Fightin' Ninth. Reporters began looking ahead on the schedule to see when and where the real test for Wilder would come. Conveniently, in its second full week, Wilder's tour looped into Southside — and his first full day there would take him onto the home turf of A.L. Philpott.

What a perfect symbol of Virginia conservatism, this laconic, pipe-smoking country lawyer from Bassett. What a perfect symbol of the Democratic establishment, this speaker of the House whose famous scowl is said to be enough to kill a bill or bring order to a rancorous chamber. What a perfect symbol of Virginia's racial past and present, this Southside politician known to sometimes utter racial epithets.

One would be hard-pressed to find another Virginia politician with whom Wilder had sparred more frequently. They were "two old warriors who had rarely marched to the same music," wrote the *Virginian-Pilot* in Norfolk. "For years, [they] have served as protagonist and antagonist in some of the state's most publicized debates on race."

"A.L. I love," says Jay Shropshire, "but he had fought Wilder basically on everything for the past ten years. On the Martin Luther King bill, A.L. stacked the committee and killed it nine years in a row. A.L. had said the word 'nigger' in print before."

Once Wilder accused the speaker of having a "magnolia mentality" and even threatened to campaign against Philpott in his own district. Another time Philpott had called black legislators "boys." Of course, Philpott called everyone "boy" — but that didn't quiet the storm that followed. In 1985, Philpott had once again managed to run afoul of blacks. In June, a veteran white legislator in Portsmouth had been defeated in a primary by a black challenger. Asked to comment on his friend's loss, Philpott lamented that voters had chosen "color, not quality." That stirred up everything all over again; the state NAACP demanded Philpott's resignation. Wilder steered clear of this latest brouhaha, but the smell of yet another racial controversy involving Philpott was still in the air as Wilder's tour neared Henry County.

Speculation mounted: Would Philpott be there when Wilder came through?

Jay Shropshire was the key.

He was Philpott's political protege. He was Wilder's best friend.

Shropshire and Wilder had been talking strategy even before Wilder's announcement back in 1984. One thing Shropshire always had in mind was trying to bait former Gov. Mills Godwin into the campaign with some sort of racial statement that would help put the election in the stark context of the past vs. the future.

A newspaper photograph of his two buddies Philpott and Wilder might do the trick, Shropshire thought. Godwin, he hoped, would see that, fear that even trusted conservatives were lining up behind Wilder and conclude the only way left to save the commonwealth was to beat the racial drum, thereby turning off moderate voters.

But getting Philpott's endorsement was crucial from Wilder's point of view — even if Shropshire hadn't had a secret plan to bait Godwin into a racial strategy. Before the tour had started, Goldman had talked with Shropshire about Philpott and the inevitable questions that would arise when Wilder went through Henry County without seeing the speaker. Wilder simply had to be seen with Philpott.

"Would he do it?" Goldman asked.

"He's a good Democrat," Shropshire said. "He'll do it."

Goldman also talked to Virgil Goode, whose senatorial district included Philpott's Henry County, about what it would take to get Philpott out in public with Wilder. "Goode said Doug ought to call him direct. 'He'll like that,' " Goldman recalls. "But Doug was a little reluctant. 'I don't want to ask him and have him say no; it would get out.' " But Goldman kept pressing and eventually Shropshire cleared the way for Wilder's call.

"I was up front with Mr. Philpott," Shropshire recalls. " 'He's coming down there. You're gonna need to do something for him. Everybody's gonna be looking. You can't escape it. It'll catch up with you sooner or later.' Mr. Philpott was great about it. He understood it. He's been in politics all his life. So after I talked to Mr. Philpott, then the question was who was really going to ask him. I said to Doug, 'You call.' "

Wilder was at a country store just outside Grundy when he decided he couldn't put it off any longer. This was Tuesday, Aug. 6. The weekend papers had been filled with long, glowing accounts of Wilder's first three days in Southwest Virginia. In Henry County, Philpott was so shocked by what he was reading that he had called friends out in the coalfields to see if the stories were true. "Most said Doug had sold himself, they hadn't," he recalls. That news made a big impression on the speaker.

That afternoon, Philpott and Wilder chatted amiably about how the tour was going. The speaker kidded the candidate about the press coverage he was getting. Finally, Wilder eased around to the subject of coming through Henry County the next week. "I said, 'I'm on my way. I'd like to talk to you,' " Wilder says. "He said, 'Let me see what we can do.' "

So what would the speaker do? "He could have just had Wilder come by his office, and I think that was all Wilder expected," Goode says. "He just wanted to meet him" — and have his picture taken.

Philpott waves off that suggestion. "That wouldn't have done him any significant good," he says. What Wilder needed, Philpott decided, was to be introduced to the leaders in the community so they could see he wasn't some wild man. The speaker recognized the politics involved. "I certainly wasn't going to let it be said when he came to this county he was ignored and not given an opportunity to sell himself," he says.

Nevertheless, it was a completely stunned Michael Brown who two days later received a call from the speaker's secretary — with all the details already taken care of: Philpott will sponsor a breakfast for Wilder on Thursday, Aug. 15 in Collinsville, just outside Martinsville. The speaker will handle all the arrangements and pay the bill. All Wilder needs to do is be there. If there are any questions, please call.

By the time Brown got through scribbling down all the details, about all he could stammer out was "yes, ma'am."

A breakfast was a shrewd idea. It put Philpott on record supporting Wilder and gave his friends a chance to meet Wilder in a comfortable, informal setting. But Philpott also was hedging his bets, Shropshire says. "A.L. knew most people had to go to work at nine, so he knew wouldn't but so much happen. He didn't realize Wilder would settle for a handshake."

Breakfast, lunch, dinner, Goldman didn't care. It was the speaker and that was all that mattered. "Philpott was the key to the tour," Goldman says. "He symbolized that whole part of Virginia that was totally against Doug Wilder on the basis of race and there was no need to discuss it."

Shropshire was thinking the same thing. "I knew if I could pull off that breakfast, all the blue bloods and ultraconservatives would get in line. I knew if I could pull that off and we had a picture, it was half over. Bingo, we hit the bull's-eye."

Goldman started putting out the word among reporters. By the time he was done, reporters from every major newspaper in the state were crowding into the back of the room.

Poor A.L. Philpott. "I had no idea," he says. "I thought it would be Doug and three or four of his staff." Philpott had his secretary call the *Martinsville Bulletin* and thought that would be sufficient press coverage. Next thing Philpott knew, his office was besieged by calls from reporters wanting to know about the breakfast.

A flustered, angry Philpott got on the phone to Shropshire: "What the hell is the *Washington Post* coming down here for?" the speaker demanded to know. Shropshire grins about it now. "Mr. Philpott had no idea that the press would all come down there like that."

Jay Shropshire always knew when the speaker was mad at him. Philpott would ring him up and, as soon as he was put through to Shropshire, would never call the Senate clerk by name. Instead, Philpott would just light right in. The day before the breakfast, the phone buzzed in Shropshire's office. The speaker calling for you, the secretary said. Right away Shropshire could tell this was one of those calls.

"God damn you, get your ass down here," Philpott snapped, according to those familiar with the conversation who related the incident afterward. "Get down here tonight."

"Why?" Shropshire asked.

"Get down here tonight. We've got to rehearse this thing."

"Rehearse what?" Shropshire asked. "You know Wilder."

That wasn't the point, Philpott said. With all these reporters descending on Henry County like locusts, the speaker didn't want any missteps. He wanted things choreographed. "Now you're going to be master of ceremonies," Philpott said. "This is the way it's going to be. I'm going to introduce Virgil. Virgil will introduce you and you introduce Wilder."

That sounded fine by Shropshire. So what needed to be choreographed? But Philpott insisted Shropshire come down that night to go over the arrangements, anyway. Like a teen-ager angling with his father to stay out late, Shropshire talked his way out of it so he could go to the Wilder dinner in Rocky Mount.

"Meet me at 7 o'clock tomorrow morning then," Philpott said before he hung up. "We gotta rehearse this."

When A.L. Philpott arrived at the Dutch Inn in Collinsville, the place was crawling with reporters. Even though the speaker had had fair warning that his little breakfast would draw attention from more than the local paper, he still had no idea it would be like *this*. "I'd never seen such an entourage of news people," he says.

The first thing Philpott did was find Jay Shropshire. They ducked into a men's room to rehearse.

By now, the tiny hallway was filling up with white-haired old gentlemen in dark suits, roly-poly middle-age men hailed as "young fella" by their elders, a smattering of blacks. It practically took a shoehorn to squeeze them all into the room.

Philpott had limited the invitations to the Henry County and Martinsville Democratic committees, a sizable enough contingent already, especially if any number at all agreed to come. It wasn't long, though, before Philpott's secretary realized the breakfast would be a sellout. "I think she was as surprised as anybody," Philpott says. "When we started calling people, it was a unanimous response. Normally, to get 'em to breakfast, you have to drag 'em kicking and screaming. Whether they came out of curiosity or an honest desire to help, I don't know, but they came."

Mike Cannaday, a Collinsville lawyer, offers another explanation: "They couldn't say no to this. I get invitations from the governor. You can turn those down if it's not convenient. But you don't turn down the speaker. When you get a call from his secretary, who says, 'We're having a breakfast for Doug Wilder Thursday at the Dutch Inn. Are you going to be there?' you say, 'Yes, ma'am.' I don't mean that dictatorially. I mean that respectfully."

Philpott commands that kind of respect in his home county, where a town and a reservoir bear the Philpott name. "In this county, its Democratic machine is not a Democratic machine," Cannaday says. "It's personally loyal to A.L. Philpott. It's the same people, thirty years older, who elected him commonwealth's attorney thirty years ago. They're not Democratic with a capital D. They're loyal to A.L. People are either part of his group or not active in politics in this county. That was what his breakfast was for. It told me, 'I'm a party Democrat, Doug Wilder is our nominee, I'm supporting him, you put your people on it.' I don't know how many votes it changed in Northern Virginia, but it did in the Fifth District. He was saying, 'It's all right, come on, get in line.' "

Philpott and Wilder sat side by side at the head table. The speaker stood and said a few inconsequential words of welcome, referring to Wilder only as "a man of high intellect, ability and experience" and "one of the more capable and articulate members of the Senate." Then he turned things over to Goode. Soon it was Shropshire's turn.

With a sly grin on his cherubic face, Shropshire turned to the one-time antagonists at his side and quipped: "Looking at my two buddies here, I feel like President Carter did when he finally reached the Camp David accords. This is a monumental day in Virginia politics." The ripple of laughter that went around the room was slightly nervous, but welcome.

Then Shropshire jumped in head-first, tackling a subject others had sought to tiptoe around or ignore completely. "Times have changed," Shropshire said again and again, a phrase that didn't have to be explained to anyone — and a phrase that nicely turned the racial question aside. But as Shropshire ran through Wilder's resume, he focused directly on race and the discrimination Wilder faced growing up.

"His grandfather was a slave," Shropshire said. "He couldn't go to any college he wanted. He couldn't get into any law school he wanted to. I'm not crying on your shoulder, but he couldn't." Wilder served his country in Korea and won a Bronze Star for heroism in combat. "But he came back home to Richmond and he had to ride on the back of the bus."

Although race seemed to be the overriding theme of Shropshire's talk, there was another message there, one the reporters missed, but one his hometown listeners didn't. Shropshire's introduction of Wilder wasn't so much a racial guilt trip as it was a presentation of Wilder's hard-working, up-from-poverty career in terms a conservative, rural white audience might identify with. "People where I'm from are discriminated against, too," Shropshire explains. "Other people think they're hicks, so I knew when I said Doug Wilder was deprived of his right, that would get their attention and they could relate to that because they're deprived, too. They don't have the same educational system you do, say, in Fairfax County."

Shropshire also indirectly countered Wilder's liberalism and, once again, in a way a stubborn rural crowd could sympathize with. "You're not going to agree with him on everything. That's politics. But regardless of whether you agree with him or not, he tells you what he thinks. He means what he says and he says what he means." Shropshire compared Wilder to Pete Rose, then closing in on Ty Cobb's record for career hits. "When he came up people thought he was a hot dog and couldn't do it, but he's doing it right now."

Wilder was in the on-deck circle. He came up to bat with the most direct talk about race in the whole campaign.

Nodding toward Philpott, Wilder pointed out, "To the pundits, to the naysayers, to those who said it could never happen, we are here together today . . . We can, in fact, bring all the disparate elements of this state together. To those who said it never could be, we are gathered here today to march on to victory."

Wilder noted indirectly, as Shropshire had directly, that times had changed. He spoke of his tour and the encounters he had had so far out on the road. "People said I was crazy because I could be spending time doing better things like going to fund-raisers, but I never had a more rewarding experience in my life. Whether it is going into a barbershop or a coal mine, it means a great deal to hear what people have to say." He spoke of going to Bob Lambert's home in Abingdon and seeing "the biggest Confederate flag I have ever seen" flying in the yard, yet coming away with a handsome contribution. "There are those who would look down on the past, but that's a part of Virginia," Wilder said. He joked that if that's the kind of reception he should expect beneath a Confederate flag, then he'd like to know where he could find some others, a line that drew a hearty laugh from this Southside crowd.

Wilder's talk was one of the best of the campaign — smooth, reassuring, acknowledging race yet dispensing with it in a subtle way. His comments about the Confederate flag were a way of telling his conservative audience that yes, he was black and they were white; that he realized they had come through some rough times together, but there were no hard feelings; that he was not interested in debating the old issues of the past, but in moving on to the new ones of the future. He talked about roads and jobs and schools, practical sorts of things his listeners cared about far more than making a social statement. Finally, of course, Wilder's delivery was so pleasing, so perfect, he could have read the phone book and made a favorable impression. He sat down to a round of genuine applause.

Then something unusual happened. Philpott, who had leaned back during Wilder's speech, puffing leisurely on his ever-present pipe, rose and delivered an impromptu political benediction. Turning to Wilder, he said, "It's obvious we are giving you an education into the problems of Virginia and when you are finished, you'll be better for it and we'll be better for it." It wasn't exactly a tub-thumping endorsement, but it was more than the laconic Philpott needed to say.

The breakfast over, the reporters, who had been pressed into the back of the room, swarmed in like buzzards, buttonholing people for comments.

The locals weren't sure what all the fuss was about. "Mr. Philpott is a good Democrat," said Ward Armstrong. "He's all behind Wilder's campaign. He told me that personally."

Reporters kept bringing up Philpott's old clashes with Wilder and asking what had changed. The speaker kept his pipe clenched between his teeth, grinned mischievously and said as little as possible. "If I were going to comment on every disagreement I've had with every politician in Richmond, I wouldn't be there."

Ah, but that was exactly what the reporters wanted, some kind of comment on Wilder, race, controversy, changing times. The same question was rephrased every way imaginable. What prompted Philpott's sudden change of heart? What did his breakfast this morning have to say about the state of race relations in Virginia? "He's the Democratic nominee and I support the nominee of my party," Philpott said. But that wasn't good enough. "These are changing times in changing environments," Philpott finally, grudgingly acknowledged. "Doug Wilder is proof of that. You have got to change with them if you are going to survive."

Asked if he was "enthusiastically" supporting Wilder, the speaker scowled his famous scowl. "That's an unfair question," he snapped. Then he smiled faintly and added: "But I got up at 5:30 this morning and I don't usually get up at 5:30 in the morning. I'm here, aren't I?"

Philpott left town soon after the breakfast to give a speech in Williamsburg. But he left Wilder in the hands of escorts he had personally arranged — and what escorts they were. In Henry County, it was Philpott's cousin. In Martinsville, it was his brother.

Shropshire drove back to Richmond that afternoon for a meeting with a business group. Their talk turned to the breakfast down in Collinsville that Shropshire had just come from. The businessmen raised their eyebrows and looked at one another. "The talk among them," Shropshire says, "was if A.L. could come out for him, 'I guess I can, too.'"

Aug. 16, 1985

Del. Bernie Cohen, D-Alexandria, was eating breakfast, flipping through the *Washington Post*. There, staring him in the face, were two photographs of A.L. Philpott and Doug Wilder. In one, both had their heads reared back in a gigantic belly-laugh. In the other, Philpott was seen whispering to Wilder some private word of wisdom. "I almost fell off my chair," Cohen says. He called to his wife: "Can you believe this?" he said, waving the newspaper. "This is history being made in Virginia. This is important. What you see here, this article and this picture is very, very important."

In Baliles headquarters in Richmond, there was still grumbling about Wilder's ragtag campaign as his tour moved into his second week. All that changed on the morning of Aug. 16. "I think the realization of the brilliance of the tour began to sink in the day the Post ran the big picture of Wilder and Philpott together, sort of knee-slapping," says adviser Alan Albert. "In the realm of the possible, if you envision a picture that embodies the New Dominion [Baliles' campaign slogan], I don't think you could have chosen a better one. We were very happy."

In Durrette headquarters, the reaction was exactly the opposite. Press secretary Don Harrison nearly threw the morning papers down in disgust when he saw all the stories and photographs. "Forget it," he said. "You want signals? You just got one of the biggest signals ever sent in this state."

Jay Shropshire got his picture of Philpott and Wilder together, all right. The Philpott breakfast was front page news in every major morning newspaper in the state except the *Richmond Times-Dispatch.* The Wilder campaign couldn't have bought publicity like this.

The news coverage magnified Philpott's simple breakfast from a political event into a social happening, a cultural milestone. "It was the plantation owner inviting the servant in," Cannaday says.

Shropshire has another analogy: "It was like Archie Bunker and Martin Luther King." Yet now here they were, laughing and carrying on in the pages of the *Washington Post* like old friends: "Old Adversaries Embrace in Virginia."

"The psychological effect of that breakfast on the right wing of the party was tremendous," Cannaday says.

"That made Wilder a lot more acceptable to the establishment," says Durrette campaign manager Bruce Miller.

The result? "I think from that point on, the campaign had credibility," Wilder says.

It also dispirited the Republicans. The Philpott breakfast was a sign, Harrison says, that the Democrats were "willing to get their act together and we in the Republican Party weren't. Philpott, by barely opening his mouth and just being in the picture, had managed to do for Wilder what more unfortunate comments by Philpott's counterparts [Mills Godwin later in the campaign] did for us in the negative."

In an interview a few months before his death, former Gov. John Dalton reflected on how the Philpott breakfast made it difficult for the Republicans to brand Wilder as a liberal and make the label stick. "The record he made for sixteen years in the Senate was just buried in the ashes."

A.L. Philpott sits in his Bassett law office tamping down his pipe and smiling a rare smile. "I've heard more about that breakfast than I want," he says. "I caught a lot of flak over that from various sources." He smiles again, then resumes meticulously tending his pipe.

Philpott says there was never any doubt about whether he'd support Wilder. "I've always worked for the ticket and worked for the whole ticket. I couldn't see where I had any alternative. If you're on the team, you have to play with the players on that team.

"Wilder and I, on a professional level, get along well. He was forever making cracks about anything connected with race. He was always quick to brand me as a racist. As for working with him, I worked with him as easy as any member of the Senate. I don't guess we ever agreed on anything that dealt with social issues. Certainly he's liberal on social issues, but I have never found Doug to be that liberal when it comes to fiscal responsibility and nothing he's done since has changed that. Certainly he has his own constituency and anyone who doesn't look after that is stupid."

So Philpott was quite ready to do his duty as a good Democrat and support Wilder, long before the famous breakfast was organized, he says. Sometimes other legislators would call him, worried about how Wilder would go over in their districts, wondering what the speaker thought they should do about it. "I got a lot of those calls. I reminded them that Doug Wilder was the Democratic nominee."

Still, Philpott says he was under no illusions about how Wilder would go over in his district. "In the beginning, I did not expect him to go over at all here," Philpott says. Race, the speaker says, was a secondary consideration to ideology. "Everyone perceived him as an extreme liberal."

Instead, complaints were few and they were soon quashed. "There were certain people after that breakfast, they'd get into an argument about him being a liberal on social issues," Philpott says, "but most of the whites there at that breakfast counteracted that and it never amounted to anything."

The speaker says all this in his customary laconic way, but one can just imagine some poor fellow in Henry County complaining about that so-and-so Doug Wilder and getting quickly put in his place by one silent blast of Philpott's famous scowl. And if that's not a signal, then nothing is.

Aug. 17, 1985

For the second time in just over a month, Baliles ambushed Durrette at a mountaintop resort.

At their Wintergreen debate in July, Baliles had boxed the Republican into saying he wouldn't commit himself to full funding of the Standards of Quality in education. Fiscally, Durrette may have been on the high ground. But politically, his budgetary caution was costly. Voters got the impression that Baliles was pro-education while Durrette wasn't.

Durrette, if he wanted to have any chance at all of winning in the suburbs, whose young adults were prime Republican voters, had to make over his image on education. The Virginia Bar Association convention at the Greenbrier, just over the state line in White Sulphur Springs, W.Va., was where he was going to do it. Instead, Baliles once again put Durrette on the defensive and stole the next morning's headlines.

In the end, none of this really would have mattered much if it weren't for what all this led to a month later. With their candidate on the defensive, Durrette's staff desperately looked for a way to seize the initiative in this campaign. Their panic would lead to Durrette's ill-fated September swing through Southside, in which the Republicans wound up helping Doug Wilder far more than the Democrats ever could.

Wilder's station-wagon tour continued.

The media missed what was happening, even though they were part of it. A *Times-Dispatch* story Aug. 18 ripped the tour. "Wilder is hurting himself with corn-pone campaign stops at virtually every dot on the map" when he should be out raising money, it said. "The spring was the time for such tours, not now," agreed University of Richmond political analyst Tom Morris. He admitted Wilder was getting a lot of attention, but dismissed that as a fad that would pass by Labor Day. "By then, it will be clear that Wilder is a long shot and attention will be turned to other contests." Other analysts agreed: "I don't think Wilder has a chance, no way," Larry Sabato told the *Daily Press* of Newport News Aug. 25. "Wilder will go down in a disastrous defeat," predicted Old Dominion University analyst Thomas Wells.

The Republicans missed it, too, so the Chichester campaign did nothing to push Wilder off center stage. "I think they failed to understand the importance of Doug's trip," Albert says. "It looked like a stunt. Here's another Goldman stunt. Henry Howell's Winnebago brought a decade forward."

But the tour was making Wilder a celebrity — while Chichester remained an unknown.

And if you compare the number of stories about Wilder to the number about Chichester — well, there was no comparison. In August:

• The *Times-Dispatch* devoted six major stories to Wilder, none to his opponent.

• The *Washington Post* devoted four major stories to Wilder, none to Chichester.

• The *Virginian-Pilot* in Norfolk devoted four major stories to Wilder, none to Chichester.

• The *Roanoke Times & World-News* was the only paper to run a separate story about Chichester's campaign to balance the tour coverage, but even so, it still ran five stories about Wilder.

"I can't remember when there has been a greater imbalance of coverage for a statewide race," U.Va.'s Sabato complained at the time. "It's as though the press is making sure Doug has a chance to win."

Morris, the University of Richmond analyst, doesn't believe the media had impure motives, though — just practical ones. "Your profession got excited by him during the summer when things were slow," Morris says. "Others were out organizing and it's hard to report that, so there was this great imbalance in the press. It was just something the press stumbled into. The tour was the best story of the summer."

The Wilder campaign sensed that — and was quick to exploit one of the few advantages it had.

As it turned out, the coverage Wilder received was highly favorable and a big boost to his campaign. But the intense focus on Wilder could just as easily have hurt him. Suppose Wilder had met with a chilly, if not outright hostile, reception in Lee County? Suppose voters had refused to shake Wilder's hand — or freely admitted they couldn't support a black? Given the herd instincts of the journalistic pack, the stampede to write stories about racist Ol' Virginny rearing its ugly head and hooting Doug Wilder out of town would have been so fierce it would have made the Old West cattle drives seem like tame strolls to the market — and Wilder's campaign would have been over. For better or worse, the media spotlight inevitably magnifies what it's focused on. This time, it just happened to work out to Wilder's advantage.

In any event, the Chichester campaign simply couldn't compete with Wilder for publicity. The reason wasn't an allegedly biased media, but the Chichester campaign's own internal problems — the debilitating personality clash between the candidate and the campaign manager and the campaign's inability to raise money and get out from under its convention debts. In August, the Chichester campaign simply wasn't in a position to pick up on Wilder's building momentum and come up with a clever response. Plus, at the time, it didn't seem necessary.

Ironically, about the same time the Democrats began to realize the tour was not such a dumb idea after all, it was effectively over.

By the time of the Philpott breakfast, every major newspaper in the state had published, or had in the works, a major story on the tour. The idea that Wilder had embarked on a great journey, and was being well-received in unlikely places, was firmly planted in the public's mind. The Philpott breakfast reinforced it in dramatic fashion. "The tour was very successful for the first fifteen days," Goldman says. "After that, it had served its purpose."

By then, most papers had already written all they were going to write about the tour. So with reporters no longer literally looking over their shoulders every step of the way, Wilder and Goldman let things slide. Oh, they'd still have a local escort. But no longer did they map out every second of the day as they had with Edgar Bacon and A.L. Philpott. Sometimes they had no formal schedule at all, beyond a nighttime dinner or reception with local campaign workers.

Yet every time a newspaper ran a campaign story and mentioned in a background paragraph, "Wilder, now in the third week of his two-month station-wagon tour across the state," or "Wilder, campaigning in the Shenandoah Valley on his 3,408-mile trip across the state, could not be reached for comment," the image of his marathon was reinforced. "The key to free publicity is the same as paid," Goldman says. "You need repetition. You could have twenty-five stories on twenty-five different things and it would mean nothing, but a couple stories on the tour, that builds on a theme."

After the early burst of stories, every newspaper reader in Virginia probably felt he knew about Wilder's trip firsthand. So what if Wilder was only meeting a few people here, a few people there? Voters imagined a much more colorful campaign, of a gutsy underdog barnstorming the back roads, than really existed. The mere idea of the tour soon became more important than its reality.

"The tour, it's all folklore," Goldman laughs. Wilder really didn't meet all that many people. But the major newspapers covered the early part of the tour so heavily that people began to talk about it, Goldman says. Wilder's campaign wasn't based on issues, it was powered by image — an image that the news media and voters' imaginations helped create.

"He probably personally saw no more than one thousand people, but everybody heard about it and everybody thought they were a part of it," says former GOP legislator Ray Garland, now a newspaper columnist. "That was what Chichester was up against. Wilder was a phenomenon. He was a novelty. He was a neat guy, he was a cool guy and his day had come."

Paul Goldman may have thought it up, Edgar Bacon may have started it off right and A.L. Philpott may have provided an unexpected exclamation point, but there were three other people who were crucial to the tour's success.

The first was Doug Wilder himself. He turned out to be one heck of a campaigner.

"I hate to use the word charisma, but he's got it," says Bruce Miller, Durrette's campaign manager. "When people met him, they saw they had nothing to fear."

"Doug is very gregarious in a very dignified, sophisticated way," says Del. Chip Woodrum, D-Roanoke. "There hasn't been a better handshaking politician in Virginia since [former Gov.] Bill Tuck."

And in the country stores of Southside and Southwest Virginia, Wilder simply shined. He was a natural. "One thing that impressed me about Doug, him being black and being from Richmond, he was able to blend in with us people down here," says Wise County Democratic Chairman Glenn Craft.

The second unsung hero of the tour was someone who wasn't even on it — Michael Brown.

"Michael actually played a pivotal role in the campaign," Goldman says. "I don't know of anyone else who could have played it. Michael had to deal with all the phone calls, make it seem like we had a dozen people. He had to deal with the towns we were setting up. Michael was the guy representing us in Richmond during August and September, a dicey period. Michael had to take the brunt of complaints and that was no small factor."

In the evenings, Brown usually had help from Jackie Epps, who helped set up fund-raising events along the tour route. But by day, Brown *was* the Wilder campaign. He was a combination scheduler, travel agency, long-distance advance man and field coordinator, telephone switchboard, office manager and probably a dozen other things no one ever realized. If you called Wilder headquarters with a question during August or September, Brown was probably the only person in the office who could answer it. Who knows? He might even be the one who answered the phone.

For so many people who were skeptical of the tour, Paul Goldman and the whole campaign setup, Michael Brown was the one sensible person they could turn to.

"Without him, Doug Wilder would not be lieutenant governor," insists David Temple, one of Wilder's two Northern Virginia organizers. "In so many ways, Michael Brown was the hero of that campaign."

"He was the glue that held it all together," agrees Pat Watt, the other Northern Virginia organizer.

The final key figure behind the scenes of Wilder's tour was Jay Shropshire. Besides setting up the Philpott breakfast, the Senate clerk served as Wilder's personal consultant and a one-man information center for political insiders.

"I think Jay deserves a lot of credit," said George Stoddart, Robb's press secretary. "I think a lot of people think Jay did it just because Doug was a senator. But a candidate needs someone they can call to see if his message is getting across." And Shropshire was the friend Wilder could call on.

"Doug's first question when he called was always, 'Well, what's up?' My line was, 'Well, where the hell are you now?' " Shropshire recalls. He had the day's papers from throughout the state spread out on his dining room table and he'd go through them, one by one.

"I'd give him a rundown of what was happening. He knew what issues they were raising. So Doug was current. He wouldn't call until 11, 11:30, or 12 at night. When he would call, I'd tell him bang-bang-bang what was in the news. Every night. Sometimes I'd have the 11 o'clock news on and I'd just put the receiver up to the TV and I'd channel hop."

Wilder, in turn, would pass on glowing stories from out on the road. "He would call me and say, 'Jay, we had a crowd of seventy-five today for lunch.' The numbers were turning out. But were they doing it out of courtesy? In the beginning, I thought it was courtesy; then the crowds began to grow."

Shropshire saw for himself at Rocky Mount the night before the Philpott breakfast and concluded the response was genuine. Pretty soon, everyone down the line knew it, too. The Senate clerk doubled as chairman of the Compensation Board — the board that set salaries for local courthouse officials — and Shropshire used his considerable contacts to advance Wilder's tour. Shropshire was on the phone constantly to local officials in the next county, making sure they knew how big were the crowds Wilder had been getting, not-so-subtly letting them know they'd better do just as good or they'd look bad. The Philpott breakfast was simply the most dramatic, and most visible, result of Shropshire's behind-the-scenes work for Wilder.

For countless other local politicians, Shropshire was the unofficial communications center for the Wilder campaign. "Senators and delegates started calling me, saying 'Doug did really well down here,' they began to grasp that the guy was not going to embarrass them," he says. From one county to another, word began to spread.

And a few days after the Philpott breakfast, Wilder called Shropshire from somewhere in Southside and for the first time made a prediction: "Jay, we're going to win. I can feel it."

Aug. 27, 1985

George Austin put on his only three-piece suit. The thirty-five-year-old policeman in the little Tidewater city of Poquoson was about to face the toughest fire he'd seen since 'Nam and he wanted to look nice — as he told the capital press corps that for the first time, the Fraternal Order of Police was endorsing candidates for statewide office and it was backing the Democratic ticket, Wilder included.

The FOP traditionally has been only a social organization in the South, not involved with labor and political issues as it is in the North. That started to change in 1984 when Austin, a patrolman in Poquoson, was elected president and brought in a slate of young, politically minded officers determined to make the FOP into a stronger lobbying force in Richmond.

The endorsements of Baliles, an attorney general, and Terry, a former prosecutor, weren't all that surprising. The Wilder endorsement was. Here was a black man generally perceived to be a liberal on all the standard law-and-order issues — yet he was being backed by Southern cops.

The endorsement had little to do with ideology, though, and a lot to do with clout. "Wilder's up in the hardball league," Austin says, "Chichester was a nobody." Plus, Wilder had always been helpful to the police, sometimes simply in personal ways, whenever they had come to the General Assembly. "We were rubbing shoulders with big, powerful lobbyists and power brokers," Austin says. "We were always intimidated. Wilder would point us out, recognize us, take us back to his office, take time to discuss bills."

So now here was Austin with Baliles on one side, Terry on the other. But it seemed the only questions the reporters asked were about Wilder, on tour in Northern Virginia.

"The questions started coming, practically asking what time of day we did it," Austin says. "They kept on and on about Wilder. They wanted me to slip up. Finally, I pulled a Reagan and said, 'Thank you, ladies and gentlemen,'" and took no more questions.

That evening Austin was back in Poquoson, sitting in his patrol car, numbed by the day's events. "Here I am in Richmond, facing UPI, AP and the capital press corps and here I am in Poquoson at the library, writing parking tickets." Two months later, every Virginian with a TV set turned on would know about the FOP's Wilder endorsement — and George Austin would find his group was suddenly getting more attention than he could ever have imagined.

Aug. 29, 1985

Wilder was causing trouble for Robb again. Labor Day was coming up, time for the traditional weekend appearances at black churches in Tidewater. But Goldman had threatened not to put them on Wilder's schedule, reasoning Wilder had nothing to gain by appealing to blacks. He needed to be out talking to whites.

The Labor Day schedule threw the Robb staff into a small crisis. A firm but solicitous David McCloud finally tracked Wilder down in Winchester and tried to explain the importance of all three candidates appearing together. We'll do whatever it takes, McCloud assured Wilder. We'll pick you up anywhere you want, fly you to Norfolk, then return you wherever you need to be. Wilder agreed, figuring it was a no-win situation. "If I don't go, they would just say I'm taking them for granted," he said. Goldman counted the Labor Day scheduling crisis as just another example of Robb's staff meddling in the campaign, not being very helpful, worrying more about appearances than raising money. McCloud saw it as another catastrophe averted, just one more time that Robb's staff had rescued the bumbling, amateurish Wilder campaign from itself.

Not long after the FOP endorsement, Michael Brown was working in the basement when he heard someone coming down the steps. He looked up — and saw a stern-faced white police officer marching his way. "I thought, 'Oh Lord, what have I done now?' This guy came downstairs with jackboots on."

But then he asked for some Wilder literature. He'd heard about the FOP endorsement and wanted to do his part.

Over the next several weeks, Brown saw a whole parade of police officers come down the steps unannounced, saying they'd heard about the FOP endorsement and they wanted some literature to take with them. "I'm not talking black policemen, either," Brown says. "I'm talking white police officers, with short hair styles. The stereotype image."

But the small parade of policemen trooping by Wilder's Church Hill law office wasn't the only sign of something strange happening in Virginia as the summer began to turn toward autumn.

Just after Labor Day, Jay Shropshire received a call from one of Wilder's state Senate colleagues, broaching a sensitive subject of Senate protocol. He realized it was unlikely, this senator said, trying not to make himself look too foolish, but just in case Wilder happened to win, did Shropshire think he could arrange for this senator to be assigned Wilder's coveted corner office in the General Assembly building and/or his front-row seat beside Ed Willey on the Senate floor?

11

The Criminal's Interest At Heart

Sept. 2, 1985

Late at night, Paul Goldman was skulking around the UPI office in downtown Richmond. He was trying to peddle a story about Wilder's tour reaching the halfway mark. He was hoping with the holiday being a slow news day that he might be able to score some free publicity on the radio news during Tuesday morning's drive time.

While he was at UPI, Goldman glanced up and saw a story that had been ripped off the wire machine. It was a news brief about a Chichester press release that had gone out over the weekend, something about Chichester accusing Wilder of having "the criminal's interest at heart."

This was the first Goldman had heard of it. "I remember looking at it," he says. "I said, 'This is Chichester's press release?' They said yeah. I said, 'Really? I can't believe it.' " He asked if a copy of the original release was still around the UPI bureau. It wasn't.

Goldman, when he gets an idea in his head, is relentlessly single-minded. He simply *had* to have a copy of the release. And right *now.* He might have even driven out to Chichester headquarters for one if he had thought he couldn't find one another place. Instead, he drove up to the State Capitol. It was nearly midnight but he was able to get into the press room. There, stuffed into one of the pigeonholes, was the Chichester release. Goldman plucked it out and went home a happy, scheming man.

The agreement Dennis Peterson and John Chichester had struck was that the Chichester campaign would go on the attack in September.

The way Peterson saw it, September was the key month for the Chichester campaign. Chichester had gotten virtually no ink all summer. Ordinarily, that wouldn't be so bad, but the Wilder tour had dominated the political news in August, building up an unexpected reservoir of goodwill with the voters. Peterson figured that by October the gubernatorial campaign would be so hot the candidates in the other two races would have difficulty getting attention. So whatever was going to happen in those campaigns had to happen in September. Peterson told Chichester that if he hadn't won by the World Series, he was in big trouble. But not to worry. With Wilder's sixteen-year voting record to work from, it wouldn't take long to expose him as a liberal — and then Durrette could go into the final month tying Baliles to the sinking Wilder.

This was the Chichester strategy — and over Labor Day weekend, the Chichester campaign fired its first volley, a stinging press release charging that Wilder was soft on the death penalty. Unfortunately, it was lost in the Labor Day shuffle — until Paul Goldman stumbled upon it one night in the UPI bureau.

Sept. 3, 1985

Wilder and Goldman rode up to Charlottesville Tuesday morning to start the second half of the tour. Chuck Nichollson was behind the wheel — and the whole way up Wilder and Goldman talked about Chichester's press release.

They both found it a fascinating little document, amazingly shrill and sometimes grammatically incorrect:

"Referring to Wilder's votes *against* adding mass murders to the list of crimes for which the death penalty is allowed as punishment, Chichester said, 'Senator Wilder must not consider mass murder a serious enough injustice against mankind that it should be punishable ny [sic] the death penalty.'

"'Tough talk on crime is not enough. For too long now some lawmakers have always had the criminals [sic] interest at heart, and this shows in my opponents [sic] record. My consistant [sic] support of the death penalty is indicative of my strong commitment to strengthning [sic] the criminal justice system.'"

Chichester also charged that Wilder's opposition to allowing prosecutors to appeal their case in capital crimes is "another one of Senator Wilder's votes for the guilty criminal."

Goldman had been expecting the Republicans to go after Wilder's law-and-order record. This press release was curious, though. Calling a candidate soft on crime was one thing, but accusing him of having "the criminal's interest at heart"? What was the Chichester campaign up to?

Goldman laid out the options to Wilder on the ride to Charlottesville. "There were two ways of thinking," Goldman says. "One was to let it drop. No one had picked up on it." No reason to publicize the opposition's charges.

On the other hand . . . "We had to focus on his charges rather than our record," Goldman says. "Turn it around. Force him to defend his charge and call it mudslinging. Make him answer that charge, make him produce the evidence. Throw him off stride."

Wilder liked it. He and Goldman worked up a statement, which Goldman scribbled out on a legal pad. When they got to Charlottesville, Goldman got on the phone, ringing up reporters around the state — calling Chichester's attack "an all-time low," demanding that Chichester meet Wilder in person within the next seven days to explain in person this "unprecedented" personal attack.

For most of the reporters Goldman was calling, who'd been on vacation over Labor Day and were just now opening up the weekend's mail, this was the first they'd heard of Chichester's press release.

They'd hear of it plenty more in the next few days.

Sept. 4-10, 1985

The Wilder-Chichester flap earned a four-paragraph story in the *Times-Dispatch:* "The state's candidates for lieutenant governor traded some unusually sharp comments yesterday, as Republican John H. Chichester compared Democrat L. Douglas Wilder to 'some lawmakers [who] have always had the criminals' interest at heart' while serving in the state Senate . . ."

Goldman liked it.

So did Peterson.

The Chichester campaign, having belatedly scored on press release No. 1, now readied volley No. 2.

It came out Thursday, Sept. 5.

In this release, Chichester dismissed Wilder's demand for a debate as "just my opponent asking for time to make excuses. There is nothing debatable about my opponent's weak support for law-and-order issues." Then he went on to attack Wilder for being the only state senator to vote against mandatory jail time for repeat offenders.

No sooner had this release hit reporters' desks than Goldman was on the phone, in his best indignant tone. He didn't want to talk about the votes Chichester was talking about, he wanted to resurrect the phrase the "criminal's interest at heart" and rail about it some more.

"When we put in the anti-drug paraphernalia bill, did we have the criminal's interest at heart?" Goldman fumed. "When the FOP endorsed us, did they have the criminal's interest at heart?"

Then he put Wilder on the line. He called Chichester's attacks "scurrilous" and the lowest he'd ever heard. He said Chichester was acting "out of jealousy and out of desperation" because the Fraternal Order of Police had endorsed Wilder instead. Asked about the specific votes, he claimed Chichester was "distorting" his record, that the issue was not as simple as it sounded, that the bill was poorly written.

Goldman was angling for ways to keep the "criminal's interest at heart" phrase going — and he was getting lots of help from the Chichester campaign. Every other day for the next week the Chichester campaign issued a new press release attacking Wilder for being soft on crime in some way; and just like clockwork, Goldman was on the line to reporters, trying to turn the attack around, getting the focus off Wilder's voting record, harping instead on Chichester's "mudslinging" and how he had accused Wilder of having "the criminal's interest at heart."

On Saturday, Sept. 7, Chichester addressed the Republican State Central Committee. "Throughout the summer months there has been an effort to sell Doug Wilder to Virginia as a mainstream Virginia candidate. When he is questioned about his voting record and political philosophy of the past, we are told that this is the new, improved Doug Wilder. Well, my friends, you and I know those excuses won't work. Did millions of dollars in advertising make the New Coke taste any better? Of course not, and packaging Doug Wilder as a conservative isn't going to change his record either."

Chichester's retort got little attention in the Sunday papers.

But on Monday, Sept. 9, Wilder made virtually all the papers when he called Chichester's original "criminal's interest at heart" line "a personal attack of extreme proportions" and demanded that Chichester meet him 12:30 p.m. Wednesday at the Capitol.

On Tuesday, Sept. 10, Peterson dismissed Wilder's call as "just some theatrics." Chichester had no intention of meeting Wilder, he said.

That Wednesday Wilder made his appearance at the Capitol, decrying what he called Chichester's "baseless personal attacks."

Wilder also noted that Chichester had dismissed the FOP endorsement as meaningless, saying the police group was more interested in collective bargaining than law enforcement. Wilder called this an attack on the integrity of Virginia's law enforcement officers and "such an attack on the police is unprecedented by any statewide candidate for either the Democratic or Republican parties."

By the time Wilder got through, you'd have thought Chichester was some kind of desperate hypocrite, wildly flailing away at both the police and fellow Republicans, not to mention making "baseless personal attacks" on Wilder, the loyal defender of Virginia's police officers and the state's tradition of dignified campaigns.

Peterson said Wilder should have been "embarrassed" by his wild account.

The truth is, it was the Chichester campaign that should have been embarrassed. Maybe the Chichester campaign hadn't noticed yet, but its first major offensive had gone seriously awry, doing far more damage to Chichester than to Wilder. Instead of convincing voters that Wilder was a dangerous liberal, the Chichester campaign had only given Wilder a chance to play the role of the calm, dignified Virginia gentleman the voters had come to expect in their office-holders.

Meanwhile, the public's first real glimpse of Chichester was that of a shrill, faceless politician screaming that his opponent had "the criminal's interest at heart." Voters may not have been real sure what all the fuss was about but they did know the charges were so bad that Wilder called them "scurrilous" and unprecedented personal attacks.

"In politics, for an unknown to launch an attack and succeed is risky at best," says Durrette adviser Judy Peachee. "There has to be a credibility factor. John, because of lack of earned media [news coverage], was never able to establish strong enough credibility with the voters prior to launching the attack.

"So what happens? It solidified Doug's base stronger than anything I have seen. Independents were saying, 'Why is he doing that? We saw Doug Wilder on Main Street the other day and he gave me an autographed post card. He seemed like a nice man.' " By contrast, the good-natured Chichester inadvertently "came across as petulant, maybe a little mean," says former GOP legislator Ray Garland.

And the phrase "criminal's interest at heart" stuck in the public's craw — and every newspaper story — like a sharp bone that wouldn't go down.

September was supposed to be John Chichester's month, the month he blew Doug Wilder away.

But three things would go very wrong for John Chichester in September 1985.

This was just the first.

The Republicans helped Doug Wilder more than they will ever know.

First they ignored him for a month, letting him build up a month's supply of favorable publicity. Then they attacked him, but that just gave him more favorable publicity, too.

"We did exactly the opposite of what the experts said to do," Goldman says. "They said to focus on Chichester and make him the issue. They didn't think we could sell Doug." By attacking the Republicans, Wilder would presumably get the focus off race. "But by making us the issue, he played into our strategy," Goldman says. "Doug can sell himself. They made Doug Wilder the issue and we said 'great' and nobody was going to change it."

From here on, whenever Chichester even dared criticize Wilder's record, Wilder hollered that it was mudslinging. Wilder protested so loudly, and so effectively, that people believed him. All he had to do was point back to the "criminal's interest at heart" phrase. "That haunted him through the campaign," Goldman says. So what happened? How could the Chichester campaign be so clumsy as to say Wilder had the "criminal's interest at heart"?

Confusion might be the best answer. The "criminal's interest at heart" episode was simply one of the first public products of the bitter internal disputes that wracked both the Chichester and Durrette campaigns.

"At the beginning of the fall campaign we laid out a strategy," Peterson says. 'We had several issues and drunk driving was the most palatable. Eight bills — here's Doug Wilder's position. It was pretty bland stuff. We planned a series of ads, one on the Supreme Court upholding the state Bar's reprimand of Wilder, one had to do with drunk driving — Mary Sue and Buster O'Brien fought the campaign out on that issue — the spousal abuse votes and his property."

But the series of newspaper ads was never published.

Chichester didn't want to be talking about Wilder's Bar reprimand, the rundown vacant houses he owned in some poor parts of Richmond, so that knocked out three of the proposed ads. And he thought the initial one, on drunken driving, didn't amount to much. "It was a flimsy ad," Chichester says. "It stated Doug Wilder was the weakest man on drunk-driving laws." But Chichester didn't think Peterson had come up with very hard evidence. "There were something like twenty bills in the hopper on drunk driving and he and another person had only voted for seventeen of 'em. That didn't make him weak at all, but since he had voted for only seventeen of twenty, they wanted to spend $10,000 to $20,000 and put it all over the state. I said heavens no."

Instead, Chichester — influenced by his brother, the commonwealth's attorney in Stafford County — wanted to run the campaign on law-and-order issues.

"That was nuts," Peterson contends. We told him that in August — you're not going to win the election on that. To spend all summer and fall talking about who's toughest on crime when the other guy has an endorsement that mutes all that" doesn't make sense. Still, Peterson gave in and agreed to use law-and-order issues for a while and Chichester, in turn, agreed to go on the offensive. This hybrid strategy led the campaign toward its first disaster. "The 'criminal's interest at heart' came about because of his faulty decision to go after Wilder on law and order," Peterson says.

The ultimate irony is that neither Chichester nor Peterson ever intended to say "criminal's interest at heart."

"It was an accident of poor editing," Peterson says. "I had a summer intern writing press releases and this was the last thing he did. It came across my desk. I read it to John [over the phone] and he authorized it. I recall quite clearly the context in which it came up. It was a very hyper time. An intern wrote it, we were on deadline to get it out, John was hyper and crabbing about something."

The phrase slipped through without Peterson or Chichester noticing.

But while they agree it was dumb to say that Wilder had "the criminal's interest at heart," many Republicans also blame the media — for not following up on Chichester's charges and investigating them, for not forcing Wilder to defend his record instead of hiding behind the "mud-slinging" charge.

"We couldn't get anything out," Chichester says. "Among the large newspapers — the *Times-Dispatch,* Norfolk, the *Roanoke Times,* the *Post* — there was an informal, I hate the word 'conspiracy,' but decision that what we're gonna have to do is save Doug's hide and get the moss off our back and elect a black."

"Some parts of the media made a deliberate decision to counter-balance what they perceived to be the racial liability Doug had," Durrette argues. "His rhetoric in '85 was markedly different than in the past and he got away with it. Because of the velvet glove treatment with the media, he was able to switch views with impunity and campaign as a nice, friendly guy."

But while the media didn't hound Wilder about his record, the Republicans didn't, either.

Behind the scenes, the tug of war over strategy continued. Chichester says once he ripped up a speech Peterson had written and handed the pieces back because it was too strident. "All the Durrette people were saying 'attack,' but the people who knew me best, here at home, said no and my own political instincts said no," Chichester says. "What happened was, Dennis would say, 'Attack on this,' and I'd say no. So then out of the blue, someone would call and say, 'I think you ought to attack on this.' " Chichester was convinced Peterson was going behind his back. Once when that happened, Chichester found the nearest phone and called his head-quarters. "I remember telling Mike Thomas, 'Mike, is Dennis there? No, well, will you tell him if he ever goes behind my back again, he's fired.' "

Peterson admits he frequently would lobby Chichester's friends to talk the candidate into doing something. "I had to have people he had confidence in. I did that a lot. I would call his brother. I had several people I would call." But on this particular case, Peterson laughs ruefully, "I was innocent."

Meanwhile, the Durrette campaign was growing increasingly upset with Chichester. "We spent an inordinate amount of time trying to get surrogates to do John's job," says press secretary Don Harrison. "Some-body has to go after Doug."

But there were few surrogates to be found willing to attack Wilder.

"We asked for help all the time and nobody minded saying anything good about John," Peterson says, but after what happened to Durrette in May when he accidentally called Wilder a liberal and in turn was branded a racist, few wanted to say anything bad about Wilder.

So Chichester stood alone, reluctantly attacking Wilder on the wrong issue. "It was a race between two people the state never got to know very well," says Durrette media adviser Ed DeBolt. "Doug Wilder shielded himself very well and the people never got to know John Chichester very well."

Sept. 5, 1985

Doug Wilder was deep in Southside's tobacco country, with a Richmond TV crew trailing him from country store to country store.

They made their way up Virginia 49, a two-lane road that rolls up and down over the gentle hump-backed hills of Lunenburg County. By late morning, they came to the N&P Grocery. It was a hot day, the tobacco was sweet and ripe and men were coming in from the fields after a morning of harvesting the leaf. Wilder and Co. descended on the unsuspecting N&P just as the lunchtime crowd was arriving to get something at the grill.

Wilder was a hit with the farmers. One big, hairy-chested fellow — everyone knew he was hairy-chested because he wasn't wearing a shirt — ambled up to Wilder and the two chatted while TV cameras captured the scene for the evening news.

Out beside the brick store was a metal outbuilding with a pool table inside. Some of the fellows were in there knocking the balls around. Wilder caught sight of the pool table and couldn't resist. "Doug loved it and the camera crew loved it," recalls Wilder's escort for the day, former state Sen. Jim Edmunds. "He walked in. There was a fairly difficult shot on the table. He said, 'Mind if I try it?' He tried it and made it." With the cameras rolling.

The story in the newspapers that day might be some tedious account about Chichester bashing Wilder on a certain crime bill back in 1977, but the story on the evening news would show Wilder glad-handing with sweaty farmers coming in from the fields. Guess which one made the bigger impression.

Sept. 8-13, 1985

Paul Goldman picked up Sunday's *Washington Post* with trepidation. Tom Sherwood, the *Post's* Richmond correspondent, had been working on a Wilder story and the word was it wouldn't be favorable. Goldman braced himself for the first negative coverage of the campaign.

"The Pluses and Problems of L. Douglas Wilder" was the headline. It touched on all the sensitive subjects — Wilder's Bar reprimand, his dilapidated property, his divorce.

Republicans blame the *Washington Post* for many of their media troubles in the 1985 campaign, but they conveniently overlook Sherwood's story — which was accompanied by the first published photograph of one of Wilder's boarded-up town houses on Church Hill that later became so controversial.

"The first thing the story said was he got the nomination because he's black," Sherwood says. "That should hardly be positive. The second thing the story said was he was a millionaire. No one else was saying that. The third thing the story said was the house and a messy divorce. I thought the story would be Xeroxed and a million copies mailed all over the state. George Stoddart told me he was shocked I'd written such a nasty story."

The flash point of the story was one the Virginia newspapers had let fester on the inside pages — Wilder's property problems. Earlier in the year, the city had cited a garage at one of Wilder's four boarded-up town houses in Richmond's Church Hill neighborhood as "unsafe." A judge dismissed the citation after Wilder told him the property was being fixed up.

The *Post* story, however, quoted some of the neighbors, who complained that Wilder had done little to clean up the property, infested by two-foot-high weeds and piles of rotting construction debris. "It's an eyesore," one woman said. "I can't think of a worse neighbor," said another.

Goldman read the story closely and sighed. Well, he figured, if that's the worst they're going to say, it's probably not too bad.

On Sept. 11, Wilder called his "empty chair" news conference at the State Capitol to accuse Chichester of making "scurrilous" personal attacks and refusing to show up and apologize.

On Sept. 13, the *Virginian-Pilot* blasted Chichester on its editorial page. Chichester's strategy, the editorial contended, is to "throw the mud and run."

Mid-September 1985

Baliles had been on TV for about two weeks now and still was unanswered by Durrette, a void that became more noticeable with each passing day. The riverboat gambler Baliles had ventured a calculated risk. He nearly emptied his treasury on TV in late August and early September. But by beating Durrette to the tube by a full three weeks, it was Baliles who made the first impression and made it clearly. Soon the internal polls started showing Baliles inching away and the money men, sensing they had a winner on their hands, started opening their wallets for an even bigger TV blitz in October.

Terry and O'Brien wouldn't bring out their TV guns until later. Chichester was already running radio spots and had TV in the works. The question turned to Wilder: What would he do? He had already all but said he wouldn't be able to afford TV — and everyone from Robb on down, with the exception of a sharp-eyed Dennis Peterson and Tom King, believed it. "We were all in the dark," says Bobby Watson, the Democrats' executive director. "We didn't know they were raising all this money."

In the Democrats' weekly joint campaign meetings, the debate alternated between fear that Wilder might indeed come up with the money to go on TV and the fear that he wouldn't. Sometimes it was hard to tell which was more pervasive.

"People were scared," says Terry campaign manager John Jameson. "The one chance Wilder had to win was that people not know he was black. People were saying if he organized quietly and did radio spots or had surrogates on TV," then maybe he could sneak in with a Democratic sweep.

But all the consultants wringing their hands and offering advice didn't matter. The only campaign strategist who mattered was Doug Wilder. And he insisted on going on TV. "I said I'm not going to run a charade campaign," he says. "People are going to know who I am."

And so, in mid-September, very much in secret, Wilder filmed his TV commercials.

Sept. 12-13 1985

Wilder's commercials had their genesis in the spring through a friend-of-a-friend arrangement. Wilder had a friend in Arlington named Dr. Beth Stone, a speech professor at the Howard University Law School. She in turn had a friend named Dr. Tommie Jones — a Washington film maker who specialized in documentaries. In the spring of 1985, Stone suggested that Jones might want to do some TV work for Wilder. She had a documentary in mind, but Wilder ended up hiring the two women to do his TV commercials — something neither of them had done.

Their filming began early one morning in Appomattox, but their attempt at filming a commercial featuring Wilder and state Sen. Madison Marye talking about their grandfathers — one a slave, one a Confederate officer — had gone poorly. Cameraman Gerald Scheeler blamed Goldman. "We got there and he really didn't know what he wanted," Scheeler says. "He would kind of be writing these speeches. I realized then it was all unrehearsed and I felt really uncomfortable."

Eventually, the spot was scratched and the caravan carrying the candidate and his camera crew moved on to the Lunenburg County Courthouse. The plan here was to film Wilder with the Lunenburg sheriff and some of his white deputies in a double-barreled attempt to neutralize both race and Chichester's law-and-order attacks.

By now, "It was hot as willy ned," Jones recalls, and the sheriff's spot wasn't working very well. The plan was for a police car to pull up, three deputies to get out and then the sheriff would introduce them to Wilder. This was one of Goldman's ideas and it was stiff and awkward. Between the heat of the aging morning and their acting roles, the deputies were getting uncomfortable. Goldman had other complaints with the footage. "I hate to say it, but they didn't look like cops," he says. "The sheriff was thin. I kept seeing Don Knotts. I was thinking this ain't gonna cut it. I need something out of 'In the Heat of the Night.' " The filming had been halted for a few moments so everyone could figure out what to do next.

"Then Paul Goldman disappeared," Scheeler says. "He had this habit. He was always looking for a phone booth. I was very nervous about the whole thing."

And then it happened. Joe Alder, the town cop in Kenbridge, was at the courthouse that morning testifying. When he was done, he exited out the side door — and entered Virginia history and political folklore.

Who spotted Alder first is a matter of some debate. But what they saw is certain: a beefy, slow-talking white Southern lawman, straight out of the stereotype.

Alder was ambling down the sidewalk to his cruiser when Stone spotted him. "When we looked around and saw him leaving, it seemed like a concerted feeling that this was the guy," she says. "The man was getting in his car and nobody was doing anything to stop him. I ran over and said, 'That certainly is a pretty uniform you have. Why is yours blue and theirs brown?' That's the only thing I could think of."

Alder, no doubt blushing, replied that he was a town cop while the others were county deputies, but still he kept moving toward his cruiser, not sure why all these people were suddenly gathering around him. "What's the difference?" Stone asked, still stalling for time.

Wilder and Goldman had been standing in the shade under a tree, talking things over. Goldman says he spotted Alder the moment he walked out. "I thought he looked great. With his blue uniform, he looked like a state trooper. I thought 'home run!' — this is it."

The next thing poor Joe Alder knew he was shaking hands with a candidate for lieutenant governor and being asked if he'd agree to do a TV commercial for him, right then and there.

Alder, whatever his appearance, was no country bumpkin. He'd been a page in the General Assembly years ago. And while professing to be nonpartisan, he had paid close attention to the unfolding 1985 campaign. In particular, he'd already made up his mind to vote for Doug Wilder. "The man deserves to be where he is. Anybody who started at the bottom and worked his way up, why hold him back, whether he's black, green or yellow?" Alder says. "I had just followed the campaign and every time they found anything he'd ever done, they tried to put him down."

Wanna do a TV commercial for Doug Wilder? Sure, Alder said.

Alder was worried about one thing, though — whether it was proper to do the commercial in uniform. Goldman whispered to Edmunds, "We've got to have this guy." Conveniently, Edmunds, besides being Fifth District Democratic chairman, was also the town lawyer for Kenbridge. "It's OK," Edmunds assured Alder. "I'll talk to the chief." With that impromptu legal advice, Alder agreed.

Goldman took out his legal pad, leaned on the hood of Alder's police car and wrote out a script in about five minutes.

Stone hurried to get Alder to sign a model release. Before Alder knew it, his sunglasses were lifted off his face and someone was powdering the little pink indentation his glasses had left on the bridge of his nose. Taking off Alder's sunglasses had a significant impact on the subsequent commercial. "He said he couldn't see," Stone recalls. "That's why he was squinting and looked mean."

Action!

Goldman's script was simple and to the point: "I'm a Virginia police officer. Every day I put my life on the line," it began, ran through a couple more lines then ended with: "The Fraternal Order of Police endorses Doug Wilder."

But getting it all down on film was excruciatingly difficult. Alder was a joy to work with. "If he'd blow a line, he'd apologize profusely," Scheeler recalls. But he was no actor, which became quickly clear. "Joe said he'd rather be chasing criminals than this," Jones remembers, as the takes started adding up and the sun kept beating down. "He said chasing criminals was easier." Eventually Stone wrote his lines out on a legal pad, held them up as cue cards and Scheeler filmed the spot one line at a time.

When they were finally done and Alder was excused and everyone piled into their cars and vans to head to the next stop, Wilder turned to Goldman and said: "This will win us the election."

It did.

That night in Richmond, Jay Shropshire ushered the TV crew into the Senate chamber. The idea was to film Wilder working at his desk on the Senate floor. "This is where it really got bizarre," Scheeler says. He suggested that Goldman really ought to get something to show the outside of the Capitol and its gleaming white steps. Perhaps in the morning they could film Wilder walking up the front steps of the Capitol. Goldman thought Scheeler had a good idea, but there was one tiny problem. He didn't want anyone to see the filming. After all, officially Wilder wasn't supposed to be able to afford TV commercials. "Yeah, it's a good idea," Goldman told him. "Why don't you show up at 7:30 before anyone gets here, no tripod, hide in the bushes so no one will see you and Doug will come in and go up the steps?"

Scheeler just sort of stared down at Goldman, waiting for a laugh, a grin, anything to indicate that Goldman was really just joking. But he wasn't. He really did want Scheeler to hide in the bushes so Wilder could sneak up the front steps of the Capitol.

Scheeler told Goldman his idea was crazy. And it was so late at night, and it had been such a long day, that this time not even Paul Goldman was in a mood to argue.

The next morning, they filmed Wilder trotting up the front steps of the Capitol, and Goldman didn't make Scheeler hide in the bushes. But to satisfy Goldman's demand for secrecy, Jones and Stone kept well away from the scene, so as not to make any passers-by curious.

The morning was heating up and Wilder, after running up and down the Capitol steps a dozen or more times, had worked up quite a sweat. "Doug said if he'd went up the steps once more, he'd drop dead," Stone says.

The Durrette campaign started coming apart in public.

"During the campaign," says *Washington Post* reporter Sherwood, "I'd call up Republicans to ask about X and they'd say, 'Oh, you ought to know about Y' and Y was far more damaging."

That was what happened on Sept. 13, when disgruntled Republicans handed Sherwood what became a running theme of the Durrette campaign: dissension and disorganization.

The key complainer: None other than Durrette's chief fund-raiser, Smith Ferebee, an old chum of Mills Godwin and key figure in the Main Street crowd.

Ferebee complained vigorously about the Durrette campaign's inability to devise a coherent strategy and put it into practice. "I'll be damned if I can find two or three people to agree," he said.

The headline the next morning: "Internal Disputes Said to Hinder Durrette's Race for Governor."

But that wasn't all.

Baliles had just started a new round of TV spots, including one comparing Durrette's stands on certain issues over the years to a looping roller coaster.

Durrette still wasn't on the air. He wouldn't go on until Sept. 16 — buying about half the air time Baliles had.

By then, it didn't matter. "Once Baliles was on the air around Labor Day with those ten-second spots and they went unanswered, that was the beginning of the end," says Jeff Gregson, O'Brien's campaign manager.

The contrast between the Democrats and the Republicans couldn't have been more striking or more ironic — the Democrats, progressive, well-organized and united; the Republicans, hidebound, disorganized and squabbling.

Behind the scenes, the Democrats had to put up with a lively amount of conflict, crisis and controversy. They just managed to keep theirs hidden.

And almost all of them involved Doug Wilder.

This was the Democratic campaign the public didn't see.

What really aggravated the bad feelings between Wilder and Robb, between Goldman and the joint campaign committee, was the secrecy with which Wilder and Goldman cloaked their every move. "No one knew what would be in the paper the next day," says Bobby Watson, the party's executive director. "I don't think we ever 100 percent knew what they were doing," says Baliles fund-raiser Bill Wiley.

Plenty of top Democrats thought it was time for a father-to-son talk with the Wilder campaign.

Wiley was designated to have a chat with his old buddy Goldman. "I talked to Paul about it," he says. "Doug's doing well, he's getting good numbers, he's getting good press. But there was a perception that someone would write a story about how this campaign was only two or three people in the basement with no scheduler."

Robb, too, fretted that the shoestring Wilder campaign would come untied in public; that's one reason why "looking after" Wilder became his staff's top political priority.

Just like a couple having marital problems and heading toward divorce, most of the domestic disputes between Robb and Wilder involved money.

Robb and chief of staff David McCloud, of course, had pressed Wilder all during the summer to hire both a professional campaign manager and a professional fund-raiser, but neither Wilder nor Goldman showed much interest in the subject.

On the Labor Day campaign swing Robb again tried to convince Wilder that he needed some professional campaign help. To emphasize the point, when Robb returned to the governor's office on Sept. 4, he wrote Wilder a page-and-a-half letter. In it:

1 — Robb told Wilder he had contacted one of his Democratic friends

in California "and asked him if he would agree to raise some hopefully significant sums of money for you from some of his contacts on the West Coast and around the country. He said he would be delighted to do so and asked that you send him some of the campaign materials and brochures that he could give to potential contributors."

2 — Robb told Wilder he had also talked with Vernon Jordan, the former Urban League president, "at some length" and that Jordan had agreed to increase his fund-raising efforts for Wilder. (Goldman dismisses Jordan's work, saying he raised only a couple of thousand dollars for Wilder.)

3 — Robb again pleaded with Wilder to beef up his campaign staff. He noted that Jordan had agreed "to try to find some additional professional fund-raising assistance, which, as I indicated to you on Monday, is also essential if you're going to run a credible campaign and have any chance of raising the kind of money you'll need between now and Election Day."

But Robb wasn't finished with his sermonette:

"I can't overemphasize the importance of hiring full-time professional assistance in this arena as quickly as possible. I hope by now all of the outstanding factors for the Sept. 15th fund-raiser have been resolved. David McCloud had a meeting of several of my key staff members yesterday to discuss this matter and to see whatever additional assistance we can provide, but the key decisions and action have to be yours and those of your professional finance staff."

The Sept. 15 fund-raiser Robb mentioned in his letter was a particularly sore point. To Robb staffers, it was a classic example of how the governor had saved yet another Wilder fund-raiser from disaster; to Goldman, it's a classic example of how the governor didn't do nearly what he could to help Wilder, but tried to hog all the credit later.

Here's what happened, more or less:

Marie Ridder, who married into the Knight-Ridder newspaper family, lives in Northern Virginia and is a good friend of Robb's. During the summer, Wilder and Goldman visited her and it was agreed that she would hold a fund-raiser for Wilder sometime in the fall. Meanwhile, Robb had promised to appear at a fund-raiser for Wilder in Northern Virginia and at some point the Robb fund-raiser and the Ridder fund-raiser became one and the same.

That's the first Goldman complaint — Robb really didn't hold a fund-raiser for Wilder in Northern Virginia, he just took over one that was already scheduled.

Robb staffers contend the Ridder fund-raiser wouldn't have come off if it hadn't been for the governor's personal involvement. "The governor had to pick up the phone and call Doug to pick a date," says Carolyn Moss, because no one could get Goldman to commit himself to a specific day.

The Ridder fund-raiser netted about $14,000 for the Wilder campaign. Robb staffers thought they had done a great job of pulling the fund-raiser together at the last minute. Soon afterward, though, Goldman called Judy Griswold, his official contact on Robb's staff, and complained about how little money had been raised there. Goldman called it "chump change." As for Robb, "he ought to be ashamed if that's all the money he can raise," Goldman said.

Goldman pressed his complaint with a relentlessness that infuriated the governor's staff. "It was a tactical thing," he says. "Why tell anybody you were happy, especially when you know every time you criticize 'em, they'll jump out of their skin."

Robb staffers thought the Wilder campaign had unrealistic expectations of what kind of money was available. Candidates for lieutenant governor typically find money scarce, but Wilder carried an additional burden and it didn't have anything to do with his skin color, says Laurie Naismith, Robb's secretary of the commonwealth. "Part of it was Doug. He had burned an awful lot of bridges with people or didn't have them to start with."

Sept. 18, 1985

The AFL-CIO was getting antsy. "We didn't know how much money Doug had. We were afraid he couldn't get on TV," says Danny LeBlanc, the union's secretary-treasurer. For weeks now, LeBlanc had been trying to get a straight answer out of Goldman. First, Goldman was out of town on the tour. And when Goldman did bother to return LeBlanc's calls, he was less than revealing. By now, labor was worried. Wilder was the only statewide candidate it had endorsed and it wanted to help — but first it needed to know what the Wilder campaign was doing so the two could coordinate their efforts. Unable to pin down Goldman, the AFL-CIO leadership demanded a meeting with Wilder and Goldman.

On the appointed morning, four labor officials — president David Laws, LeBlanc, political committee chairwoman Pauline Huffman and Scott Reynolds, the public relations man — drove out to Wilder's home. Wilder came bouncing out the door as if he had been up for hours. Goldman straggled along behind him, still dressed in his jogging suit and spooning up mush from his cereal bowl. Wilder squeezed in the front seat. Goldman clambered in, too, and they rode off, six people in one car.

On the way out to Hanover County, where Wilder was to address a breakfast meeting, LeBlanc tried to broach the subject of Wilder's disorganized campaign. "Listen, we've got to talk about your schedule."

"Talk to Paul," Wilder said.

LeBlanc rolled his eyes.

Soon they were at the Hanover House restaurant. The labor officials could hear thunderous applause coming from the room where Wilder was having his breakfast. Meanwhile, Laws, LeBlanc, Huffman and Reynolds were having breakfast at a table in the dining room with Goldman, trying to grill him about what in the devil the Wilder campaign was up to.

"Dave opened up and complimented Paul on the campaign so far," Reynolds remembers. He also remembers Goldman squirming and fidgeting in his seat, wondering what else was to come.

The labor people had a list of fifteen questions and they went over each one. Almost all were embarrassingly basic. Why can't they get a copy of the candidate's schedule? How much money did the campaign have? How could the union get posters and bumper stickers and other materials to distribute? How's fund-raising going? Will he be able to afford TV?

"Dave and Danny were asking specific questions and he was responding with real general answers," Reynolds says. "Like, 'Paul, where will the candidate be on such-and-such a day?' and he'd go into nauseating detail about why Doug Wilder was a war hero and this is a thematic campaign."

Huffman tossed a state road map on the table. "Show us where you're going to win," she wanted to know.

Goldman scratched his head. "Well, we're going to do real well in Tidewater and we've got something going in Northern Virginia and we're talking to some people in Roanoke and we're gonna surprise some people in Southwest Virginia."

"Yes, Paul," she said, "but where are you going to *win?* Which congressional districts? Show me on the map."

Goldman scratched his head again. "Well, like I said, we're going to do very well in Tidewater . . . "

Exhausted, the labor officials moved on to money. Three times Laws asked Goldman how much money the Wilder campaign had and three times Goldman gave an evasive answer. How much money are you raising? Laws would ask. "Fund-raising is going very well," Goldman would say. Three times they went through this little charade. By now, Laws was steaming. He leaned across the table and looked Goldman in the eyes and said, slowly, firmly, like an angry father dealing with a truant son, "How much money do you have in the bank right now, Paul?"

Goldman leaned back and grinned. His eyes wandered around the room before coming back to Laws. "That's a state secret," he said simply.

Damn it, Goldman! Laws exploded. A state secret! What in hell is that supposed to mean? We're supposed to be your friends. We're on your side. We're trying to help you and you won't even tell us how much money you have? Laws covered his face with his hands and gave up.

Are you going to have TV? Goldman grudgingly gave an inch. Yes, he said.

Who's doing it?

"Someone Doug knows."

After his breakfast was over, Wilder was even more buoyant than before. The labor officials were disgusted. When they got back to their union office on West Broad Street, the four got together to talk over their disastrous non-interview with Goldman.

Laws summed up the attitude when he declared: "Well, we know one thing for certain. Doug Wilder's biggest problem isn't the fact that he's black."

12

Carry Me Back

Sept. 18, 1985

For Wyatt Durrette, this was to be the week his campaign finally got going. He had been stumbling ever since the summer and that ambush at Wintergreen, where Baliles beat him to the punch on education. Then Baliles beat him to TV, by an incredible three weeks. Durrette had come back to issue a detailed position paper on education to regain some of the ground — and his first TV commercials focused heavily on schools.

With the education issue presumably behind him, Durrette was ready to go on the offensive. On Tuesday, Sept. 17, he and Baliles would meet in their first televised debate. The next day Durrette would join former Gov. Mills Godwin for a series of campaign stops through rural Southside, where Durrette would talk about agriculture and try to make that issue his own while Godwin would attack Baliles for being a big spender.

Instead, the trip marked the biggest one-day disaster of the Durrette campaign. "No candidate had ever done what I had done on agriculture,"

Durrette says. "We had a good position paper — and we paid a heavy price."

So did Chichester.

From midsummer on, whenever the phone rang in Durrette headquarters, "We were pulling our hair out," says press secretary Don Harrison. "Is this it? Is this the Godwin bomb? You don't know the terror and anxiety we went through wondering when the Godwin bomb would hit. If the phone rang, do I turn pale or answer it?"

The Godwin bomb.

Some Republicans remembered all too well the bomb Godwin had dropped on them at the very end of the 1981 campaign. Godwin had never been fond of GOP standard-bearer Marshall Coleman. After the 1981 convention, the former governor went home to Chuckatuck and didn't do a thing for the Republicans all fall — while many Old Guard conservatives defected to support Robb. Only when President Reagan made a special call to Godwin did he make an appearance on Coleman's behalf. His belated appearance did little to reassure conservatives skeptical of Coleman, though. To make things worse, Godwin used the occasion to denounce Robb for supporting a constitutional amendment giving the District of Columbia two U.S. senators, voter registration by post card and keeping Virginia under the federal review of the 1965 Voting Rights Act. Godwin's comments were widely interpreted as his way of warning that Robb had strong black support and blacks would likely have a lot of influence in a Robb administration. Instead of helping Coleman, Godwin's appeal to Virginia's Old Guard backfired. Blacks, who had been skeptical of the moderate-conservative Robb, were suddenly energized in a way they never had been before. On Election Day 1981, blacks turned out in record numbers and provided Robb's margin of victory.

For the first time in his long political career, an endorsement by Mills Godwin had turned out to be a handicap, and his past as a legislative leader of Massive Resistance in the 1950s had returned to color his remarks. What would happen in 1985, Harrison wondered with more than a twinge of trepidation, when the Republicans had nominated a ticket clearly to Godwin's liking and the Democrats had nominated a black candidate?

By mid-September, though, the Durrette campaign was in such poor shape on its right that it plainly needed Godwin's help, Harrison explains, however risky that might be among moderates. The problem was Robb: He had shown the business community that not all Democrats were free-spending liberals. Baliles seemed a Robb clone, so many conservatives felt no urgency in either electing Durrette or defeating Baliles. One place where Durrette's early polls showed him doing especially badly was Southside, which set off warning bells in Durrette headquarters. If Durrette couldn't carry conservative Southside, then where could he carry? Durrette's mid-September swing through Southside to promote his position paper on agriculture, with Mills Godwin at his side thumping the tub of fiscal responsibility, was a rescue mission to stir up the rural conservatives.

Nevertheless, sending Godwin out to campaign with Durrette — on one of the most widely advertised trips of the campaign — was a mistake.

"Anybody who would put a seventy-some-year-old man out on the road all day in the hot sun in a politically charged campaign and not expect him to say something unprintable ought to have their head examined," says Alan Albert, a Baliles adviser. "Sending Godwin through that territory, when race had become a subject, was a questionable message to send."

The Durrette advisers understood the risk, but not clearly enough. They had someone — they won't say who — talk to Godwin privately before the trip. This emissary gently explained that this was a campaign trip for *Durrette,* that Durrette's strategy was not to even mention Wilder's name, that it was up to Chichester to attack his opponent, and therefore, since this was a campaign trip for *Durrette,* it would be greatly appreciated if the former governor would confine his remarks to Durrette's opponent and not mention Wilder's name at all.

But all the precautions and all the position papers didn't much matter. The way the trip came across to many Virginia voters, Godwin looked like an old dinosaur thrashing through the woods, caged up in Southside like some dangerous animal so he wouldn't frighten voters in more cultured parts of the state. The Durrette campaign desperately wanted plenty of reporters along on the trip to play up Durrette's farm policy and his fiscal conservatism, but the Republicans hadn't counted on the media being far more interested in something else.

"We had *beaucoup* reporters going along and their sole purpose, they told this to me," Harrison says, "was to see Mills Godwin screw up again."

The day began beautifully, with Godwin telling a group of Suffolk farmers that Baliles had proposed new programs costing more than $2 billion and that he'd have to raise taxes to pay for them. Godwin assured his listeners that Durrette doesn't believe in "throwing money at every problem that comes along." This was exactly what the Durrette staffers wanted Godwin to say. They couldn't have been happier as the entourage moved on to a luncheon in South Hill and a tobacco auction in Danville, and Godwin kept up his attacks on Baliles' budget proposals.

Along the way, the reporters pressed Godwin to comment on the

Democratic ticket and Doug Wilder in particular. But Godwin was a model of gentlemanly restraint. All he would say about the Democratic ticket was it "certainly does not represent mainstream Virginia." Pressed on why not, Godwin skillfully noted Wilder's voting record. "Surely one would not judge the present nominee for lieutenant governor as one who had followed the conservative line." The most important attribute for a candidate for lieutenant governor, Godwin stressed, is that he "have the qualities that enable him to succeed the governor in the event of a vacancy." But when someone asked directly if Wilder's color was a problem, Godwin quickly backed off. "I don't think the color and the race has anything to do with it." Clearly there would be no repeat of the 1981 Godwin bomb today.

Late in the afternoon, many reporters decided they'd heard enough and peeled off from the pack, heading back to Richmond. The Durrette-Godwin entourage went on to a nighttime appearance at Hampden-Sydney College, just outside Farmville, but nothing new was expected.

If the tour had ended here, it would have been a striking success. "To see what the tour could have been, read Marge Fisher's story," Durrette says. "She left just before Farmville. Just compare her article to the others. You can't begin to measure the impact that has on your campaign."

Fisher's story in the *Roanoke Times & World-News* was exactly what the Durrette campaign had been looking for out of the trip:

"Godwin preaches the fiscal gospel,

says Democrat Baliles is non-believer"

"SOUTH HILL — Former Gov. Mills Godwin unsheathed the dagger of fiscal conservatism Wednesday and stuck it to the campaign spending promises of the Democrats' candidate for governor, Gerald Baliles.

"On a swing through Southside Virginia with the GOP gubernatorial candidate, Wyatt Durrette, Godwin depicted Baliles as one who could not be trusted to carry on the state's longstanding tradition of fiscal responsibility and limited government."

If the Southside tour had ended there, "you can use your imagination and imagine a very different campaign," Durrette says.

Unfortunately for Durrette, though, the tour — and plenty of other reporters — continued on to Farmville.

Hampden-Sydney, one of only a handful of all-male colleges left in the country, is the very essence of the Virginia establishment. Of the 850 students, a full 85 percent belong to the College Republican Club. Here at this little patch of aristocracy set down in hardpan Southside, the Durrette-Godwin tour ended with a reception on the lawn.

By now, the reporters who remained had heard the same speeches over and over again. Some were already typing out their stories, keeping one ear half-cocked for any deviation from the day's script, though not really expecting any. Suddenly they instinctively stopped their typing and looked up. They'd waited all day — and now he was doing it, talking about Wilder, right here in front of them.

Godwin was tired. It had been a long day. And tonight, he looked out on a friendly Southside audience and simply got carried away. He started talking about Wilder and all the reasons he was out of step with conservative Virginians. Godwin assured his audience that he wasn't being personally critical of Wilder, but cited his record on crime, right-to-work and collective bargaining as evidence of his liberalism. But that wasn't all.

There are two different versions of what Godwin said next.

According to the *Richmond Times-Dispatch* he said: "I have a hard time seeing how Jerry Baliles could ask for and espouse the record of this man. Why, he actually introduced a bill to repeal the state song. He wanted to repeal the song 'Carry Me Back to Old Virginny.' "

According to the Norfolk *Virginian-Pilot,* Godwin said: "I can't resist the opportunity to say to you that he actually introduced a bill in the state Senate to repeal our state song, 'Carry Me Back to Old Virginny.' He was the only patron of the bill."

Either way, it hardly matters. Godwin had done it. He had made race an issue. Republicans would argue otherwise, but how could they deny the obvious? Admittedly, someone could make the case that Wilder's opposition to the state song was an indication of how unpredictable and loud-mouthed he could sometimes be, especially early in his political career. But everyone knew why Wilder had tried to repeal the Reconstruction-era state song back in 1970. Its nostalgic references are clearly offensive to blacks. Wilder's repeal attempt got nowhere, and the song retains its official status. But, as Wilder loves to point out, "they don't play it anymore."

Durrette remembers thinking at the time, "Hmm, this could be trouble if the press gets a hold of it and waves it around." Even as he was thinking that, reporters clustered around Godwin. The former governor must have sensed he had done something wrong when they quizzed him about the racial connotations of the state song. "I don't believe that people refer to it with racial connotations," Godwin said. "I was simply citing the record of one of the bills he put in and I have no further comment."

Durrette press secretary Don Harrison was one of those who had caught a plane back to Richmond and missed the Hampden-Sydney reception. When he got back to Durrette headquarters, he could tell right away something was wrong, terribly wrong. "[Adviser] Frank Atkinson was absolutely pale," he says. "That's when I found out. The assistant press secretary was going bonkers trying to handle the damn calls. Not more than forty-five minutes had elapsed" since Godwin had said what he said.

"I have never seen Frank Atkinson any more frustrated or just heartbroken," Harrison says. "I had a feeling in my bones. I thought we lost the campaign right there."

Sept. 19-20, 1985

Don Harrison picked up the morning newspapers and found even more trouble than he had imagined. Someone inside the Durrette campaign, apparently trying to prod the Republicans to change their tactics, had leaked to the *Washington Post* the results of an in-house poll that showed Durrette falling nine points behind Baliles, 43 percent to 34 percent. And then there was the Godwin story. Just as Godwin's 1981 remarks overshadowed President Reagan's appearance on Coleman's behalf, this time his comments bumped his attacks on Baliles' spending plans out of the news. The *Times-Dispatch* even made a direct comparison to "the racially charged tactics the former governor" used in 1981.

This was just the beginning, too. Newspapers jumped on the state song controversy and rode it for days. Republicans and Democrats alike sat stunned when they saw how the press had seized on Godwin's brief remark about the state song. Democrats secretly couldn't have hoped for better news. "If we could have put Mills Godwin on our payroll, we'd have done it," says Bobby Scott, the state senator from Newport News.

Democrats, though, decided this was one time discretion was indeed the better part of valor. Wilder — safely out of reach somewhere on the tour — would have nothing to say now, though Goldman promised Wilder would respond "in the near future," which only insured that the controversy would live on until he did.

Two days after the Southside tour, one day after the leaked poll and the state song hit the papers, Durrette appeared with Baliles in Virginia Beach. By now, under Durrette's master plan for the week, he had hoped to be on the offensive. Instead, he was even more on the defensive than before, as reporters pestered him with questions about both his sagging polls and whether he thought the state song was racist. His chin-up attitude didn't help change the spin on the stories: "Durrette not discouraged by nine-point lag in poll" was one headline.

Moreover, the controversy over the state song had taken on a life of its own and all the Republican denials and explanations only kept it going. Chichester wisely tried to steer clear of the controversy. But try as he might to avoid it, Chichester was becoming inexorably drawn into the turmoil, if only because he was Wilder's opponent.

Ed DeBolt just shakes his head when he remembers looking at the first Durrette polls to come in after the Godwin bomb was dropped. "That was catastrophic," he says. "We went down nine points in one day, fourteen in Northern Virginia." Durrette eventually made up the lost ground, but used up valuable time doing it.

Durrette blames the media for exaggerating the importance of Godwin's comments and making them into something they weren't. "The *Washington Post* was very flagrant, just unpardonable" in its coverage of Godwin, Durrette charges. Godwin's progressive 1966-70 administration was overlooked and instead he was invariably identified in the context of his role in Massive Resistance. "They created a monster in the minds of Northern Virginians. If you didn't read the stories very closely, you wouldn't know when he was governor and you would know nothing about his accomplishments. You would think here was the architect of Massive Resistance and a former segregationist out plying his racism. They created an image far from the man himself. And how do voters in Northern Virginia know any different?" Most are from out of state, Durrette notes. "Probably half of them didn't live in Virginia before his second term." So all they know about Mills Godwin is what they read in the *Washington Post*.

If "the criminal's interest at heart" was the first thing to go dangerously wrong for Chichester, the state song controversy was the second. Simply by being an ex-Democrat, by having had Godwin's nod at the convention, Chichester was automatically — though unfairly — pictured as an extension of the Old Guard that was now seen as trying to stir up racial animosity. The state song controversy did more than anything else to make the Chichester-Wilder campaign not simply a campaign to elect a lieutenant governor, but a referendum to decide how racist Virginia still was.

From here on out, the 1985 campaign would be increasingly viewed as a contest between the past and the future. The Baliles campaign highlighted the contrast, running a sepia-toned film of an antique car running in reverse. Let's not go backward, the announcer said.

Godwin and other Republicans had wanted to make Wilder the issue and now they had, but not quite the way they had intended. "It's like the 1960 West Virginia primary," says Baliles adviser Alan Albert. "With religion in the back of everyone's mind, Kennedy would be dead. But when religion became the issue, people are very averse to admitting they're bigots."

Sept. 22-23, 1985

Being out on the tour was a godsend — the Wilder campaign was simply inaccessible. Had Wilder been running a regular campaign, speaking at the same type of events his running mates were, the TV cameras would have shone on him and microphones would have been thrust in his face and he'd have been on the evening news that night, or in the next day's paper, whether he liked it or not. Instead, Wilder could afford to meander around the rural Northern Neck.

Goldman had promised that Wilder would have something to say on the Godwin incident but when and where he would surface next was something the big-city reporters could only guess. For that matter, the Baliles and Terry campaigns didn't know either. In the days immediately after the state song controversy, the Democratic camp was gripped by fear. "The conservatives were deathly afraid we would utter a word about Godwin," Goldman says.

In public, Wilder was the very model of charm and decorum. "Doug said, 'They'll never get me to pop off in front of a camera. They don't think I can do it,'" Goldman says.

In private, though, Wilder was plenty worked up. "Wilder said many times, 'I wish, I really wish, I could wade in there,'" says Michael Brown. "It was getting to him."

Robb saw a glimpse of the emotion behind Wilder's serene public front. "Doug and I had any number of conversations. He wanted to fire back at Mills Godwin and others. I said, 'You do that and you lose the election. Most people don't know you. If they catch you with violent or angry words, that will reinforce stereotype images. If you give them any reason [to vote against you], it's all over.'"

Nevertheless, Robb says, Wilder was in a swivet throughout the fall. "People would say things and he'd say, 'I want to get him.' The desire to strike back was there throughout, all through the campaign."

When a reporter for the *Roanoke Times & World-News* finally caught up to Wilder on Sept. 22, though, he played it cool, and formally declined comment on Godwin: "In keeping with the positive tone of my campaign, I think it is best left to the past. I don't intend to go back fifteen, one hundred, three hundred years to talk about what used to happen in Virginia. I'm concerned with moving on."

In Richmond, Democratic strategists sighed in relief — for now.

The Republicans, too, were torn over how to respond to the state song controversy.

Backers of Wyatt Durrette tried again to seek an endorsement from former Gov. Linwood Holton. "They had seen their polls and knew they were in trouble," Holton says. A Holton endorsement, better than anything else, would send a strong signal that Durrette was not simply the candidate of the Old Guard.

"They put tremendous pressure on me," Holton says of his fellow Republicans. "I was hesitant to do it because of the race issue. I didn't know what the people who were raising the money would influence those candidates to do. About that time, they gave me an out. [Godwin] made a statement that Doug Wilder was the candidate who had tried to amend our sacred state song. This was the sort of thing I thought was objectionable and unacceptable."

Late in September, Ed DeBolt went to lunch with Holton. "What do I have to do to get you working?" he asked.

Holton thought he saw a way not only Durrette but also the whole Republican ticket could get out from under the burden of the state song controversy. He made a list of positive, specific issues he thought the Republicans should identify themselves with — education, economic development, women's issues, a proposed state zoo in Roanoke.

But mostly he thought the Republicans should do something about the state song. Holton reluctantly agreed to do TV commercials for Durrette on one condition. "Tell Wyatt before I do it," Holton says he told DeBolt, "he must issue a statement saying the words 'massa' and 'old darky' are offensive to him and if he's elected he'll appoint a commission to look into changing it. If he does that, I'll get out here and work and work very strongly." Holton also insisted that Chichester and O'Brien sign off on the statement to show GOP unity.

Some Republicans privately scoff at Holton's "ultimatum," suggesting he purposely made demands he knew could never be met. Holton disagrees. "I was not being coy. I was not just offering a device to get myself off the hook. There were three things the candidates needed. They needed to show middle voters they were independent and could stand on their own two feet. Secondly, it would clearly show they were serious about saying they were not racists and would do overt action in office to eliminate a racial problem. Three, it would get the campaign much-needed attention among middle voters who were drifting to the Democratic side.

"The negative side of it would have been to make some of the fund-raising people mad. But I had been approached by strong financial backers in the Northern Virginia area to support the ticket and I felt they would have made up the difference if the Main Street crowd in Richmond pulled back money. And I agreed if they did these things and it did hurt the financial effort in Richmond, that I would get out actively and help make up the difference. But I never got any answer."

"I dutifully took the list back to Judy [Peachee] and Bruce [Miller] and they said no, it can't be considered; we can't insult Mills Godwin," DeBolt says.

But even as his fellow Republicans were rejecting his demands, the Democrats were courting Holton in a way. Baliles called him once just to chat. "He's a friend," Holton explains. "I think he just called to keep me out." And Holton did tell Baliles to pass on a message to Wilder: "Tell him make sure he doesn't lose his temper."

Meanwhile, Robb talked with Holton several times about the possibility of endorsing Wilder. "We finally decided in the last week that it would be more divisive if he did it, but that was one of a number of things I had in my pocket," Robb says. "I have no doubt he'd have done it if I had asked, but we decided he was doing more good by not saying anything. He and I discussed it with some frequency."

Holton sounds less sure. "All those who were professionals knew I was not in a position to endorse a Democrat without any special cause," he says. "I'm a Republican. I'm still a Republican. I want the party to occupy the ground I delineated for it in my two campaigns and in my administration. And I don't think people should be bouncing back from party to party. I think they recognize there was not much chance Holton would endorse a Democrat."

Still, for those who followed the nuances of Virginia politics, Holton's "golden silence" was deafening. "It was funny," Holton says. "Toward the end of the campaign I saw Bobby Scott at William and Mary. He said, 'I've been hearing a lot about you and some TV commercials.' I said, 'I haven't done any TV commercials.' He said, 'That's what I hear.' "

Sept. 20, 1985

Two days after the state song controversy, the third disaster to overtake John Chichester's campaign would become public — charges of conflict of interest.

Paul Goldman first heard about Chichester's fine by the State Corporation Commission — Virginia's chief regulatory agency for business — back in April, but won't say who told him. Meanwhile, at least three high-ranking Robb staffers — adviser Phil Abraham, press secretary George Stoddart and chief of staff David McCloud — were busy researching Chichester's voting record, looking for some weak spot Wilder could exploit.

McCloud cites this research as a prime example of how the Robb staff did the nitty-gritty work for the Wilder campaign. "Stoddart had the principal ore on that [the conflict-of-interest]," McCloud says. "Without us, they couldn't have gotten that." On this particular issue, McCloud is right — Robb's staff deserves the credit for digging up the dirt on Chichester.

Specifically, it was Stoddart who, on Goldman's request, went to the SCC and got the file on Chichester's case. These weren't confidential papers, but considering the almost paranoid secrecy under which Virginia's most powerful regulatory agency operates, it can be extremely difficult for anyone without the proper contacts to lay their hands on exactly what he's looking for, especially if it involves detailed accounts of businesses being fined. Stoddart had the proper contacts, and so, by the end of August, Goldman had what he needed — documentation of how Chichester had once been fined for a minor technical violation of the state's insurance law.

Goldman's plan was to hold the information until October and then leak it to the press. "Saving our ammunition" was the way he described it. Goldman's idea was that if the Republicans starting making some headway against Wilder with the Bar issue, then Goldman would make sure Chichester's SCC fine became public. Then, Goldman says, "I could say here's a man fined for violating the law. OK, maybe we're not the greatest lawyer in the world, but he's not the most ethical insurance man, either. A plague on both your houses." Chichester's $250 fine, the minimum allowed — the business equivalent of a $25 traffic ticket — was hardly in the same league with Wilder's reprimand and the harsh language in the state Supreme Court's ruling. Still, it was the only way Goldman could see to handle Wilder's Bar problem.

Then came the Sept. 8 *Washington Post* story, "The Pluses and Problems of Wilder," which focused mainly on the problems, specifically the Bar and his vacant property.

Goldman decided he'd better get Chichester's fine out in public now. Meanwhile, the Robb staff had dug up something else. Phil Abraham found out that after he had been fined, Chichester had introduced a bill to change that part of the law. This put an entirely new, and potentially more damaging, spin on Chichester's otherwise meaningless fine.

What happened is that in July 1980 Chichester's insurance agency bought out a rival. One of the companies the Milton B. Graves agency had represented was the Wisconsin-based Dairyland Insurance Co. After the merger, some agents of the new Chichester-Graves firm continued to sell Dairyland policies. The agents had licenses to represent Dairyland. However, the new Chichester-Graves agency did not; Graves' old license did not carry over to the new company, something Chichester discovered only when his firm was fined. Chichester had strongly protested the fine, calling it "excessive" for an unintentional error and writing the SCC: "You have given us a fine for driving under the influence of alcohol, when in reality, all we did was let a parking meter expire." Two years later, Chichester introduced a bill that gave insurance agencies a grace period to write policies for out-of-state companies while waiting for their licenses to be processed in Richmond. The bill passed both houses unanimously.

This was hardly the stuff of political malfeasance. But, in the midst of a campaign, details aren't nearly as important as the broad outlines. And the broad outlines of Chichester's SCC troubles could be made to look pretty bad without too much effort. Chichester *had* been fined by the SCC for a violation of state law. And Chichester, an insurance agency owner, *had* introduced an insurance bill that would change the law he had violated. When presented to busy, distracted voters that way, Chichester's technical oversight could look entirely different.

Goldman asked for Stoddart's help in leaking the story. The governor's press secretary was in a perfect position to do so. "Reporters were always coming around asking if I had anything," Stoddart said. This time he would.

Before long, the *Richmond Times-Dispatch* had the story: "Chichester fought law he violated."

Sept. 20, 1985

"That's an issue almost impossible to deal with," Mike Thomas, Chichester's No. 2 man, says of the conflict-of-interest charge. No matter how flimsy the accusation, the headline is damaging enough and suddenly there were headlines all over the state as other papers scrambled to catch up:

"Chichester voted to change law he violated"

"Chichester is accused of conflict of interests"

"Va. candidate sponsored bill affecting his company"

Then came the rebuttal, which only dug the hole a little deeper:

"Insurance bill sponsorship is defended by Chichester"

"Chichester says '84 bill not related to his fine"

"If people even see the explanation in the first place, they may not understand it," Thomas says. The result is, no matter how weak the evidence and no matter how strenuous the denial, the charge sticks. In Chichester's case, "he didn't have a strong positive image established ahead of time," Thomas says. For some voters, the first impression was of him denying he had a conflict of interest. "So you get voters who'd say, 'Yeah, I've heard of him. Doesn't he have a conflict of interest?' "

The conflict-of-interest stories came at an especially bad time for Chichester. The first two weeks of September had been devoted to his "criminal's interest at heart" attack, which quickly backfired. The next week he kept a low profile. Then came Godwin's state song comment, which raised the issue of race and began to elevate the lieutenant governor's race to a social referendum. And just two days after the state song furor came the first conflict-of-interest stories. The Chichester campaign had planned to go back on the offensive about now, but "we were thrown off by the stories about John's supposed conflict of interest and we had to devote time to that," Thomas says.

Another bad thing about the timing of the conflict-of-interest story, which broke Sept. 20 in the *Times-Dispatch* — it overshadowed another story that Friday about another politician's possible wrongdoing: Doug Wilder had been charged by Richmond's building inspector with "maintaining an unsafe and hazardous condition" at one of his Church Hill houses.

Sept. 22-24, 1985

Fighting off the conflict-of-interest stories, Chichester *finally* was going back on the offensive.

This time Chichester accused Wilder of supporting two bills that would have let many rapists "get off the hook." It looked like a pretty good hit for Chichester:

"Chichester says Wilder was lenient on rapists"

"Chichester criticizes Wilder's record on rape-related bills"

It wasn't a hit at all, though.

Goldman had someone look up the bills and quickly came up with two easy retorts. The 1972 bill Wilder had introduced "by request" of a social services group in his district, but Wilder had declined to support it. As for the 1982 bill, look who else opposed the bill — Buster O'Brien. Goldman went into a frenzy. "I'm amazed. This man attacks his own running mate. I can't think of any election where a candidate has attacked his own running mate."

In Chichester's hometown paper, the second-day headline read: "Chichester charge may have backfired."

Sept. 25, 1985

In late September, Paul Goldman dropped off the tour and spent his days on the road between Richmond and Washington, where Wilder's TV spots were being produced.

Goldman was becoming ever more single-minded about the TV spots. On one trip between Richmond and D.C., Goldman was busily spooning up yogurt and chattering with his driver — sent over from the Baliles campaign — about the spots when a lens popped out of his rickety wire-framed glasses and ... ploop ... disappeared into the yogurt. The driver started to laugh when Goldman, without missing a beat in his long monologue about the campaign, fished out the errant lens, licked the yogurt off and fit the lens back into his glasses as if nothing out of the ordinary had happened.

No wonder the people producing the TV commercials found Goldman strange to work with. Cameraman Jerry Scheeler, who did the preliminary editing, and Goldman argued even by long distance. For the spot with Wilder running up the steps of the Capitol — the one for which Goldman had wanted Scheeler to hide in the bushes — Goldman wanted a few seconds of Wilder running, then a freeze frame to put some words on the screen or some narration about Wilder's experience, then show Wilder running up a few more steps, freeze frame again, then run some more ...

Scheeler tried it and was horrified. "I thought he looked like Bojangles dancing up the steps. I had the footage and I refused to give it to him [Goldman]. We had these long, anguished phone calls. I said I can't find it. I really felt we were trying to protect him from this guy's bad idea. The commercials were close to being a fiasco. The things that got on the air, 100 percent, none of that would have existed if we had done what Paul Goldman wanted us to."

Meanwhile, a camera crew was dispatched to film Robb. Tommie Jones couldn't make it; Beth Stone, who had no video experience, was in charge. Robb saw it as yet another example of the Wilder campaign's incompetence. "Usually they send you a script," he says. "Usually I reject them but at least they're thinking about you. But they just sent someone over with a camera with no script, so I made up my own. At that point, I was used to the fact there was no campaign. I said, 'Give me a couple of minutes to think about what I want to say.' " Robb even found himself having to suggest camera angles. "Any campaign I've ever done has thought it through. Here, nothing."

Still, the material was steadily accumulating and working its way through the system. Four spots were emerging: one with Robb, one about the tour (using footage of Wilder shaking hands), one about Wilder's experience (using the footage of Wilder running up the Capitol steps), and lastly, Goldman's favorite, the one with Joe Alder, the Kenbridge cop.

It was almost 11 one night late in September when a rough version of the cop spot, with narration added, was put together in Richmond. Jones called Goldman to come over to the studio and look at it. As he watched Joe Alder come on the monitor with his uniform, and then heard not only Alder's thick Southside drawl but the narrator come on and intone the crime-fighting virtues of Doug Wilder, a big grin broke out on his face. "I sure wanna see their faces when this comes out," Goldman said.

Still, there were some frenzied, last-minute complications. Goldman went over each frame and threw out all the ones that made Wilder look "too black" or showed other blacks. Goldman insisted that Wilder look as light-skinned as possible. "We were trying to get him lighter and lighter until the grass that was green was turning different colors," says Beth Stone.

Meanwhile, Goldman had other concerns about the TV commercials. How to announce them, mostly. "I remember sitting around thinking, 'I've got to condition the press for us going on TV.' I said all along the odds are against it. Was that an untruth? If you look at the words, it's not." But Goldman had misled the media back in July into thinking Wilder was too poor to afford TV, when, in fact, Wilder had plenty of money — a ruse Goldman cheerfully pleads guilty to.

On Tuesday, Sept. 25, an anxious Goldman, citing "frugal management," finally announced that Wilder would make a $200,000 TV buy — throughout the state, including the expensive Washington market — in early October. "The odds have changed," Goldman gloated.

Chichester campaign manager Dennis Peterson tried to score some points out of Goldman's announcement. "For the entire campaign, on numerous occasions, Senator Wilder has said, 'We're very broke — poor old us, the Republicans are going to outspend us.' They've deliberately misled the public on the integrity issue. To say they've squeezed out $200,000 through frugal management — give me a break. Personally, I think it's an example of what I believe is a lack of honesty with the public."

Peterson was right but nobody bit. More importantly, Peterson conceded that Chichester didn't have much money set aside for his TV campaign and furthermore, Peterson didn't know if his candidate would be able to afford buying time in Northern Virginia.

The *Richmond News Leader* reported:

"Goldman's announcement that Wilder planned to go on TV to carry his message to Virginia voters appeared timed to coincide with a sense of momentum building up in the Wilder camp . . .

Momentum? Pat Caddell had just completed the first poll the Baliles campaign had done since July. It showed numbers the Democrats could scarcely believe: Baliles was ahead 42-27, Wilder was ahead 33-26 and Terry was ahead 30-24.

Sept. 26, 1985

John Chichester was finally going to have a chance to do things his way — positive and upbeat. Flanked by former Gov. John Dalton, Chichester called a news conference in Richmond to play up his plan to use the lieutenant governorship to become a roving ambassador for economic development. "We can be more aggressive" in recruiting new employers to the state, Chichester said, and a visit by the lieutenant governor would impress out-of-state executives.

But one of the first questions was what is the state doing now on economic development? Chichester said he didn't know.

The next morning the *Richmond Times-Dispatch* reported:

"State Sen. John H. Chichester, the Republican nominee for lieutenant governor, said yesterday that he would use that office to lead a campaign for business expansion in the state but admitted he does 'not know what the state government already does' to recruit new industry."

Late September 1985

In Charlottesville, analyst Larry Sabato was starting to feel something was seriously out of sync. "I can never remember having to back up and make a 180-degree turn like I did in September 1985," he says. "It first dawned on me not too long after Labor Day. The first or second week after Labor Day, Mike Hardy had a piece in the *T-D* about how well Wilder was doing. Suddenly it dawned on me Chichester hadn't done anything and had no plans to do anything. And with Durrette's decline, which became very apparent by the end of September, and I realized Terry was starting to move, the worst-case scenario started to spin, that Chichester might lose, too. But then I thought 'nah, it won't happen.' "

Still, something strange *was* happening and lots of people, scarcely believing their own eyes and ears, were starting to notice it.

Charlottesville's Democratic chairman, Tom Vandever, had organized a poll for the Democrats' local candidates and threw in questions about the three statewide races.

When the results came in, Vandever's reaction was the same one John Jameson had had when he saw the first Terry poll in July. This poll has to be wrong. It shows Wilder ahead.

Until this poll, "I don't have any memories of anyone saying Wilder was going to win unless it was from someone I considered totally naive," Vandever says. But now he started to wonder. What if the poll was right? He tried not to even think about the possibility, but it kept teasing him and wouldn't go away. What if the poll was right? What if ... ?

It was a question starting to tease a fair number of Democrats.

Sept. 28, 1985

The governor's staff wanted to meet with Wilder. The result was chronicled in Robb's angry post-election letters as "a very frustrating occasion."

The meeting grew out of the Northern Virginia fund-raiser that Robb's staff had arranged in mid-September. They felt they had saved the event from disaster; Goldman complained it had raised only "chump change."

To make sure that kind of misunderstanding didn't happen again, and to get straight just what needed to be done in the final month of the campaign, top Robb aide David McCloud arranged a meeting for the last weekend in September. He even envisioned this as the first of a series of weekly meetings to oversee the hapless Wilder campaign the rest of the way in to Election Day. "I felt we had to ensure we had our act together," McCloud says. "If the election had been lost, Chuck Robb would have gotten a lot of blame from the press."

At least seven Robb staffers were in the governor's office for the meeting. McCloud was presiding. A little after 5 p.m. Paul Goldman and Michael Brown showed up. But no Wilder. "We called his home three or four times and personally told him we were waiting," Griswold wrote in her post-election memo to Robb.

Goldman and Brown wanted to start the meeting without him, but McCloud ruled otherwise. He wanted Wilder present so there would be no chance of any misunderstanding about the extraordinary effort the Robb staff was trying to make on his behalf.

Wilder finally showed up about 6:30 p.m. and from all accounts an upbeat and productive meeting followed. Press secretary George Stoddart recalled that everyone walked out with an assignment in hand. It was agreed that Wilder couldn't glad-hand his way through the whole campaign, that he needed to speak out on some issues. To take care of that, Phil Abraham was assigned to research and write two issues papers, one on ports and one on high-tech industry, so Wilder could hold issues-oriented news conferences in Tidewater and Northern Virginia. McCloud assured Wilder that Robb would be at his side in both of them.

Others were assigned to redouble efforts on fund-raising. "A concerted effort was done that was more than was done for anybody else," Stoddart said. "We left with marching orders on what to do and we did it."

Griswold's memo tells the rest: "The meeting went very well and everyone agreed to meet weekly. [However] because of scheduling conflicts with Wilder, no other meeting was held. This type of episode was not unusual, but was very frustrating to those of us trying to get a little feedback on what we were volunteering to do."

Sept. 30, 1985

Monday morning's *Washington Post* brought more bad news to the Republicans' doorstep:

"Controversy creeps into Chichester campaign"

"When Virginia Republicans met in Norfolk this summer to pick their nominees for the fall elections, many said they wanted one thing in their candidate for lieutenant governor: a lack of controversy.

"Wary of the conflict-of-interest problems that had plunged their nominee into an unexpected defeat four years ago, the party turned to state Sen. John H. Chichester, a relatively unknown legislator from Stafford County . . .

"In recent weeks, however, Chichester (pronounced Chee-chester) has brought controversy and, perhaps, liabilities to the Republican ticket."

13

Freeze Warnings in Hell

Back in the spring, University of Virginia political analyst Larry Sabato was invited to speak to Democrats in Orange County. One of the things Sabato said that night, remembers party vice chairman Hubert J. "Buzz" Rider, was that Doug Wilder "doesn't have a snowball's chance in hell."

But now it was autumn. And in the first ten days of October came the unmistakable signs that hell was indeed starting to freeze over. Each new day seemed to only bring more bad news for the Republicans in general and for John Chichester in particular:

On Oct. 2, Wyatt Durrette revealed that he supported teaching creationism in the public schools, setting off a round of newspaper stories that made the Republican gubernatorial candidate a laughingstock, especially among suburban voters.

On Oct. 3, the Republican National Committee attempted to run an ad in the state's major newspapers attacking Wilder for allegedly being soft on wife-beating. But the ill-conceived newspaper campaign backfired when the *Richmond Times-Dispatch* refused to run the ad and the *Roanoke Times & World-News* demanded that it be rewritten — drawing attention to the clumsy GOP name-calling instead of Wilder's record.

On Oct. 4, Wilder and Chichester appeared in their only televised debate of the campaign, a debate that most neutral observers agreed Wilder won.

On Oct. 5, the *Virginian-Pilot* blasted the Republican with an editorial headlined "A desperate Chichester."

On Oct. 6, the *Times-Dispatch* published the first public poll to show Wilder with a lead. Though it was a scant 2 percent, this was the first evidence most Virginia voters had that this really was a close race.

On Oct. 7, Wilder and Chichester debated before high school students at St. Catherine's, a private girl's school in Richmond's exclusive West End. Despite the conservative locale, the smooth, charming Wilder won the girls' hearts and was cheered loudly while Chichester was given only polite applause — an incredible reception that was near the top of all the TV news shows in Richmond that night.

On Oct. 8, while downstate papers were reporting Wilder's remarkable success at St. Catherine's, the *Washington Post* was raising more conflict-of-interest questions about Chichester.

On Oct. 9, President Reagan crossed the Potomac to attend a Republican fund-raiser in Arlington. But the president's visit was overshadowed by the release that morning of a controversial poll by the *Post,* which gave Wilder an unbelievable twenty-two-point lead.

On Oct. 10, Mills Godwin, silent since the state song controversy, leveled a blistering attack on Wilder that further tied the Republican ticket to the Old Guard and Virginia's racist past. Meanwhile, Chichester's and Wilder's television commercials hit the airwaves. Chichester's were forgotten almost immediately, but Wilder's TV spots became some of the most enduring images of the 1985 campaign.

From the Republican perspective, it would be difficult to even imagine a worse series of events than the one that overtook the Chichester campaign in early October. From the Democratic perspective, it would be difficult to imagine a more fortuitous run of luck and circumstances.

The timing was everything. Early October was the time when, in the natural order of things, the Wilder boomlet should have started to fade and the Chichester campaign take hold. Instead, the opposite was happening. What's more, it quickly became apparent — through Wilder's reception at St. Catherine's and the reaction to his TV commercials — that this was becoming a test of how modern Virginians, confronted once again with the touchy subject of race, wanted to view themselves.

All of this, of course, was being kicked around deep in the murky subconscious of Virginians who, one by one, were just beginning to pay attention to the campaign and figure out who the candidates were and what the issues were all about. But, Sabato observes, "The public just takes in the broad outlines and when you looked at the broad outlines, Wilder was on the move, doing things, getting very little negative publicity. Most of the bad things were on the Republican side. It was the 'Bad News Bears' for the Republicans. The only cues voters were receiving were pro-Democratic and anti-Republican."

And by the time this started to happen, it was almost too late for the GOP to do anything about it. The Republicans had figured Wilder would be such a pushover that they never had a strategy for dealing with him as a serious candidate. Laments Durrette adviser Judy Peachee: "All of a sudden they were on top of us and we'd left all our ammunition at home."

Oct. 2, 1985

While the Durrette campaign was trying to ride out the first day of the creationism crisis, the Chichester campaign was trying, again, to get back on the offensive. Once again, the issue was crime. The plan was to call a news conference at the Arlington County Courthouse in Northern Virginia to announce the formation of a "Law and Order Committee for John Chichester" — including several Democrats. Included in the press packet was an eight-page analysis comparing Wilder's voting record with Chichester's on twenty-nine bills relating to crime and law enforcement.

It was an impressive bit of typing, if nothing else, to prove that Wilder was indeed soft on crime.

Too bad only one reporter showed up.

While Chichester was getting stood up by the Northern Virginia media, his campaign was surreptitiously trying to ambush Wilder another way. Wilder, the Chichester campaign had discovered, hadn't paid his 1985 personal property taxes. What's more, he had been late paying his real estate taxes for three years in a row. Why, in 1983, he'd been ten months late paying the taxes on one piece of property he owned.

Here was a godsend for the whole Republican ticket, which sorely needed some Democratic trouble to point to. But even with this, Chichester and campaign manager Peterson clashed on how to handle it.

"I'd always admonished Dennis to stay the hell out of the press," Chichester says. "Here it is Oct. 1 and Doug hadn't paid the taxes on his Mercedes back in January. I said, 'Dennis, the one to drop this on is ole Dave Miller of WRVA [radio in Richmond], but don't tell him where it came from.' Fine. So the morning news has Dave Miller blasting off on the air about taxes, and in the written media it's lost in the back pages. The next night, I'm watching Channel 12 [in Richmond] and there's Dennis Peterson in my office blasting Wilder for it. I could not believe my eyes."

For one day, it looked like Wilder's late payment of taxes was going to be big news.

WRVA radio had the story that morning and the afternoon *Richmond News Leader* jumped on it right away. Within an hour after the newspaper called Wilder's office for comment, someone from Wilder's office hand-delivered a check for $1,315.93 to cover the delinquent taxes and penalty. Goldman blamed the problem on "a clerical oversight."

Maybe so, but this still could be made to sound like a scandal — and Peterson wasted no time trying.

Peterson told the *Times-Dispatch* that the late payments suggested Wilder had a habit of being irresponsible: "Producing city tax records, Peterson said that in 1985 Wilder was two months late in paying real estate taxes on seven properties, most of them in the East End. In 1984, the senator was from three weeks to two months late in paying on two properties, Peterson said, and in 1983 he was ten months delinquent in paying on the property adjoining his law office in the 2500 block of East Broad Street."

The tax story couldn't have been better timed for Chichester. It broke just a day before Wilder was scheduled to go to court for the building inspector's complaint about his vacant house.

But before the Republicans could even move to exploit Wilder's late payment of taxes for a second day, the hard-luck Chichester campaign had yet another public relations disaster on its hands — the wife-beating ad.

Oct. 2-3, 1985

Oct. 2 was not a good day for the Chichester campaign. The ticket's standard-bearer was looking like a fool for advocating creationism. Chichester's big law-and-order pitch in crucial Northern Virginia was a humiliating flop. Peterson was high on Wilder's tax problems — until the phone calls started coming in late that afternoon about "the ad."

Back in the summer Peterson, arguing that Chichester had to go on the attack, had proposed a series of five newspaper ads attacking Wilder on various issues. Chichester vetoed the plan. But the idea of the spouse abuse ad — attacking Wilder for opposing some bills designed to aid battered wives — survived into late September.

Peterson was desperate for his candidate to go on the attack. "At that point, we were losing," he says. The Bar reprimand, the boarded-up houses and the late taxes were the most scandalous things the Republicans could get on Wilder, but Peterson, hamstrung by Chichester's desire to run a positive campaign, couldn't use them directly. Instead, Peterson spent a good bit of his time trying to interest reporters, off-the-record, in the Bar reprimand especially. So far, though, no one had taken the time to do more than merely mention the reprimand in the context of bigger stories on Wilder.

Meanwhile, Peterson eyed the spouse abuse bills. The way he saw it, putting together a newspaper ad asserting that Wilder was unsympathetic to the plight of battered women had potential.

"What one thing was John known for if you knew anything at all about him?" Peterson asks. "ERA. [Chichester's vote had been the one to kill it in the state Senate.] We had trouble with women. This ad was designed to invoke a common bond with women voters. My job as campaign manager is to move voting blocs. We had a weak demographic group that we needed. Doug Wilder had a record that was irrefutable — his votes. The thing was deliberate, to hit just prior to the debate, so we could discuss spousal abuse in the debate."

Much research went into the ad to figure out which bills to cite. "John did participate in discussions of the ad," Peterson says. "He did decline to run it when the campaign would pay for it, but it was also very clear he did not object if someone else ran it."

So Peterson went to the Republican National Committee, which bought ads in the Thursday, Oct. 3, editions of the *Richmond Times-Dispatch, Virginian-Pilot* and *Roanoke Times & World-News.* Or at least the RNC attempted to buy ads in those papers.

The Norfolk paper happily took the Republicans' money. But the Roanoke paper cringed at the wording and demanded a slight rewrite. And the Richmond paper simply refused to accept the ad.

What caused problems in Roanoke was almost academic quibbling over the original wording of the ad:

"WHY DID DOUG WILDER NEGLECT THE NEEDS OF BATTERED WIVES?

"Should a beaten wife have to flee her home to protect herself — and her children?

"It doesn't seem fair.

"That's why most state senators voted to strengthen our laws in 1982. They wanted to allow an abusive spouse to be ordered out of the house by a magistrate, to leave wife and children in peace.

"But Doug Wilder opposed this badly needed reform. Twice. Why?

"No Virginian supports wife beating. Not Doug Wilder's constituents. Not anyone else.

"When Doug Wilder voted to do nothing to help the battered wife, he neglected an opportunity to protect some of the most vulnerable citizens in our Commonwealth.

"Why does Doug Wilder neglect the people he is supposed to represent? He owes ALL Virginians an explanation. We're waiting.

"DOUG WILDER.

"HIS RECORD SPEAKS FOR ITSELF."

The Roanoke paper objected on the grounds that the ad was misleading. Virginia law already allowed a judge to order a husband out of the house if his wife testified that he was beating her, so the paper demanded — and the RNC agreed — to rewrite the one line to read "they wanted to allow an abusive spouse ordered out of the house by a magistrate *until a circuit court judge has time to act.*" (emphasis added) The paper also wanted to add — and the RNC went along with — the word "further" to make another line read: "When Doug Wilder voted to do nothing *further* to help the battered wife . . ." All in all, pretty picky stuff.

What caused problems in Richmond was something darker. The newspaper's ad director said only that the company decided not to print the ad on the advice of its lawyer. But those who have been around Virginia politics a while quickly suspected the paper's reluctance stemmed from some of the rumors that had floated around about Wilder's divorce. The records in the case are sealed and Wilder's standard reply is that he was never required to pay any alimony, which ought to be answer enough, he says. But WRVA radio had once made reference to some possible allegations of spouse abuse in the case, a reference repeated in the *Washington Post's* September story, "The Pluses and Problems of Wilder." With that inside information, the Chichester campaign's decision to make an issue of wife-beating looked far more sinister than it actually was — and the Richmond newspaper apparently wanted no part of it. "It was suggested to me they thought Chichester was getting at the wife-beating charges Dave Miller had made on WRVA during the divorce case," Goldman says.

As reporters caught wind of the refusal and started calling for comment, Peterson tried desperately to direct the subject away from the *Times-Dispatch's* decision not to run the ad and back to the issues at hand. But he wasn't having much luck.

Meanwhile, Goldman had another opportunity to shout "mudslinging." He called the ad "a gross distortion of the facts" and proof that Chichester "has nothing positive to say. It's kind of sad that [the Chichester campaign] has gotten this low. I'm disappointed."

But not when he read the newspaper accounts the next morning: "Two newspapers balk at ad from Chichester."

Having generated stories like this, clearly the ad failed to achieve its purpose of making Chichester politically attractive to women. But it did worse than simply fail. It backfired. "Most people never saw it," Peterson says. "It just ran in two papers. Most people just heard it was so bad the *Times-Dispatch* wouldn't run it." Skeptical voters need only look to the staid and trusted *Times-Dispatch* for confirmation that yes, Chichester must be running a very dirty campaign indeed.

The way Chichester sees it now, "that crackpot ad" was the beginning of the end. "That was the turning point. That was the decision to lose the campaign. Even if it was true, it's not my style. I've never conducted a campaign railing against my opponent. What it did was polarize the campaign."

It also polarized the already-strained relations between Chichester and Peterson. "I was infuriated," Chichester says. "The thought was to have a news conference and apologize and terminate those responsible, but in politics, the best thing to do is let it die as quickly as possible and say nothing about it." So Chichester was forced into defending an ad he detested and a policy he fundamentally disagreed with.

Meanwhile, a few days after the ad ran, Paul Goldman received a most unusual letter in the mail. It was from Eunice Wilder, the candidate's ex-wife. "She said she didn't like what people were saying about the family. She understood it was politics, and if we ever needed her to say or do something to set the record straight, she would do something to stop all the lies."

But Goldman never told Wilder about the letter. Within a day, the two campaigns had moved on to other controversies.

Oct. 3, 1985

Wilder had started the final leg of his tour, across the Chesapeake Bay Bridge-Tunnel and up the Eastern Shore, earlier in the week with state Sen. William Fears, D-Accomack. Though more than two months had passed since Wilder took the strange but likewise distant Southwest by storm, Fears was still skeptical how Wilder would go over in his truck farming district. "Bill would go up to a country store and say to me, 'Now this is a hard group, but we'll go in, Wilder.' We'd go in and shake hands and when we came out he'd say, 'I think we made a lot of friends there,'" says Wilder, who was amused by Fears' down-home pessimism.

Fears stayed with Wilder for part of the second day but he had to go off to practice law, so for a while, it was just Wilder and driver Chuck Nichollson, inching northward on the peninsula. They headed toward the final stop of Wilder's two-month odyssey: Greenbackville, a dust-spot community backed up against the Maryland line.

When they got there, Nichollson took a picture of Wilder standing beside a sign to authenticate the visit. From Greenbackville, they could look across the water at the houses of Chincoteague and also across the state line into Maryland. It was a beautiful fall day, with the afternoon aging comfortably. The sun was starting to slant down toward the western horizon Wilder had left so long ago. But now his tour was just about over, with just one final ritual yet to be done.

Greenbackville's store was closed, so Wilder picked out the post office. Effie Williams, postmistress and great-grandmother, had just finished putting up the mail for the day when Wilder came in. He introduced himself while effortlessly signing one of his post cards. "He told me where he started," Williams recalls. "I remember wishing him good luck."

Wilder and Nichollson got back in their station wagon and turned back south toward the bridge-tunnel that would take them into the thick of the campaign.

Back in Richmond, Dennis Peterson was finally sensing a turnaround. This was Wilder's day in court on the alleged housing violations.

Ever since the housing inspector had filed charges in September, Republicans had been complaining that the media weren't devoting enough attention to the "scandal." But most newspapers treated the housing problems as a local issue and gave little play to the stories; Chichester's conflict-of-interest charges, which seemed more job-related, were given prominent display.

Still, there was potential fallout. "Paul was going rabid over that house," Michael Brown says. "Sell it, bomb it, give it away," Goldman would shout at Wilder and sometimes no one in particular. "I don't need this issue. Why must I continue to deal with this issue?" Brown remembers Goldman's pointed warning to Wilder: "If any issue can hurt you more than any other, this is it."

Wilder appointed Brown to take care of things and he spent several weeks pestering what he considered a lazy contractor into cleaning up the property. Eventually, the building materials scattered in the yard were hauled away. When Wilder's law partner Roger Gregory explained this in court, the judge dismissed the charges.

Still, the court appearance kept the house issue in the news. Peterson thought the media were finally overcoming their reluctance to criticize Wilder.

Wilder and Nichollson swung through the Tidewater cities to Chesapeake, a booming suburb-in-the-swamps. Wilder had agreed to go to some event there with state Sen. Bill Parker, a conservative good ole boy developer. Wilder didn't know much about what the event was supposed to be. The information he had suggested it would be some small community festival. "We'll stop in and see what's going on," Wilder told Nichollson, with the unspoken assurance that this wouldn't take long at all.

What was going on, though, was only one of the biggest events of the year in Chesapeake, an annual fall festival sponsored by the Ruritan Club.

When the station wagon eased onto the grounds, Wilder saw a huge crowd — that turned out to be simply the hangers-on in the parking lot. An even bigger crowd lay beyond, maybe as many as 3,000, working their jaws over barbecue and civic matters. Waiting in the parking lot, more than a little anxious, was Parker. Wilder, as usual, was running late and Parker was afraid he wouldn't make it. A weary Wilder got a second wind when he saw all the people. This was quite a change after two months of working small knots of curious voters in country stores and small-town Main Streets. "You watch," he told Nichollson, "we're gonna work this crowd."

Parker grabbed Wilder as soon as he got out of the car so fast that Nichollson, trying to keep up, didn't even have time to get his customary supply of literature to pass out. Wilder sent Nichollson back to the car to get some while he waded into the crowd with the eager Parker.

Parker hadn't been sure what kind of response Wilder would get at the barbecue, but whatever it was, he knew it would be representative of Chesapeake voters. "I thought it would be an excellent sounding board," Parker says. But even he was shocked at the reception. "What struck me was the many people who came up to him voluntarily. That just doesn't happen. But this night, it did. People I did not even know would walk up, shake hands and voluntarily say, 'I'm gonna vote for you. What can I do to support you?' I've never in my political career seen that happen."

That night, when Nichollson checked in with headquarters, he told Michael Brown about how Wilder had been mobbed. "I can't believe it," Nichollson said. "If this is any indication of the rest of the state, Doug's gonna do real well." But for Parker, there were no "ifs" about it. "From that day, I felt Doug Wilder had an excellent chance of winning the lieutenant governorship."

Oct. 4, 1985

Wilder and Chichester met in Richmond in their first televised debate. Neither candidate was very impressive. Larry Sabato recalls that Chichester "was laughable and Wilder was not much better."

Wilder, for all his celebrated flair in the courtroom and Senate floor, started hesitantly, almost nervously. He tried to score points by calling Chichester's wife-beating ad "totally misleading, totally repugnant" and solemnly invoked the name of the state's newspapers who had objected to it, but got some of them wrong.

Wilder also seemed to have difficulty adjusting his style to television, constantly wagging his finger at the camera whenever he made a point as if he were lecturing a jury.

However unimpressive Wilder was, Chichester, though, looked worse. The TV lights kept flashing off his glasses whenever he looked up. Chichester was also the victim of circumstance and necessity. Wilder had come to the debate to reassure moderate whites by acting dignified and senatorial. He simply had to look the part, a decidedly easier task than what faced Chichester, who had to prove his point that Wilder was a liberal. And the only way to put Wilder on the defensive was for Chichester to be on the offensive — but being an aggressor wasn't Chichester's strong suit.

On that score, there is bipartisan agreement.

Chichester had been pumped full of research, issues and preparation. Wilder had declined any full-scale rehearsal. His job was simply to deflect Chichester's attacks and he was more than ready.

When Chichester tried to score points on the spouse abuse bills, Wilder had only to point out the "totally repugnant" newspaper ad that had offended even the *Richmond Times-Dispatch.* And when Chichester tried to zero in on the specifics of the bills, rather than the newspaper ads, Wilder stole a line from Ronald Reagan. "There my opponent goes again, not knowing what the law is," Wilder said with a sweet smile, painting himself as the voice of experience and reason and noting he voted for what he called a more comprehensive bill two years later.

When Chichester started talking about his "jobs for Virginians" program, Wilder put him in his place with devastating ease. Wilder held up a copy of the *Times-Dispatch* story reporting Chichester's since-forgotten economic development news conference of the week before. The story, Wilder said, quoted Chichester saying he does "not know what the state government already does" to recruit new employers. "Now he's been there [in the state Senate] seven years," Wilder said, "and either hasn't taken the time to try to find out what the state is doing or he didn't care. Now all of a sudden" he gets interested in jobs. "I find it almost unbelievable." Then Wilder ticked off a list of job-training programs he had worked with.

The highlight of the debate, though, came when Chichester tried to unmask Wilder as a supporter of collective bargaining for public employees. When Wilder made the traditional statement in opposition, Chichester held up a sheaf of papers and announced: "You have just heard my opponent say he is opposed to collective bargaining for public employees. I must say I am shocked, because in 1972, 1974, 1975, 1978, 1979, 1980 and 1984 my opponent sponsored and co-sponsored legislation for collective bargaining for public employees.

"Now how can one come to this studio tonight, how can one look at the camera, at thousands of people, and say 'I don't support collective bargaining'? . . . I am aghast."

Wilder coolly asked Chichester to hand over the paper he was waving so he could read the bills aloud. Chichester declined.

Wilder went into an impassioned, but still carefully restrained, denial, insisting the bills never mentioned the words "collective bargaining." "I have never introduced any bill calling for collective bargaining in Virginia," Wilder said. "Never. Never . . . I have made it as clear as I know how to make it. I am for maintaining the right-to-work law just like it is and not to do anything at all with it. Period."

The Chichester staffers were elated at this carefully-planned exchange. But they were about the only ones who thought this was a great victory. Instead of looking like a candidate in command of his facts and stripping Wilder bare of excuses, Chichester looked to TV viewers as if he was simply ranting and raving. "I thought Doug beat the shit out of him," O'Brien's campaign manager Jeff Gregson says bluntly. More important, though, was Wilder's staying low-key despite the attacks. "Here was another time that went by without him losing his cool," Gregson says.

Oct. 5, 1985

"Here," Goldman said to a visitor, passing around an already dog-eared copy of the morning's *Virginian-Pilot*. "Have you seen this?"

It was an editorial, the harshest yet of the campaign: "A desperate Chichester."

"In his latest and most virulent ploy, Mr. Chichester wants you to believe that Senator Wilder coddles wife beaters," the editorial said. The RNC ad, the paper declared, "is an attempt at character assassination. A candidate would not do this unless he was desperate."

The phone rang and Goldman sprawled out in a nearby chair to talk to a reporter from the *Times-Dispatch,* whose first poll was due out tomorrow. Suddenly Goldman's grin became even wider.

"So how big is our lead?" he asked.

Oct. 6, 1985

For conservative Virginians, the story could only have seemed a bad joke. Here, on the front page of the respected *Richmond Times-Dispatch,* was the newspaper's own poll showing the state's most prominent black politician *leading* in his campaign for lieutenant governor over a good conservative ex-Democrat turned Republican. It was just a two-point margin, but this was still the first public poll to give Wilder a lead. Clearly, the natural order of things was being turned upside down. But the Republicans quoted throughout the story offered reassurances that nothing was wrong, that voters simply hadn't begun to pay attention to the lieutenant governor's race, that Wilder, with 38 percent, had a solid base but one he was unlikely to expand. (Baliles, meanwhile, led by 41-38.)

Comforted by those pronouncements, conservatives breathed easier, confident that Wilder's lead was a statistical blip that would eventually straighten itself out.

Oct. 7, 1985

The most incredible event of the 1985 campaign took place this sunny Monday afternoon on the tree-lined, red-bricked campus of an exclusive girl's school in Richmond's West End.

Maybe no more than a dozen registered voters — mostly reporters and teachers — watched as Wilder and Chichester sat on stools and patiently answered questions from the fresh-faced girls who squeezed into the chapel and sat cross-legged on the floor before them when all the seats were taken. But the impact of the "debate" at St. Catherine's, conveyed through the cruelly honest pictures on the TV news, and the stories that buzzed through Richmond and beyond, nearly knocked the meter off the state's political Richter scale.

"There was an event that nicely capsulized the whole campaign," says analyst Larry Sabato. "It capsulized how charismatic Wilder is and how wooden Chichester is in a place where Chichester should have the advantage if assumptions had held."

At this Episcopal school for the daughters of Richmond's elite, the state's most prominent black politician was greeted with teen-age squeals fit for a pop star. And that night every TV station in Richmond took the mob scene into Virginians' living rooms.

The irony is that neither Wilder nor Chichester wanted to accept the invitation to talk to the students at St. Catherine's. The irony is only compounded by the fact that it was Smith Ferebee, the conservative financier, who talked Chichester into it.

"The way it came to me was, 'Would you talk to some young people at St. Catherine's?' " Chichester recalls. It sounded to him like just another one of countless "candidates day" sessions scheduled by overeager civics classes around the state. "I turned it down. I didn't have time. Then Smith Ferebee calls and said it would mean a lot to me if you speak to a group at St. Catherine's. I said 'OK, I'll do it for you, but it'll cut me close.' " Chichester can now only shake his head sourly. "Ferebee got hoodwinked," he says.

Wilder, meanwhile, had reservations of his own, never explicitly stated but well imagined. "In the beginning, the senator was not all that keen about participating," says Michael Brown. "It was not high on his agenda." But one of the teachers at St. Catherine's was a Democratic worker and she kept at Wilder. "I think you'll find it to be a receptive audience," she told him. Eventually a reluctant Wilder gave in.

Michael Brown drove the candidate out to the school. "When we got there," Brown says, "we expected an assembly, but it looked like every child that day had said, 'I'm not gonna play hooky.' " The big meeting room was packed, with pink-and-green preppies and little Madonna look-alikes crammed into every chair, bench and empty spot on the floor all the way up to the small raised platform where the candidates would sit, dreadfully exposed to this expectant assembly before them.

Wilder was momentarily taken aback. "I saw John [Chichester] and it dawned on me, this was a double appearance. I knew they were trying to get him but I had no indication it would be a debate." But the importance of this innocuous little civics lesson before a roomful of teen-age girls was suddenly becoming very apparent to Doug Wilder.

Taking up the front row were reporters from every TV station in Richmond and a handful of major newspapers.

The girls yelled and screamed when the two candidates appeared, but there was something odd about their reception. Chichester noticed it right away. "It was a set-up," he fumes. "The students were coached. You could tell. You could walk into the room and feel the hostility. I've never felt hostility from young people before."

The two candidates' opening statements gave a hint about what was to come. Wilder was his usual soaring self. He also got in a dig against Chichester. "I have not nor will conduct a negative campaign," he declared. "I will not be involved in mudslinging. The people of Virginia reject it and elective office does not mean that much to me." The sustained applause that greeted his opening statement seemed cranked up a notch from the triumphal entrance for both candidates.

But where Wilder talked to the girls as equals, Chichester tried to establish a bond as a father figure. "It's indeed a pleasure to be with you. It's like being around the house. I have a teen-ager at home . . . "

Give the opening round to Wilder.

Then came the first question from the crowded floor, one that gave a broad hint at what the two candidates would face for the next hour.

"Mr. Wilder, what is your opinion toward nuclear arms?"

While reporters grimaced and snickered among themselves, the quick-witted Wilder jumped right in with a skillful "all things for all people" answer, saying he was in favor of a strong national defense, talking about his tour of duty in Korea, then cleverly segued his answer into why he was opposed to uranium mining in Virginia.

Chichester talked about Pearl Harbor and Grenada.

Make that Wilder, 2-0.

Sitting next to Chichester on the platform, Wilder sensed that his opponent was uncomfortable. "He was as nervous as a tick," Wilder says. "Dennis Peterson said John won the debate but lost the audience. I thought he lost both."

Before long, the rout was on — as Wilder bested Chichester on one subject after another, many of which had little to do with Virginia issues.

"We have about ten minutes," history teacher Bob Hiett finally announced.

The ordeal was nearly over.

But here it came.

A meek girl rose and asked what would become *the* question: "Mr. Wilder, what is your stand on abortion?"

Wilder was reluctant to get mixed up with too many social issues. "The question is not what my stand is," he said, explaining that the Supreme Court decision was the law of the land and he would abide by the court's ruling.

But the girl pressed him for an answer. Specifically, she wanted to know about periodic efforts in Virginia to pass a law requiring parental consent before girls under eighteen could have abortions. Again, Wilder, who opposed a parental consent bill, seemed to be begging off the question with a minimum of comment. "I reserve the judgment for those persons who are affected." Then he said it: "Being somewhat physically different, I won't ever have to be confronted directly with the question."

Suddenly the whole room burst into thunderous applause.

"I think of some young girl who would be raped by the inmate of some mental institution if you will" — some of the girls giggled, others gasped — "and there are those who would say this girl would have no say so in it at all. When I'm speaking young — thirteen, fourteen — but let's carry it to what some advocates want to carry it to — sixteen, seventeen, eighteen . . . That this person has absolutely no say so at all in whether she should be forced to carry the baby of someone that has brought the vilest repercussions to her . . . Ruining her life is bad enough . . . I have strong reservation about foisting my will on those persons directly affected."

When he finished, the room was deathly silent, but the silence spoke its own approval.

Chichester began awkwardly. "Let me see what I think your question is . . . The measure that was before us would allow a child, and God forbid a child find themselves in that situation — " Chichester had just called all these teen-age girls children.

He went on to explain that if any of the students in the room hurt themselves at school and needed stitches, the doctor would need their parents' permission before treating them. "Therefore, I think some guidance along the other line, in abortion, some guidance there by your parents would be to your advantage."

There was no applause.

A question about the drinking age followed, then came another abortion question for Chichester.

"You said that you supported guidance and counseling in abortion. Do you support guidance to help the child to make the decision or to make the decision [for the child]?"

"Guidance to make the decision," Chichester said, as rumbles went around the room.

A capital punishment question came up, then came the closing statements.

When Wilder finished, the girls whistled, screamed and yelled. Chichester was given only the obligatory round of applause.

As both candidates exited stage left, a jubilant Wilder waved to the girls, who whistled and screamed back. A grim Chichester rushed to find Dennis Peterson, who hustled him away before reporters could get to him.

Wilder, though, lingered on the sidewalk outside, surrounded by stunned reporters looking for insight. "It's a new day," he said, as he had said often before, but this time there could be no disputing him.

Once Wilder got back to his law office, the first thing he did was phone Jay Shropshire.

"Jay, you won't believe it," he said. "I can't believe it."

Shropshire sat dumbfounded as Wilder described the tumultuous reception he had received coming and going. "I didn't believe it, either," Shropshire confesses, "until I saw it on TV."

The St. Catherine's debate overshadowed another revealing tidbit of political news that Monday. Campaign finance reports, the first since the summer, were due by midnight.

Baliles had raised more money than Durrette — $2.7 million to $2.6 million. Interestingly, Durrette had just taken out a $100,000 loan, borrowed against the money expected to be generated by Wednesday's presidential visit.

In the attorney general's race, Mary Sue Terry had just passed the $1 million mark in her fund-raising campaign, leading Buster O'Brien by almost 2-1. The Terry money-and-media juggernaut, which surprised no one, was starting to roll.

But even more interesting was the financial status of the two candidates for lieutenant governor. Chichester had raised more money, though, not that much more: $604,000 to $454,000. But the significant figure here was the one Tom King had seized on back in the summer.

Chichester had only $12,820 free and clear. Wilder had $296,000.

Oct. 8, 1985

John Chichester was driving into Richmond to a breakfast meeting with local businessmen when the radio crackled out news:

The *Washington Post* that morning had just uncovered three more cases of potential conflicts-of-interest against him.

"He came in ashen," Peterson says.

What the *Post* had this morning were more highly complex insurance bills that would have limited competition for state and local government contracts, although the story made things plainer than perhaps Chichester would have liked:

"The bills were introduced in 1983 and 1984 when Chichester, who owns a Fredericksburg insurance firm, [was] losing thousands of dollars in local and state government contracts."

Chichester denied there was any conflict of interest between his private business and his duties as a legislator because none of the bills was introduced to benefit his own firm.

The *Post* had wanted to interview Chichester about the bills. Chichester — against Peterson's advice — steadfastly refused. "It got to be silly, running down sidewalks to avoid talking to the press," Peterson says. Eventually Chichester relented, somewhat. "Tom Sherwood even came over to the office one night before he was ready to break another story, the one on school boards," Chichester says. "Even Walt Disney in his wildest imagination couldn't make conflict of interest out of it, but they did."

And then Chichester heard the damning headlines on the radio news.

Later that day, Dennis Peterson talked with his old friend, Larry Sabato. "He was at wit's end with Chichester as much as anyone," Sabato says. "Dennis said no matter how well prepared he is or unprepared he is, he just can't do well. He wouldn't go with a prepared text because he thought it was unmanly. I really thought Dennis at that point was plunged into the depths of despair."

The Wilder campaign couldn't afford to be too happy over Chichester's troubles, though. Wilder's house was back in the news. Eight neighbors had filed a petition with the court, asking for a special grand jury to be impaneled to investigate the problem. And a Richmond judge agreed. He asked the Richmond commonwealth's attorney to present evidence in the case on Oct. 17. The Wilder campaign declined comment.

What the grand jury would do was something Goldman would fret over — and Republicans would fantasize about — for the next two weeks.

The big political news of the day came out of the Durrette campaign. The GOP announced that former Sen. Harry F. Byrd Jr. — a Democrat turned independent — was endorsing Durrette and Chichester.

Byrd's endorsement came in a letter which, as the *Times-Dispatch* described it, "said nothing about the Republicans' qualifications but strongly suggested that the candidacy of state Sen. L. Douglas Wilder, the Democratic nominee for lieutenant governor, played a key role in his decision."

Byrd argued that the candidates for governor and lieutenant governor must be considered in tandem. "For three decades, with an occasional exception, the lieutenant governor has been a strong right arm of the governor, his chief spokesman in the legislature and a participant in the making of policy. Indeed, the lieutenant governor is only a heartbeat away from the governorship."

But Byrd pointedly made no endorsement for attorney general, saying that office "deals largely with legal technicalities [and] generally is not a policy-making one." Maybe so, but his "golden silence" on the attorney general's race was yet another indication of how Mary Sue Terry had neutralized the state's conservative establishment.

Democrats, after "privately" suggesting to reporters that Byrd was using racial code words, smiled. If the Republicans were having to pull out the old "heartbeat away" argument against Wilder, then they must truly be frightened.

That night, Goldman was back up in D.C. to keep an eye on his TV commercials. During a break, Goldman called his friend Barry Rose in Richmond. Rose had some news for Goldman. The *Washington Post* was set to release its first poll the next day. The numbers were already floating around Democratic circles in Richmond and Rose couldn't resist telling Goldman.

First he told Goldman the poll would show Wilder with a lead.

Goldman asked how much.

"I don't know if this is right," Rose began cautiously, "but twenty-two."

Goldman burst out laughing. He thought Rose was joking. "He laughed for five minutes," Rose says. " 'OK, tell me another one.' "

Oct. 9, 1985

If the first eight days of October had been a steady drumbeat of bad news for the Republicans, Wednesday was the day the cymbals crashed.

The headlines weren't pretty, as downstate papers picked up on the *Post's* conflict-of-interest stories about Chichester: "Bills he supported posed no conflict, Chichester says." Or "Chichester bills would have cut bid competition."

But the most dreadful news was the *Post's* incredible poll, which showed Baliles with a nineteen-point lead (50-31), Wilder with a twenty-two-point lead (48-26) and Terry with a sixteen-point lead (43-27). It was so far out of line with the other public polls it was laughable. When Bobby Watson, the Democrats' executive director, first heard the numbers, "I distinctly remember I thought someone was on drugs."

But there it was.

One reason for the inflated leads was the newspaper's belief that

Wilder's presence on the ticket would spur an unprecedented black turnout — a debatable proposition. Nevertheless, the poll was yet another example of the bad luck that dogged the Republicans.

It just happened to be published on the day President Reagan went to Arlington to speak at a fund-raiser for the GOP ticket. Virginia Republicans swore later the *Post's* poll was intentionally timed to embarrass the president. That's not so, but the *Post* poll certainly upstaged him, especially on the Washington TV broadcasts, where the poll got equal billing with Reagan's river-crossing. What a powerful cue it was to Northern Virginia voters, who may have had no real feel for how ridiculous the poll seemed downstate.

Reagan's visit to Arlington only continued the GOP's bad luck streak. He had been scheduled to come to Richmond for a big fund-raiser in the summer but his cancer operation forced the White House to send George Bush instead. The Republicans had been counting on a big haul from the president's visit to carry them through the fall, but the Bush fund-raiser fell short of expectations, forcing Durrette to go on TV late and eventually borrow money. Reagan's October visit to Arlington did raise $500,000, but a brief hop across the Potomac didn't generate nearly the publicity that a presidential visit to Richmond or another downstate city would have.

And just as the lunch at the Crystal City Marriott Gateway was starting, the hotel's fire alarms started clanging. For a moment, there was fear the Secret Service would have to evacuate the building. They didn't. It turned out to be a false alarm. But in the back of the room, one reporter whispered: "This campaign is star-crossed."

After the luncheon with Reagan was over, about fifteen heavy-duty Republican contributors and strategists convened a super-secret meeting in a suite upstairs to talk about what was wrong with the Durrette campaign and how to set it right.

This was the final rout of the moderates who had urged an upbeat campaign. The money men decided that Wilder simply couldn't be ignored any longer. Chichester obviously couldn't be counted on to do the job. And with Durrette falling further behind every day, it was high time he and other top Republicans start slicing up Wilder and make Baliles answer for his running mate.

14

The Cop

By mid-October, the smell of doom was starting to drift through the Republican campaigns like the stench of burning leaves. "A guy on the Durrette staff, in the top four or five, which is a telling story, three weeks before the election calls a friend of mine in Washington, a consultant, and says: 'Can you find me a job after the election?' " says one Republican strategist. "My friend says, 'You're not giving up?' The guy on the Durrette staff says 'yeah.' "

The O'Brien campaign had given up, too. "It was a classic case of being able to buy an election," says O'Brien campaign manager Jeff Gregson. "She [Terry] had about as much money as the candidates for governor. That's really unheard of." Gregson had three polls 2½ weeks before the vote. All showed O'Brien losing by fifteen to eighteen points. "That's when I stopped spending money on media," Gregson says. "There's no way to close that gap. We just tried to pay off as many bills as we could. I don't think I even told Buster I had those three polls."

Only the lieutenant governor's race remained in doubt. With just three weeks to go, here was Wilder, still hanging tough while Chichester continued to stumble. Republicans withered. Democrats gulped the cold air and found it invigorating.

"Beginning in October, Paul and I talked a number of times about ways he could win," says Bill Wiley, a fund-raiser for the Baliles campaign. "After Labor Day, because Mary Sue was running so strong and Jerry Baliles was running so strong and the polls were saying we had the right themes, we began to think there just might be a sense out there that there was a New Dominion and that this ticket was a symbol of the future.

"We began to think in early October if that feeling caught hold, then Doug Wilder could sneak over the line. The factor for me was the *Washington Post* poll. It had Jerry Baliles up nineteen points. We very quickly disclaimed that and said our polls showed us only up 5 percent. Bullshit. Our polls showed us up 19 percent, too. Paul had always said Doug would win if Jerry Baliles got 55 percent. The problem was, no one thought Jerry could get 55 percent. A Republican like Durrette should have gotten 47 percent. As a Democrat, Baliles was more acceptable than Robb was four years ago, but in between there had been the big Reagan landslide and new voters registered in Northern Virginia and Virginia Beach. Polls showed 4 percent more identified themselves as hard-core Republicans."

Now, though, it looked as if Baliles might indeed crack the 55 percent threshold — and give Wilder the statistical opening he needed. "There was no question in my mind going into that last three weeks," Wiley says, "that the race was at least 50-50 and he'd either win by half a percent or lose by half a percent."

But as much as Wiley and others in the Baliles campaign tried to offer Goldman help, sometimes there seemed little they could do. "Most campaigns are won on a tactical level," Wiley says. "But this campaign had a life of its own. It moved faster than any of us could keep up with it."

Even as they saw the opportunity for a sweep opening before them, Democrats had good reason to be uneasy about the Wilder campaign.

There were so many things that could still go wrong. The long-awaited Republican bombshell, for one thing. What would it be on? The house? Taxes? The Bar reprimand? Some dark scandal no one knew about? "Every day I was cringing," recalls Wilder's law partner, Roger Gregory. "I was expecting the Big Bomb. What will it be? Will it come a week before the election when there's not time to respond? I remember that was tense."

And though the state song flap had hurt the Republicans, no one knew what voters really thought about a black man running for office. When questioned about their racial attitudes, voters insisted, oh, no, they weren't prejudiced, it was the next guy. "I thought people were lying," says Tom

Vandever, the Charlottesville Democratic chairman. "They're too embarrassed to confess over the phone they're not going to vote for Doug Wilder. Even when it was close, I thought the bottom would fall out."

Republicans and racism were things the Democrats could do nothing about, which made the anxiety only worse. And now it was getting too late to do anything about Wilder's other problem — his ragtag campaign.

Democrats found themselves on the verge of a historic breakthrough — and the Wilder campaign was still nothing more than a station wagon and a prayer.

"We couldn't get materials for Wilder," Vandever complains. "We had to manufacture them. Someone would find a [favorable] newspaper story and copy it. In Charlottesville we were dying to do something for Doug but couldn't." A few weeks before the election, one man went to Richmond to scavenge for supplies. "He had been to Wilder's law office," Vandever recalls. "Somehow he had gotten some materials out of them. He had a little box cradled under his arm. It was like gold. He just opened it a little bit so I could see them." What the man had found was a box of fliers put out by the joint campaign committee. On the front was a photo of all three Democratic candidates. The flier then folded out, with an individual portrait of each candidate. "He said look what we could do, fold it over and make it a Wilder piece" with Wilder's photo on the front, Vandever says. "We thought we were so clever we had thought of that."

Vandever's makeshift Wilder fliers would be funny if the Wilder campaign itself hadn't been doing the same thing.

All through the fall, Michael Brown kept requesting more flyers from the joint campaign committee, until eventually he had requisitioned some sixty cartons. Committee worker Barry Rose was curious. What was Brown doing with all these fliers? One day Rose went over to Wilder's law office and saw the answer. The boxes were sitting open. Some of the fliers were the way the joint campaign had them printed, with the ticket photo on the front. Others had Wilder face up. "He had had volunteers fold 85,000 of 'em so Wilder's picture would be on front," Rose says. "That's what they were using for literature because they had none of their own."

As polls showed all three Republicans doing steadily worse, the pressure on Chichester to "go after" Wilder increased — and the rift between candidate and campaign manager widened even more.

The Durrette campaign was torn along the same lines, too.

"The sad part about this election is that a lot of thoughtful people won't know why they lost," says Durrette media adviser Ed DeBolt, one of those urging an upbeat campaign. "They think it's because they weren't nasty enough or not right-wing enough." Instead, he says, Republicans lost because they never projected any positive themes or identified themselves with any issues that voters cared about. That goes double for Chichester, he says. "When 18 percent of the people in mid-October have a favorable opinion of you, that's not even half the Republican Party." But those who urged an attack-oriented campaign cite those same figures, saying if Chichester couldn't attract Republican voters by being positive, then the only alternative was to rally them by attacking the Democrats.

Whichever side is right may not matter, because "I don't think we ever adopted a strategy and stuck to it," says GOP Chairman Don Huffman. "John Chichester was pulled in very opposite directions by prominent people and factions in the party" and ended up pursuing both strategies, doing neither very well.

But that still doesn't explain why the Republicans were so clumsy in manipulating campaign symbols. For some reason, the GOP could not see that the campaign was being cast as a choice between the past and the future. Because they couldn't, they first sent Mills Godwin out on the stump, which resulted in the state-song furor. Then, on Oct. 11, the Republicans compounded their error by bringing in South Carolina Sen. Strom Thurmond to tour the state. For the Republicans to cozy up to the South's original Dixiecrat while the Democrats fielded a New South ticket with a black and a woman could only make the contrast between the two parties even starker — but not in a way that favored the GOP.

The Republican rhetoric that day was just as clumsy. Chichester praised the GOP ticket as one composed of three like-minded candidates, in contrast to the "diverse" Democrats. "A diverse ticket is not what Virginia wants," he said.

Oct. 13, 1985

For Democrats, this Sunday was a time to shift their campaign machinery into a higher gear. For Republicans, it was a time to regroup.

Wilder, for the first time in the campaign, began devoting his Sundays to attending black churches. On a more public note, his second — and most powerful — TV commercial went on the air across the state. Meanwhile, a claque of high-powered Republicans met to discuss the Chichester campaign and agreed it was time to quit playing Mr. Nice Guy. And for once, Chichester relented.

For Doug Wilder, the week since the incredible debate at St. Catherine's had faded into a blur of fund-raisers and ordinary campaign appearances. Wilder's campaign was run exactly backward from a conventional campaign. In August, Virginians could hardly pick up a newspaper without reading about his exploits. In September, when other campaigns "went public," Wilder stayed discreetly out of the public's eye, still plugging away at his tour. "This is just a guess," says Buster O'Brien, "but Doug Wilder probably made fewer public appearances than any statewide candidate I can remember. And most of the things Doug Wilder said were through his campaign manager." In October, Wilder's only major public appearances were the debates with Chichester. Instead, he let his TV commercials do the campaigning for him while he spent his time quietly raising money.

"The story" in the Sunday papers was again dissension in the Republican camp, specifically disputes about what to do about Wilder. But the stories themselves were part of the problem. Whenever people didn't get their way on strategy, DeBolt complains, they leaked it to the press. The headline in the *Virginian-Pilot:* "Durrette urged to take aim at Wilder's record." The *Richmond Times-Dispatch* agreed: "Attack on Wilder's record may be key to GOP hopes."

"It's twenty minutes to midnight on the doomsday clock for the Republicans," U.Va. analyst Larry Sabato told the *Times-Dispatch.* "The trends now are so strongly in the Democratic direction."

He blamed the media for not being more critical of Wilder. "Doug Wilder's pulled one of the greatest transformations in politics since we had the 'old' Nixon and the 'new' Nixon," Sabato said. "Wilder's gone from being the old liberal Doug to the new Wilder, who's in the Robb-Baliles moderate-conservative mold, espousing all the right Virginia virtues. It's incredible."

As if on cue, Chichester's finance committee and other GOP money types — about twenty people in all, including Godwin — met at the Farmington Country Club in Charlottesville Sunday afternoon to plot strategy. The meeting was Peterson's idea. "That was the only way I could get him to make decisions, to surround him with people I felt were in agreement," Peterson says. "He never was comfortable doing negatives." But now that's what Peterson wanted to insist on.

It's unclear whether this happened before the Oct. 13 meeting or afterward, but about three weeks before the election, Peterson confronted the candidate with a poll he had just received. "The numbers made me wince," Peterson says. Wilder was running in the mid-fifties, with Chichester thirteen points down. A change in strategy was the only alternative. "He had been running positive, positive, positive, talking about being a cutting edge [in attracting new industries]." But he was going nowhere. "I said you have more to gain by being negative against Wilder than being positive about yourself. It's the Republicans who are abandoning us. We hadn't even inspired our own base. Sometimes you have to say something about the other guy [to get your own people fired up]."

Peterson went over the poll by phone. "I said 'John, it's my duty. I've got to tell you where you are.' He said, 'Are you finished?' and he hung up on me."

Whether this conversation happened before or after Oct. 13 hardly matters. By the time the meeting convened, Chichester was already convinced he was going to lose: "We had no money, bad commercials, Dennis was off on a tangent. I'm wanting to get positive on TV, he wants to get negative and we have no money to do either. And Wilder has just upped his TV buy in Washington to $250,000, more money than we had to spend in all. Even if you didn't know either of us, he was going to win there" in Northern Virginia, simply on the basis of greater exposure. "After the last three weeks, I never thought I was going to win."

So Chichester wasn't in much of a mood to argue in Charlottesville. "The agreement [earlier] was John was to do negative advertising and he resisted it," Peterson says. "All these finance folks said we thought you were going to talk about the reprimand, we thought you were going to talk about not paying taxes. They said if you'll do these spots, we'll get the money. This was the collective wisdom of twenty people."

Chichester relented. "I agreed to do one round of negatives, three weeks out. I thought it was lost, so what the hell? We couldn't build up ourselves. We had no [decent positive] commercials."

Peterson thought he had won a major battle. He had a TV crew standing by and dispatched it immediately to film Wilder's run-down property.

The phenomenon that became known simply as "the cop" began that Sunday.

In Manassas, Chuck Colgan Jr., the Draft Bagley organizer, was slumped over in his chair half asleep with the TV on about 11 p.m. when Joe Alder came on the screen. Colgan vaguely remembered a beefy Southern lawman testifying on Wilder's behalf, but thought he was dreaming. Suddenly the phone rang, jarring him awake.

Dawn Hunt, president of the Manassas Young Democrats, had been sitting at home watching "M*A*S*H" when Joe Alder appeared. "When I saw it, I went nuts," she says. "It was really wild to see that. I always holler a lot but I know I did it then."

She was so excited that she immediately called Colgan. "Hey, did you see that Wilder ad?" she shouted over the phone. Colgan wasn't sure —

but, very much awake now, he watched the rest of "M*A*S*H" in hopes of seeing the commercial again. Sure enough, it came on again at the end. By the time Alder was through drawling about how "the Fraternal Order of Police endorses Doug Wilder," Colgan was standing up and cheering. "Super!" he shouted. "Super!"

All over Virginia, Democrats reacted with similar delight when they first saw Wilder's show-stopping TV commercial that he had stumbled upon back in Lunenburg County the month before.

The Republicans, naturally, weren't nearly as excited when they saw it. "The production wasn't very good but it was the best commercial of any of the campaigns," says Ed DeBolt. "My reaction was that's gonna take away the criminal law issue and that's the best one John had," Durrette says. "It was that good." Chichester could say whatever he wanted to about Wilder's record on law and order, but after Oct. 13, it didn't matter. Who were the voters going to pay more attention to, Chichester citing votes on obscure bills in the newspaper, or the cop in their living room? "They wound up running against our commercial," Goldman says.

From here on, the campaign the candidates waged became increasingly irrelevant. The campaign now was almost strictly on television, between Wilder's cop and Wilder working his way to the top against Chichester getting out of his airplane and calling a staff meeting to combat beach erosion. "If the opposition had run a campaign to match them on the air, then you might be writing a different ending to your book," says Terry's media adviser Bob Squier. But the Republicans had nothing to match the cop.

No wonder, after the election was over, Wilder credited two things for his upset victory: his station-wagon tour and the cop commercial.

And with all that money in the bank, voters saw a lot of the cop.

"One of the great myths of this campaign," says G.C. Morse, then a *Virginian-Pilot* editorial writer, "is that Wilder had no money. Hell's bells, he had plenty of money and he had it to spend when he needed it most."

Chichester raised more money than Wilder had — $882,000 to $696,000 — but the margin turned out to be insignificant. While the Chichester campaign, with staff to pay and literature to print, spent only $220,000 on television, Wilder spent about $550,000 — nearly 80 percent of what he took in.

The shrewd Goldman found another way to make his money last longer, too. Most campaigns buy their TV time through ad agencies. It doesn't cost any more; the agency makes its money from the 15 percent discount that TV stations offer to ad agencies. But, Goldman reasoned, why pay an agency if he could get that discount on his own and have an extra 15 percent to put back into the campaign? So he set up his own ad agency — with himself and Michael Brown as the partners. It was a corporation that existed only on paper, but it was all perfectly legit. TV stations didn't know any better when Goldman called and identified himself as the media buyer for Virginia Media Group. Goldman ran himself ragged the last month of the campaign, trying to figure out which shows to buy and at what frequency. But the dummy agency stretched Wilder's media dollars by 15 percent, so with about $550,000 cash, Goldman was able to buy the equivalent of $632,500 worth of time. "No one noticed, but the last few weeks we were on nearly as much as Mary Sue was," Goldman says.

But frugality and finagling don't answer the original question: Where did all of Wilder's money come from?

Two places: Jackie Epps and Chuck Robb.

The political professionals discount Epps' role. In campaigns geared toward pulling down contributions $5,000 and $10,000 at a time, the mere discussion of a fund-raising campaign based on $25 and $50 and $100 contributions is considered naive. However, "that's part of the national importance of this race," Goldman says. "We raised a lot of money off the tour and nobody ever paid any attention to it. We raised a lot of money in October. We had a lot of $2,000, $4,000 fund-raisers. It adds up. You can't raise $4 million like that but the point is you can raise $300,000-$400,000 indigenously from blacks in a state like Virginia. It's probably not enough, but enough to run a credible campaign [and serve as seed money]. It demonstrates to Democrats a source of money to be tapped in the future. People have missed the emergence of the black middle class."

When the infamous "Robb letters" were released about a year after the election, the attention focused on how much work Robb's staff had done for Wilder, especially fund-raising. But in an interview in April 1986, long before the letters were released, Wilder thoroughly discounted Robb's role. He estimated Robb's staff raised only 3 or 4 percent of his money. By contrast, Epps raised about 40 percent, making her — by Wilder's accounting — ten times more important to his fund-raising efforts.

Indeed, in his April 1986 interview, Wilder sounded especially bitter about what he saw as Robb's lack of help. "First of all, I wanted him to help me raise money" before the convention, Wilder said. "Then after that, to help me raise money. He never flatly refused," but Wilder makes it clear he believes Robb never did much, either. "When the polls started looking good, he made a call or two. I'm not being critical of Robb, I'm just trying to put a perspective on the facts. We knew the Terry people were already greased up with those people. The doors were open. Billy Thomas and [Al] Smith and [Al] Diamonstein — they may have decided they didn't want to spread themselves too thin. They all helped, but it was a question of degree."

So what did Robb do?

Sorting out assistance from interference was difficult even at the time it was going on, much less later after so much bad blood had been shed in public between the two men. "I would hear the Robb people and then I would hear the Wilder people and it was a night and day difference," says Larry Framme, who chaired the joint campaign committee.

Goldman describes Robb's role this way: "He was never an advocate of Doug's candidacy. He only came to it when it was inevitable. He gave some support in the summertime, but you have to understand, the Democrats couldn't afford us having no chance." So of course, Robb was going to say nice things about Wilder, Goldman reasons. But he contends Robb never went "above and beyond the call of duty" to raise money. "If we hadn't raised that TV money and fended off those attacks, by the time the final decision to put the shoulder to the wheel was made, we wouldn't have been in that position. I think of all the people who worked so hard for us. Robb likes to bask in the glow of victory but wouldn't lift a hand to turn on the switch. What they did in October, as it turns out, maybe it didn't matter."

"Wilder always felt Robb should have unleashed his people, whatever that means," says Robb's chief of staff, David McCloud. The irony, McCloud says, is Robb already had. How important their help was to the Wilder campaign can be debated but clearly the Robb staff did spend an enormous amount of time in October working on Wilder's behalf.

"I was on the phone, I'd venture to say, once a day" to the Wilder campaign, says Judy Griswold. So were others. "I can assure you that the governor's office, between Phil Abraham and Jordan Goldman and Ben Dendy, was out there beating the bushes and shaking the trees," says Carolyn Moss, Robb's director of minority business enterprises. Moss herself was often on the phone to black businessmen. "There must be a thousand people in this state who think the governor personally asked me to call them and contribute because that's the line I used," she says. "There were some people in the governor's office who were very sensitive afterward because they didn't get a call, a thank-you [from either Wilder or Goldman]." Instead, what they got was a bitter blast in the newspapers. "It was not easy to get contributions," Moss says. "We had to call and beg and I'm not sure Doug fully appreciates that fact."

Two postscripts to the cop commercial: Joe Alder, the anonymous hero, and George Austin, president of the FOP.

Alder never heard anything from the Wilder campaign after he had filmed the spot and soon forgot about it. One October morning, though, he was at Mildred's Meals diner in Kenbridge when a friend called out across the restaurant: "Hey, I saw you on TV last night."

Alder couldn't figure out what the man was talking about.

"Yeah, I saw you on TV," the man insisted.

Before long Joe Alder was the talk of his little Southside town. Blacks "were tickled to death," he says. "My 2-year-old son, he screamed out, 'Daddy, daddy, daddy's on TV!'"

But Alder remained an anonymous celebrity. Reporters who pestered Goldman for the cop's name were given a runaround. The Wilder campaign was getting all the mileage it needed out of the commercial, why risk the cop saying something stupid? Ironically, by the time reporters found out who Alder was, he was long gone. He voted Election Day morning, then took a week off to go bear-hunting. He returned home to find half a dozen newspapers wanted to interview him.

And not until after the election did Goldman learn something about Alder — the cop who had solemnly intoned "the Fraternal Order of Police endorses Doug Wilder" wasn't even a member.

Meanwhile, for George Austin, the Alder spot was an unexpected bonanza. It gave power to the FOP's endorsement. But it also was an unexpected headache. "I'm still going around the state putting out fires with twenty-year Republican state troopers," he said in the summer of 1986.

Oct. 14, 1985

Dennis Peterson flew to Philadelphia to produce the negative TV spots Chichester had agreed to the day before.

"While I was in the studio, John called," Peterson told the *Washington Post* in a post-election interview. "He had changed his mind — we could make one thirty-second commercial, but twenty seconds of it had to be something like him and [his wife] Karen walking, holding hands. The last ten seconds could be negative. But for every time we ran the negative spot, we'd have to run three positive ones."

Peterson ignored Chichester's directions and went ahead and produced the negative spots he had intended.

Oct. 15, 1985

Peterson drove to Hampton to meet Godwin and played the new commercials for the former governor. He liked them. "We'll pay," he told Peterson. But when Peterson told Chichester this, the candidate "was furious. 'Keep him [Godwin] away from me. I don't care how much money they have.' "

Chichester describes it this way: "I looked forward to those ads coming back and when they did, they were nothing like I had described to him, not even kin to it. And one was just awful. I wouldn't let him run it. There was nothing but venom in those commercials."

Now what was going to happen?

On Tuesday night, Wilder and Chichester met for their third debate — this time before the Richmond Jaycees.

Chichester calls the opening statement he read that night the worst thing he had to do in the whole campaign. He hated it because Peterson insisted he attack Doug Wilder. Chichester's attacks stuck strictly to legislative issues, though — no mention of the house or back taxes.

Chichester made the usual attempt to paint Wilder as a liberal, accused him of being a friend of labor unions, a supporter of collective bargaining for public employees, an opponent of tough crime bills. But the hour-or-so question-and-answer session produced no new issues.

Once a Jaycee planted by the Chichester campaign asked Wilder a leading question about his support of law-and-order measures. "I somewhat anticipated the question, as I saw you had to read it," Wilder said with a grin. Then he opened a file folder of his own and began reading a list of the crime bills he had supported.

More telling, though, was the way the two candidates handled themselves. Whenever Wilder was speaking, Peterson rushed over to Chichester and gave him a folder or a piece of paper or advice on what to say next. But Wilder, when he wasn't speaking, simply stood to the side of the lectern, sometimes waving to people he knew in the hometown audience.

Chichester would draw no blood tonight.

Oct. 17, 1985

The polls showed the Democrats starting to pull away. Two Democratic polls completed in midweek gave Baliles a sixteen-point lead and showed Terry ahead by as much as nineteen points. But Wilder remained the surprise. In just a week's time, his lead had ballooned from nine points to nineteen. In a Pat Caddell poll for Baliles, Wilder led 43-24.

No wonder the headline in the *Washington Post* on Thursday morning took on tones of panic:

"Va. GOP scrambles for strategy on Wilder"

"RICHMOND — Virginia Republicans are increasingly frustrated and at odds over strategies to attack state Sen. L. Douglas Wilder, the Democratic candidate for lieutenant governor and the first black to be nominated by a major party for statewide office."

"The Republicans for years have shouted 'liberal, liberal, liberal,' and now they've got one and don't know what to do with him," Sabato said.

In Richmond, the special grand jury appointed to investigate Wilder's row house on Church Hill was sworn in, but so far Republicans seemed unable to capitalize on the slumlord charges. "That's enough to sink a battleship," Sabato told the *Post*. "A white candidate would have been finished months ago."

Oct. 19, 1985

Wilder spent Saturday campaigning in Northern Virginia with Baliles and Terry, the first time all three candidates had campaigned together since Labor Day. What an odd feeling it was. Early in the summer, people had wondered if Baliles and Terry would shy away from Wilder once he started sinking in the polls. Wilder's two-month tour had rendered the question moot in August and September. Now, here it was, just over two weeks before the election, and Wilder wasn't sinking, he was soaring in the polls. Wilder's reunion with his ticket mates on this sunny Saturday afternoon seemed to give them all a boost.

By the time the day was over, Wilder was worn out. He wanted nothing more than for Chuck Nichollson to take him straight home for a long night's sleep. One problem, though. One event remained on his schedule. Some little black church in Culpeper. Neither Wilder nor Nichollson knew much about it. This was something Jackie Epps had set up.

Going to Culpeper meant a significant detour. And Wilder was already late. He was supposed to be there at 8 p.m. It was almost 8 now and he was still stuck in Northern Virginia. Wilder wanted to cancel.

But he didn't.

Epps was waiting in Culpeper at the Antioch Baptist Church. The church was packed — the aisles were jammed, the choir stall was filled up and the crowd spilled out into the street, the basement and even the parish hall. It was a stifling hot night and there was no air conditioning. The only breath of air came from people fanning themselves. Epps assured everyone Wilder would soon be there, even as she kept looking at her watch. Where was he? She had already called Michael Brown at the office and he hadn't heard a thing.

Eight soon turned into 8:30 and 8:30 soon turned into 9. Epps was amazed — no matter how many minutes slipped by with no sign of Wilder, the church members still sat patiently. In the reception room, punch and cookies had been carefully laid out, but no one got up to sample them. A busload of people who had come in from neighboring Orange County left, but only to go out to sit on the bus and cool off. Nine turned into 9:15, but still no one thought of leaving.

All the local white bigwigs were waiting, too. "We had local politicians get up to pump 'em up but we ran out of politicians," Epps says.

Still she kept looking at her watch and still no one got up to leave.

Finally, at 9:20 p.m., Wilder's car bounced into the parking lot. "When we got there, she ran out and kissed me and kissed Doug," Nichollson recalls.

If Wilder hadn't expected much out of this little church, his expectations were soon changed when he saw the crowd milling outside — then caught a glimpse of the even bigger crowd waiting inside.

The church roared when Doug Wilder came down the aisle and was introduced by the sheriff. Though it had been a long day, Wilder seemed renewed. "He gave one of the best speeches I've ever heard a politician give," says Culpeper lawyer John "Butch" Davies. "The crowd energized him." When Wilder was done, the sheriff jumped up and asked the crowd, "Who in here would disagree that it was worth waiting for?"

The crowd roared again.

It took nearly an hour for Wilder to shake all the hands that night, but now he didn't seem to mind at all. For all the perfunctory campaigning a candidate must do, this was one time Wilder was truly moved. "People believed," Epps says. But Nichollson and Epps remember something else, too. They took in $3,000 from that little church. Yet, says Nichollson, who counted the money that was tossed into the collection plate, "there was not a single check over $25 and no $100 bills, either." Epps remembers little children who came up with money, sometimes carefully stuffed into envelopes. "We'd open up the envelope and see crumpled up three $1 bills. You wonder, 'My God, where has this money been?'"

Oct. 20, 1985

Only two full weeks remained. Still the Republicans had yet to unleash the attack dogs they had promised. The negative spots that Peterson had flown to Philadelphia to produce had yet to air, though they would soon. Meanwhile, Wilder's two initial spots — running up the steps and the cop — were soaking into the voters' collective consciousness as Goldman busied himself buying more TV time.

"In mid-October, the Baliles and Terry campaigns began to realize Wilder could win," Goldman says. "The *Post* poll [Oct. 9] jogged a lot of people but they quickly dismissed it. When TV went on, we went up. The cop was big time. You could feel it. We got up there in the stratosphere. We were sensing what everyone else was sensing. Then we started to top out. We could get 42-43-44-45 and top out. Then Chichester was back on with [negative] TV. Baliles and Terry, they started to share information with us, talking numbers with us and this was very much invaluable, but no one came to us and said how much do you need? Robb didn't come and say 'OK, we see you can win, what do you need? Will another $75,000 buy the time?' "

Nichollson remembers Wilder's enthusiasm building two weeks out. "He said, 'I can't believe the Richmond papers are leaving me alone. They beat Henry Howell up. They're not eating me alive, calling me a liberal Communist.' I was nervous as a tick. Paul was all wired up, but Doug was cool. He'd come through the office and say, 'Let's go, men.' Mike and I joked that he thinks he's still in Korea leading the charge. Everything was 'men.' 'Men, are you ready?' Every evening he'd come through, 'Men, are you ready to go?' And he always said 'we' would win. Not 'I' but 'we.' "

But oh, those last two weeks would feel so long.

By now, pessimism was rampant in the Republican Party. "Dennis Peterson kept his cool, but he panicked by the third week of October," Sabato says. "All at once his confidence ebbed away. He saw the numbers weren't changing. And Wilder was outdoing Chichester in every public appearance. He knew then he was managing a campaign that would go down as blowing one of the surest things in history."

Even the candidate had given up. About two weeks before the election, Peterson asked permission to rent a suite of rooms on Election Night at the Marriott, for the GOP victory party. Chichester said no, provoking yet another argument with his campaign manager. "I knew how that election would come out," he says. "I didn't want to be around any frivolity in a losing effort."

The Sunday papers were full of more gloom and doom for the Republicans. The *Washington Post* and *Richmond Times-Dispatch* had more internal polls, from both sides, but all with the same result: The Democrats were ahead, though the GOP poll put Wilder up by only 3 percent.

In the *Roanoke Times & World-News,* meanwhile, Sabato was busy blaming both the Republicans and the media for Wilder's strong showing. Chichester, Sabato said, has been "inept, afraid and unable" to attack Wilder. In addition, Sabato said the news media had "done everything possible to help Doug Wilder and hurt Chichester. It has been the most imbalanced and unfair picture of an election I've ever seen."

Oct. 21, 1985

Fifteen days out. For Richard Dickerson, field commander of the Democrats' get-out-the-vote blitz, it was time to field his army. Starting today, he took a leave of absence from his job as a consultant in the state Department of Education. His assignment was to organize the campaign the Democratic National Committee had paid for with its unprecedented $110,000 grant to the joint campaign. Framme's committee had targeted 130 precincts that traditionally vote 70 percent or better Democratic. All were black. Most were confined to the state's "black belt" that began in Richmond, swept down through Petersburg and eastern Southside — Southampton County, Greenville County, Emporia — and into Tidewater — Suffolk, Chesapeake, Portsmouth, Norfolk, Hampton and Newport News.

The Virginia Democratic Party had been so disorganized in the 1970s that it had never set up a formal network of black leaders who could turn out the votes on Election Day. Not until the Robb campaign in 1981 was one created. "We could not have done it in '85 had we not had the success we did in '81," Dickerson says — just another example of the debt Wilder owes Robb, many would contend.

Using the contacts made during 1981, Dickerson says, "I did the chicken-and-chitlins circuit hiring flushers," the people who go through black neighborhoods on Election Day "flushing out" the voters like so many quail. He also made sure black ministers planned to deliver a pro-Democratic message the Sunday before Election Day.

By the end of the week Dickerson had his thousand flushers hired and the Democrats' secret weapon — its GOTV army — was a week away from hitting the beaches.

Oct. 21-24, 1985

The next-to-last week before the election rushed by with surprisingly little news. By now, the campaigns were being fought almost entirely on TV screens and in living rooms, not on the campaign trail. But signs of Wilder's surge were apparent nearly everywhere.

In Southwest Virginia, Wise County Democratic Chairman Glenn Craft was at an auto parts store when he ran into the same old man he'd talked to at the garage back in July, an old man who had been a Democrat all his life but who swore he could never vote for a "nigger."

Now the old man looked up at Craft and grinned. "You know," he said. "I feel we got a pretty good man in that black man." Craft was ecstatic. "I felt if he was turning, a lot of others were, too."

Charlottesville lawyer George Gilliam remembers a call he received one day in mid-October from a conservative businessman he knew. Out of the blue, this businessman called Gilliam and said he wanted to talk about Doug Wilder. Gilliam readied for the worst.

"I don't think we're doing enough for Doug Wilder," the man said. "What do you think would be appropriate?"

Gilliam almost dropped the phone.

The man sent Wilder $200.

Gilliam thinks much of the Wilder momentum came from voters who wanted to purge Virginia of its racist past. "When Godwin said what he said about 'Carry Me Back,' that was not a particularly nasty thing to say, but I think a lot of people thought, 'I thought Virginia was beyond that. I don't know much about Wilder but he's endorsed by the police. He seems a nice, clean-cut guy. Maybe it's about time.'"

Former GOP legislator Ray Garland is more indelicate. "People devote a lot of energy to self-deception," he says. "Everywhere I go I encounter a lot of racist attitudes, but people don't want to say that and voting for Doug Wilder was a good way to show they weren't racists."

Whatever the reasons, clearly something was happening as the election neared. Doug Wilder was catching on. Supporting him was no longer the unthinkable taboo. Indeed, laments Bruce Miller, Durrette's campaign manager, "it almost became the socially acceptable thing to do."

The underdog had suddenly become the front-runner. Now, as Chichester prepared to unleash his long-awaited final offensive, the question was: Could Wilder hold on?

15

Stalled Out

With two weeks left in the campaign, Wilder was leading in the polls, sandwiched between two candidates who were pulling away. He was blanketing the state with some dynamite TV commercials — and he had plenty of money to keep them on the air.

Ironically, at the same time the public was beginning to believe in the Wilder miracle, the Wilder campaign was waking up to a sobering statistical reality. As close as Wilder had come, an actual upset was going to be excruciatingly difficult to achieve.

"Nobody believed the polls," says Larry Framme, the Democrats' joint campaign committee chairman. "The predication was, if he won, he needed 15-16 percent black vote [as a percentage of the total electorate]."

But, thanks to Wilder's decision not to appeal directly to blacks, along with the low intensity of the whole campaign, the earlier prospects of a big (20 percent or more) black turnout now seemed dim — which meant Wilder's chances rested with the diminishing pool of undecided, mostly moderate-conservative, white voters and, Framme says, "nobody ever believed he would pull the percentage of white votes he did."

On Monday, Oct. 28, Chichester finally unveiled his negative TV commercials. His main spot pounded Wilder on the vacant house on Church Hill. Equally harsh spots on the Bar reprimand and his late payment of taxes were known to be ready and waiting. Democrats cringed at the thought of how much these attacks would cut into Wilder's soft support among middle-of-the-road white voters.

But even before Chichester's spots had a chance to register, the polls that had been looking so good for Wilder were beginning to belie a deeper, more disturbing truth. Wilder was running out of momentum — just when Chichester was starting to make his move.

The Democratic polls showed Wilder in the mid-40s, with better than a ten-point lead. "The problem was, by late October, we were stalled out and it looked like what was left were Republicans who hadn't heard of Chichester yet," Goldman says. "We made our move with the cop but couldn't seem to get over 50. We couldn't get higher." The other Democratic campaigns were getting worried.

Now Chichester's negative spots threatened to boost his numbers and cut into Wilder's at the same time.

For the next week — right up until noon on Friday, Nov. 1, the deadline for placing TV commercials for the last weekend of the campaign — the Wilder campaign, indeed the whole Democratic hierarchy, would be consumed by one question: How should Wilder respond to Chichester's attacks? Specifically, should he go negative?

A lot of people thought so — virtually all the high-powered consultants to the other Democratic campaigns. Against this solid front of campaign wizards, only the unlikely duo of Robb and Wilder argued against going negative, on the grounds it would ruin Wilder's upbeat image. Somewhere in the midst of this frenzied tug of war was Paul Goldman, run ragged by the do-it-yourself campaign, his usually quick mind dulled by the frenetic pace. "Paul was really confused," says Barry Rose. "He didn't know what to do."

This was the scene as the campaign spiraled to its end at a dizzying pace — a ragtag Wilder campaign stretched to the breaking point, the prospect of a historic victory so tantalizingly near yet the margin of error so narrow that one wrong move could tip the campaign into the abyss of heartbreaking second place and perpetual regret. But who knew which was the safe course — for Wilder to attack his opponent and risk alienating voters? Or do nothing and hope he could simply hold on?

Said Robb press secretary George Stoddart: "The last ten days were as tough strategically as anything I've been involved in."

Oct. 25, 1985

Doug Wilder's fund-raising campaign marched on. Wilder joked with driver Chuck Nichollson that he'd raise $20,000 on this little jaunt through Northern Virginia.

The Friday began in Winchester, with a breakfast sponsored by Robb's right-hand money man, Del. Al Smith. Wilder and Nichollson got to the restaurant, though, and couldn't find Smith. All they saw was a sign in the lobby announcing something called "Cash Management Group."

Suddenly Smith appeared, smiling. "Cash Management Group" was the name he had reserved the room under and he seemed to enjoy the little in-joke. The man who had refused to take Wilder to the Commonwealth Club during the Pickett crisis, the man who had come to Wilder last December and begged him to drop out of the race, now ushered Wilder into a private breakfast with about a dozen Democratic contributors. When Al Smith speaks, wealthy men open their wallets.

From Winchester, it was on to Northern Virginia and a fund-raiser sponsored by another Robb money man, lawyer Bill Thomas.

That night in his hotel room, Wilder handed Nichollson his ever-present briefcase. Nichollson opened it and saw the briefcase was stuffed with checks Wilder had collected. Wilder told Nichollson to count the money while the candidate took a shower. While Nichollson counted, he could hear Wilder singing.

Sometime later — by now it was close to midnight — Wilder came out of the shower, all steamy and refreshed. Nichollson told him the amount. Wilder beamed at his prescience. "Didn't I tell you we'd raise $20,000 up here? Didn't I tell you?"

Oct. 26, 1985

While the Democratic candidates appeared before the NAACP state convention in Norfolk, the Republicans were having a rally in Roanoke.

While reporters peppered Durrette with questions about his faction-ridden campaign and who was really in charge, party Chairman Don Huffman had plans of his own. He was convinced Durrette was a goner. His worry now was saving Chichester. Huffman had stayed up late the night before working on a speech. "I was going to take Wilder on on those three issues," he says — the house, the Bar reprimand, the late payment of taxes. Before the breakfast, he showed his speech to Durrette, who thought it was fine but suggested Huffman ought to clear it with Chichester first. "I don't know," Chichester said as he looked over it, "let's show it to John Dalton."

But former Gov. John Dalton firmly said no. No way should the Republicans be seen beating up on a black candidate, he warned. Huffman reluctantly put his humdinger of a speech back in his coat pocket and it went undelivered. Once more, the Republicans let Wilder go untouched.

Out in the crowd at the NAACP convention, some blacks were grumbling. "Wilder is taking black voters for granted," said Wymond Mitchell, former president of the Nottoway County branch in Southside. "Even though they're going to vote for him, they resent it."

When it came time for Wilder to speak, only half the delegates gave him a standing ovation. Clearly, this election had generated little enthusiasm from any quarter.

But the talk of history had already started. "We have come a mighty, mighty long way," Wilder told the crowd. "I'm going to win the election," a line that, for once, brought some heat to the lukewarm convention hall.

Oct. 27, 1985

The last Sunday in October was bright, blue and clear. The little airplane Wilder was riding found some light gusts of wind and rode them over mountain after mountain, all the way from Roanoke to Wise County. Below him, the mountains were turning from burnt orange to a denuded brown. In the higher elevations, autumn had passed through. The passing of the seasons was a solemn reminder that the campaign was near its end.

He had flown to Roanoke that morning to speak at a black church. Now he was flying back to far Southwest Virginia for the first time since he had left it by station wagon in August. That seemed a long time ago and much had happened since. Wilder wondered again how he would be received in those hard, dark coalfields.

Russ Axsom, the AFL-CIO vice president from the Newport News shipyards, was waiting at the airstrip. The union had sent him back to his native Southwest Virginia to spend the last few weeks of the campaign working for Wilder.

Axsom was hoping Wilder's entourage would be bringing campaign literature to pass out. Axsom had run out long ago. But when Wilder traveled alone, that's what he meant. "He had no staff, no literature to hand out," Axsom says, still aghast.

Axsom hustled Wilder into the car and drove on to the rally at the Wise County fairgrounds. A country music band was playing. Axsom led Wilder through the crush, but the candidate was mobbed by people who had met him on the tour and people who had wished they had. The crowd was so thick, "he was holding onto my arm pretty tight," Axsom recalls. Even coal operators were reaching out to grab one of Axsom's "AFL-CIO for Wilder" stickers.

Finally, Axsom maneuvered Wilder up to the grandstand. Wilder looked out on the huge crowd of Southwest Democrats, every bit as accepting and enthusiastic as they had been in the summer. "I knew then I'd won," he says. "I was convinced then, things would be all right."

The sky was black as ink by the time Wilder flew back to Roanoke for a nighttime reception at the home of black businessman Byron Smith. Somehow signals got crossed. About 8 p.m., the house was filling up with people — both black and white — when the phone rang. Joe Hancock, a black California political consultant who had grown up in Roanoke and come back to do volunteer work in his hometown for the last weeks of the campaign, answered it. Doug Wilder was on the other end and he wasn't happy. "Who's supposed to pick me up?" Wilder snapped.

"He was fit to be tied," Hancock recalls. Hancock said he'd rush right over to the airport, but Wilder said no, he'd take a cab. Hancock was waiting when the taxi pulled up in front of Smith's home. Hancock reached into the car to pay the driver. Wilder angrily pushed his arm out of the way and paid the cabbie himself. Hancock could feel the power in Wilder's well-exercised arm. Hancock stepped back and let Wilder go by.

"I've never seen him so livid," says Hancock, who first met Wilder when the latter was a young lawyer just starting his practice. Later in the evening, when Wilder had cooled off, he apologized to Hancock. He was tired, he explained, and his normally steady nerves were starting to fray.

Del. Chip Woodrum thought the fund-raiser was a homecoming of sorts, as Wilder seemed to speak directly to the blacks in the room. "He said it meant so much to be here at Byron's with you. He never said I haven't paid as much attention to you as I like. But at the same time, the unspoken innuendo was, 'I am of you, but I can't be speaking only to you,' and everybody understood. He said, in so many words, 'I have got to court white voters,' and everybody understood that."

Oct. 28, 1985

"We do not find a nuisance, your honor."

With those words from special grand jury foreman Robert Ellett

Dandridge, the investigation into Wilder's Church Hill housing came to an end.

But the controversy didn't. That Monday night, Chichester's negative commercials finally went on the air. The camera zeroed in on Wilder's boarded-up Church Hill house, weeds shooting up in the yard. "He's been publicly reprimanded by the state Supreme Court," the narrator gravely intoned. "He's been hauled before the general court of Richmond for maintaining hazardous properties." It was the mildest of the three spots Peterson had prepared, and with only eight days left before the election, that wasn't much time for the housing issue to sink in. Still, Chichester had a chance to pull out a victory if enough voters saw the commercial and began to have doubts about Wilder's character.

At first glance, the latest Baliles poll — completed Sunday night — seemed encouraging for Wilder. It showed Durrette's support slipping and Baliles closing in on 50 percent. He now led 49-27. Wilder led 45-26.

But other numbers showed deeper trends that were discouraging to Democratic strategists. About 30 percent of the voters were still undecided. These undecideds were overwhelmingly white, over forty, right-leaning moderates and conservatives, Reagan voters in '84. Even with Baliles and Terry landslides developing, these undecided voters could be expected to break heavily for Chichester. Wilder needed one in five to put him over the 50 percent mark, but even that number seemed exceedingly difficult. Could Wilder realistically expect to get 20 percent of the vote from a pool of white Southern independent conservatives who had voted for Reagan in '84? Probably not, many Democratic strategists feared.

What's more, could Wilder even hold onto the 45 percent he already had? Chichester's negative TV spots hadn't started to move voters yet, but they had started to change perceptions — the first step. Since the Oct. 23 poll, Wilder's unfavorable rating had shot up dangerously fast in Richmond, where Wilder's housing had received the most attention. Generally when a politician's negative rating is half his favorable rating, he's in big trouble. Wilder's 40-30 favorable-unfavorable rating there was not simply dangerous, it was deadly.

Chichester's TV commercials were now spreading the news about Wilder's house all over the state; would voters' reaction elsewhere be the same as in Richmond? With just barely a week to go, did Chichester have enough time to cut the celebrity hero Wilder back down to size? And with more than a week to go, had Wilder perhaps peaked too soon?

On Monday night, with the election now just eight days away, Goldman also fired his last round of TV — a spot featuring Robb. The commercial with the popular governor emphasizing that Doug Wilder has "a clear edge" in experience was a powerful image to project in the campaign's decisive days. Saving the Robb spot until last was designed to motivate those reluctant Democrats and independents still undecided about Wilder to come on, let's vote for him, Robb says it's OK. But despite the thirty takes it took to film the governor, the spot came up short. About twelve seconds short, to be exact. To fill the gap, Goldman tacked on Joe Alder leaning up against his cruiser, saying "the Fraternal Order of Police endorses Doug Wilder."

Goldman could only hope the Robb-and-Alder spot — Wilder's two strongest spokesmen — would be strong enough to blunt the Chichester negatives on the house. Terry media consultant Bob Squier, though, was convinced Wilder needed to go negative and offered to produce a last-minute spot if Goldman wanted one. At party headquarters, executive director Bobby Watson was insistent that if Wilder didn't want to dirty his own hands, then the party should be allowed to do something. Meanwhile, both the Baliles and Terry campaigns were passing on the daily tracking polls. Wilder's numbers continued to be flat, stalled out in the high forties. "All the experts were saying we had to do something," Goldman says. "The traditional wisdom is if you let someone run unanswered negatives on you, you'll lose a lot of votes."

Goldman had the money to do whatever needed to be done. The new finance reports showed that during October Wilder took in almost as much money as Chichester did. More importantly, Wilder used virtually all of that money to buy additional TV time; Chichester still had bills to pay. With Wilder holding a commanding lead in TV time, one question both sides had to ask was whether enough people would see Chichester's negatives for them to do any good.

Goldman decided tomorrow he would have to take a look at Chichester's TV and then figure out what to do.

Oct. 29, 1985

About noon, Goldman and Jay Shropshire drove out to the Channel 6 studios on West Broad Street. Back in the control room, an engineer queued up the Chichester cartridge and played the three commercials on the pack.

One focused exclusively on the house on Church Hill. "Douglas Wilder maintains these nests of urban blight." A second focused on the Bar reprimand, citing Wilder's "unprofessional conduct" and "inexcusable procrastination." It ended with: "Today, a course of study still given all candidates for the Virginia State Bar cites Wilder's conduct as an example of how not to practice law." The third spot was the one that had gone on the air the night before, briefly mentioning both the Bar reprimand and the house.

Wilder and Shropshire didn't know it, but Chichester so far had agreed to let only one of these spots go on the air. Even if they had known, it might not have made a difference. The spots were there, in the studios, just waiting for the word from Dennis Peterson to put them on.

Goldman returned to the law office in a quandary. The Chichester negatives were worse than he had imagined. "The roughest ones I've ever seen," he says. Election Day was now one week away. Before that, there was another deadline — Friday noon, the deadline for scheduling TV spots over the weekend. The decision the Wilder campaign made in the next three days would likely determine the outcome of the election. But which way? That was the question Goldman was now debating with the other campaigns — and with himself.

"With seven days to go, it really set in," Goldman says. " 'You've got to do something.' They were honest. They'd been doing this for a long time. They said, 'We analyze these all the time. We see this all the time. You can't get over 50. It's all gonna come crashing in. You've got to go negative. You've got to stop the undecideds from going to Chichester.' "

"I argued forcefully, [Terry pollster Harrison] Hickman argued forcefully, Squier argued forcefully," says Terry consultant Tom King. "The professionals were arguing, go negative. It got intense. We were banging away on him."

Goldman was starting to agree with them. But Goldman also decided to stall for time. He'd wait for another day's worth of tracking polls, maybe two days' worth, and then decide.

Meanwhile, Goldman and Bobby Watson cut a deal, one that solved a number of problems. Each of the three Democratic campaigns was supposed to contribute money to the joint campaign committee. The Wilder campaign had adamantly refused. Goldman didn't believe he needed the joint campaign's get-out-the-vote effort. Hell, he wanted the joint campaign to give *him* money so Wilder could buy more TV time. So the deal between Watson and Goldman was this: Watson would cut a radio spot attacking Chichester and the joint campaign committee would buy the time, so technically it wouldn't be a Wilder spot. In return, the Wilder campaign would pay the joint campaign committee $8,000 — the amount the committee had expected from Wilder anyway.

Goldman's interest in a counterattack was increasing. He helped Watson write and produce the spot. It opened with the sound of breaking glass and an announcer saying: "Everyone knows if you live in a glass house, you shouldn't throw stones." It then accused Chichester of hypocritically slinging mud at Wilder "when he himself is the only state legislator who has been fined for unfair business practices."

Finally, Goldman decided to make his own negative spot. He went to a nearby construction site, loaded up a bucket of dirt, poured water in it and mixed up a gooey batch of mud. He found a Wilder bumper sticker, pasted it on a board, got a cameraman. Then splat, he threw the mud on the Wilder sticker.

"Why is John Chichester throwing mud at Senator Wilder? The Norfolk *Virginian-Pilot* says it's because he's desperate. Two major newspapers in Richmond and Roanoke have refused to run his advertisements. Chichester is hoping his mudslinging will hide his own record, for he's the only statewide candidate to be fined by the SCC for unlawful business practice."

But while the other campaigns were warning Goldman that he had to go negative or lose the election, he was getting exactly the opposite advice from Robb and his staff. "Stoddart got to the point, he'd answer the phone and say 'No, no negatives,' " Goldman says.

"Paul was very divided in his own mind," Stoddart said. "Paul said this is a Catch-22. Either we stay positive and get clobbered or go negative and if people react negatively, we lose the race."

Regardless, Robb's advice was firm. Stay positive. Don't hit back.

Goldman kept running the polling numbers through his mind. It wasn't simply a matter of looking at the polls and figuring out how many undecided voters were left; you had to first consider the poll's presumptions. Specifically, what percentage of voters on Election Day were going to be black? In 1981, when the black turnout was considered large, 15 percent of the voters were black. In 1985, there was a black candidate on the ticket but little had been done — outside of Richard Dickerson's last-minute GOTV campaign — to organize the black vote. So what would it be? Most Democratic strategists were looking at 15-16 percent and putting their polls together on that basis. "It ended up being 14 percent," Goldman says. "If they'd known that, they'd have demanded the negative." As it was, pollsters were warning that even if 16 percent of the voters were black, they could project no better than a 50-50 split. "It'll go right down to the money," Terry pollster Harrison Hickman said.

It was a rainy Tuesday night in Roanoke, a city Wilder seemed to be spending a lot of time going in and out of as the campaign wound down. The Sixth District, the old mountain-valley Republican district, was now the state's premier swing district. And the neighboring Ninth District of Southwest Virginia was where Wilder needed a big turnout among straight-ticket Democrats to offset deficits elsewhere.

Wilder was scheduled to speak at a Democratic dinner before going home to Richmond. At the head table, Wilder sat next to lawyer John Edwards, the city's Democratic chairman. "He turned to me," Edwards says, "and said, 'I've been getting a lot of advice to go negative. What do you think?'" Edwards was aghast. "Don't do it," he implored. "That would ruin you." Wilder said that's what he thought, too.

After dinner, Wilder was mobbed. But the plane he needed to catch was a commercial flight and he had to pull himself away before everyone had a chance to shake his hand.

As state Sen. Granger Macfarlane sped Wilder to the airport, he tried to reassure the candidate. "Doug, I've talked to a lot of people and you're doing fine. Just keep it up through Tuesday."

Wilder seemed pessimistic. "Who's telling you that? Your friends?"

'No, other people," Macfarlane said. "I've been asking around." But just don't hit back, Macfarlane urged.

Wilder agreed, but acknowledged the uncertainties. The word he used was "patsy." If he didn't hit back, would he look like a patsy who didn't have any counter-arguments?

"You're doing fine, you're doing fine," Macfarlane counseled. "Just keep to the high road."

Macfarlane got the airport with time to spare. Wilder leaned against the airline counter and waited. "I just grit my teeth," he said. "And Paul, I have to hold him in. You know he wants to hit back. I'll always wonder. I always will."

Oct. 30, 1985

Maybe it wasn't politics but social graces that tugged at Virginians' consciences.

Virginia is a conservative state — but also a polite one. Under ordinary circumstances, Virginians would have been quick to vote against a black candidate. But now that Wilder was leading in all the polls, Virginia had shown it was indeed ready to elect a black. To back off now would be a social gaffe that would expose Virginians as rednecks and racists, something proper Virginians are quick to avoid. The only correct thing for Virginians to do now was to go ahead and elect him and get it over with and avoid the controversy of explaining why he was defeated.

Plus, there was the powerful lure of history. Virginians may have been starting to feel a tingle of excitement at the prospect of electing Wilder. Virginia is such a history-conscious state, but most of the things Virginians like to recall were a century or more old. Most of the recent history is rather embarrassing — Massive Resistance and all that. Now here was a rare chance to make history again — and what history it would be. In one day, Virginians could wipe away all the ugly stains of the past. Virginians could boast at how progressive and enlightened they were — and the beauty of it is, it's only for lieutenant governor. If Wilder turned out bad, he couldn't do too much harm. Perhaps some Virginians could not resist the urge to do what their forefathers did and *make history*.

But the history-making was still a week away. And a week can be a long time in politics.

Wilder was back in Richmond. Whenever anyone came into his law office — and by now the finely appointed lobby of Wilder's office was a virtual revolving door of politicians — Wilder took them into the meeting room in the back, turned on the VCR, showed them the mudslinging spot Goldman had prepared and asked what they thought.

"The bulk of the people said 'run 'em,' " says Michael Brown. " 'You ought to do it. Fire back at Chichester.' "

Wilder went to see Robb. "Doug came in to see me and said 'we're all ready to go [with negative TV],' " Robb says. The governor was horrified. "I said, 'Don't do it. You've got the election. It's a very volatile situation.' "

"If he popped off just once, he'd have lost the election," Robb says. "I'm very skeptical of negative advertising, but in this particular election especially."

Robb says Wilder gave him the clear impression he favored running the negative spots; the way Robb describes it, he was practically begging Wilder not to run them.

While Wilder was giving Robb the impression he was determined to fire off his TV rounds at Chichester, he seemed more reflective to those back in his law office. "The senator took a lot of time," Brown says. "He listened to all the arguments. It wasn't Paul's decision, it wasn't Mike's decision, it wasn't Jay's decision. It was Wilder's decision. Paul argued until he was blue in the face."

Wednesday afternoon, a Richmond radio station obtained part of the final Mason-Dixon poll, always the most Republican-leaning of the public polls: Baliles was up 48-39, Wilder 41-40, Terry 42-39.

In Wilder headquarters, the new poll numbers did little to make things clearer. Eventually, the whole confused scene came down to nine men standing around the TV in the meeting room, studying the mudslinging spot.

Wilder stepped out of the room while the others watched the spots so he wouldn't influence them. Then came the debate.

Shropshire and Wilder's law partner, Roger Gregory, were the strongest for not using the negatives. "We looked at 'em twice," Shropshire remembers. "They were good spots, but that would have propelled all the editorial writers to say he was just like all the others. It would have taken that issue away from Wilder."

Wilder also felt going negative was wrong, even if it worked. "I kept thinking about [former U.S. Sens.] Bill Scott and Bill Spong and who I would rather be. In this campaign, there was no question who I'd rather be. I have to tell people who Bill Scott is, while Spong's reputation is renowned." (Scott, of course, used a last-minute TV blitz of negative ads to upset Spong in 1972.)

The meeting broke up with no formal decision. But the sentiment — not to use Goldman's mudslinging spot — was clear.

Goldman wouldn't take no for an answer, though. He had until Friday noon to decide. He wanted to see another day's worth of tracking polls.

Oct. 31, 1985

Chuck Nichollson came by Wilder's home that morning to have breakfast before they went on the road to Tidewater. While Nichollson was waiting, Jay Shropshire called. Nichollson told him Wilder was still in the shower, to call back later. In a few minutes, Shropshire called again. Wilder was still upstairs.

"Who was that who called?" Wilder asked when he finally came downstairs.

"Jay," Nichollson said.

Wilder smiled. "Guess he's a little nervous, huh?"

Who wasn't at this point? Wilder seemed calm, but his questions over breakfast seemed to betray the debate going on his own mind. "Did I ever say anything to you about going negative?" Wilder asked.

No, Nichollson said, wondering what was coming next.

Wilder seemed almost to be talking to himself. "That's what I've been trying to tell everybody."

He asked Nichollson what he thought.

Nichollson chose his words carefully. "It would be a shame if you lost because of negatives," he said. Wilder nodded. He seemed to like that answer.

By Thursday afternoon, Goldman was dragging. "I had been up two straight days, two-three hours sleep a night." He kept sniffling back a cold he felt coming on, hoping it wouldn't be worse. He was on the phone to Stoddart a couple of times a day. "No," Stoddart kept saying. "No, negatives." Then Goldman would call the other campaigns and get the opposite advice.

Finally, Goldman called Bob Squier in Washington. Squier already had studio time booked that night and was itching to make a negative spot for Wilder. At last, Goldman gave in. He wasn't ready to commit to using it, but at least he'd have it ready. The final tracking polls were due later that night. "If they showed deterioration, I could go back to Doug and demand the negative," Goldman says. He and Squier wrote the spot over the phone, attacking Chichester for his SCC fine.

Wilder's day ended with a $50-per-person Halloween night fund-raiser in Newport News. Robb staffers cite this as the final example of the governor's office saving Wilder from embarrassment. The fund-raiser had been scheduled long before but, without anyone in Wilder headquarters to supervise it, little if anything had been done. "We had about two days to turn it around," says Carolyn Moss.

Despite the late and bungled start, the event came off beautifully. And while the Robb staffers privately shook their heads at the Wilder campaign's incompetence, Wilder sparkled. "If there were any doubters, they came to see that night," says Del. Alan Diamonstein, D-Newport News. "Wilder was very well received. He put a lot of himself into the campaign and it showed that night."

Thursday night came and the tracking polls Goldman had been waiting for hadn't come in yet. Wilder had just gotten back into the office from the fund-raiser at Newport News and was busy signing thank-you notes to contributors. Wilder was absorbed in his task and wasn't paying much attention to Goldman pacing around his office, talking up the negative spot he had written with Squier. "Paul was hammering away at him for forty-five minutes. 'Let me show 'em to you,' " Brown remembers. "The senator said no. We're not going to run 'em. He was in control. He was not in the hands of a political consultant." Eventually, Goldman gave up — for tonight, anyway. He stomped off downstairs and left Wilder signing thank-you notes.

About 11 p.m., Squier called to say the spot was done and he was ready to ship it out to the TV stations. Goldman gave him the news: Wilder had vetoed it. Squier was disappointed but understood. What should we do with all the spots then? he asked. "I said 'send 'em to me,' " Goldman says. "Doug wanted all the copies, but I said, 'You keep some.' In the back of my mind, I was thinking I might need 'em yet." Squier said he'd put the spots on the Greyhound bus to Richmond that night.

Across town at Baliles headquarters, Bobby Watson and Larry Framme had a funny feeling they were about to be cheated. The "breaking glass" radio spots that Watson and Goldman had written were scheduled to start tomorrow. The joint campaign committee had already paid for the air time. But Goldman had yet to send Watson the check he had promised. Without the money from the Wilder campaign, there wouldn't be money in the bank to cover all the checks the joint campaign had written.

Watson got on the phone to Goldman. Where's the money? he wanted to know. Goldman was evasive. Wilder doesn't want to do the negative radio spots, he said. But what about the money? Watson asked. And then they went 'round and 'round.

"When Watson got off the phone, you could tell he had been through the ringer," Framme says.

But Watson had at least wrung one concession out of Goldman. He would be at the Greyhound station about 2 a.m. If you want your check, come get it then.

Framme had to go home that way anyway so he agreed to follow Watson to the bus station — moral support so the slippery Goldman would be outnumbered.

Watson and Framme walked through the desolate bus station, their heels clicking on the tiles. They laughed nervously among themselves. What in the world were they doing in a bus station in the middle of the night?

They looked for Goldman but couldn't find him.

Eventually they found Goldman back in the baggage express. He was hunched over a big stack of boxes, filling out forms. Goldman had decided to ignore Wilder's orders about Squier's negatives and was going to send them out to the TV stations anyway with instructions not to use them unless he gave the word. Goldman mumbled something and ignored Watson and Framme until he was finished filling out all his forms.

"Then," as Watson remembers it, "there was this long, tedious process of avoiding the subject and beating around the bush."

Framme could barely stifle a laugh as he watched Watson and Goldman fence with each other.

Watson's demand was plain: He wanted the money and he wanted it *now*. "I can't have these checks bouncing all over Virginia," he said.

Goldman shrugged. Wilder didn't want the spot run. "Tell 'em you're not going to do it," he said. "It's no big deal."

Watson was furious. He couldn't cancel the spots on this short notice. A long argument followed.

"I want the money tonight," Watson said. "I want to put it in a night deposit tonight."

The conversation went on and on. Goldman was wearing down. Finally, he gave up and said he'd pay Watson the money. Watson should meet him up at the law office in a few minutes.

Goldman, meanwhile, went to a pay phone and called Wilder at home. The candidate was still up.

"Look, I'm exhausted," Goldman says. "I don't want to argue with Watson anymore. Let's give him the $8,000. I'm beat."

On the other end of the phone, Wilder laughed as he pictured his bedraggled consultant haggling with Watson. Go ahead and pay Watson, Wilder said, but cancel those radio commercials immediately.

It was maybe 3 a.m., 3:30 a.m. by the time Watson and Goldman finally got back to the law office. "We were all exhausted," Watson says. "We talked about a lot of things that weren't necessary at this hour. It was stalling for time on his part."

Finally Goldman rummaged through Wilder's safe, produced a signed, blank check the candidate had left him for emergencies and started to write it. But he wrote the amount in the "pay to the order of" blank.

Goldman laughed weakly as he tore it up. "This is the last check."

Watson threatened him again. "Your life won't be worth a plug nickel."

Goldman grinned and found another check. This one he made out correctly. Then they both started laughing and Goldman played the negative spot Squier had just sent him.

Nov. 1, 1985

About 7 a.m., Goldman called state Sen. Granger Macfarlane in Roanoke. Macfarlane was still asleep but that didn't stop Goldman from launching into a mile-a-minute explanation of why Wilder needed to respond to Chichester's house commercial.

"How do you intend to respond?" Macfarlane asked.

"We've cut some spots," Goldman said. "I'd like for you to take a look at 'em."

Macfarlane was still groggy. Goldman said the spots were already on the way, in fact they should be at the bus station by now.

Del. Benjamin Lambert stopped by Wilder's home before he went to his optometric office that morning. The night before Lambert had been out in rural Goochland County, where he had spoken for Wilder at a meeting of local blacks. Lambert had collected $300 for the Wilder campaign and now he came by to deliver the money.

Wilder was relaxed and confident as he let Lambert in, but there was a seriousness to his voice.

"You better get ready to run for my seat," Wilder told him. Throughout the fall, friends had been asking Lambert whether he would run for the state Senate if Wilder won. Lambert hadn't paid much attention to the talk. Now Lambert was taken aback.

"You really mean that, Doug?" he asked. Lambert wasn't asking as much whether Wilder thought Lambert should run as whether Wilder really thought he was going to win.

"Yes, I really mean it," Wilder said. "There's no way Chichester can beat me. If I were you, I'd get myself ready to make some sort of announcement."

Macfarlane went to Roanoke's Channel 7 to look at the TV commercials. The engineers put the first spot up on the monitor. Macfarlane thought it was awful. "Let's see it again," he said. The TV people played it again. "All right, let's see the other one," Macfarlane said. It was just as bad.

Macfarlane got on the phone to Goldman. "I think it's a mistake," Macfarlane told him. "You've come so far and the candidate made a strong promise not to run a negative campaign.

"Then we had this long conversation," Macfarlane remembers. "Paul repeated the advice he had been getting and I'd repeat what I'd just said. That it would have been suicidal to run those commercials. It was just out of character. The opposition would have had three to four days to say, 'I told you so. Put him under pressure and see what happens? He cracks.'"

Goldman said he'd call back — and left Macfarlane waiting at the TV station.

The tracking polls Goldman had been waiting for since last night had finally arrived. They were inconclusive: Wilder was still holding in the high forties. Chichester was somewhere in the thirties and coming on strong. And the undecideds were all people unlikely to vote for Wilder. But maybe some could be persuaded to vote *against* Chichester . . .

Goldman saw a problem with the polls, though. "The problem was the 16 percent black vote. That bothered me. What if it was only 13 percent black? Or it could be 20 percent like the *Post* said. Who knows? It had some of the earmarkings of a classic collapse at the end."

Goldman showed Wilder the negative spot Squier had done. By now, both Wilder and Goldman were laughing as they argued back and forth on the same subject they'd been over and over all week. Finally, Wilder said: "Look, I'm not going to do it. If I lose, I'll tell everybody you wanted to run the negative commercials and I wouldn't let you. We've been taking the punches so long, don't you think I'd like to say something? We've come this far, let's go with the positive message. It'll work out. I feel it."

Goldman was still angling to run the negative. "You have to make the decision now," he said. The TV deadline was now only minutes away.

"Good," Wilder laughed, slapping Goldman on the back. "You won't have to worry about it anymore."

It was about 11:50 a.m. when Goldman finally called Macfarlane, still waiting at the TV station in Roanoke. "The TV guys were saying we gotta close the books, you gonna use it or not?" Goldman recalls. He told Macfarlane the word from Wilder was no.

Macfarlane was relieved. "I think you made the right decision," he said.

The hands of the clock swept past 12 and headed into the afternoon. For better or worse, the TV spots were set from here to Tuesday. Goldman got on the phone and called all the people who'd been giving him advice.

With less than ninety hours left before the polls opened at 6 a.m. Tuesday, the campaign was now finally, and irrevocably, out of Goldman's hands. For the first time since he had arrived in Richmond last December, there was nothing he could do to influence the outcome. No more TV spots to cut, no more TV time to buy, no more issues to float in the press. Wilder was flying out of town this afternoon for the traditional campaign's-end round of appearances with the ticket in Southwest Virginia, so even the candidate would be gone. In other campaign headquarters, the GOTV machinery was gearing up, but Goldman wasn't the least bit interested in that. For him, the campaign was over and he could only mark time between now and Tuesday night. The campaign was on automatic pilot, rushing headlong toward Election Day.

"Friday afternoon I just sat there," Goldman says. "A lot of reporters were calling for their Sunday stories" so he talked to them. And soon the figures from the poll the *Times-Dispatch* would publish Sunday were floating around town, which gave Goldman some numbers to crunch, though there was precious little now that could be done about them. On the surface, the poll was encouraging, but actually mirrored the tracking polls that had the Terry consultants convinced Wilder was headed for defeat unless he gave one-third of the undecideds some reason to vote against Chichester:

Baliles 45; Durrette 40
Wilder 45; Chichester 36
Terry 50; O'Brien 31

In other quarters, too, confidence in Wilder's ability to pull it out was starting to wane. State Sen. Buzz Emick, D-Botetourt County, always a cynic, gave a reporter this off-the-record assessment Friday afternoon: "Doug Wilder is my friend and I'm sorry to see him lose. I think John Chichester has run a sorry-ass campaign and when I see him in January, I'm going to tell him that. I'm going to tell him he ran a sorry campaign and he didn't deserve to win."

Virginia tradition dictates that candidates spend the last weekend of the campaign in the hollows of Southwest Virginia, bouncing from one noisy rally to another — with both parties trying to outdo the other and make their rally the biggest one in town. So Friday afternoon, reporters started converging on Southwest Virginia. The forecast wasn't good: the clouds hung low, wrapping themselves around the mountains and drizzling on the valleys below. There was a question whether the helicopters would even be able to fly in this weather. Maybe both parties' entourages would have to travel by car, a queasy thought for anyone familiar with Southwest Virginia's mountain roads.

Before he left, Wilder went to a "homecoming" in Richmond at the Flamingo Lounge, traditional meeting place of the city's Crusade for Voters, a black voters' group. "We're going to win," Wilder told the cheering crowd. "It was very emotional," Nichollson remembers. "People were crying."

Nov. 2, 1985

The first in the long series of Ninth District rallies started at noon Saturday in Radford. The crowd that packed into the courtroom was one hundred-strong and loud.

The biggest response was for Wilder, now the sentimental favorite. "He got a standing ovation," recalls state Sen. Madison Marye. "For the others they stood politely, but he got a standing ovation. There was that much excitement."

From Radford, the Democrats went on to Pulaski for more of the same. At last, the Democrats felt comfortable talking about their diverse ticket. "This ticket is part of Virginia's renaissance," Baliles told the cheering Pulaski crowd. "I don't just read history, I make it."

After Pulaski came Wythe County — with three hundred Democrats shoehorned into Fort Chiswell High School. Rep. Rick Boucher said the crowd was one of the biggest he'd ever seen in that Republican county. Then it was on to Marion, where the courtroom was so crowded not everyone could get inside. A bluegrass band played, the twang of Southwest Virginia was in the air and Doug Wilder was getting nostalgic. "While the others were on vacation, we were out walking and driving across this state," he said. "There was those who said when he went out there . . . they predicted woe, said he was going down there and he might never come out." The audience laughed and Wilder laughed along with it.

Back in Richmond, Wilder's law office was filling up with volunteers for the first time in the campaign. In the campaign's one attempt at organization, Wilder wanted to make sure he had his own supporters out working the polls in Richmond on Election Day. It was up to Michael Brown to organize them.

The last week of the campaign, sometimes it seemed like the whole neighborhood was coming in, volunteering to help. Brown remembers the scene: "People were coming in, saying, 'I need bodies in this area,' 'Can you do this?' 'Where's the staple gun?' Dwayne Yancey's on the line. Dale Eisman's on the line. This TV reporter wants an interview. The Swedish press is calling, the English press. Party people are calling up. The candidate is tired. His nerves have become frayed. Everything's bugging him."

Meanwhile, as Baliles strategists went over the polling numbers that weekend, their confidence in a Wilder upset began to ebb. "At the very end, because of the margin of error and the undecideds, two things had to happen or Doug would lose," says deputy campaign manager Sandy Bowen. "One, he had to take a large percentage of the undecided vote or we had to have a record-breaking GOTV. Well, we knew it would not be a record-breaking GOTV, even though it was a first-class effort."

With that in mind, Baliles consultant David Doak gave Goldman this analysis: If 15 percent or less of the voters on Election Day are black, then Wilder will lose. If blacks account for 16 percent or more of the voters, then Wilder will win. That's how close he would be cutting things.

In Chichester headquarters, the mood was still upbeat, but an uncomfortable darkness was beginning to seep in. "It never dawned on me" that Chichester might lose, says Harvey Gulley, the campaign's press secretary. "I began to worry about ten days out that we had some serious problems." But he put them out of his mind. Sure, Chichester had had a tough time getting his message out. Nevertheless, Gulley says, "I'd have given you 9-1 odds or better that the undecideds would break for Chichester."

But Saturday night Gulley had dinner with a campaign worker from Tidewater who broke the news: Chichester was in deep, deep trouble. "He told me that unless something changed radically within four days' time" it was all over. Gulley didn't believe it. He couldn't believe it.

In Durrette headquarters, it was now every man for himself. This was the ultimate irony for the GOP. It was the Republicans who had pledged to run a ticket-oriented campaign, one for all, all for one, and now it was the Durrette campaign that felt dragged down by its running mates while Baliles was basking in the same history-making glow as Wilder and Terry.

At 5:30 p.m., the Democratic caravan arrived at Abingdon High School. "That last week so many of the candidates looked tired," says Fred Parker, the Washington County Democratic chairman. "Doug Wilder didn't look tired, though. He looked like he was just starting."

Just as he had been in Radford and Pulaski and Wythe County and Marion, it was Wilder who was the favorite of the 350 or so Democrats at the Abingdon High School cafeteria for a hot dog dinner. "All got a standing ovation, but his response was much warmer," says Kurt Pomrenke, the Bristol Democratic chairman. Many Democrats "felt Jerry had been terribly upstaged," Parker says.

Earlier in the day, Northern Virginia car dealer Don Beyer Jr. had bumped into a *Washington Post* reporter who hinted that the poll coming out in Sunday's paper would be a surprise to Democrats. Beyer knew that could mean only one thing — bad news. Baliles' Northern Virginia organizer was so worried about what the poll would say that he drove into D.C. that night to the Post building, to wait outside until the first edition came off the press about 11 p.m. "My heart was in my throat as I walked up to the stand," Beyer says. The poll was there on the front page. It was a surprise all right, but this was the kind Beyer liked.

"2 Democrats widen leads in Va. races"

The *Post* poll in early October had been laughed at because it showed such huge Democratic leads, but now they were even larger:

Baliles 56; Durrette 37
Wilder 58; Chichester 34
Terry 61; O'Brien 29

Beyer was ecstatic as he drove back to Falls Church. "I was so excited, I got on the phone at midnight and called people I thought would still be up."

But there was one figure in the poll he missed, a figure that threw the whole thing off. The *Post's* sample was 20 percent black.

The crowds got larger and louder as the Democrats moved deeper into the Southwest. In the day's finale at Honaker in Russell County, five hundred noisy Democrats turned out for speeches, dinner and country music.

When the rally was over, Wilder went back to Abingdon to spend the night with state Sen. Jim Jones. The rest of the entourage spent the night in Lebanon. After they had filed their stories, a handful of reporters sent word to Terry that they'd be waiting for her in the lobby if she wanted to come down and chat. Somewhat to their surprise, the candidate joined them.

"I just got off the phone with my pollster and we're in good shape," she announced, smiling, when she arrived.

"What about Doug?" someone asked.

'Doug's going to be all right," she said. "Doug's going to be all right."

Nov. 3, 1985

Mike Musick, the University of Virginia student who had been Wilder's advance man for the first leg of the tour back in August, was one of the drivers in the Democratic caravan the final weekend. His job Sunday morning was to pick Wilder up at Jim Jones' home and take him to the airport, where helicopters would brave the fog between there and Grundy, the first stop of the day.

Wilder came bounding down the steps, said his goodbyes to his hosts and climbed into the van. Musick barely had time to say anything before an animated Wilder launched into a monologue:

"You know, Mike, it's going well." Wilder said. "I said, 'I'm so tickled that they're saying you're ahead.' He grinned real big and said, 'I am ahead and you know, people are gonna hear that I'm ahead and they're going to vote for me. It's solid. I feel it.' " Musick noticed that Wilder was clenching his fist, not in anger, but in expectation. "Yes, I really am ahead," Wilder said. "Early on, they tried to brand me as a liberal and I dared them to make it stick."

The Republicans began the last Sunday in Weber City, a small town in

Scott County on the Tennessee line. There was brave talk of momentum and a last-minute rush to the Republican ticket "unlike anything I've ever seen before," Durrette told forty-five early-morning supporters. But the Republicans' underlying frustration was evident.

"Certainly, it has been a difficult campaign," Chichester told the crowd. "It's been tough to discuss the issues, to talk about his softness on crime and capital punishment. They say he'd be a heartbeat away from the governor's chair and the press says it's a racial appeal." Then Chichester switched to the past tense, as if the campaign were already over: "It was like running into a brick wall."

There were maybe five hundred people jammed into the high school gym at Grundy. Once again, the loudest cheers were for Wilder. This last swing through the coalfields was a homecoming of sorts for him. "Everybody was waiting for Doug to come back," Musick says.

Wilder did not disappoint them. "I know something's going to happen on Tuesday and I can't wait," he told the cheering throng.

Privately, Terry told reporters at Grundy: "We've all been excited for so long that you wouldn't let yourself say certain things. Now we're beginning to let ourselves feel happy."

And Wilder was happiest of all. For all of his inner passion, though, his speeches that weekend were models of restraint. As an editorial writer, G.C. Morse of the *Virginian-Pilot* was under no constraints of objectivity and didn't mind haranguing the politicians he disagreed with or encouraging the ones he did. Once on the final swing through the Southwest, Morse went up to Wilder and urged him to really fire up the next crowd. "Give 'em hell, give 'em a real ringer," Morse said. Wilder shook his head no. "It was very clear what he was doing," Morse said. "He was coming over very calmly, but with some feeling." The pitch was the nearness of history. Wilder needed only to point that out, not shout it.

While the Democratic tour was taking on all the aura of triumphal procession — loud cheers for Robb, the man who led them out of the wilderness, louder still for the prospect of making history in Jerry Baliles' New Dominion — the Republican tour was more like a death march through enemy territory. The fog that invigorated the Democrats and made their final swing seem such a playful adventure wrapped around the Republicans like a damp, gray shroud. The Democrats braved the weather with helicopters. The more conservative Republicans were grounded, forced to ride over slick and winding mountain roads that became ever more dreadful as they inched deeper into the coalfields.

Chichester found that last weekend the most trying in the whole awful campaign. He knew he was going to lose, yet here he had to parade himself before the cheering crowds, in the rain, in the fog, in Democratic country. He felt trapped — by the mountains, by his manager, by tradition itself. He desperately wanted to break out and do his own thing. But he couldn't, especially not now. It was too late. All he could do was go through the motions and it was so useless. "The worst thing was going out to Southwest Virginia," he says. "Somehow the Democrats have talked us into going into Southwest Virginia, their own back yard, the last weekend, when we'd better spend that weekend in another area with more media."

From Richlands, the Democratic candidates flew on to Big Rock for lunch at the home of a local coal baron. By 4:30, the Democrats were airborne again. Parts of the day were oddly sunny when the helicopters would break out of the clouds and the sun would shine down on the mountains. Other parts were pure drizzle. From Big Rock to Big Stone Gap, the helicopters were in and out of the clouds, the worst yet. Sometimes the helicopters would lose sight of each other as they disappeared into the gray mist. Near Big Stone Gap, the choppers ran into a nasty spot of rain that pelted them like stones.

Wilder didn't seem to be bothered by the rain, though. His thoughts were far away as he peered out the windows. Rob Eure of the *Roanoke Times & World-News* noticed Wilder's excitement even in his silence and asked him about it. Wilder rubbed the palm of his left hand on the back of his right hand. "This," he said, looking down at his black skin and then back up at Eure, "means nothing. It's the qualifications."

It was nearly 5 p.m., dark and dank, when the Democrats' little air force came buzzing over Big Stone Gap. When the helicopters tried to land, the pilots found the clouds had sunk nearly all the way to the ground.

Soon afterward the Democrats decided they would go by ground to the last stop, in Clintwood.

The crowd at the Big Stone Gap Armory was the biggest yet, maybe six hundred people in all. It also was the loudest. People had driven in from neighboring Lee and Scott counties, the first two counties on Wilder's summer itinerary. This was Wilder's real homecoming. "I think those people particularly turned out in such large numbers because Doug started campaigning here," says Ninth District Chairman Jack Kennedy. "They took pride. Here we were forty-eight hours before the polls opened and it all started and ended here."

One local politician exhorted the crowd with typical Fightin' Ninth frenzy. "We're going to beat the hell out of the Republicans," he exclaimed, emphasizing the "hell" so much it startled even the reporters. "Those Republicans have put on ads so negative they're libelous."

Even the cautious Baliles seemed excited here as he urged Democrats not to be lulled by favorable polls and discouraged by bad weather: "When the Baliles-Wilder-Terry ticket was nominated last June, people in the ivory towers said that fog will envelop that ticket. They were preaching gloom and doom. But on Tuesday, we're going to break through that cloud into the sunshine of victory."

It was 7 p.m. by the time the final rally, at Clintwood Elementary School, got started — with a prayer that rivalled the political speeches for attention. "One of these old Primitive Baptist preachers came out in the middle of the floor, got on his knees, humbled himself and started talking to his God," recalls Glenn Craft, the Wise County Democratic chairman. "It sounded like a sermon. It went on for ten or twelve minutes."

As soon as the speeches were over at Clintwood, the candidates were gone. Baliles and Terry flew off to Roanoke, where they'd begin the final day of the campaign Monday morning. Wilder and Robb flew back to Richmond.

And still the rain fell.

Nov. 4, 1985

On the day before an election Chichester supposedly could not could lose, a sense of doom settled over his headquarters like a pall. "I felt fine right up until Monday morning, about 8:30 or 9," Gulley says. He was greeted by word around the office that some polling data that had come in over the weekend didn't look good. "I went in and somebody grinned and said, 'I got a feeling this is going to be embarrassing,'" he recalls.

Dennis Peterson tried to keep the staff's spirits up but it wasn't easy. His brave talk could only depress them more. "We're going to surprise some experts tomorrow," Peterson was telling reporters who called for last-day stories. That was how far things had come — now it was Chichester's campaign that was talking about surprising the experts with an "upset."

"Let's face it," Gulley says. "The impossible had happened. We were on the bridge of a ship that was going down."

Meanwhile, the candidate was, quite literally, in deeper water. Chichester was supposed to spend Monday making his flying "Victory Tour," barnstorming in a series of Western Virginia cities — conveniently, all with TV stations — in a last-minute effort to rally the mountain-valley Republicans. But the weather out west was still foul and getting fouler. The "Victory Tour" never got beyond Bristol. All flights were grounded in the heavy rain, now in its fifth day. Chichester, if he wanted to get home at all, would have to leave his plane there and come back for it later. His only way out Monday morning was a rental car. So along with his wife, Karen, and brother Richard, Chichester started the long, dreary ride back home. Actually, they could only drive as far as Charlottesville, because there wasn't a place to return the Budget car in Fredericksburg. His other brother, Dan, would have to meet him there.

"It was terrible," Chichester says of the ride back, "but when you're in a situation like that, you're just glad for it to be over. I knew in two days, I could stay in bed in the morning or come home at 5 p.m."

In Richmond, Sue Fitz-Hugh, secretary of the state Electoral Board, had just come to work at 8:30 a.m. Monday when she got a call from the registrar in Nelson County, near Charlottesville. "She said they had been put on an alert. That registrar wanted to close her office and walk out the door." Fitz-Hugh tried to discourage her from doing anything rash until she could call Emergency Services to find out what was going on. Emergency Services didn't know anything about any emergency being declared, though. But then other calls started coming in, a trickle at first, then finally a flood.

Wilder spent the last day of the campaign in his law office, calling friends he had made around the state and offering last-minute encouragement. Baliles and Terry, though, set off on the traditional "fly-around" to the major media markets. As the two candidates finished their first stop in Roanoke and headed for the airport, the rain was coming down so hard that water was coming up through the manhole covers.

There were long delays at the airport as the pilots waited for a hole to the storm. The planes carrying the candidates eventually taxied down the runway and disappeared into the storm, although not many people could find the hole the pilots were supposed to have been waiting for.

Not long after the planes were airborne, it looked like someone had suddenly turned the faucet on full blast. The clouds ripped open and dumped their full load.

Three inches fell in just two hours, but the storm wasn't over yet. In all, more than 6 inches of rain pounded the Roanoke Valley. The ground, already soaked from four straight days of rain, couldn't handle it.

The flood of '85 — one of the worst in Virginia's history — had begun.

"I was sure by 10 a.m. we had a serious situation," says the Electoral Board's Fitz-Hugh.

By 1 p.m. it was a full-fledged crisis. Fitz-Hugh didn't quite realize how much of one, though, until the registrar in Salem called. She had just been evacuated. "I said, 'Did you get the voter list out?' She said 'no.' I said, 'We'll have to get the National Guard to bring you one.'" Soon the computers started the hour-long process of printing out a new roster of Salem voters.

Meanwhile, calls were coming in from other registrars in other Western Virginia communities. "These people had panicked," Fitz-Hugh says. "It was a matter of calming them down. Yes, I know your polling place is under water, but we have to hold this election, even if you have to do it in someone's house. The National Guard will take officers of elections and equipment to polling places." But no, the Guard can't transport voters. In Roanoke, which had been hit the worst, three or four voting machines had been washed down river. The city didn't have enough paper ballots to make up for the loss. Fitz-Hugh told officials it was all right to photocopy ballots, provided they were all embossed with the official seal.

The law didn't say anything about moving polling places, but Fitz-Hugh took it on herself to give registrars the authority to set up new polling places if the old ones were under water. And from Roanoke to Rockingham County — virtually the whole Sixth District — lots of them were.

The flood was now roaring through the valleys of Western Virginia. In the Roanoke Valley, private helicopters were being pressed into service to pluck people off the roofs of stores and houses. Radio and TV stations already were reporting the flood's first fatality — a Salem rescue worker who had waded into water to help evacuate people and been swept away himself. Hours later, Joe Cunningham was found in a tree downstream — cold, wet, stunned but still very much alive. But before the day was over, twenty people would be drowned in Western Virginia.

In Richmond, Democratic worker Keech LaGrande was busy organizing Baliles' "homecoming," an outdoor event at his suburban home. About 4 p.m., she called Pat Michaels, the state climatologist.

How long would it be before it started raining in Richmond? she asked.

"Keech," he said, "you've got ninety minutes."

In Roanoke, Del. Chip Woodrum came home about 6:30 p.m. The Democrats' downtown headquarters had been flooded and he had spent the afternoon moving campaign supplies to a motel room on higher ground. But he still didn't know just how bad the flood had been. He found out when he heard on the kitchen radio that Del. Vic Thomas' grocery store had been washed away. The whole store!

"Jesus!" Woodrum shouted when he heard the news.

He got on the phone and called Thomas at home. "God, what happened, Vic? I heard about the store."

Thomas was calm, or perhaps simply stunned. "That's the least of my worries," he said. "I'm just glad to be alive."

Then he told Woodrum about how the waters from tiny Tinker Creek had risen so fast, he and some store workers had to climb onto the roof of his grocery to avoid being drowned. A Channel 7 helicopter, filming the flood for the evening news, heard the distress call over the police radios and swooped into the rescue. It took two trips to pluck everyone off the roof. Thomas was the last one off. Below him, he could see muddy water swirling around his beloved store, peeling off bricks as if they were paper. Not ninety seconds after Thomas was in the helicopter, his store collapsed into a heap and was no more.

Doug Wilder had spent the afternoon calmly shaking hands at two supermarkets in Richmond, one on Cary Street downtown, the other out in suburban Bon Air. "The reception was so good," Wilder recalls. "I picked those two in particular," because both the West End and South Richmond were notoriously conservative. "That's supposed to be some kind of bellwether."

Wilder didn't know about the weather out west, but his bellwether was telling him the political forecast was good.

"People were coming up to him saying, 'How are you Mr. Wilder?' " Chuck Nichollson says. "They were saying, 'You don't have to introduce yourself, I know who you are.' "

When Wilder finally tired of handshaking, he decided to go buy some groceries to have something to fix for supper when he got home. He was standing in the checkout line clutching his purchases when the cashier looked up and recognized him. "Are you Doug Wilder?" she asked. As soon as she asked it, another cashier and two bag boys clustered around him. Wilder asked if Nichollson could scrounge up four stray war cards in the car — the two cashiers and the two bag boys wanted his autograph. He happily signed the cards, paid for his groceries and carried them outside.

Back in the car, Wilder was euphoric. "Can you believe this?" he asked Nichollson as they rode to Baliles' homecoming. "We're going to win this thing."

The storm that climatologist Michaels had predicted hit right on time — and with incredible fury. All the lights went off in Baliles' neighborhood. Someone had brought generators, though, and the show went on.

The crowd chanted "We want Jerry!" Baliles spoke, to great applause. Then Robb. Now suddenly the crowd started chanting "We want Doug! We want Doug!" Wilder was a little embarrassed. This wasn't his party. He clambered onto the stage, waved to the crowd, flashed a double V-for-Victory sign and the crowd cheered louder still. Robb leaned over and asked Wilder if he wanted to speak. Wilder shook his head no and disappeared back into the crowd, surrounded by well-wishers. "I'll be just a minute," Wilder told his driver, but it took him another thirty to disengage himself from the crowd. People wouldn't let go of him. Wilder was a little worried. Even Doug Wilder knows better than to show up the head of the ticket at his own homecoming.

Paul Goldman hung around the law office Monday night, watching Michael Brown race about making last-minute preparations, until he finally realized there was nothing more he could do to affect the outcome of this campaign.

He'd wracked his mind, and wracked his body, for almost a year now, in pursuit of an impossible dream — to elect a black man in the state that was the capital of the Confederacy. Amazingly, he had come close. Wilder had intimidated his way to the nomination. Wilder had gone into the supposedly backward hollows of the Appalachian coalfields and come out a hero. Wilder had gone into the lion's den of the crusty old speaker of the house and been feted as one of the boys. For two months, Wilder had criss-crossed Virginia in a borrowed station wagon, with Goldman at his side, shaking hands, plotting strategy, lucking into a white Southern cop out of Central Casting to be in his TV commercials. And now here they were, on the brink of history. But Goldman knew the numbers as well as anyone, he knew them forward and backward, and he knew that the difference between 51 percent and 49 percent was oh, so slim and oh, so wide. And who knew which side of the brink they would be standing on tomorrow night?

16

Virginia Votes

Nov. 5, 1985

Beneath the blanket of night, not all of Virginia was sleeping. Beyond the Blue Ridge, the flood was still raging. In Roanoke, the floodwaters didn't crest until sometime after midnight and by then much of the valley was under water, swirling, angry water that carried cars, trucks, mobile homes, anything it could wash away. Power stations were under water and electricity was off in parts of town. At the *Roanoke Times & World-News,* workers were pumping water out of the pressroom while upstairs reporters listened to the police radios crackling with emergencies. They could hear the calls for houses that were burning down because fire trucks were blocked by floodwaters.

In Richmond, election chief Sue Fitz-Hugh was up all night, fielding calls from frantic western registrars. "Every time I laid my head down on the pillow, the phone rang," she says. "Finally, I stayed up because my husband wasn't getting any sleep." At 4 a.m., she remembers precisely, Republican lawyer Bill Hurd called. He was demanding a list of all the polling places that had been moved. Fitz-Hugh said she couldn't give him a complete list yet, that changes were still coming in. Instead, she offered to meet him at her office at 5:30 a.m. and give him a list. "Their lawyer proceeded to tell me he'd sue," she recalls. "I said, 'I'm sorry, I'm doing the best I can.'"

The black, vicious night faded to reveal gray, leaden clouds. No one was sure whether they had been wrung out or not. In Roanoke, radio stations were reading off lists of voting places that had been moved; the recitation sounded like a list of school cancellations on snow days. In Richmond, Jackie Epps, Wilder's valiant fund-raiser, woke up at 6 a.m. to find a light drizzle outside. When she arrived at Northside Richmond's Precinct 603 to vote, no one was there passing out literature for Wilder. Nor were any Wilder posters up. "I was frantic," she says.

Epps got to Wilder's law office a little after 7. Wilder's law partner, Roger Gregory was already there, handling the day's first crisis. Poll workers at one precinct near Azalea Mall had run out of Wilder posters. Gregory grabbed a bunch and was out the door.

Epps settled down behind the phone. Volunteers were filtering in, picking up posters and going back out. Soon there was constant traffic in and out. Before long, the Wilder campaign had run out of election day handouts. Epps took the last one, raced down to Copy Cat and ordered two thousand copies.

Richard Dickerson, the Democrats' get-out-the-vote commander, had his first crisis at 7 a.m. A sharp-eyed poll worker called in to report that Republicans at black precincts were passing out sample ballots that looked exactly like the Crusade for Voters sample ballots — but calling for a Durrette-Wilder-O'Brien ticket. The sample ballot, attributed to something called "Black PAC," was illegal under Virginia law because it didn't list an address or identify who its treasurer was. "Immediately you're calling around the state," Dickerson recalls. "'We've got illegal sample ballots, here's what to look for, alert the commonwealth's attorney.'" Dickerson walked a couple blocks down to the polling place at the downtown library and found a GOP poll worker handing them out. He took a copy, then raced away to Sue Fitz-Hugh's office to file a formal complaint. She had precincts washed away, still other precincts she couldn't even contact, and here was Dickerson, arguing over some silly sample ballot. But it wasn't silly to the Democrats' GOTV chief. Soon, he had lawyers gearing up for an injunction.

Chuck Nichollson arrived at Wilder's home in tree-lined Northside

Richmond at 7 a.m. for the final trip of the campaign — to the polls. At Precinct 304 at Northminster Baptist Church, the media were waiting and Wilder was mobbed. It was 7:30 a.m.

Afterward, Wilder had Nichollson drive him to the Aunt Sarah's Pancake House on Broad Street, where he was supposed to meet Jay Shropshire for breakfast. Wilder and Shropshire had planned this to be a private breakfast, but their table soon turned quite public. "Doug could hardly eat breakfast," Shropshire recalls. "All the waitresses kept coming up saying, 'We're with you.' Blue-collar people would come up and say, 'We haven't voted yet but we will.' "

Before long, Paul Goldman, still in his jogging suit, straggled in to join them. Goldman had been out running at the University of Richmond track, trying to kill time until tonight.

He ordered oatmeal.

Bobby Watson, the Democrats' executive director, went to vote, saw the long, discouraging lines in the heavily Republican suburb of Mechanicsville, and decided to come back later. Until then, he spent the morning riding around Richmond with Billy Hudgins, an old buddy from the Davis campaign. Watson had a phone in his car. A master of imitations, he couldn't resist calling up the Love Brothers — the drive-time show on EZS 104. Watson, in his best Southside drawl, identified himself as Mills Godwin and went through a side-splitting routine. "Ahm fed up with Wyatt Durrette," Watson said. "Ahm supporting the whole Democratic ticket," The DJs were loving it. "This is a hot flash," they laughed. "We'd better put this on the wire."

"Yessuh," Watson was saying. "I listen to you all all the time down here in Chuckatuck."

Watson and the DJs seemed to get a kick out of it. As Watson and Hudgins drove around, checking on polling places, they wondered if the Love Brothers would dare put the Godwin impersonation on the air. Watson figured they wouldn't. "Just then they came on and said, 'We're very fortunate, we've got Mills Godwin on the line.' Billy Hudgins was driving and he almost drove off the road" they were laughing so hard.

At Chichester headquarters, Dennis Peterson came in, hung up his coat and tried to rally the staff. "I think we're gonna kick a lot of hind ends today," he said hopefully.

It didn't work.

"About 10 a.m., I did not feel good about it," Harvey Gulley says.

The morning rush hour over, things settled down for the long midday lull. It was deceptively quiet. The Democrats' expensive GOTV machinery was starting to hum. At 9 a.m., the phone bankers started dialing and didn't quit until the polls were nearly closed. The calls were into black households and the pitch was hard for Wilder. "Governor Robb asked me to call. Doug Wilder's election looks very close and we need your help," was the standard line.

Even through the confusion of an election headquarters, the sense of history in the making was unavoidable. "We had a lot of blacks calling up our office for rides to the polls," remembers Debbie Oswalt, who ran the Democrats' GOTV push around Richmond. "That was funny, seeing some of our yuppie and suburban people with maps driving around Church Hill."

From the coast to the Cumberlands, Democrats and Republicans alike stood in front of schools, town halls, churches, sometimes private homes, shaking hands with voters, passing out literature, hoping for some last-second converts.

In precinct after precinct, it seemed to be the Democrats who were better organized and more excited. The Republicans were stumbling toward the end of a disappointing campaign. The Democrats were out to make history.

In Hanover County, the mood among Republicans was the same as the weather. "It was bad, real bad," says Montpelier insurance man Ron Steele. No one from Durrette headquarters had bothered to call Steele — one of the key GOP contacts in the county — about what he should do on Election Day. Steele called some of his GOP friends. None of them had been contacted, either. So he figured he was on his own. He, his wife and a neighbor gathered up some materials and went out to the Locust Creek precinct, just across the line in Louisa County. "Usually there's a barrage of Republicans [handing out literature] and nobody was there," Steele remembers. "I got a real cold feeling."

Fred Parker, the Democratic chairman in Washington County, saw the same phenomenon from the other side of the state. He spent the day going around the Abingdon-Bristol area, delivering coffee to Democratic poll workers. He made it to fifteen of eighteen precincts and encountered only one "incident." When he gave a sample ballot to one elderly woman he knew, she pulled him over to the side and asked: "Freddie, which one is the black guy?" And the way she said it, he knew there wasn't any point in trying to get her to change her mind.

But elsewhere, "even the Republicans knew what was coming," Parker says. At his home precinct of Ray Valley, "usually they're racing to give out sample ballots. It's really a competitive deal. This year they sat in their trucks or chairs all day. Their morale was really low."

In Buckingham County, Nellwyn Morris of Appomattox saw the Democrats' organizational strength firsthand.

At the firehouse in Arvonia, poll worker Morris greeted an elderly white woman who was coming into vote and reminded her to please vote for Watkins Abbitt Jr. for the House of Delegates.

'Is that Wat Sr.'s son?" the old woman asked.

'Yes," the poll worker said. She noticed the old woman straining to look down her hand. Something was written there. Watkins Abbitt Sr., the former Southside congressman, had called the old woman the night before to remind her who to vote for. To make sure she wouldn't forget, she had carefully written them out on her hand — Baliles, Wilder, Terry, Abbitt.

After breakfast at Aunt Sarah's, Wilder went to the law office and Jay Shropshire went to his Senate office. There, the Senate clerk went through his Election Day routine of calling constitutional officers around the state at 10, 2 and 5. "My mood that day, as of around noon, was good," Shropshire says. "People were calling me from areas where a black should not get a vote of any consequence, Southside, Southwest, and saying there was a big turnout that appeared to be Democratic."

The sense in the Democrats' GOTV headquarters was exactly the opposite, though.

For the Democrats there were three important times during the day — 10, 12 and 3, when they called around the state, compiled the latest turnout figures and compared them with '81. On the wall at the Terry/GOTV headquarters, the walls were covered with big charts listing the hour-by-hour '81 figures, with blanks to fill in the '85 comparisons. The 10 a.m. checks told Democrats all they needed to know. Turnout was way down, especially in black precincts. "It became apparent we had a problem," says Larry Framme, who headed the Democrats' joint campaign committee which was in charge of GOTV. "Flushers were not scheduled to hit the streets until noon, but we got them out early."

By 11 a.m., Richard Dickerson was deploying his troops. Riding shotgun, as it were, Dickerson rode the chartered bus out to Virginia Union University to pick up the students he had recruited and drop them off in their assigned neighborhoods. Dickerson's formula was for a team of ten people to scour each precinct. Once the flushers were off the bus, they fanned out, according to plan, knocking on doors, reminding voters it was Election Day, leaving leaflets on unanswered doors.

His foot soldiers in place, Dickerson was heading back to his command center when he went by a crowded black barbershop and decided to duck inside to remind the men to vote today.

Around noon, Larry Sabato went through his Election Day ritual, calling the campaign managers — all of them except Paul Goldman — to trade predictions.

"Everyone had kissed off Durrette and O'Brien," Sabato recalls. "The only question was, 'Can Wilder make it?' One of the Republican managers" — he won't say which one — "said to me, 'As far as I'm concerned, it's just a matter of how many racists there are in Virginia. Chichester has given no coherent reason to vote for him.' At that point, he practically indicated to me he had voted for Wilder."

Sabato, significantly revising his infamous 100-1 odds against a Wilder victory, was now privately predicting a Democratic sweep — Baliles with 54 percent, Wilder 51, Terry 57. Baliles campaign manager Darrel Martin was a tad more cautious and gave Baliles 53. But he declined to predict a margin for Wilder. "I refuse to do it," he told Sabato. "I've never felt comfortable saying Doug can win. It can go either way."

Sue Fitz-Hugh counted seventeen counties and cities where polling places had been moved or couldn't be opened on time because of the flood. In the Augusta County village of Deerfield and the Botetourt County village of Glen Wilton, election officials couldn't get to the polling place until 9 a.m. In the state's smallest precinct, Big Valley in Highland County, where there were all of thirty-six registered voters, election judges couldn't get in until noon. In other precincts, there was no electricity and voters cast their ballots by candlelight.

Then Fitz-Hugh was on her way to court. The Democrats had rounded up a judge to hear their argument against the Black PAC ballots. In a hearing at his home, he issued an injunction and the Democrats went away happy.

For John Chichester, Election Day was funereal, in more ways than one. A friend had been killed in an auto accident on Saturday and today he went to the funeral. Chichester had been advised to tour the state on Election Day to try to get some last-minute attention, but now his plane was grounded in Bristol and he wasn't interested anyway. At noon, he was at White Oak precinct in Stafford County, having a bowl of soup with campaign workers.

While Chichester waited grimly for the worst, the Wilder camp prepared for victory. Del. Benjamin Lambert stopped by Wilder's law office that afternoon to see how things were going. He found Wilder eating

Brunswick stew and pound cake a friend had brought him. Wilder and Lambert had a long talk about the election and the Richmond state Senate seat Wilder was sure he would soon vacate. "He was so confident, I really believed he was going to win," Lambert says. "He said, 'You ought to think about what you're going to do tonight when I win.' "

In the town of Wise, county Democratic Chairman Glenn Craft had spent the day standing out in the rain, passing out sample ballots and cajoling the undecideds. By 2 p.m., Craft was feeling good despite the chill. "People were responding and our turnout was good," he says. "A lot of the Republicans didn't come out. They felt they had nothing to vote for."

In Richmond, the mood was exactly the opposite. As the early afternoon turnout reports filtered into the Democrats' GOTV headquarters, they showed only 12 percent to 20 percent of the blacks registered to vote had been to the polls yet. Usually by this time, the turnout should be well above 20 percent, maybe as high as 25 percent.

The turnout figures meant only one thing: Doug Wilder was going to lose. Even the most generous estimates for how well he would do among white voters meant little if black voters didn't turn out in strength for him. No one could tell what white voters were doing in the privacy of the voting booth, but everyone studying the wall charts could see what black voters were doing. They weren't voting.

For the next two hours, the Democrats running the GOTV campaign, both for Richmond and the whole state, were in a panic. "That was a very grim couple of hours," recalls Baliles adviser Alan Albert. "The GOTV effort seemed to be disintegrating at that moment." All day the radio news had been reporting low turnout around the state. "But everything I saw in Richmond looked worse than what the public reports were," Albert says.

'It was scary, really hairy," Dickerson remembers. Not only that, but now he was running low on flushers, too. Some hadn't shown up to begin with, and others hadn't re-grouped when they were supposed to.

So Dickerson decided to go out and hire new flushers. He commandeered a van and headed out to Virginia Union University. "I was hiring people literally almost off the street," he says. "I hired twenty-five or thirty-five people right on the spot."

In mid-afternoon, Marian Tucker got a phone call from Michael Brown, the first time Norfolk's chief Democratic organizer had heard from the Wilder campaign all fall. Tucker laughs about the belated interest. "He wanted to know how things were going. I thought, nice of you to call."

Soon after Tucker got off the phone with Brown, Baliles consultant David Doak called, urgency in his voice.

"Doak calls and says black precincts are down from '81," says Marian Tucker. "I said oh? Well, maybe it's because we haven't seen any of the candidates? We never had anybody to energize it. We saw Wilder only twice and he never got close to the black community here. It would have helped if [Wilder] had done some churches. It would have turned people on."

But Doak wasn't in a mind to hear excuses, however valid. He wanted something done. Only four hours were left and if things kept on this way, Wilder would lose the election. Do something. Tucker, who had thrown everyone she had into GOTV, did the only thing she could. The Norfolk phone bank message had been a party pitch. Now she called and changed it to "Doug Wilder needs you to get out and vote." It wasn't much but what else could she do?

About 4 p.m., while Democrats in Richmond were scrambling to make sense of the latest turnout reports, Mike Musick, making the rounds in Russell County, arrived at Drill, a tiny precinct back in the hollows. Drill was an old coal mining town and reliably Democratic. "The numbers were heavy," Musick says. "That made me optimistic. Almost everybody who was expected to vote had voted." Cheered by this news, Musick began the long drive back to the courthouse to wait for the returns.

Richard Dickerson studied the latest reports. Black turnout was up to 24, 25, 27 percent in some areas. "We were getting calls from all around the state. I was so scared for an hour and a half. Then at 4, I saw the numbers coming up," he says. "In my heart of hearts, I felt we were OK. The big vote is from 5 to 7. If we were at 24 percent at 4 p.m., we'll be OK."

Reports were now coming in every half hour. Dickerson was on and off the phone, redirecting sound trucks, redirecting flushers. Calls kept coming in with new statewide numbers. Turnout seemed to be inching up.

At 4:45 p.m., Dickerson, forever studying the turnout reports, turned to Alan Albert and grinned. "We got these bastards."

Others weren't so sure.

Out in the streets, the flusher operation went on.

"You win an election between 4 and 7," Dickerson says. "You have some people who vote come hell or high water. Joe Smith, who owns his house, college-educated. His wife a teacher. He'll vote come hell or high water. But six blocks down and three streets away you've got Mary Anderson and next to Mary Anderson you have Pete Johnson. Mary is a female head of household, two kids. She's moderately inclined to vote. She gets off work at 5:30, catches a bus to work, gets home at 6, she's tired when she gets home. She didn't vote on the way to work. She knows a black is running, wants to vote, but is basically alienated, doesn't believe his winning will make a difference. People like that, flushers make a difference. The guy next to her votes sporadically. He always sees politicians in church at election time . . . He's more concerned with what's happening in his neighborhood than in the governor's office. It's out of his milieu. Knock on his door, say make history today. He's a proud black man, aware of the history of this state. He says yeah, let's do it."

By 5:30 p.m., "we were at 52 percent or better in all the [Richmond] precincts," Dickerson says. If he could keep this up for the next hour and a half, Wilder would get his black base. Then the question would be how well he had done among whites.

Rush hour jammed the interstates of Tidewater. At Democratic headquarters in Virginia Beach, volunteers were pouring in, looking for something to do. Democratic organizer Maxine Cook hustled them to the phone bank operation nearby. "I don't want to see y'all until the polls close," she told volunteers.

That wouldn't be long now.

In Richmond, Sue Fitz-Hugh thought all her flood crises were over. But at 6 p.m., there came another. The floodwaters that had hit farther west the day before were now rampaging downstream through Lynchburg, where they had ripped loose some chlorine tanks from an industrial park. The tanks were now headed for Riverville in Amherst County and authorities were evacuating the area — including the polling place. The registrar called for instructions. He was on his own, Fitz-Hugh informed him. He couldn't close the polls, though. He'd have to set up somewhere else and notify late voters the best he could.

Paul Goldman, freshly barbered at the Hotel John Marshall's prestigious barbershop, returned to the law office and called around town, to the other Democratic headquarters. All reported the turnout was low, dangerously so. "They were all concerned, real concerned," he says.

There was nothing Goldman could do now. But sitting around the office was killing him. About 5:30 p.m., Joel Harris — a Republican operative who had switched parties and spent the fall helping out both Baliles and Wilder research the GOP candidates' voting records — came by and volunteered to drive Goldman around town to see what the evening rush hour turnout was looking like. They went to some black precincts on Richmond's Southside but couldn't tell much in the falling darkness.

The car radio could pick up the audio from the Channel 6 evening news, which had an exit poll. Baliles and Terry were going to win but the Wilder-Chichester race was still too close to call. The exit poll did show, however, Wilder was getting 42 percent of the white vote.

Goldman thought a bit, then turned to Harris: "If that's the case, we're not going to make it."

In the little James River town of Buchanan, about thirty miles north of Roanoke, the greatest get-out-the-vote effort of the whole campaign was about to happen.

Railroad worker Tommy Jordan had tried to get to the Springwood precinct in the morning but couldn't reach it for the high water. His wife, Debbie, had gone to work in Roanoke but found her office closed because of high water. Instead, she spent the day at the Democrats' headquarters, where there was little to do but sit around and watch others doing the same. Every so often she tried calling neighbors in Buchanan to see if they could get to vote, but no, the roads were still closed.

Eventually she went home. About 4:30 the Jordans gathered up a kerosene heater and some other supplies and drove them down to the Presbyterian Church in Buchanan, one of the local evacuation centers. It was a pitiful sight. The room seemed full of old widows. One woman was over one hundred. She had managed to escape with her dog and eighty-some-year-old daughter. Just down the street, the James River roared. "You could stand on Main Street and reach out and touch the flood," Debbie Jordan says. "It was scary."

The Jordans got back home at 6:30. Daughter Sherry, fourteen, met them with the news: The state police had called a half-hour ago to say the road was open to the polling place at James River High School. Just after the police had called, Glynn Loope — a local college student working for the Baliles campaign — had called to see if the Jordans had been able to vote yet. When Sherry told him the road was now open, Loope told her to go tell all her Democratic neighbors. Within a few minutes, Sherry Jordan had covered half a mile and three Democratic households. Loope, meanwhile, raced up the interstate to find voters of his own to drive to the polls.

The Jordans turned around and drove to the high school to vote. A half-mile from the school, the state police had set up a checkpoint. "If we're not back in fifteen minutes, you come get us," Debbie Jordan joked.

The state trooper wasn't joking. He grimly took down the Jordans' name and address and they rode into the unknown.

The high school was still full of students and teachers who had spent the night. As the Jordans came in, students crowded around them. What's the town like? they asked. They asked about local landmarks. Is Big Daddy's still there? Debbie Jordan didn't have the heart to tell them Big Daddy's, a local hangout, was simply gone, washed down the river. "We're not sure," she stammered and went in to vote.

When she finished, it was only a few minutes before 7.

Larry Framme was at Richmond City Councilwoman Claudette McDaniel's home when the polls closed. "Flushers were coming in, going over the figures. A couple big precincts did not turn out. I was pretty down. A fellow came up to me and said, 'Doug did not come into the [black] community.' Blacks and whites vote for the same reason. There has to be a certain level of enthusiasm. You can't turn out a lot of people with a last-minute effort. There has to be enthusiasm over time."

Framme was glum as he drove to Baliles headquarters. "I thought we'd lose Doug by a short margin. I'd seen turnout figures and thought we were short."

Downtown at the Marriott, Republicans were straggling in for what had been billed as a victory party. Few were under any illusions, though. State GOP Chairman Don Huffman was wearing a black suit. "Mourning clothes," he called them sourly.

Not far away at the John Marshall, giddy Democrats were starting to gather. Talk of a sweep was in the air.

Shortly after 7 p.m., Goldman heard another exit poll. This one put Wilder's share of the white vote at 46 percent, giving Wilder a 53-47 lead. That made Goldman feel better, but he thought the numbers were too high. He'd suspend his judgement, and his excitement, until he saw some real numbers. He got in his car and drove off to the Grace Place, his restaurant hideaway in the Fan.

All around Virginia, doors were being locked and voting machines were being opened.

Bobby Watson had seen the exit polls but he had also seen the turnout figures. "Turnout was scary, discouraging, very frightening." Watson showed the exit poll to David Doak. "He was still scared."

Richard Dickerson got back to Terry headquarters after 7 p.m. He looked over the turnout figures and thought things would be OK. "Numbers don't lie," he says, and it seemed the Democrats had the numbers. "I thought Doug had done really, really well. I thought it would be incredibly close, ten thousand votes, fifteen thousand votes and I thought maybe he could win."

At the Grace Place, Goldman ordered a bowl of beans, some rice and two pieces of carrot cake and took them to the Commonwealth Park, a hotel overlooking Capitol Square where Wilder had decided he would wait for the returns.

Goldman arrived at 7:30 to find he was the only one there. He sat alone in the suite, eating his beans and rice, watching TV. No one had any returns yet. He picked up the phone, dialed Michael Brown and Baliles headquarters to see what they had. They didn't have anything yet, either. He also phoned Wilder at home. Wilder was getting dressed and said he'd be there soon. Goldman hung up the phone and went back to his lonely beans and rice.

Wilder's law office was deserted. Only Michael Brown was left to answer the phones that now seemed to be ringing all at once. Tonight, he came up from his basement bunker, went upstairs into Wilder's ornate office and sat behind the senator's desk so he could answer the phones and watch the returns on TV at the same time. As soon as Brown answered one call, another line seemed to be ringing. Every so often, he called down to the Commonwealth Park and talked to Goldman. Together, they tried to piece together the picture but right now neither knew enough to even guess.

"Come on down," Goldman said.

Brown begged off. He had phones to answer.

And the pace was picking up. The people calling in were so excited they'd forget to say where they were calling from. "They'd say 'Hey, down in the county we've got 32 percent for Chichester and 68 percent for Wilder.' I'd say, 'What's the county? What's the vote? I need numbers.'"

In Norfolk, Marian Tucker was waiting. As is her custom on Election Night, she had a box of tissues and a scotch on the rocks, precautions enough to cover any outcome. In 1981 she was off alone in a corner of the headquarters when Del. Tom Moss came in and found her crying. "Oh, my God," he shouted, "have we lost?" "No," she said through tears and scotch, "We won!"

Tonight, the first precinct came in at 7:20 p.m. It was Precinct 10, from Norfolk's fashionable Ghent district. Upper class whites and apartment dwellers. A swing district. Wilder carried it.

"We're gonna win," Tucker proclaimed.

A few minutes later, one of Norfolk's blue-collar precincts came in. Wilder had lost, but only by about a hundred votes. "There weren't too many people in headquarters who didn't know what that meant."

In Roanoke, Del. Chip Woodrum arrived at Democratic headquarters about 7:30 p.m. Not long afterward, the two South Roanoke precincts —

old money — reported. Chichester had carried both, but his margin was no bigger than any other Republican would normally get there. Woodrum knew right then Wilder had won. In the confusion, he got up and gave a little speech about how Virginia had done something the whole nation should imitate.

At 7:42 p.m., news about the exit poll swept through the crowd gathering in the John Marshall ballroom. Not far behind this rumor was Bobby Watson, grinning now that he had seen some early returns. "They're big," he said. "The numbers are big — if the exit polls hold up."

Larry Framme left Claudette McDaniel's house, convinced Wilder had lost. He stopped by Baliles headquarters, thanked everyone for their help on the joint campaign, then left for the John Marshall. As he stepped up the first step of the hotel, he tripped and somehow ripped his dress slacks from the crotch all the way down.

Framme remembers it was exactly 7:55 and now, damn it, he'd have to go home and change his pants. Inside, the lobby was crowded, important people were coming up to shake his hands and he was trying to leave with at least a little dignity.

The 8 p.m. report on Richmond's Channel 12 came with 8 percent of the vote in. Baliles was leading 56-44, Wilder 52-48, Terry 62-38. Wilder's totals put him up 46,482-42,254, not nearly as comfortable a margin as the percentages would indicate.

Wilder arrived at the Commonwealth Park at 8:15. His son, his two daughters (who had spent the fall either in college or at work) and Joel Harris and Harris' wife came along. Wilder had known Harris since the latter was a Senate page a decade before. Wilder sat on the sofa with Goldman. The children and the Harrises found chairs. No one said very much. Goldman was on the phone constantly, calling his friends at AP and UPI to see what the latest returns said and where they were from.

TV put the race back at 50-50.

'It's in the bag," Goldman kept saying between phone calls.

"Doug was a little tense," Goldman remembers. "Not tense tense, but anxious tense. Doug was always upbeat [during the campaign]. Only once I saw Doug not his usual smile-up. That was Election Night. I could see how much he wanted it."

"Where are our votes?" Wilder kept asking Goldman.

"Hey, our good areas are still out," Goldman said. He explained these early returns were disproportionately from Richmond suburbs, Southside and the Piedmont, all the Republicans' best areas. Tidewater and Northern Virginia had yet to be heard from in strength. Nevertheless, Wilder kept asking Goldman, "Where are those voters you keep saying are out there?"

"They're coming," Goldman said, "they're coming."

In Charlottesville, Democratic headquarters was uncharacteristically subdued. Four years before, when the Third Congressional District — Richmond and suburbs — came in for Robb, one of the city's most prominent lawyers had led the crowd in a chant of "Fuck the *Times-Dispatch.* " Tonight, though, things were quiet and respectful.

City chairman Tom Vandever got up every so often to announce the latest returns — Wilder first, because his margin was the slimmest, then Baliles, then Terry. But suddenly in the statewide returns Charlottesville was getting, Chichester pulled ahead. The mood turned somber. "We were thinking, here it comes," Vandever said. Two out of three. Oh well, we tried.

The AFL-CIO had its own vote-counting room set up at its state headquarters in Richmond. Calls were coming in from locals all over the state. Labor organizers who gathered on West Broad Street were prepared for the worst. "They were used to losing," says state political director Pauline Huffman.

Between 8 and 8:30, the votes started pouring in. The Channel 12 report now had 23 percent of the vote in. Baliles was up 55-45, Terry up 62-38. Wilder's race had tightened a bit, to 51-49. His margin was almost exactly 8,000 votes — 142,826-134,827.

Out in Russell County, Democrats had started converging on the courthouse about 7 p.m. to wait on the returns. Most were downcast, expecting Wilder to lose. The first returns came in from Moccasin, a Republican precinct, which didn't help the mood any. But then other precincts started trickling in, with the Democrats winning most of them.

Soon someone called a friend in Grundy to see how things were going in Buchanan County. Buchanan's reputation as the most racist county in all of Virginia was hard to live down. That made the news from Grundy all the more hard to believe. Wilder had not just beaten Chichester in Buchanan County, he had buried him — 4,094-2,451. "That was one of the big items of conversation," Mike Musick remembers. Why, Wilder even got sixty-eight more votes there than Terry got, one of the few places in the state where he led the ticket. All around the Russell County Courthouse, there was a buzz. Hey, listen to this, Wilder carried Buchanan County by 2-1, can you believe it?

Robb aide Judy Griswold had spent the day in Newport News, running GOTV, making sure the early morning "lit drops" were done on time, making sure the flushers were out in the neighborhoods. By 4 p.m.,

Griswold had decided she'd done as much as she could do in Newport News and drove back to Richmond.

Now she was in Baliles headquarters, where a desk was set up to tabulate returns for each part of the state. Griswold hovered over the Tidewater desk, studying even the smallest scraps of information. About 8:30, some Norfolk precincts came in, from Larchmont — conservative white neighborhoods. Wilder had won all but a couple of precincts there and in the ones he lost, he came tantalizingly close. Griswold looked up from the numbers and announced to those standing around her: "Doug has won."

She immediately got on the phone to Michael Brown and shouted in his ear: "Y'all have won!" Then she gave him the Norfolk numbers she had.

Brown was his usual cool self. No, can't be sure, he said. Griswold was jubilant. This is it, she tried to tell Brown. This is it. Wilder has won! But Brown wouldn't buy it. Griswold didn't care. As far as she was concerned, the election was over and Wilder had won. She left Baliles headquarters and drove straight to the John Marshall. As soon as she got into the lobby, she told everyone she recognized that Wilder had won.

"Nobody believed it, though," she says.

A bus was waiting outside Democratic headquarters in Virginia Beach to take people to Richmond for the victory party. "I had a hard time holding people back," Maxine Cook says. "They wanted to get on the bus at 7 p.m."

She wanted to wait until the Beach returns were nearly complete. And what returns they were. Mary Sue Terry had beaten Buster O'Brien in his hometown 32,469-28,707. The other Republicans had won, but just barely. Wilder lost Owen Pickett's Virginia Beach by only about 3,000 votes, 31,620-28,317.

The bus rolled out at 9 p.m. with about thirty people on board. "It seemed like the longest bus ride in the world," Cook says. The singing and shouting all but drowned out the radio, which was giving more returns as the bus sped toward Richmond.

In Norfolk, House Majority Leader Tom Moss, who a day before had declined the governor's invitation to go to Richmond to watch "history being made," looked on in amazement as the returns came in. "When the Virginia Beach returns came in, I said, 'Christ, the man's going to pull it off.'

"You can throw away the books," Moss told everyone.

"I kind of wish I had gone now," he says.

The road from Manassas to Woodbridge wound back and forth through patches of Northern Virginia countryside that had yet to be suburbanized. Chuck Colgan Jr., the one-time Draft Bagley organizer, and two Democratic friends — one of them black — were headed for a victory party for the Democratic candidate for the House of Delegates. They were all knee-deep in politics, but the only returns they had heard were what they could pick up on the radio, which was precious little. Just then a batch of returns came in from Southside's Fifth District, showing Wilder hanging on to a 51-49 lead there.

"My God, if we carry this, we can't lose," Colgan shouted.

His black friend slapped the seat beside him. "I'm proud of Virginia!"

At 9 p.m., Channel 12 in Richmond went on the air full-time with election returns. More than a third of the votes were now in. The numbers were virtually unchanged from a half-hour before, Baliles 55-45, Wilder 51-49, Terry 61-39.

Analyst Larry Sabato pronounced Baliles and Terry the winners. "It's only in the third race that we might be here for a while, but it is leaning to Wilder. Baliles has achieved enough of a percentage statewide to perhaps pull Wilder in."

Shortly after 9 p.m., Buster O'Brien telephoned his congratulations to Mary Sue Terry, then went downstairs at the Marriott to concede.

About the same time, Larry Framme, new pants and all, arrived back to the John Marshall. He was dumbfounded at what he saw in the ballroom. "No one was entertaining on stage, yet people were just packed in there, waiting on results. It took twenty-five minutes to get from the door into the ballroom to the side of the stage. Yet people weren't complaining. It was euphoric, the thought that this was going to happen. They were just mesmerized. The only time people were upset were when some cameramen came in and blocked their view. Those people had been standing there two hours. I didn't have a drink the whole night yet I was as high as I've ever been."

In UPI headquarters in Richmond, reporter Jeff Shapiro had been studying the returns. He had some favorite communities to watch. Lee County, where Wilder had started his tour, came in. Wilder had won big, 3,688-2,545. "Hampton is a nice little city to watch," he says. Wilder had won there, too, 16,526-10,618. Two normally Democratic areas had gone Democratic big. No surprises there.

Shapiro turned his eyes toward the Sixth District, stretching from

When Hell Froze Over

Roanoke to Harrisonburg. Once the redoubt of mountain-valley Republicanism, this was now the state's premier swing district. With a late afternoon surge of voters, the flood didn't dampen turn-out there as much as expected. In any event, the key remained the populous Roanoke Valley — especially suburban Roanoke County. At 9:15 p.m., the signal came. All three Democrats had carried Roanoke County. Terry won by 13,249-6,717. Baliles by 10,710-9,332. And Wilder by exactly two hundred votes — 9,995-9,795. That did it. Shapiro was ready to call the election.

State news editor Tom Kapsidelis was more cautious and wanted to wait. But fifteen minutes later, an eternity in wire service time, Kapsidelis sat down and typed out the code that sent a prepared bulletin out to all the UPI wires, declaring Wilder the winner.

Sometime after 9 p.m. a friend with the Rainbow Coalition in Tidewater called Michael Brown with the numbers from Virginia Beach.

"Lord have mercy," Brown muttered when he heard how close Wilder had come.

But his doubts weren't entirely erased until the calls started coming in from Northern Virginia. They were huge. Wilder had carried Alexandria 14,819-8,579. Wilder had carried Arlington 25,375-14,701. Wilder had carried Fairfax County 82,634-73,425. The two congressional districts there were his, by big margins. Wilder was winning 54 percent of the vote in the Eighth, 56 percent in the Tenth. With Wilder running as close as he was in such Republican strongholds as Virginia Beach and Southside and with such a big margin in Northern Virginia, even Michael Brown had to believe.

"I was in shock, a kind of controlled shock," he says. "Here was a relative of mine. I was proud of that. And proud that here's a black person, accepted in this state, and he's coming through."

Brown sat a while in Wilder's office, alone, watching the phone lines light up. He called down to the Commonwealth Park one more time. This time the phone in the suite rang and rang without answer. Finally the switchboard operator came back on and asked who Brown was calling for.

"Oh, they just left five minutes ago," she said.

Brown cut off the TV and hit the lights as he went out the door. Behind him, the phones were still ringing.

It was a short drive up to the John Marshall from the Commonwealth Park, but one long thought held Wilder's mind: "It looks like I'm a winner. What if something happens? Jammed machines? Missing reports?" After so many years of the Byrd Machine running the state's election machinery,

Wilder harbored secret fears. That was one reason he wanted to lead from the beginning. If there was going to be any fraud, he wanted them to have to take it away from him.

Jay Shropshire met Wilder in the lobby of the John Marshall and took him upstairs to the official suite.

Brown, arriving soon afterward, tried to follow. But as he approached the stairwell he spotted John Jameson arguing with a security guard. "But I'm Mary Sue's campaign manager," he could hear Jameson repeating, but the guard wasn't buying it.

Brown decided it wasn't worth the hassle and went up to the balcony overlooking the crowded ballroom. All around him, people were hugging and cheering. He stood alone by the railing, looking down at the mob, as alone as anyone could be in that crowd. "My eyes got swelled up with tears," Brown says. "I didn't cry." But still, it was all a little sad. It was over.

"Wyatt didn't believe he was going to lose until 9, 9:30 on Election Night," says his press secretary, Don Harrison. Then the returns from Vienna came in. The Northern Virginia district he had once represented in the General Assembly had gone overwhelmingly for the Democrats. That did it. Fifteen minutes later, Durrette went downstairs at the Marriott. He conceded at 10:35 p.m. By then it wasn't even two down and one to go.

At 10:32 p.m., The Associated Press declared Wilder the winner.

On Channel 12, Sabato was laughing at himself. "Every political analyst keeps file of tasty crow recipes on hand and Doug Wilder can call me up and ask for any one he wants," he said.

In the Democrats' suite upstairs at the John Marshall, a tug of war was developing. Wilder was the object. Robb wanted the whole ticket to go downstairs and claim victory right before 11 p.m. to make a dramatic showing for the late night news. But Wilder was hesitant to go down until he was absolutely certain he had won.

"Chuck kept saying, 'Come on, Doug,' " Wilder says. "I said, 'No, I'm not gonna do it.' I thought of a lot of ways to hold 'em up. I'd go wash my hands or go to the bathroom."

When the governor saw he was making no progress with the recalcitrant candidate, "Robb got Al Smith to go to him," Shropshire says. Smith made the same pitch that Wilder was going to win, so he should go down in time for the news.

But the Senate clerk whispered to Wilder: "Stay here. Period."

Wilder stayed.

Robb and his crowd fumed on the other side of the room, tense now with both anticipation and annoyance. With three winning candidates and a governor in the room, says Terry media adviser Bob Squier, "you didn't have to send to room service for egos."

In the midst of all this, Robb came up to Goldman. "I never said you're not a good strategist," the governor told him. Goldman gave Robb a quizzical look. "What were you saying then?" Goldman laughed.

It was 10:45. "Pat Caddell came over, said, 'Hey, you're up by 4 percent, there's about 4 percent outstanding, only fifty thousand votes or so left. It's just not gonna happen.' " Goldman agreed. "I can't argue with that," he said.

The Democrats assembled to go downstairs to claim their share of history.

Squier escorted Terry onto the freight elevator with the others, then dashed down the steps to be there at the bottom when the slow-moving elevator arrived. Squier had a pocket TV with him, a habit acquired from years of working election nights. While waiting for the elevator to creak down, Squier watched the news. TV just now had the news that AP had declared a Democratic sweep. The elevator opened and the candidates spilled out. Squier grabbed Wilder and pulled him aside: "I just saw a report on TV," he said. "You've definitely been declared the winner."

Wilder says he didn't go down until he was absolutely certain he had won, but Squier saw his expression change nonetheless. "He was still worried about it," Squier says. "When he got out of the elevator, he still had a question mark on his face. He didn't quite trust what people had been telling him."

Now Wilder, visibly brightened, swept by him and out onto the stage, into the full glare of history.

What happened next is difficult to describe. The Democratic victory party in the John Marshall was the center of attention for a whole state, but the thousands of people sardined into the ornate old ballroom where Doug Wilder once waited tables knew less about what was happening than ordinary citizens sitting at home by their TV sets and radios in the distant valleys of Lee County. Three big screens had been set up around the room, one for each network. But the pictures were so fuzzy even the numbers were hard to read and the sound was so bad it was drowned out in the general din. The TV screens became irrelevancies. All anyone knew about how the vote count was coming out was what they heard from rumors and snatches of conversations, and after a while even they were forgotten, replaced simply by expectation. Everyone knew things were looking good, but . . . had it really happened? Had they made history?

By 10:50 p.m., the crowd was crammed in so tight it was but a single being — sweating, standing, waiting . . . waiting for something, waiting to be a part of history.

And then it happened . . . much commotion about the stage, people coming and going, curtains rustling, and then Robb and the three candidates came out, waving, smiling, Wilder flashing a double V-for-victory. Was this it? Had they won? Had they *all* won?

The crowd roared.

Robb leaned into the microphone and shouted: "Fellow Democrats, fellow Virginians, may I present the attorney general-elect of the commonwealth of Virginia!"

The crowd roared some more and chanted: "Mary Sue! Mary Sue!"

"Governor Baliles . . . " More roars. "Lieutenant Governor Wilder." Now the roar was a shriek. It was true.

Terry's acceptance speech was unremarkable until the end. Then, Terry turned to look at the black man behind her. "I know something of the joy felt tonight by one member of this winning ticket. He has spent the last year hearing all of the so-called experts say that he would be a drag on the ticket. Well . . . " The cheers drowned out what she had to say next.

Robb seized the microphone again. "My fellow Virginians, my fellow Democrats, may I present the lieutenant governor-elect."

"Doug! Doug! Doug!" the crowd chanted.

Wilder flashed his double V for victory. The crowd eventually quieted, almost eerily, as it waited to hear what Wilder would say, in this, his moment of supreme triumph.

"I never prepared any statement one way or another," Wilder explained later. "I wanted it to be what I felt at that moment. I had no idea that many people were out there. It was an amazing thing to see so many people out there. We had touched people. You could see it in their faces. Only when I saw the group did I know what I was going to say."

Throughout the campaign, Wilder had taken pains not to discuss race or the historical implications of his campaign. Others had always been the ones to mention his rags-to-riches story. Of himself, he had said only that he was qualified. So tonight it was somewhat surprising when Wilder, reaching into himself to say what he honestly felt, spoke quite plainly about the sweet ironies of history:

"I could not begin to tell you how happy, how pleased, how thrilled I am with this moment. Many, many years ago in this room, there may be some of you were here with me" — you could hear the crowd collectively suck in its breath — "when I used to listen to political speeches as I would wait tables on this floor as well as in the gallery — " The room broke into cheers. "Little did I believe one day I just might be your lieutenant governor."

Another roar.

Wilder gave thanks to the countless Democratic workers around the state. He also gave thanks to A.L. Philpott. In Henry County, Philpott, watching on TV "nearly fell off his chair when he heard that," says one man who was there.

And Wilder also gave thanks to God. But then the personal tone of this moment shone through again.

"I can only hope that my mother and father were here to witness this moment, but I can see my mother's face as clear as if she were, she would say, 'Don't let your head get too big' " — cheers — " 'because you know you didn't get there by yourself.' "

More cheers.

And then Wilder pulled one last shocker. "Doug just kept telling me during the week, on Election Night, you're going to be on the stage," Goldman says. "On Election Night, I want you with me. I said I don't know, I've got things to do, he said no, stay near me all the time, so obviously he had something in mind. He said he had something in mind. I had no idea." Then, as the official party came down the freight elevator, Wilder pulled Goldman on stage with his three children and the ever-present Jay Shropshire. They crammed onto the stage with wives, children, assorted relatives of the other candidates.

Now Wilder grinned and looked over his shoulder. "Let me close by saying, nothing ever is accomplished alone and I know many have maybe seen what used to be called my campaign consultant" — laughter — "he never had the title of campaign manager. Many of you wouldn't recognize him tonight anyway" — more laughter — "but I'd like Paul Goldman to step forward, please."

"I thought he deserved it," Wilder said later. "He's caught enough grief all these years in Virginia politics. I never told him what I was going to do. I wanted him to be there to raise his hand in victory and he loved it."

Out in the crowd, though, Goldman's friend Barry Rose felt old hostilities bubble up. "People were pissed he did that. I heard a lot of people bitching. 'He forced Howell on the party, then Edie (Harrison) and now Doug.' "

After Wilder and after Terry, Baliles seemed almost an anti-climax. Even the governor-elect had to frame his victory within the context of his running mates:

"Two hundred years ago, Virginia led the nation. We were the writers and the fighters and the thinkers. What we did set the course for the nation. Tonight, we proved we're doing it again."

All night long, AFL-CIO staffer Scott Reynolds had been at a motel on the Eastern Shore, where he had been working for the Democratic challenger in a House of Delegates campaign. Reynolds might as well have been in another state. The motel room in Accomac where the Democrats were awaiting returns had no TV. The only returns anyone could get were by radio and they were sketchy at best. Whenever Democrats carried a local precinct, someone got up and rang a bell. But the bell wasn't ringing many times. Every so often, Reynolds called labor headquarters in Richmond to find out what was really going on. When he called at 10:30 p.m., all he learned was that Wilder was leading, but hadn't been declared the winner yet.

About 11:30 p.m., Reynolds made his final call. This time Danny LeBlanc didn't even bother to tell him Wilder had won.

"Brother," he said, "welcome to Virginia. Virginia has just walked into the twentieth century."

17

The Signs We Should Have Seen

So why did it happen? Why did Doug Wilder, the grandson of a slave, win election in Virginia, the state that less than a generation ago gave the South the strategy of Massive Resistance? How could any black candidate best known for infuriating the leaders of his own party on racial issues win election in a Southern state in a campaign whose vote was noteworthy principally for the extraordinarily low turnout of black voters?

The short answer is that Virginia voters decided Wilder was more qualified than his opponent.

That's not an answer skeptics are likely to accept at face value, but it's true. Of course, many voters had to take the long way around before they finally came around to seeing the campaign in those terms, but that's the contrast Wilder succeeded in setting up.

"One thing Virginians have is a sense of inbred fairness about them," says state Sen. Madison Marye, D-Montgomery County. "People say, 'I don't mind hiring blacks as long as they can do the job.' Well, here was a black who could do the job and better than the white could. It finally got down to voting against him because he's black." And dignified, fair-minded Virginians couldn't bring themselves to do that.

Still, it's remarkable that Virginians came to see such a clear, dispassionate choice — between a qualified black and a less-qualified white — and do it without any apparent consternation. It's even more remarkable when you consider the other factors at play.

Race, remember, was just one of what should have been three powerful strikes against Wilder, the other two being his liberalism and a variety of business problems, ranging from the Bar reprimand to his late payment of taxes and housing code violations. In the beginning, conventional wisdom held that any one of those should have been enough to do Wilder in. Yet race never became a public issue, as such, in the campaign and apparently wasn't much of one in the privacy of voters' minds. Republicans were never able to prove Wilder was a liberal; indeed, after he called liberalism a racist code word, they were even afraid to call him one. Likewise, many Republicans were afraid to exploit Wilder's business problems and those that were publicized, such as the house, weren't enough to hurt him.

Instead of focusing on Wilder's negatives, the campaign focused almost exclusively on Wilder's three strongest positives: his experience, the enormous popularity of Gov. Charles Robb (which, in effect, made the Baliles-Wilder-Terry trio a ticket of the status quo) and, thanks to the station-wagon tour, Wilder's celebrity status. The negatives in the campaign belonged to the Republicans, who seemed clumsy and unknown amateurs who couldn't even run their own campaigns, much less hope to run the state.

So in the end, the short answer to why Virginians elected a black candidate is that they really did decide Wilder was more qualified.

The long answer, of course, is much more complicated. And even if Wilder's experience was the deciding factor, why did voters come to see the election that way and not some other?

One of the biggest reasons, University of Virginia analyst Larry Sabato noted in his post-election analysis, was that "Wilder cleverly shaved the liberal edges off his public record, instead focusing on his legislative achievements, on his Korean War record, and on the patriotic virtues and moderate-conservative Virginia values he claimed to possess." Wilder didn't actually run as a conservative, but he didn't object one bit if voters concluded that he was one.

And both the Republicans and the news media let him get away with it. On top of that, Wilder outspent Chichester about 2.5-1 in television, and the "cop spot" neutralized GOP suggestions that Wilder was soft on crime.

So it's almost a wonder that Wilder didn't win by a bigger margin than he did. But Sabato reminds us that the election was a close call: "Had the

Republicans succeeded in painting Wilder ... with liberal hues, the election results might well have been different."

For that reason, Randy Flood, the Washington lobbyist who attempted to organize the Draft Bagley movement, grouses that Wilder's election proves nothing: "His election was a fluke in that his record was never exposed. The laws of Virginia elections never became applicable."

The Wilder-Chichester campaign was fought almost strictly on image and many contrasts were drawn between the two candidates — but a contrast between Wilder the liberal and Chichester the conservative was never one of them. Instead, the contrasts were between Wilder, the General Assembly insider, and Chichester, the minority party back-bencher; between Wilder, the cool and dignified celebrity statesman and Chichester, the loud and clumsy politician; between Wilder, whose historic victory would symbolize Virginia's future, and Chichester, whose Byrd and Godwin connections became a symbol of its sullied past — all contrasts that worked to Wilder's advantage.

But there are several other reasons that go a long way toward explaining Wilder's election:

Virginia has changed. It's become more urban, more cosmopolitan — more progressive. Four out of every ten voters now live in Northern Virginia or Tidewater, and odds are, they moved in from out of state. To them, "Virginia tradition" is not necessarily something worth emulating.

The Democrats succeeded, and the Republicans failed, in understanding this "New Dominion" of suburban Virginia. These suburban voters may be nominally conservative but the tenor of that conservatism is much different from that of Ole Virginny. They are fiscal conservatives who pride themselves on being socially progressive. The old symbols — Byrd, Godwin — mean little here and if they mean anything at all, they stand as symbols of a backward and discredited era, spokesmen who should be repudiated, not heeded.

"The suburbs are no longer the Old South," says Ed DeBolt, Durrette's media adviser. "They look at who can solve the problems, who can build the roads, who can build the schools." The Democrats identified themselves as practical, problem-solving, forward-looking politicians; the Republicans identified themselves with creationism, school prayer, aging Dixiecrats and the echoes of Massive Resistance.

As a result, Wilder took 48.8 percent of the suburban vote, a stunningly high figure for a Democrat. For comparison, Robb in '81 won 49.5 percent; Baliles in '85 took 51.5 percent.

Under Larry Sabato's Cocktail Party Theory of Virginia Elections — Virginia voters will vote for the candidate they'd most like to invite to a cocktail party — Wilder's strong showing in the suburbs was hardly a surprise. By campaign's end, Wilder would indeed have been the favored guest — he was a celebrity, charming and articulate, provocative but in a tasteful way. His presence would ensure a large and curious crowd, yet he could be counted upon not to bring up any impolite subjects, such as asking the hostess why her children went to private schools. Chichester, though, might be either a dreadful bore or start ranting about who had "the criminal's interest at heart."

Virginia voters in 1985 weren't angry at anybody. They liked Robb specifically and they liked the way things were going generally. "Unfortunately for the Republicans, their president had done too good a job," observes Del. Richard Cranwell, D-Roanoke County. Virginia Democrats benefited from the Reagan recovery. People were generally satisfied and Wilder's upbeat campaign matched the mood of the times better than Chichester's harsh "criminal's interest at heart" campaign did.

The Democrats nominated good candidates and the Republicans nominated terrible ones. Baliles looked like a Robb clone, cautious, pro-business, well-intentioned. Durrette was a two-time loser who hadn't won an election in a decade. Wilder had an impressive resume and was a gifted orator. Chichester was obscure and inarticulate. Terry had a strong resume as an ex-prosecutor and champion of tough drunken-driving laws. O'Brien had his macho reputation as a college football star but fumbled that advantage early in the game and instead became only a jock.

Wilder wasn't simply a good candidate in the conventional sense; he had charisma. "Wilder's problem was to allay fear, some vague, non-specific fear, to be comfortable with him," says Larry Framme, who after the election became state Democratic chairman. The fact that Wilder was such a charming, likable fellow enabled Goldman to disregard the conventional wisdom and make Wilder the central issue in the campaign — and get away with it.

In some ways, then, the lieutenant governor's race was nothing more than a personality contest. Wilder's charisma, combined with his historic status and his unorthodox station-wagon campaign, soon made him a celebrity. Voters were curious about him; they wanted to meet him, maybe even ask for his autograph. Who was John Chichester but just another boring politician?

The Democrats were united; the Republicans were not. Baliles' nomination secured the patronage of business, while blacks, liberals and labor were bound to be excited by Wilder's candidacy. All segments of the party were satisfied. By contrast, the GOP was rife with internecine warfare. Moderate Republicans felt disenfranchised by Chichester's defeat of Coleman and Giesen at the June convention, which no doubt contributed to the low Republican turnout in November.

The Democrats ran better TV campaigns than the Republicans did. The Republicans wasted money on radio and ineffective television spots. All three Democrats looked good on TV and Wilder, with his famous cop spot, came off best of all.

The Democrats ran better campaigns, period, while the Republicans were thoroughly inept. The Wilder campaign, in particular, had a clear strategy from the beginning and carried it out relentlessly; the Chichester campaign changed its mind from day to day and, as a result, never did anything well.

"Sometimes campaigns don't mean anything," says Tom King, the Terry consultant from the Democratic National Committee. "In Virginia, the campaigns meant everything. The Democrats ran great campaigns and the Republicans ran lousy campaigns."

"They were the three worst campaigns I've ever seen and we've worked in a lot of states," says Bob Squier, Terry's media consultant.

Low voter turnout helped Wilder. Turnout was down 12 percent from the 1981 governor's race, and, as Sabato writes, it was down "in ways that directly benefited Democrats and hurt Republicans. Central cities (heavily Democratic) provided a larger share of the statewide vote, the Republican-leaning suburbs less so." It was the Republican voters who were staying at home and if they had turned out, Chichester might have won.

Race actually helped Wilder. Because he was black, many Republicans didn't take Wilder seriously until it was too late. Even then, they were afraid to attack Wilder too hard for fear they'd be called racists. Thus the issues the Republicans could have used to prove Wilder morally unfit for office — his housing problems, his Bar reprimand, his late payment of taxes — were never used in the way they could have been. Neither were the Republicans unable to prove Wilder politically unfit for office, and they failed completely in their attempts to prove Wilder was a liberal.

Media coverage helped Wilder. Republicans say the press was biased; Democrats and reporters say the Republicans deserved the bad publicity they got. Either way, Wilder undeniably came off looking better than Chichester. "It was just as new to the press to cover a black as it was to run against a black," Chichester says, "then throw in the bias of a handful."

The siren's song of history was irresistible. Once Wilder proved himself harmless, the prospect of being able to "make history" and expurgate the stain of Massive Resistance was a very real motivation for many voters. And since this was, after all, "only" the lieutenant governorship, many voters no doubt believed they could make a positive statement by voting for Wilder without having to worry about what he might do once in office.

And so the thing Republican adviser Judy Peachee feared the most came to pass: "When Doug Wilder first started talking about running, I made the statement, 'Don't underestimate Doug Wilder, it may become the chic thing to do to vote for him,' and that's probably what happened. Nobody presented a reason why it shouldn't happen.

"It was a unique set of circumstances in Virginia politics," she says. "There were two people in Virginia politics that all the stars came together for. One was Bill Scott and the other was Doug Wilder."

Before we go further in understanding why Wilder won, we should take a look at just how Wilder won.

The best analysis of the 1985 returns is by Sabato in his "Virginia Votes" series, published by the University of Virginia. Most of the following figures are taken either from his report or the state Board of Elections. To begin with, the basics:

Baliles	741,438	55.2%
Durrette	601,652	44.8%
Wilder	685,329	51.8%
Chichester	636,695	48.2%
Terry	814,808	61.4%
O'Brien	512,569	38.6%

Baliles and Terry scored a sweep unprecedented in recent times by winning all ten congressional districts. In 1981, Robb had won nine.

Wilder surprised nearly everyone, including himself. He carried seven congressional districts and two of the three he lost — the Fifth in Southside and the Third in and around Richmond — he lost by narrow margins (a mere 3,585 votes in the Fifth, which would most closely resemble a red-clay district of the Deep South). Only in the Seventh, stretching from Winchester to Hanover County, was he soundly defeated.

Wilder won through a combination of cutting his losses in Southside and the Richmond area and winning by big margins in the Northern Virginia suburbs, the Tidewater cities and the Southwest Virginia coalfields. His best congressional district was Northern Virginia's Tenth, where he polled 56 percent of the vote. "The old three-corners strategy," Goldman quipped on Election Night.

Interestingly, some of Wilder's biggest margins came in two of the whitest parts of the state — suburban Northern Virginia and Appalachian Southwest Virginia.

Demographically, Wilder's victory was just as broad as it was geographic. Perhaps the most significant statistic is this: Wilder received 44 percent of the white vote; Robb in 1981 had won only 46 percent; Baliles in 1985 won but 48 percent.

Just as interesting is this figure: In 1981, blacks accounted for 15 percent of those who voted. In 1985, with Wilder on the ballot, blacks were expected to account for an even greater share of the voters; the *Washington Post,* in its polling models, had estimated as many as 20 percent of the voters would be black. Instead, black turnout was down — to 14 percent. The Democratic strategists who had warned in the closing days of the campaign that Wilder would lose unless at least 16 percent of the voters were black were wrong.

However, without the well-financed get-out-the-vote campaign that Goldman protested so loudly, black turnout likely would have been even lower than it was. Some Democrats say that the irony of the 1985 campaign is that it was the Democratic establishment's efforts to organize black voters that, in the end, may have saved Wilder from defeat.

No doubt the low black turnout was a direct result of the general lack of enthusiasm that marked the entire campaign. The Democrats set out to run a low-key campaign to minimize the emphasis of their "rainbow" ticket. In the process, the Democrats succeeded in boring the public. In 1977, when the choice was between liberal crusader Howlin' Henry Howell and John Dalton, 62 percent of Virginians registered to vote actually did. In 1981, when the choice was between two photogenic, high-profile young men named Robb and Coleman, 65 percent of Virginians cast a ballot. In 1985, only 53 percent of the voters bothered to go to the polls.

By evoking so few emotions, Democrats did nothing to alarm their opposition, but they also numbed many of their own supporters — in this case, blacks. In 1981, when Godwin's last-minute comments gave blacks added incentive to vote for Robb and against the Republicans, black turnout was 68 percent, a significant 3 percent better than the overall turnout. But in 1985, only 53 percent of blacks registered to vote went to the polls, the same percentage as Virginians as a whole. The Wilder campaign, which had counted on a big black turnout simply because Wilder was on the ticket, was nearly caught short. Wilder had spent so much time running a racially neutral campaign that, by Election Day, his campaign seemed no more important to blacks than it was to whites.

After the election, Wilder credited two things — the tour and the cop commercial — for his victory. From a strategic standpoint, that's true. From a tactical standpoint, though, Doug Wilder should give a small prayer of thanks for Richard Dickerson and his GOTV network.

Some other statistical insights into Wilder's election: There was no "gender gap." Wilder won 52 percent of the vote from both men and women. Goldman, who booked lots of time on "Dukes of Hazzard" reruns, credits the "cop spot" for winning back conservative, white males.

The real gap in the election was a generation gap. The Reagan Youth of 1984 became Virginia Democrats in 1985. In 1984, voters eighteen to twenty-four gave Reagan the biggest vote of any age group in Virginia. In 1985, they were the second-biggest age group for the Democratic ticket, giving Wilder 54 percent of their ballots. And Wilder got 58 percent of the vote among those in their thirties.

After the election, armchair analysts were quick to credit Robb for "moderating" Virginia by appointing blacks to scores of prominent offices.

Not all of the credit should fall on Robb, though.

Perhaps Virginia simply is not quite as racist as it has been perceived. Instead of being one of the last Southern states where a black would be expected to win (given its relatively low black population of 19 percent), perhaps Virginia should have been expected to be the first. In some ways Wilder's election was not the great upset it seemed. There were, in fact, some signs we should have seen that Virginia was a natural to lead the way.

Even before 1985, white Virginians had already voted for blacks in several significant local elections, electing state Sen. Bobby Scott in a whitemajority district in Newport News and electing black mayors in Roanoke, Fredericksburg, Danville and Martinsville, all cities with white majorities. "One thing I sensed before this campaign started was that racial-line voting is non-existent in Virginia," Scott says. "If you run a racially neutral campaign, you can get racially neutral results. Running as a Democrat or Republican will polarize things more than race does if you run a racially neutral campaign. So it was always funny to me to hear people saying things like Chichester's likelihood of winning were equal to his actuarial chances of being alive on Election Day. Doug's challenge was to get past the color of his skin, to get where people think of you as not the black candidate, but the candidate who took the tour, the candidate who was endorsed by the FOP, the candidate who was the Korean War veteran."

Explaining how this could possibly happen in a Southern state requires an examination of Virginia's unique social and political climate.

Make no mistake, Virginia is fundamentally a conservative state, but it's not a fundamentalist conservative state, Jerry Falwell and Pat Robertson notwithstanding. Virginia's conservatism has always been more of a business conservatism, an aristocratic conservatism — not a redneck populist conservatism. This is the key — and something the historian V.O. Key stressed in his masterpiece, "Southern Politics," in 1949:

"The political distance from Virginia to Alabama must be measured in light years. Virginian deference to the upper orders and the Byrd Machine's restraint of popular aberrations give Virginia politics a tone and a reality radically different from the tumult of Alabama . . .

"Virginians . . . conclude that to succeed in high-level politics a person must enjoy a relatively high social status commanding at least a measure of respect. In a word, politics in Virginia is reserved for those who can qualify as gentlemen. Rabble-rousing and Negro-baiting capacities, which in Georgia or Mississippi would be a great political asset, simply mark a person as one not to the manor born. A public attitude favorable to this type of leadership . . . represses most of the crudities commonly thought to be characteristic of Southern politics. Virginia leadership is ingenious in strategems to maintain political decorum. Thus, in 1948 Henry Wallace met eggs and tomatoes and anti-segregation laws in many parts of the South in his campaign tour. Virginians calmly construed his political meetings to be private gatherings to which segregation laws did not apply."

It was exactly this genteel attitude, almost forty years later, that kept race from becoming the dominant theme of the Wilder-Chichester campaign. Virginians noticed Wilder's skin color, but they were just too polite to mention it — and they weren't about to make a big to-do over it in public. The surprise, of course, is that once in the privacy of the voting booth, they didn't exercise their native prejudices. But while the casting of an individual vote is a secret process, an election is an inherently public display and by Election Day 1985, Virginia knew quite well that the whole nation was watching to see what it would do. With Wilder so far ahead in the polls, for Virginians to defeat him now would make for lots of embarrassing questions the day after — and if it's something proper Virginians hate more than anything else, it's to be embarrassed in public. No, the only polite thing they could do was go ahead and vote for him and hope he didn't embarrass them. Others took an even more chauvinistic attitude and voted for Wilder simply to prove Virginia's superiority over sister Southern states.

Here, then, is why Wilder's victory shouldn't have been such a surprise: Virginians are more cautious than they are conservative.

In the mind of a genteel Virginia voter, the Republicans came off looking like loud-mouthed, fundamentalist crazies; the Democrats looked like polite, proper, responsible leaders the state had known before, even if one of them was black and another a woman. Given this choice, V.O. Key wouldn't have been surprised one bit by the outcome. He tried to predict in 1949 what Virginia politics would be like when the Byrd Machine was no more: "It seemed certain that Virginia's politics would retain a character all its own; a character fixed perhaps by a pervading belief that the upper orders should govern. That belief, incidentally, also infects the Negroes who take pride in being Virginians and look down on lesser peoples." So Key might well have also predicted the tone of Wilder's campaign — reflected in the *Times-Dispatch* cartoon showing Wilder as a Southern colonel, asking for a mint julep.

If conservatism was all that mattered, the Republicans would have won easily. The Democrats certainly weren't conservatives but in 1985 they were the cautious choice. This is where Wilder must thank Robb, as painful as that may be. The great leap of faith Virginians made was not in electing a black and a woman in 1985 but in electing Robb in 1981. For a decade, Virginians had seen a Democratic Party run by liberals. But in 1981 Virginians gambled that Robb was what he said he was — a moderate.

Bob Crouch, former Fifth District Democratic chairman, makes the argument that Virginia may have been *socially* ready to elect a black to statewide office before 1985. However, one doubts that Virginia would have been *politically* ready to elect a black until after Robb was elected.

Had Wilder run in the 1970s, his race might not have defeated him but his party affiliation would have. Until Robb came along, about all Republicans had to do to win was call their opponent a Democrat and voters right away believed he was a liberal. But that tactic didn't work after Robb became governor.

Robb made it respectable to be a Democrat in Virginia again. He reopened doors that had been shut to business and the money crowd; he firmly established the proposition that it was possible to be both fiscally responsible and socially enlightened. Robb did not so much "moderate" the state socially as he redefined what it meant to be a Virginia Democrat. It was Robb's ability to recast the image of the party of Howell into the party of Robb, to emphasize the difference between irresponsible national Democrats and reponsible Virginia Democrats, that made Wilder's victory possible. John Alderson, the 1984 Reagan-Bush coordinator in Virginia, voices some of the frustrations Republicans felt in 1985. "We couldn't stand on the ramparts and say hide your dogs and women, the liberal Democrats are coming. Chuck Robb didn't damage any of the sacred institutions of Virginia. He didn't go on a wild-eyed spending spree. The Republicans could not show where the state would be better off under their leadership and we're still grappling with that."

But before we go too far and make Virginia sound like it has eradicated racism from its civic soul, let's not overlook the public's capacity for inattentiveness. State Sen. Buzz Emick, D-Botetourt County, says he wouldn't believe this except it happened so often: "After the election, I heard a number of times from people who told me they didn't know Wilder was black."

So who really knows why Wilder won?

Perhaps the key question is not so much how Wilder won but can his victory be duplicated — in Virginia or in other states?

It's useful to remind ourselves how rare Wilder's feat of winning a statewide election is. In post-Reconstruction times, only California and Colorado have elected a black as lieutenant governor; only Massachusetts has elected a black to the U.S. Senate; no state has elected a black governor. Only three other Southern states — Alabama, Florida and Georgia — have elected blacks to statewide office, all judgeships.

The year after Wilder's election, Paul Goldman served as media consultant to Dwight Evans, a young black state legislator seeking the Democratic nomination for lieutenant governor in Pennsylvania — and encountered great difficulties in exporting the Wilder phenomenon. "Virginia is light years ahead of Pennsylvania on race; I can't believe it," Goldman says. "His [Evans'] opponent said he was not a serious candidate, he was just a black leader. Can you imagine someone saying that about Doug Wilder? The guy saying that wouldn't have gotten a single vote. In the South, if you get past race, you have to look hard for the next prejudice. Up there, you have ethnicity, religion, neighborhoods, ward leaders. So much in the South is put on that one arbitrary distinction so when you bust through that, you get voters who are a little more honest."

Still, Wilder's 44 percent share of the white vote is tough for a black candidate to match. When Michael Espy won election to Congress from Mississippi's Second District, he took just 20 percent of the white vote — considered a breakthrough by Deep South standards. And despite all the hullabaloo over Jesse Jackson's breakthrough in 1988, he usually won only about 15 percent of the white vote — in a Democratic primary.

Was Virginia uniquely situated for Wilder's victory, far enough south that he didn't have to deal with the complications of Northeastern ethnic politics but far enough north that he didn't encounter racism in the streets, Forsyth County, Ga.-style?

Certainly Virginia's sense of Southern aristocracy and genteel politeness may have made it the ideal place for a black — one shrewd enough to play to the state's sense of history and decorum — to win a statewide election in the South. And certainly Wilder benefited from a fortuitous set of political circumstances — a popular incumbent, a lackluster opponent, his own impressive campaign and all the rest.

Other black candidates in other states will have to run in states with different cultures and different circumstances. But certainly Wilder's campaign provides a blueprint that prospective black candidates in other states would be well advised to study. On a tactical level, Evans in Pennsylvania took a tour similar to Wilder's to dramatize how he wanted to be a candidate for all the people; Espy in Mississippi copied the cop commercial almost exactly to win over conservative rural whites. Strategically, the Wilder campaign is rich with implications for other black candidates. Perhaps the two most important lessons are to position oneself as a moderate to win white voters and to tap the black middle class for contributions.

As for whether Wilder's victory can be duplicated in Virginia or whether it was a fluke, the question may be moot.

Wilder describes the importance of his victory this way: "They'll never again take a poll to ask if a black can win in Virginia." Indeed, from now on, the poll will have to ask can this specific black win? That's a far different question, which is the way it should be.

It is not necessarily a question that will help future black candidates, or even Wilder, though. Having shown how progressive they are in electing Wilder, voters may now feel they have purged themselves of their racism and will study future black candidates more closely than they did Wilder. That will be the challenge facing Wilder himself as he seeks to move up from the ceremonial post of lieutenant governorship to the governorship. Wilder will no longer be a pleasant symbol of Virginia's progress whose presence in office was unlikely to disturb the commonwealth. He will have to be a candidate with specific plans for how he would exercise the immense powers of the Virginia governorship. Patronage and promises and philosophy may have far more to do with how far Wilder advances in Virginia politics than pride and prejudice — and that, too, is the way it should be.

Henry County lawyer Mike Cannaday, a Democrat, likens the Virginia of 1985 to a teen-age girl asked to the prom by a date she's not crazy about. "Voters said, 'OK, you take me, but I don't know if I'll dance with you. I'll stand there and eat cookies and drink punch. You come over later and ask me if I want to dance.' " Will Virginia want to dance with Doug Wilder? "We'll find out in 1989."

Epilogue

On the day after the election, the street outside Doug Wilder's law office atop Church Hill was jammed with traffic. Couriers wheeled up to deliver batch after batch of Mailgrams, folks from the neighborhood came in to share in the glory and shake hands with the man who had dared to act on his dreams. And Main Street's money men belatedly decided they'd better learn their way up Broad Street on the other side of the tracks.

Michael Brown stood in the lobby with nothing to do but look on bemused as the unlikely parade of lobbyists and other favor-seekers coming to pay court to the lieutenant governor-elect filed through.

"All these people were driving up saying, 'I knew you were gonna win; I meant to give you this.' The joke was we'll take in more money today than the rest of the year. People were driving up in Lincolns, Cadillacs, BMWs, those kind of cars. The senator was standing around, making himself available. People were coming on, 'Oh, Doug, you did it, I knew it all along, here's a little something for you.' "

Doug Wilder's term as lieutenant governor can be divided into three parts — the first half of 1986, when he received nearly unanimous praise;

the second half of 1986, when he was mired in controversy; and then 1987 and 1988, when he stayed out of the news, except to carefully build a record as a crime-fighter and tax-cutter to use to run for governor.

In the weeks following Wilder's election, Virginia basked in the glow of favorable national publicity. Virtually all the coverage, though, played up Robb's role in Wilder's victory. An Evans and Novak column even said that Robb had handpicked Wilder as a candidate and then "personally managed the sweep." This was the flash point that set off the first public sparks between Wilder and Robb. On Nov. 17, Goldman called reporters around the state and complained that Robb was getting too much credit for Wilder's election.

Goldman's outburst, which presumably came with Wilder's acquiescence, seemed to come out of the blue — at this point, only their immediate staffs knew of the private friction that had been building between the two men for nearly a year. The next day, though, Wilder pointedly refused to join Robb in Washington where he wanted to show off the winning ticket to the Democratic Leadership Council, a group of moderates he had organized.

Those episodes passed quickly from public view. They were not so quickly forgotten by Robb, though.

On Nov. 30, the governor wrote an extraordinary letter to Wilder — six pages, single-spaced, bitterly and emphatically pointing out all the ways the governor had helped Wilder. The governor had the letter hand-delivered to Wilder (with a copy to Goldman).

Robb's letter minced few words.

Goldman's post-election blast was "one of the least gracious actions I have ever witnessed in Virginia politics," Robb wrote. He was also sore at Wilder for standing him up at the DLC. "We've been friends for many years and we've both carried water for each other when it wasn't easy, but friends don't treat friends like you've treated me and those closest to me recently. Unless you can find a way to repair the damage you and Paul Goldman did last week, there are some very large numbers of our mutual friends and supporters who just won't be there again for Doug Wilder, and I'd hate to see that happen . . . "

Finally, somewhat like a stern father to a wayward son, Robb lectured Wilder about how the governor's staff had saved Wilder's rag-tag campaign. They "turned at least three fund-raisers from what would otherwise have been complete disasters into very respectable events," Robb wrote.

Wilder didn't respond. The Robb letter was filed away, a private but sour note to the sweet melody of praise that charmed Doug Wilder's ears. Throughout the rest of 1985 and well into 1986, Wilder was on his way toward becoming a celebrity. He was profiled in *People* and *Ebony* magazines; speaking invitations poured in from around the country. At home, Wilder held the state transfixed. Scarcely a week went by without the lieutenant governor making the news — and making an image that conservative Virginians couldn't help but love:

•When a Republican senator uttered a mild "damn" in a debate, presiding officer Wilder unexpectedly rebuked him — reminding the legislator that the gallery was full of impressionable Girl Scouts. Letters to the editors hailed Wilder; he came off looking like a Virginia Gentleman defending the honor of Southern girlhood.

•Not long afterward, Wilder gave a speech to the Lynchburg NAACP in which he warned blacks against laziness, illiteracy and promiscuity. Blacks must no longer look to government but instead must solve their own problems, Wilder said. "Yes, dear Brutus, the fault is not in our stars, but in ourselves." He advised young blacks not to shun menial jobs if that was the only way to find work, to avoid "black talk" and say "yes, sir and yes, ma'am" if necessary to their white bosses.

The Lynchburg *News & Daily Advance* editorialized that if President Reagan had given the same speech, he'd have been run out of town. The arch-conservative *Richmond News Leader,* went to the trouble of reprinting Wilder's "extraordinary speech" in its entirety and called favorable attention to it.

"One of us must be doing something wrong," Wilder quipped — but clearly he was doing everything right to solidify his white support.

The moralistic tone and self-help theme of Wilder's speeches became common. At Harvard, Wilder played down racism as an obstacle. "If you know you have to be doubly prepared," he told the Black Students Law Association in March, "be doubly prepared and then get on with doing the job." At a conference on the black family at Hampton University, Wilder warned of the dangers of drugs and teen-age pregnancy. "Where have all the fathers gone? How can future generations sing of their father's pride, when almost an entire generation is going fatherless?"

Wilder's star was shining. His office was inundated by so much mail that Wilder had to ask the General Assembly for $200,000 to hire more staff. Ted Kennedy made sure Wilder got a copy of a recent speech he had given on South Africa. Former heavyweight boxing champ Muhammad Ali paid a courtesy call and exchanged autographs. Baliles sent him to Japan and Taiwan on trade trips; Ted Turner took him to Moscow; *Time* magazine excerpted his commencement address at the University of Virginia.

But once again Wilder unexpectedly locked horns with Robb. On

April 3, Robb — in his capacity as DLC chairman — gave a speech in which he urged Democrats to adopt a more moderate agenda in 1988. Invited to respond by the *Roanoke Times & World-News,* Wilder let Robb have it — loudly accusing the former governor of wanting to push certain groups out of the party and make it into a pale copy of the GOP.

Not long afterwards, Wilder tweaked Robb again. Wilder had returned from his Moscow trip in time to be the keynote speaker at the North Carolina Democratic convention, where he attacked both Robb and Jesse Jackson for tearing the national party apart. Back in Richmond the next week, Wilder suddenly took on Baliles, announcing that he opposed the governor's prison policy — specifically so-called contact visits for death-row inmates. Baliles, stung by the unexpected criticism, chided Wilder for not apprising him first, but Wilder's office made it clear he was not in the habit of clearing his comments with anyone. Then Wilder set off for Japan. When he returned, he went to Lee County to re-enact part of his famous station-wagon tour the year before. There, Wilder broke with Baliles again, this time on the road-building plan that was the hallmark of the new administration, saying it would cost more than the governor said it would.

Quipped the *Virginian-Pilot:* "L. Douglas Wilder, a man with a hectic international schedule, seems to save just enough time for politics to keep the Virginia Capitol in an uproar." A cartoon in the *Richmond Times-Dispatch* showed an aide pulling on a Civil Defense helmet and racing down the hall to the governor's office. An alarm bell was clanging and a siren was going "whoop-whoop-whoop." "Red alert, Governor!" the aide shouted. "Wilder is making another speech!!"

Before long, Robb sent Wilder a second angry letter, this chastising him for not being part of the Democratic team. Wilder wasn't deterred, though. In September, he again criticized a Baliles policy — this time the tax increases required to pay for building roads. Wilder played it safe, though, perhaps too safe. He waited until a special session of the General Assembly had approved raising the sales tax — then he came out against it. Wilder looked to distance himself from the Baliles tax increases in another way, too. He called on the General Assembly to give back part of the state's expected "windfall" from the federal tax reform Congress has just enacted — the same position state Republicans were taking. "There are those who may say that as a Democrat I had an obligation to do whatever the governor asked," Wilder explained, "but that is not how I see the role of lieutenant governor."

Soon Wilder found himself in even deeper political trouble, though. In October, *Virginia Business* magazine reported that Wilder was charging sizable fees for his speeches — sometimes as much as $1,500. Editorials accused Wilder of using public office for private gain; he soon stopped.

Things only got worse for Wilder, though.

Robb had finally had enough of Doug Wilder's sniping and grousing. In December, Robb dramatically released the two angry letters he had written Wilder. And in an accompanying interview with the *Washington Post* Robb came close to saying there was no way he'd support Wilder for governor. "He has made that very difficult," Robb said. The former governor's rare and extraordinary display of temper held the state riveted as a real-life soap opera was played out in public view.

Wilder, forced to comment, did so in style. He invited "selected" reporters to join him for dinner at the Richmond Marriott. Word leaked out, though. Before long the Marriott was swarming with uninvited reporters. TV stations in Norfolk helicoptered crews in. Richmond TV stations covered the event live on the 6 o'clock news.

When the pressure was on, Wilder was his gracious, dignified self — but refused to accept any blame for the rift with Robb. Instead, he blamed the former governor. If Robb had problems with Goldman's November 1985 comments, he should have telephoned Wilder instead of sending a letter in which "I was called everything but the scourge of God." The tone of that letter, Wilder said, made it impossible for him to respond — and Robb's August letter only made matters worse.

About two weeks later, the warring politicians finally had a summit — where they made up, publicly at least. Robb was able to inflict one final humiliation, though. Wilder had to climb over a fence in Robb's backyard to avoid the reporters camped out at the end of the driveway.

With that, Wilder's first year in office came to an end. His remaining ones weren't nearly so eventful. Wilder spent 1987 and 1988 staying out of the news — unless it was to rebuild his image as a dependable custodian of Virginia tradition. All along, Wilder has kept his eye on the 1989 governor's race and anticipated the dangers of a black Democrat running as Baliles' heir. He figured law-and-order is one issue Republicans might try to use against any black candidate. And he figured whoever the Democratic candidate is in 1989, Republicans certainly will try to tie him to the tax increases of the Baliles administration. Anticipating those twin lines of attack, Wilder has tried hard to blunt them by cultivating an image as a tax-cutter and a crime-fighter. He misfired badly in 1986 by opposing Baliles directly on taxes and prison policy. Whatever points he may have scored from his conservative positions, Wilder likely lost by the unpredictable manner in which he made them. More recently, though, Wilder has approached the image-building with more savvy — taking the unusual step of coming up with his own legislative package, for instance.

As 1988 ends, Wilder stands in a remarkable position. The prospect of becoming the first black ever to be elected governor is within his grasp. His most formidable rival for the Democratic nomination, Mary Sue Terry, declined to oppose him, opting instead for a second term as attorney general. Other likely challengers have also stayed on the sidelines, leaving only state Sen. Danny Bird of Wytheville, still struggling to establish himself as more than just a favorite son from Southwest Virginia. It's the Pickett factor at work six years later: Few Democrats dare to oppose Wilder because they fear alienating black voters.

If Wilder does succeed in winning the Democratic nomination, he'll face a tough fight from any of the likely GOP candidates — former Attorney General Marshall Coleman, U.S. Sen. Paul Trible, Rep. Stan Parris. But it's a fight that could go either way, which underscores the central premise of this book. Wilder's great upset was in 1985, when he was dismissed as a dangerous dreamer who would sink the whole ticket. Now Virginians have had almost four years to get used to the idea of a Wilder governorship. If they do elect him governor, that may be more significant, but not nearly as surprising, as when they elected him lieutenant governor.

What kind of governor would Wilder make? Former GOP legislator Ray Garland once speculated on that: "I'm not sure he's best-suited for the nitty gritty of state government, running an operation that has 85,000 people working for it and a budget of [$22 billion]. I think he's the kind of guy who's bored by nuts and bolts — unlike John Dalton or Jerry Baliles. Wilder is an artist and his greatest work will always be in the realm of the ephemeral and I don't think there's anything wrong with that. In that sense, the governorship may almost limit him — although his attainment of it would be an artistic, dramatic moment. Doug Wilder is embarked on the single most interesting political adventure of our day. It's far from certain he can pull if off and he probably won't." But then again, Doug Wilder might very well succeed in Virginia, where Tom Bradley failed before him in California. And who knows what kind of national role awaits the first black elected governor — especially one with a Southern accent and a constituency on the doorstep of Washington?